John Truby

THE ANATOMY OF STORY

John Truby is Hollywood's premier story consultant and the founder of John Truby's Writer's Studio. He has worked as a story consultant and script doctor for the Walt Disney Studios, Sony Pictures, Fox Entertainment Group, and HBO, among others, and has taught his 22-Step Great Screenwriting and Genre classes to more than twenty thousand students worldwide.

ALSO BY JOHN TRUBY

Story Development Software
Truby's Blockbuster

Classes on CD
Action Story
Advanced Screenwriting
Comedy
Crime Stories, Detectives, and Thrillers
Fantasy, Horror Stories, and Science Fiction
The Love Story
Myth
Sitcom Writing
TV Drama

For more information, go to www.truby.com

THE
ANATOMY
OF
STORY

THE
ANATOMY
OF
STORY

22 STEPS TO
BECOMING A MASTER
STORYTELLER

John Truby

Faber and Faber, Inc.
An affiliate of Farrar, Straus and Giroux
New York

Faber and Faber, Inc.
An affiliate of Farrar, Straus and Giroux
18 West 18th Street, New York 10011

Distributed in Canada by Douglas & McIntyre Ltd.
Printed in the United States of America
Published in 2007 by Faber and Faber, Inc.
First paperback edition, 2008

The Library of Congress has cataloged the hardcover edition as follows:
Truby, John, 1952–
    The anatomy of story : 22 steps to becoming a master storyteller /
by John Truby. —1st ed.
        p.   cm.
    ISBN-13: 978-0-86547-951-7 (hardcover : alk. paper)
    ISBN-10: 0-86547-951-8 (hardcover : alk. paper)
    1. Storytelling.   I. Title.

GR72.3T78 2007
808.5'43—dc22

                                                    2007023459

Paperback ISBN-13: 978-0-86547-993-7
Paperback ISBN-10: 0-86547-993-3

Designed by Cassandra J. Pappas

www.fsgbooks.com

10   9   8   7   6   5

TO JACK AND AMY

CONTENTS

Acknowledgments ix

1. Story Space, Story Time 3
2. Premise 16
3. The Seven Key Steps of Story Structure 39
4. Character 56
5. Moral Argument 108
6. Story World 145
7. Symbol Web 220
8. Plot 258
9. Scene Weave 326
10. Scene Construction and Symphonic Dialogue 373
11. The Never-Ending Story 418

Notes 423
Index 425

ACKNOWLEDGMENTS

This book would not exist were it not for my agent, Noah Lukeman, and my editor, Denise Oswald, who, along with her colleagues, showed me the first-class treatment for which Farrar, Straus and Giroux is famous.

Many people gave me useful feedback on the text and the writing process, most notably Tim Truby, Patty Meyer, Bob Ellis, Alex Kustanovich, and Leslie Lehr. Thank you.

This book also benefited immensely from my past students, whose intense commitment to the craft of writing drove me to seek a clear translation of story theory into practice.

I would especially like to thank Kaaren Kitchell, Anna Waterhouse, Dawna Kemper, and Cassandra Lane, who took time out from their writing to give me hundreds of suggestions for improving this book. A writer needs good readers above all, and they are the best.

Finally, I want to thank the screenwriters, novelists, and playwrights whose well-told tales inspired me to explore the anatomy of story. They are the stars of this book, these amazing, wonderful authors, and they have given us all an invaluable gift.

THE
ANATOMY
OF
STORY

Story Space, Story Time

E VERYONE CAN TELL a story. We do it every day. "You won't believe what happened at work." Or "Guess what I just did!" Or "A guy goes into a bar . . ." We see, hear, read, and tell thousands of stories in our lives.

The problem comes in telling a great story. If you want to become a master storyteller, and maybe even get paid to be one, you run up against tremendous obstacles. For one thing, showing the how and why of human life is a monumental job. You have to have a deep and precise understanding of the biggest, most complex subject there is. And then you have to be able to translate your understanding into a story. For most writers, that may be the biggest challenge of all.

I want to be specific about the obstacles of story technique because that's the only way a writer can hope to overcome them. The first obstacle is the common terminology most writers use to think about story. Terms like "rising action," "climax," "progressive complication," and "denouement," terms that go as far back as Aristotle, are so broad and theoretical as to be almost meaningless. Let's be honest: they have no practical value for storytellers. Say you are writing a scene where your hero is hanging by his fingertips, seconds from falling to his death. Is that a progressive complication, a rising action, a denouement, or the opening scene of the story? It may be none of them or all of them, but in any event, these terms don't tell you how to write the scene or whether to write it at all.

The classic story terms suggest an even bigger obstacle to good technique: the very idea of what story is and how it works. As a storyteller in training, the first thing you probably did was read Aristotle's *Poetics*. I believe Aristotle was the greatest philosopher in history. But his thinking about story, while powerful, is surprisingly narrow, focused on a limited number of plots and genres. It is also extremely theoretical and difficult to put into actual practice, which is why most storytellers trying to learn the practical techniques of their craft from Aristotle leave empty-handed.

If you are a screenwriter, you probably moved from Aristotle to a much simpler understanding of story called "three-act structure." This is also problematic, because three-act structure, albeit a lot easier to understand than Aristotle, is hopelessly simplistic and in many ways just plain wrong.

Three-act theory says that every story for the screen has three "acts": the first act is the beginning, the second is the middle, and the third is the end. The first act is about thirty pages long. The third act is also about thirty pages long. And the second act runs to around sixty pages. And this three-act story supposedly has two or three "plot points" (whatever those are). Got that? Great. Now go and write a professional script.

I'm simplifying this theory of story, but not by much. It should be obvious that such an elementary approach has even less practical value than Aristotle. But what's worse is that it promotes a view of story that is mechanical. The idea of an act break comes from the conventions of traditional theater, where we close the curtain to signal the end of an act. We don't need to do that in movies, novels, and short stories or even, for that matter, in many contemporary plays.

In short, act breaks are external to the story. Three-act structure is a mechanical device superimposed on the story and has nothing to do with its internal logic—where the story should or should not go.

A mechanical view of story, like three-act theory, inevitably leads to episodic storytelling. An episodic story is a collection of pieces, like parts stored in a box. Events in the story stand out as discrete elements and don't connect or build steadily from beginning to end. The result is a story that moves the audience sporadically, if at all.

Another obstacle to mastering storytelling has to do with the writing process. Just as many writers have a mechanical view of what a story is, they use a mechanical process for creating one. This is especially true of screenwriters whose mistaken notions of what makes a script salable lead them to write a script that is neither popular nor good. Screenwriters typically come up with a story idea that is a slight variation on a movie they saw six months previously. Then they apply a genre, like "detective," "love," or "action," and fill in the characters and plot beats (story events) that go with that form. The result: a hopelessly generic, formulaic story devoid of originality.

In this book, I want to show you a better way. My goal is to explain how a great story works, along with the techniques needed to create one, so that you will have the best chance of writing a great story of your own. Some would argue that it's impossible to teach someone how to tell a great story. I believe it can be done, but it requires that we think and talk about story differently than in the past.

In simplest terms, I'm going to lay out a practical poetics for storytellers that works whether you're writing a screenplay, a novel, a play, a teleplay, or a short story. I will

- Show that a great story is organic—not a machine but a living body that develops
- Treat storytelling as an exacting craft with precise techniques that will help you be successful, regardless of the medium or genre you choose
- Work through a writing process that is also organic, meaning that we will develop characters and plot that grow naturally out of your original story idea

The main challenge facing any storyteller is overcoming the contradiction between the first and second of these tasks. You construct a story from hundreds, even thousands, of elements using a vast array of techniques. Yet the story must feel organic to the audience; it must seem like a single thing that grows and builds to a climax. If you want to become a great storyteller, you have to master this technique to such a high degree that your characters seem to be acting on their own, as *they* must, even though you are the one making them act that way.

In this sense we storytellers are a lot like athletes. A great athlete makes everything look easy, as though his body just naturally moves that way. But in fact he has so mastered the techniques of his sport that his technique has simply disappeared from view, and the audience sees only beauty.

THE TELLER AND THE LISTENER

Let's begin the process simply, with a one-line definition of a story:

A speaker tells a listener what someone did to get what he wanted and why.

Notice we have three distinct elements: the teller, the listener, and the story that is told.

The storyteller is first and foremost someone who *plays*. Stories are verbal games the author plays with the audience (they keep no score—the studios, networks, and publishing houses do that). The storyteller makes up characters and actions. He tells what happened, laying out a set of actions that have been completed in some way. Even if he tells the story in the present tense (as in playwriting or screenwriting), the storyteller is summing up all the events, so the listener feels that this is a single unit, the full story.

But telling a story is not simply making up or remembering past events. Events are just descriptive. The storyteller is really selecting, connecting, and building a series of intense moments. These moments are so charged that the listener feels he is living them himself. Good storytelling doesn't just tell audiences what happened in a life. It gives them the experience of that life. It is the *essential* life, just the crucial thoughts and events, but it is conveyed with such freshness and newness that it feels part of the audience's essential life too.

Good storytelling lets the audience relive events in the present so they can understand the forces, choices, and emotions that led the character to do what he did. Stories are really giving the audience a form of knowledge—emotional knowledge—or what used to be known as wisdom, but they do it in a playful, entertaining way.

As a creator of verbal games that let the audience relive a life, the story-teller is constructing a kind of puzzle about people and asking the listener to figure it out. The author creates this puzzle in two major ways: he tells the audience certain information about a made-up character, and he *withholds* certain information. Withholding, or hiding, information is crucial to the storyteller's make-believe. It forces the audience to figure out who the character is and what he is doing and so draws the audience into the story. When the audience no longer has to figure out the story, it ceases being an audience, and the story stops.

Audiences love both the feeling part (reliving the life) and the thinking part (figuring out the puzzle) of a story. Every good story has both. But you can see story forms that go to one extreme or the other, from sentimental melodrama to the most cerebral detective story.

THE STORY

There have been thousands, if not millions, of stories. So what makes each of them a story? What do all stories do? What is the storyteller both revealing to and hiding from the audience?

KEY POINT: *All stories are a form of communication that expresses the dramatic code.*

The dramatic code, embedded deep in the human psyche, is an artistic description of how a person can grow or evolve. This code is also a process going on underneath every story. The storyteller hides this process beneath particular characters and actions. But the code of growth is what the audience ultimately takes from a good story.

Let's look at the dramatic code in its simplest form.

In the dramatic code, change is fueled by desire. The "story world" doesn't boil down to "I think, therefore I am" but rather "I want, therefore I am." Desire in all of its facets is what makes the world go around. It is what propels all conscious, living things and gives them direction. A story tracks what a person wants, what he'll do to get it, and what costs he'll have to pay along the way.

Once a character has a desire, the story "walks" on two "legs": acting and learning. A character pursuing a desire takes actions to get what he wants, and he learns new information about better ways to get it. Whenever he learns new information, he makes a decision and changes his course of action.

All stories move in this way. But some story forms highlight one of these activities over the other. The genres that highlight taking action the most are myth and its later version, the action form. The genres that highlight learning the most are the detective story and the multiperspective drama.

Any character who goes after a desire and is impeded is forced to struggle (otherwise the story is over). And that struggle makes him change. So the ultimate goal of the dramatic code, and of the storyteller, is to present a change in a character or to illustrate why that change did not occur.

The different forms of storytelling frame human change in differing ways:

- Myth tends to show the widest character arc, from birth to death and from animal to divine.
- Plays typically focus on the main character's moment of decision.
- Film (especially American film) shows the small change a character might undergo by seeking a limited goal with great intensity.
- Classic short stories usually track a few events that lead the character to gain a single important insight.
- Serious novels typically depict how a person interacts and changes within an entire society or show the precise mental and emotional processes leading up to his change.
- Television drama shows a number of characters in a minisociety struggling to change simultaneously.

Drama is a code of maturity. The focal point is the moment of change, the *impact*, when a person breaks free of habits and weaknesses and ghosts from his past and transforms to a richer and fuller self. The dramatic code expresses the idea that human beings can become a better version of themselves, psychologically and morally. And that's why people love it.

KEY POINT: *Stories don't show the audience the "real world"; they show the story world. The story world isn't a copy of life as it is. It's life as human beings imagine it could be. It is human life condensed and heightened so that the audience can gain a better understanding of how life itself works.*

THE STORY BODY

A great story describes human beings going through an organic process. But it is also a living body unto itself. Even the simplest children's story is made up of many parts, or subsystems, that connect with and feed off one another. Just as the human body is made up of the nervous system, the circulatory system, the skeleton, and so on, a story is made of subsystems like the characters, the plot, the revelations sequence, the story world, the moral argument, the symbol web, the scene weave, and symphonic dialogue (all of which will be explained in upcoming chapters).

We might say that theme, or what I call moral argument, is the brain of the story. Character is the heart and circulation system. Revelations are the nervous system. Story structure is the skeleton. Scenes are the skin.

KEY POINT: *Each subsystem of the story consists of a web of elements that help define and differentiate the other elements.*

No individual element in your story, including the hero, will work unless you first create it and define it in relation to all the other elements.

STORY MOVEMENT

To see how an organic story moves, let's look at nature. Like the storyteller, nature often connects elements in some kind of sequence. The following diagram shows a number of distinct elements that must be connected in time.

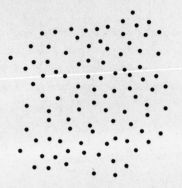

Nature uses a few basic patterns (and a number of variations) to connect elements in a sequence, including linear, meandering, spiral, branching, and explosive.[1] Storytellers use these same patterns, individually and in combination, to connect story events over time. The linear and explosive patterns are at the opposite extremes. The linear pattern has one thing happening after another on a straight-line path. Explosion has everything happening simultaneously. The meandering, spiral, and branching patterns are combinations of the linear and the explosive. Here's how these patterns work in stories.

Linear Story

The linear story tracks a single main character from beginning to end, like this:

It implies a historical or biological explanation for what happens. Most Hollywood films are linear. They focus on a single hero who pursues a particular desire with great intensity. The audience witnesses the history of how the hero goes after his desire and is changed as a result.

Meandering Story

The meandering story follows a winding path without apparent direction. In nature, the meander is the form of rivers, snakes, and the brain:

Myths like the *Odyssey*; comic journey stories like *Don Quixote*, *Tom Jones*, *Adventures of Huckleberry Finn*, *Little Big Man*, and *Flirting with Disaster*; and many of Dickens's stories, such as *David Copperfield*, take the meandering form. The hero has a desire, but it is not intense; he covers a great deal of territory in a haphazard way; and he encounters a number of characters from different levels of society.

Spiral Story

A spiral is a path that circles inward to the center:

In nature, spirals occur in cyclones, horns, and seashells.

Thrillers like *Vertigo*, *Blow-Up*, *The Conversation*, and *Memento* typically favor the spiral, in which a character keeps returning to a single event or memory and explores it at progressively deeper levels.

Branching Story

Branching is a system of paths that extend from a few central points by splitting and adding smaller and smaller parts, as shown here:

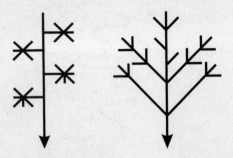

In nature, branching occurs in trees, leaves, and river basins.

In storytelling, each branch usually represents a complete society in detail or a detailed stage of the same society that the hero explores. The branching form is found in more advanced fiction, such as social fantasies like *Gulliver's Travels* and *It's a Wonderful Life* or in multiple-hero stories like *Nashville*, *American Graffiti*, and *Traffic*.

Explosive Story

An explosion has multiple paths that extend simultaneously; in nature, the explosive pattern is found in volcanoes and dandelions.

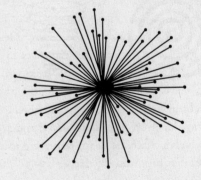

In a story, you can't show the audience a number of elements all at once, even for a single scene, because you have to tell one thing after another; so, strictly speaking, there are no explosive stories. But you can give the *appearance* of simultaneity. In film, this is done with the technique of the crosscut.

Stories that show (the appearance of) simultaneous action imply a comparative explanation for what happens. By seeing a number of elements all at once, the audience grasps the key idea embedded in each element. These stories also put more emphasis on exploring the story world, showing the connections between the various elements there and how everyone fits, or doesn't fit, within the whole.

Stories that emphasize simultaneous action tend to use a branching structure and include *American Graffiti, Pulp Fiction, Traffic, Syriana, Crash, Nashville, Tristram Shandy, Ulysses, Last Year at Marienbad, Ragtime, The Canterbury Tales, L.A. Confidential,* and *Hannah and Her Sisters.* Each represents a different combination of linear and simultaneous storytelling, but each emphasizes characters existing together in the story world as opposed to a single character developing from beginning to end.

WRITING YOUR STORY

So let's get practical: What writing process will give you the best chance of creating a great story?

Most writers don't use the best process for creating a story. They use the easiest one. We could describe it in four words: external, mechanical, piecemeal, generic. Of course, there are lots of variations on this process, but they all work something like this.

The writer comes up with a generic premise, or story idea, that is a vague copy of one that already exists. Or it's a combination of two stories that he has creatively (he thinks) stuck together. Knowing the importance of a strong main character, our writer focuses almost all of his attention on the hero. He "fleshes out" this character mechanically, by tacking on as many traits as possible, and figures he'll make the hero change in the last scene. He thinks of the opponent and minor characters as separate from and less important than the hero. So they are almost always weak, poorly defined characters.

When it comes to theme, our writer avoids it entirely so that no one can accuse him of "sending a message." Or he expresses it strictly in the dialogue. He sets the story in whatever world seems normal for that character, most likely a major city, since that's where most people in his audience live. He doesn't bother using symbols because that would be obvious and pretentious.

He comes up with a plot and a scene sequence based on one question: What happens next? Often he sends his hero on a physical journey. He organizes his plot using the three-act structure, an external imprint that divides the story into three pieces but doesn't link the events under the surface. As a result, the plot is episodic, with each event or scene standing alone. He complains that he has "second-act problems" and can't understand why the story doesn't build to a climactic punch that moves the audience deeply. Finally, he writes dialogue that simply pushes the plot along, with all conflict focused on what is happening. If he is ambitious, he has his hero state the theme directly in dialogue near the end of the story.

If most writers use an approach that is external, mechanical, piecemeal, and generic, the writing process we will work through might be described as internal, organic, interconnected, and original. I must warn you right up front: this process isn't easy. But I believe that this approach, or some variant of it, is the only one that really works. And it can be learned. Here's the writing process we're going to use in this book: We will work through the techniques of great storytelling in the same order that you construct your story. Most important, you will construct your story from the *inside out*. That means two things: (1) making the story personal and unique to you and (2) finding and developing what is original within your story idea. With each chapter, your story will grow and become more detailed, with each part connected to every other part.

- **Premise**   We begin with the premise, which is your entire story condensed to a single sentence. That premise will suggest the essence of the story, and we will use that to figure out how to develop it so as to get the most out of the idea.
- **Seven Key Story Structure Steps**   The seven key story structure steps are the major stages of your story's development and of the dramatic

code hidden under its surface. Think of the seven structure steps as your story's DNA. Determining the seven key steps will give your story a solid, stable foundation.

■ **Character**   Next, we will create the characters, not by pulling them out of thin air but by drawing them out of your original story idea. We will connect and compare each character to every other character so that each one is strong and well defined. Then we'll figure out the function each must perform in helping your hero develop.

■ **Theme (Moral Argument)**   The theme is your moral vision, your view of how people should act in the world. But instead of making the characters a mouthpiece for a message, we will express the theme that is inherent in the story idea. And we'll express the theme through the story structure so that it both surprises and moves the audience.

■ **Story World**   Next, we'll create the world of the story as an outgrowth of your hero. The story world will help you define your hero and show the audience a physical expression of his growth.

■ **Symbol Web**   Symbols are packets of highly compressed meaning. We'll figure out a web of symbols that highlight and communicate different aspects of the characters, the story world, and the plot.

■ **Plot**   From the characters we will discover the right story form; the plot will grow from your unique characters. Using the twenty-two story structure steps (the seven key steps plus fifteen more), we will design a plot in which all the events are connected under the surface and build to a surprising but logically necessary ending.

■ **Scene Weave**   In the last step before writing scenes, we'll come up with a list of every scene in the story, with all the plotlines and themes woven into a tapestry.

■ **Scene Construction and Symphonic Dialogue**   Finally we'll write the story, constructing each scene so that it furthers the development of your hero. We'll write dialogue that doesn't just push the plot but has a symphonic quality, blending many "instruments" and levels at one time.

As you watch your story grow before your eyes, I can promise you one thing: you will enjoy the creation. So let's begin.

CHAPTER 2

Premise

MICHAEL CRICHTON doesn't have the deep human characters of a Chekhov or the brilliant plots of a Dickens. He just happens to be the best premise writer in Hollywood. Take *Jurassic Park*, for example. Crichton's story might have come from this designing principle: "What if you took the two greatest heavyweights of evolution—dinosaurs and humans—and forced them to fight to the death in the same ring?" Now that's a story I want to see.

There are many ways to start the writing process. Some writers prefer to begin by breaking the story into its seven primary steps, which we will explore in the next chapter. But most begin with the shortest expression of the story as a whole, the premise line.

WHAT IS THE PREMISE?

The premise is your story stated in one sentence. It is the simplest combination of character and plot and typically consists of some event that starts the action, some sense of the main character, and some sense of the outcome of the story.

Some examples:

- *The Godfather*: The youngest son of a Mafia family takes revenge on the men who shot his father and becomes the new Godfather.
- *Moonstruck*: While her fiancé visits his mother in Italy, a woman falls in love with the man's brother.
- *Casablanca*: A tough American expatriate rediscovers an old flame only to give her up so that he can fight the Nazis.
- *A Streetcar Named Desire*: An aging beauty tries to get a man to marry her while under constant attack from her sister's brutish husband.
- *Star Wars*: When a princess falls into mortal danger, a young man uses his skills as a fighter to save her and defeat the evil forces of a galactic empire.

There are all kinds of practical reasons why a good premise is so crucial to your success. First, Hollywood is in the business of selling movies worldwide, with a big chunk of the revenue coming the opening weekend. So producers look for a premise that is "high concept"—meaning that the film can be reduced to a catchy one-line description that audiences will understand instantly and come rushing to the theater to see.

Second, your premise is your inspiration. It's the "lightbulb" moment when you say, "Now that would make a terrific story," and that excitement gives you the perseverance to go through months, even years, of hard writing.

This leads to another important point: for better or worse, the premise is also your prison. As soon as you decide to pursue one idea, there are potentially thousands of ideas that you won't be writing about. So you'd better be happy with the special world you've chosen.

KEY POINT: What you choose to write about is far more important than any decision you make about how to write it.

One last reason you must have a good premise is that it's the one decision on which every other decision you make during the writing process is based. Character, plot, theme, symbol—it all comes out of this story idea. If you fail at the premise, nothing else will help. If a building's foundation is flawed, no amount of work on the floors above will make the building stable. You may be terrific at character, a master at plot, or a genius at dialogue. But if your premise is weak, there is nothing you can do to save the story.

The big reason so many writers fail here is that they don't know how to develop the idea, how to dig out the gold that's buried within it. They don't realize that the great value of a premise is that it allows you to explore the full story, and the many forms it might take, before you actually write it.

Premise is a classic example of where a little knowledge is a dangerous thing. Most screenwriters know the importance Hollywood places on having a high-concept premise. What they don't know is that this marketing pitch is never going to tell them what the organic story demands.

They also don't know the inherent structural weakness found in any high-concept premise: it gives you only two or three scenes. These are the scenes just before and after the twist that makes your premise unique. The average feature film has forty to seventy scenes. A novel may have double or triple that number. Only by knowing the full craft of storytelling can you overcome the limitations of the high concept and tell the whole story successfully.

The first technique for finding the gold in an idea is time. Take a lot of it at the beginning of the writing process. I'm not talking about hours or even days. I'm talking about weeks. Don't make the amateurish mistake of getting a hot premise and immediately running off to write scenes. You'll get twenty to thirty pages into the story and run into a dead end you can't escape.

The premise stage of the writing process is where you explore your story's grand strategy—seeing the big picture and figuring out the story's general shape and development. You start out with almost nothing to go on. That's why the premise stage is the most tentative of the entire writing process. You are putting out feelers in the dark, exploring possibilities to see what works and what doesn't, what forms an organic whole and what falls apart.

That means you have to remain flexible, open to all possibilities. For the same reason, this is where using an organic creative method as your guide is most important.

DEVELOPING YOUR PREMISE

In the weeks you take to explore your premise, use these steps to come up with a premise line you can turn into a great story.

Step 1: Write Something That May Change Your Life

This is a very high standard, but it may be the most valuable piece of advice you'll ever get as a writer. I've never seen a writer go wrong following it. Why? Because if a story is that important to you, it may be that important to a lot of people in the audience. And when you're done writing the story, no matter what else happens, you've changed your life.

You might say, "I'd love to write a story that changes my life, but how do I know it will change my life before I've written it?" Simple: do some self-exploration, something most writers, incredibly enough, never do. Most writers are content to think of a premise that's a loose copy of someone else's movie, book, or play. It seems to have commercial appeal, but it's not personal to the writer in any way. This story will never rise above the generic, and so it is bound to fail.

To explore yourself, to have a chance to write something that may change your life, you have to get some data on who you are. And you have to get it outside of you, in front of you, so you can study it from a distance.

Two exercises can help you do this. First, write down your wish list, a list of everything you would like to see up on the screen, in a book, or at the theater. It's what you are passionately interested in, and it's what entertains you. You might jot down characters you have imagined, cool plot twists, or great lines of dialogue that have popped into your head. You might list themes that you care about or certain genres that always attract you.

Write them all down on as many sheets of paper as you need. This is your own personal wish list, so don't reject anything. Banish thoughts like "That would cost too much money." And don't organize while you write. Let one idea trigger another.

The second exercise is to write a premise list. This is a list of every premise you've ever thought of. That might be five, twenty, fifty, or more. Again, take as many sheets of paper as you need. The key requirement of the exercise is that you express each premise in one sentence. This forces you to be very clear about each idea. And it allows you to see all your premises together in one place.

Once you have completed both your wish list and your premise list, lay them out before you and study them. Look for core elements that repeat themselves on both lists. Certain characters and character types may recur, a quality of voice may seep through the lines of dialogue, one or two kinds of stories (genres) may repeat, or there may be a theme or subject matter or time period that you keep going back to.

As you study, key patterns will start to emerge about what you love. This, in the rawest form possible, is your vision. It's who you are, as a writer and as a human being, on paper in front of you. Go back to it often.

Notice that these two exercises are designed to open you up and to integrate what is already deep within you. They won't guarantee that you write a story that changes your life. Nothing can do that. But once you've done this essential bit of self-exploration, any premise you come up with is likely to be more personal and original.

Step 2: Look for What's Possible

One of the biggest reasons writers fail at the premise stage is that they don't know how to spot their story's true potential. This takes experience as well as technique. What you're looking for here is where the idea might go, how it might blossom. Don't jump on a single possibility right away, even if it looks really good.

> KEY POINT: Explore your options. The intent here is to brainstorm the many different paths the idea can take and then to choose the best one.

One technique for exploring possibilities is to see if anything is promised by the idea. Some ideas generate certain expectations, things that must happen to satisfy the audience if this idea were to play out in a full story. These "promises" can lead you to the best option for developing the idea.

A more valuable technique for seeing what's possible in the idea is to ask yourself, "What if . . . ?" The "what if" question leads to two places: your story idea and your own mind. It helps you define what is allowed in the story world and what is not. It also helps you explore your mind as it plays in this make-believe landscape. The more often you ask "What if . . . ?" the more fully you can inhabit this landscape, flesh out its details, and make it compelling for an audience.

The point here is to let your mind go free. Don't censor or judge yourself. Don't ever tell yourself that any idea you come up with is stupid. "Stupid" ideas often lead to creative breakthroughs.

To understand this process better, let's look at some stories that have already been written and play around with what the authors might have been thinking as they explored the deeper possibilities of their premise ideas.

WITNESS

(by Earl W. Wallace & William Kelley, story by William Kelley, 1985)
A boy who witnesses a crime is a classic setup for a thriller. It promises nail-biting jeopardy, intense action, and violence. But what if you push the story much further, to explore violence in America? What if you show the two extremes of the use of force—violence and pacifism—by having the boy travel from the peaceful Amish world to the violent city? What if you then force a good man of violence, the cop hero, to enter the Amish world and fall in love? And then what if you bring violence into the heart of pacifism?

TOOTSIE

(by Larry Gelbart and Murray Schisgal, story by Don McGuire and Larry Gelbart, 1982)
The promise that immediately comes to the audience's mind for this idea is the fun of seeing a man dressed as a woman. And you know they will want to see this character in as many difficult situations as possible. But what if you go beyond these useful but obvious expectations? What if you play up the hero's strategizing to show how men play the game of love from the inside? What if you make the hero a chauvinist who is forced to take on the one disguise—that of a woman—that he least wants but most needs to take on in order to grow? What if you heighten the pace and the plot by pushing the story toward farce, showing a lot of men and women chasing after each other at the same time?

Chinatown
(by Robert Towne, 1974)

A man who investigates a murder in 1930s Los Angeles promises all the revelations, twists, and surprises of a good whodunit. But what if the crime just keeps getting bigger? What if the detective starts investigating the smallest "crime" possible, adultery, and ends up finding out that the entire city has been built on murder? Then you could make the revelations bigger and bigger until you reveal to the audience the deepest, darkest secrets of American life.

The Godfather
(novel by Mario Puzo, screenplay by Mario Puzo and Francis Ford Coppola, 1972)

A story about a Mafia family promises ruthless killers and violent crime. But what if you make the head of the family much bigger, make him a kind of king in America? What if he is the head of the dark side of America, just as powerful in the underworld as the president is in official America? Because this man is a king, you could create grand tragedy, a Shakespearean fall and rise where one king dies and another takes his place. What if you turn a simple crime story into a dark American epic?

Murder on the Orient Express
(novel by Agatha Christie, screenplay by Paul Dehn, 1974)

A man killed in a train compartment right next door to where a brilliant detective is sleeping promises to be an ingenious detective story. But what if you want to take the idea of justice beyond the typical capture of the murderer? What if you want to show the ultimate poetic justice? What if the murdered man deserves to die, and a natural jury of twelve men and women serves as both his judge and his executioner?

Big
(by Gary Ross & Anne Spielberg, 1988)

A boy who suddenly wakes up to find he is a full-grown man promises to be a fun comedic fantasy. But what if you write a fantasy not set in some far-off, bizarre world but in a world an average kid would recognize? What if you send him to a real boy's utopia, a toy company, and let him go out with a pretty, sexy woman? And what if the story isn't just about a boy getting big physically but one that shows the ideal blend of man and boy for living a happy adult life?

Step 3: Identify the Story Challenges and Problems

There are rules of construction that apply to all stories. But each story has its own unique set of rules, or challenges, as well. These are particular problems that are deeply embedded in the idea, and you cannot escape them. Nor do you want to. These problems are signposts for finding your true story. You must confront these problems head-on and solve them if you are to execute your story well. Most writers, if they identify the problems at all, do so after they've written the complete story. That's far too late.

The trick is to learn how to spot inherent problems right at the premise line. Of course, even the best writers can't spot all the problems this soon in the process. But as you master the key techniques of character, plot, theme, story world, symbol, and dialogue, you will be pleasantly surprised at how well you can dig out the difficulties in any idea. Here are just a few of the challenges and problems inherent to the following story ideas.

STAR WARS
(by George Lucas, 1977)
In any epic, but especially a space epic like *Star Wars*, you must introduce a wide range of characters quickly and then keep them interacting over vast space and time. You must make the futuristic story believable and recognizable in the present. And you must find a way to create character change in a hero who is morally good from the beginning.

FORREST GUMP
(novel by Winston Groom, screenplay by Eric Roth, 1994)
How do you turn forty years of historical moments into a cohesive, organic, personal story? Problems include creating a mentally challenged hero who is able to drive the plot, have believably deep insights, and experience character change while balancing whimsy with genuine sentiment.

BELOVED

(by Toni Morrison, 1988)

The main challenge for Toni Morrison is to write a tale of slavery in which the hero is not portrayed as a victim. An ambitious story like this has numerous problems that must be solved: keeping narrative drive in spite of constant jumps between past and present, making events in the distant past seem meaningful to an audience today, driving the plot with reactive characters, showing the effects of slavery on the minds of the people who lived it, and demonstrating how its effects continue to punish years after the slavery is over.

JAWS

(novel by Peter Benchley, screenplay by Peter Benchley and Carl Gottlieb, 1975)

Writing a "realistic" horror story—in which characters fight one of man's natural predators—poses many problems: creating a fair fight with an opponent that has limited intelligence, setting up a situation where the shark can attack often, and ending the story with the hero going mano a mano with the shark.

ADVENTURES OF HUCKLEBERRY FINN

(by Mark Twain, 1885)

The main challenge facing the writer of *Adventures of Huckleberry Finn* is huge: How do you show the moral—or more precisely, immoral—fabric of an entire nation in fictional terms? This brilliant story idea carries with it some major problems: using a boy to drive the action; maintaining story momentum and strong opposition in a traveling, episodic structure; and believably showing a simple and not entirely admirable boy gaining great moral insight.

THE GREAT GATSBY

(by F. Scott Fitzgerald, 1925)

Fitzgerald's challenge is to show the American dream corrupted and reduced to a competition for fame and money. His problems are just as daunting. He must create narrative drive when the hero is someone else's helper, make the audience care about shallow people, and somehow turn a small love story into a metaphor for America.

DEATH OF A SALESMAN
(by Arthur Miller, 1949)

The central challenge for Arthur Miller is to turn the life of a small man into a grand tragedy. Problems he must solve include mixing past and present events without confusing the audience, maintaining narrative drive, and providing hope in a desperate and violent conclusion.

Step 4: Find the Designing Principle

Given the problems and the promises inherent in your idea, you must now come up with an overall strategy for how you will tell your story. Your overall story strategy, stated in one line, is the designing principle of your story. The designing principle helps you extend the premise into deep structure.

KEY POINT: The designing principle is what organizes the story as a whole. It is the internal logic of the story, what makes the parts hang together organically so that the story becomes greater than the sum of its parts. It is what makes the story original.

In short, the designing principle is the seed of the story. And it is the single most important factor in making your story original and effective. Sometimes this principle is a symbol or a metaphor (known as the central symbol, the grand metaphor, or the root metaphor). But it is often larger than that. The designing principle tracks the fundamental process that will unfold over the course of the story.

The designing principle is difficult to see. And in truth, most stories don't have one. They are standard stories, told generically. That's the difference between a premise, which all stories have, and a designing principle—which only good stories have. The premise is concrete; it's what actually happens. The designing principle is abstract; it is the deeper process going on in the story, told in an original way. Stated in one line:

Designing principle = story process + original execution

Let's say you are a writer who wants to show the intimate workings of the Mafia in America, as literally hundreds of screenwriters and novelists have done. If you were really good, you might come up with this design-ing principle (for *The Godfather*):

> **Use the classic fairy-tale strategy of showing how the youngest of three sons becomes the new "king."**

What's important is that the designing principle is the "synthesizing idea," the "shaping cause"[1] of the story; it's what internally makes the story a single unit and what makes it different from all other stories.

KEY POINT: Find the designing principle, and stick to it. Be diligent in discovering this principle, and never take your eye off it during the long writing process.

Let's take a look at *Tootsie* to see how the difference between the prem-ise and the designing principle plays out in an actual story.

- **Premise**   When an actor can't get work, he disguises himself as a woman and gets a role in a TV series, only to fall in love with one of the female members of the cast.
- **Designing Principle**   Force a male chauvinist to live as a woman.

How do you find the designing principle in your premise? Don't make the mistake most writers make at this point. Instead of coming up with a unique designing principle, they pick a genre and impose it on the prem-ise and then force the story to hit the beats (events) typical of that genre. The result is mechanical, generic, unoriginal fiction.

You find the designing principle by teasing it out of the simple one-line premise you have before you. Like a detective, you "induce" the form of the story from the premise.

This doesn't mean that there is only one designing principle per idea or that it's fixed or predetermined. There are many possible designing principles or forms that you can glean from your premise and by which you can develop your story. Each gives you different possibilities of what to say, and each brings inherent problems that you must solve. Again, let your technique help you out.

One way of coming up with a designing principle is to use a journey or similar traveling metaphor. Huck Finn's raft trip down the Mississippi River with Jim, Marlow's boat trip up the river into the "heart of darkness," Leopold Bloom's travels through Dublin in *Ulysses*, Alice's fall down the rabbit hole into the upside-down world of Wonderland—each of these uses a traveling metaphor to organize the deeper process of the story.

Notice how the use of a journey in *Heart of Darkness* provides the designing principle for a very complex work of fiction:

> A storyteller's trip upriver into the jungle is the line to three different locations simultaneously: to the truth about a mysterious and apparently immoral man; to the truth about the storyteller himself; and backward in civilization to the barbaric moral heart of darkness in all humans.

Sometimes a single symbol can serve as the designing principle, as with the red letter *A* in *The Scarlet Letter*, the island in *The Tempest*, the whale in *Moby-Dick*, or the mountain in *The Magic Mountain*. Or you can connect two grand symbols in a process, like the green nature and black slag of *How Green Was My Valley*. Other designing principles include units of time (day, night, four seasons), the unique use of a storyteller, or a special way the story unfolds.

Here are some designing principles in books, films, and plays, from the Bible all the way to the Harry Potter books, and how they differ from the premise line.

MOSES, IN THE BOOK OF EXODUS
- **Premise**   When an Egyptian prince discovers that he is a Hebrew, he leads his people out of slavery.
- **Designing Principle**   A man who does not know who he is struggles to lead his people to freedom and receives the new moral laws that will define him and his people.

ULYSSES
- **Premise**   Track a day in the life of a common man in Dublin.
- **Designing Principle**   In a modern odyssey through the city, over the

course of a single day, one man finds a father and the other man finds a son.

FOUR WEDDINGS AND A FUNERAL

- **Premise**   A man falls in love with a woman, but first one and then the other is engaged to someone else.
- **Designing Principle**   A group of friends experiences four utopias (weddings) and a moment in hell (funeral) as they all look for their right partner in marriage.

HARRY POTTER BOOKS

- **Premise**   A boy discovers he has magical powers and attends a school for magicians.
- **Designing Principle**   A magician prince learns to be a man and a king by attending a boarding school for sorcerers over the course of seven school years.

THE STING

- **Premise**   Two con artists swindle a rich man who killed one of their friends.
- **Designing Principle**   Tell the story of a sting in the form of a sting, and con both the opponent and the audience.

LONG DAY'S JOURNEY INTO NIGHT

- **Premise**   A family deals with the mother's addiction.
- **Designing Principle**   As a family moves from day into night, its members are confronted with the sins and ghosts of their past.

MEET ME IN ST. LOUIS

- **Premise**   A young woman falls in love with the boy next door.
- **Designing Principle**   The growth of a family over the course of a year is shown by events in each of the four seasons.

COPENHAGEN

- **Premise**   Three people tell conflicting versions of a meeting that changed the outcome of World War II.

- **Designing Principle**   Use the Heisenberg uncertainty principle from physics to explore the ambiguous morality of the man who discovered it.

A CHRISTMAS CAROL
- **Premise**   When three ghosts visit a stingy old man, he regains the spirit of Christmas.
- **Designing Principle**   Trace the rebirth of a man by forcing him to view his past, his present, and his future over the course of one Christmas Eve.

IT'S A WONDERFUL LIFE
- **Premise**   When a man prepares to commit suicide, an angel shows him what the world would be had he never been born.
- **Designing Principle**   Express the power of the individual by showing what a town, and a nation, would be like if one man had never lived.

CITIZEN KANE
- **Premise**   Tell the life story of a rich newspaper baron.
- **Designing Principle**   Use a number of storytellers to show that a man's life can never be known.

Step 5: Determine Your Best Character in the Idea

Once you have a lock on the designing principle of your story, it's time to focus on your hero.

KEY POINT: Always tell a story about your best character.

"Best" doesn't mean "nicest." It means "the most fascinating, challenging, and complex," even if that character isn't particularly likable. The reason you want to tell a story about your best character is that this is where your interest, and the audience's interest, will inevitably go. You always want this character driving the action.

The way you determine the best character embedded in the idea is to ask yourself this crucial question: Who do I love? You can find the answer by asking yourself a few more questions: Do I want to see him act? Do I love the way he thinks? Do I care about the challenges he has to overcome?

If you can't find a character you love implied in the story idea, move on to another idea. If you find him but he is not currently the main character, change the premise right now so that he is.

If you are developing an idea that seems to have multiple main characters, you will have as many story lines as main characters, and so you must find the best character for each story line.

Step 6: Get a Sense of the Central Conflict

Once you have an idea of who will drive the story, you want to figure out what your story is about at the most essential level. That means determining the central conflict of the story. To figure out the central conflict, ask yourself "Who fights whom over what?" and answer the question in one succinct line.

The answer to that is what your story is really about, because all conflict in the story will essentially boil down to this one issue. The next two chapters will expand on this conflict in often complex ways. But you need to keep this one-line statement of conflict, along with the designing principle, in front of you at all times.

Step 7: Get a Sense of the Single Cause-and-Effect Pathway

Every good, organic story has a single cause-and-effect pathway: A leads to B, which leads to C, and so on all the way to Z. This is the spine of the story, and if you don't have a spine or you have too many spines, your story will fall apart (we'll talk about multiple-hero stories in a moment).

Let's say you came up with this premise:

A man falls in love and fights his brother for control of a winery.

Notice that this is a split premise with two cause-and-effect trajectories. One of the great advantages of using these techniques to develop your premise is that it's much easier to spot problems and find solutions when you've written only one line. Once you write a full story or script, the story problems feel like they're set in concrete. But when you've written only one sentence, you can make a simple change and turn a split premise into a single line, such as this:

Through the love of a good woman, a man defeats his brother for control of a winery.

The trick to finding the single cause-and-effect pathway is to ask yourself "What is my hero's basic action?" Your hero will take many actions over the course of the story. But there should be one action that is most important, that unifies every other action the hero takes. That action is the cause-and-effect path.

For example, let's go back to the one-line premise for *Star Wars*:

When a princess falls into mortal danger, a young man uses his skills as a fighter to save her and defeat the evil forces of a galactic empire.

In forcing ourselves to describe *Star Wars* in a single line, we see that the one action that unites all the myriad actions of that film is "uses his skills as a fighter."

Or take the case of *The Godfather*, an epic book and an epic film. But again, if we work through the process, starting with reducing the story to a one-sentence premise, we can see the basic action clearly:

The youngest son of a Mafia family takes revenge on the men who shot his father and becomes the new Godfather.

Of all the actions Michael takes in that story, the one action that connects them all, the basic action, is that he takes revenge.

KEY POINT: If you are developing a premise with many main characters, each story line must have a single cause-and-effect path. And all the story lines should come together to form a larger, all-encompassing spine.

For example, in *The Canterbury Tales*, each traveler tells a story with a single spine. But the stories are all part of a group—a microcosm of English society—that is traveling to Canterbury.

Step 8: Determine Your Hero's Possible Character Change

After the designing principle, the most important thing to glean from your premise line is the fundamental character change of your hero. This is what gives the audience the deepest satisfaction no matter what form the story takes, even when the character change is negative (as in *The Godfather*).

Character change is what your hero experiences by going through his struggle. At the simplest level, that change could be represented as a three-part equation (don't confuse this with three-act structure):

$$W \times A = C$$

where W stands for weaknesses, both psychological and moral; A represents the struggle to accomplish the basic action in the middle of the story; and C stands for the changed person.

In the vast majority of stories, a character with weaknesses struggles to achieve something and ends up changed (positively or negatively) as a result. The simple logic of a story works like this: How does the act of struggling to do the basic action (A) lead the character to change from W to C? Notice that A, the basic action, is the fulcrum. A character with certain weaknesses, when being put through the wringer of a particular struggle, is forged and tempered into a changed being.

KEY POINT: *The basic action should be the one action best able to force the character to deal with his weaknesses and change.*

This is the simple geometry of any story because it is the sequence of human growth. Human growth is very elusive, but it is real, and it is what you, the writer, must express above everything else (or else show why it doesn't occur).

The key to doing this is to start with the basic action and then go to the opposites of that action. This will tell you who your hero is at the beginning of the story (his weaknesses) and who he is at the end (how he has changed).

The steps work like this:

1. Write your simple premise line. (Be open to modifying this premise line once you discover the character change.)
2. Determine the basic action of your hero over the course of the story.
3. Come up with the opposites of *A* (the basic action) for both *W* (the hero's weaknesses, psychological and moral) and *C* (changed person).

Going to the opposites of the basic action is crucial because that's the only way that change can occur. If your hero's weaknesses are similar to the basic action he will take during the story, he will simply deepen those weaknesses and remain who he is.

KEY POINT: *Write down a number of possible options for the hero's weaknesses and change.*

Just as there are a number of possibilities for developing your premise, there are many options for both the weaknesses and the changed person your hero will become. For example, let's say that the basic action of your hero is to become an outlaw during the story.

Starting with this basic action, you might come up with these opposites for possible weaknesses and changes. Notice that each weakness and change is a possible opposite of the basic action.

- An uptight, henpecked man becomes involved with a gang of outlaws and gets a divorce.
  W—weaknesses at the beginning: uptight, henpecked man
  A—basic action: becomes involved with a gang of outlaws
  C—changed person: gets a divorce

- An uptight, haughty banker becomes involved with a gang of outlaws and gives aid to the poor.
  W—weaknesses at the beginning: uptight, haughty banker

A—basic action: becomes involved with a gang of outlaws
C—changed person: gives aid to the poor

■ A shy, timid man becomes involved with a gang of outlaws and gets
drunk with fame.
W—weaknesses at the beginning: shy, timid man
A—basic action: becomes involved with a gang of outlaws
C—changed person: gets drunk with fame

Any of these are possible character changes that you can glean from an initial one-line premise about a man becoming an outlaw.

Let's work through this technique for a couple of familiar stories.

STAR WARS
■ **Premise** When a princess falls into mortal danger, a young man uses his skills as a fighter to save her and defeat the evil forces of a galactic empire.
W—weaknesses at the beginning: naive, impetuous, paralyzed, unfocused, lacking confidence
A—basic action: uses his skills as a fighter
C—changed person: self-esteem, a place among the chosen few, a fighter for good

Luke's initial weaknesses are definitely not the qualities of a fighter. But when constantly forced to use skills as a fighter, he is strengthened into a confident fighter for the good.

THE GODFATHER
■ **Premise** The youngest son of a Mafia family takes revenge on the men who shot his father and becomes the new Godfather.
W—weaknesses at the beginning: unconcerned, afraid, mainstream, legitimate, separated from the family
A—basic action: takes revenge
C—changed person: tyrannical, absolute ruler of the family

The Godfather is a perfect example of why you want to go to the opposites of the basic action to determine the weaknesses and change of your hero.

If Michael begins the story as a vengeful man, taking revenge on the men who shot his father will only make him seem more of the same. There's no character change. But what if he starts off the opposite of vengeful? An unconcerned, afraid, mainstream, legitimate man, separated from his Mafia family, who then takes revenge could become the tyrannical, absolute ruler of the family. This is a radical change, no doubt. But it is a totally believable one.

Note that what you end up with using this technique are only *possible* character changes for your story. Premise work, especially concerning character change, is extremely tentative. Be open to considering different character changes as you work through the writing process. We will explore this crucial story element in much greater detail in the next two chapters.

Step 9: Figure Out the Hero's Possible Moral Choice

The central theme of a story is often crystallized by a moral choice the hero must make, typically near the end of the story. Theme is your view of the proper way to act in the world. It is your moral vision, and it is one of the main reasons you are writing your story.

Theme is best expressed through the structure of the story, through what I call the moral argument. This is where you, the author, make a case for how to live, not through philosophical argument, but through the actions of characters going after a goal (for details, see Chapter 5, "Moral Argument"). Probably the most important step in that argument is the final moral choice you give to the hero.

A lot of writers make the mistake of giving their hero a fake choice. A fake choice is between a positive and a negative. For example, you may force your hero to choose between going to prison and winning the girl. The outcome is obvious.

KEY POINT: *To be a true choice, your hero must either select one of two positive outcomes or, on rare occasions, avoid one of two negative outcomes (as in* Sophie's Choice).

Make the options as equal as possible, with one seeming only slightly better than the other. A classic example of a choice between two positives is between love and honor. In *A Farewell to Arms*, the hero chooses love. In *The Maltese Falcon* (and almost all detective stories), the hero chooses honor.

Again, notice that this technique is about finding *possible* moral choices. That's because the choice you come up with now may change completely by the time you have written the full story. This technique simply forces you to start thinking, in practical terms, about your theme from the very beginning of the writing process.

Step 10: Gauge the Audience Appeal

When you've done all your premise work, ask yourself one final question: Is this single story line unique enough to interest a lot of people besides me?

This is the question of popularity, of commercial appeal. You must be ruthless in answering it. If you look at your premise and realize that the only people who will want to see your story are you and your immediate family, I would strongly caution you against using that premise as the basis for a full story.

You should always write first for yourself; write what you care about. But you shouldn't write *only* for yourself. One of the biggest mistakes writers make is to fall into the trap of either-or thinking: either I write what I care about, or I write what will sell. This is a false distinction, born of the old romantic notion of writing in a garret and suffering for your art.

Sometimes you get an idea that you simply *must* write. Or you get a great idea and you have no idea whether an audience will like it. But remember, you will have many more ideas in your life than you can possibly develop as full stories. Always try to write something that you care about and also think will appeal to an audience. Your writing should mean a lot to you personally. But writing for an audience makes it a lot easier to do what you love.

CREATING YOUR PREMISE—WRITING EXERCISE 1

- **Premise** Write down your premise in one sentence. Ask yourself if this premise line has the makings of a story that could change your life.
- **Wish List and Premise List** Write down your wish list and your premise list. Study them together to identify the core elements of what you care about and enjoy.
- **Possibilities** Look for what is possible in the premise. Write down options.
- **Story Challenges and Problems** Describe as many of the story challenges and problems that are unique to your idea as you can think of.
- **Designing Principle** Come up with the designing principle of your story idea. Remember that this principle describes some deeper process or form in which the story will play out in a unique way.
- **Best Character** Determine the best character in the idea. Make that character the hero of your premise.
- **Conflict** Ask yourself "Who is my hero fighting, and what is he fighting about?"
- **Basic Action** Find the single cause-and-effect pathway by identifying a basic action that your hero will take in the story.
- **Character Change** Figure out the possible character change for your hero, starting with the basic action (A) and then going to the opposites of the basic action to determine his weaknesses (W) at the beginning and his change (C) at the end.
- **Moral Choice** List a moral choice your hero may have to make near the end of the story. Make sure it's a difficult but plausible choice.
- **Audience Appeal** Ask yourself if your premise is likely to appeal to a wider audience. If not, go back to the drawing board.

Let's look at *Tootsie* so you can see how you might work through the premise process.

Tootsie

(by Larry Gelbart and Murray Schisgal, story by Don McGuire and Larry Gelbart, 1982)

- **Premise**   When an actor can't get work, he disguises himself as a woman and gets a role in a TV series, only to fall in love with one of the female members of the cast.
- **Possibilities**   You could take a funny look at the modern dating dance, but also dissect the deep immorality that underlies how men and women act toward each other in the most intimate part of their lives.
- **Story Challenges**   How do you show the effect of men's immoral actions against women without seeming to attack one entire gender while making the other gender look innocent?
- **Problems**   How do you make a man believable as a woman, weave several man-woman plots together and make them one, end each plotline successfully, and make an emotionally satisfying love story while using a number of farce techniques that place the audience in a superior position?
- **Designing Principle**   Force a male chauvinist to live as a woman. Place the story in the entertainment world to make the disguise more believable.
- **Best Character**   Michael's split between dressing as both a man and a woman can be a physical and comical expression of the extreme contradiction within his own character.
- **Conflict**   Michael fights Julie, Ron, Les, and Sandy about love and honesty.
- **Basic Action**   Male hero impersonates a woman.
- **Character Change**
  W—Michael is arrogant, a liar, and a womanizer.
  C—By pretending to be a woman, Michael learns to become a better man and capable of real love.
- **Moral Choice**   Michael sacrifices his lucrative acting job and apologizes to Julie for lying to her.

CHAPTER 3

The Seven Key Steps of Story Structure

*T*HE GODFATHER is a long, complex novel and film. *Tootsie* is a highly choreographed whirl of unrequited love, mistaken identity, and farcical missteps. *Chinatown* is a tricky unfolding of surprises and revelations. These very different stories are all successful because of the unbreakable organic chain of seven key structure steps deep under each story's surface.

When we talk about the structure of a story, we talk about how a story develops over time. For example, all living things appear to grow in one continuous flow, but if we look closely, we can see certain steps, or stages, in that growth. The same is true of a story.

A story has a minimum of seven steps in its growth from beginning to end:

1. Weakness and need
2. Desire
3. Opponent
4. Plan
5. Battle

6. Self-revelation
7. New equilibrium

The seven steps are not arbitrarily imposed from without, the way a mechanical story structure such as three-act structure is. They exist *in* the story. These seven steps are the nucleus, the DNA, of your story and the foundation of your success as a storyteller because they are based on *human action*. They are the steps that any human being must work through to solve a life problem. And because the seven steps are organic—implied in your premise line—they must be linked properly for the story to have the greatest impact on the audience.

Let's look at what each of these steps means, how they are linked one to another below the surface, and how they actually work in stories.

1. WEAKNESS AND NEED

From the very beginning of the story, your hero has one or more great weaknesses that are holding him back. Something is missing within him that is so profound, it is ruining his life (I'm going to assume that the main character is male, simply because it's easier for me to write that way).

The need is what the hero must fulfill within himself in order to have a better life. It usually involves overcoming his weaknesses and changing, or growing, in some way.

TOOTSIE
- **Weaknesses** Michael is arrogant, selfish, and a liar.
- **Need** Michael has to overcome his arrogance toward women and to stop lying and using women to get what he wants.

THE SILENCE OF THE LAMBS
- **Weaknesses** Clarice is inexperienced, suffering from haunting childhood memories, and a woman in a man's world.
- **Need** Clarice must overcome the ghosts of her past and gain respect as a professional in a man's world.

I can't emphasize enough how important the need is to your success. Need is the wellspring of the story and sets up every other step. So keep two critical points in mind when you create your hero's need.

KEY POINT: *Your hero should not be aware of his need at the beginning of the story.*

If he is already cognizant of what he needs, the story is over. The hero should become aware of his need at the self-revelation, near the end of the story, only after having gone through a great deal of pain (in a drama) or struggle (in a comedy).

KEY POINT: *Give your hero a moral need as well as a psychological need.*

In average stories, the hero has only a psychological need. A psychological need involves overcoming a serious flaw that is hurting nobody but the hero.

In better stories, the hero has a moral need in addition to a psychological need. The hero must overcome a moral flaw and learn how to act properly toward other people. A character with a moral need is always hurting others in some way (his moral weakness) at the beginning of the story.

THE VERDICT

Frank's psychological need is to beat his drinking problem and regain his self-respect. His moral need is to stop using other people for money and learn to act with justice. We know Frank has a moral need when we see him lie his way into a funeral of strangers in order to get business. He doesn't care if he upsets the family. He just wants to make money off of them.

One reason it is so important to give your hero a moral as well as a psychological need is that it increases the scope of the character; the character's actions affect others besides him. This moves the audience in a more powerful way.

The other reason you want to give your hero a moral need is that it prevents him from being perfect or being a victim. Both of these are the kiss of death in storytelling. A perfect character doesn't seem real or believable.

When a character has no moral flaws, the opponent, who does, typically dominates the hero, and the story becomes reactive and predictable.

Also present from page one of your story, but much less important than weakness and need, is the problem. All good stories begin with a kick: the hero is already in trouble. The problem is the crisis the hero finds himself in from page one. He is very aware of the crisis but doesn't know how to solve it.

The problem is not one of the seven steps, but it's an aspect of weakness and need, and it is valuable. Crisis defines a character very quickly. It should be an outside manifestation of the hero's weakness. The crisis highlights that weakness for the audience and gives the story a fast start.

KEY POINT: *Keep the problem simple and specific.*

SUNSET BOULEVARD
- **Weakness**   Joe Gillis has a fondness for money and the finer things in life. He is willing to sacrifice his artistic and moral integrity for his personal comfort.
- **Problem**   Joe is broke. A couple of guys from the finance company come to his apartment to repossess his car. He makes a run for it.

TOOTSIE
- **Weaknesses**   Michael is arrogant, selfish, and a liar.
- **Problem**   Michael is an excellent actor, but he's so overbearing that no one will hire him. So he's desperate.

SEVEN-STEPS TECHNIQUE: CREATING THE MORAL NEED

Writers often think they have given their hero a moral need when it is just psychological. Remember the simple rule of thumb: to have a moral need, the character must be hurting at least one other person at the beginning of the story.

Two good ways to come up with the right moral need for your hero are to connect it to the psychological need and to turn a strength into a weakness.

In good stories, the moral need usually comes out of the psychological need. The character has a psychological weakness that leads him to take it out on others.

To give your character a moral as well as a psychological need and to make it the right one for your character,

1. Begin with the psychological weakness.
2. Figure out what kind of immoral action might naturally come out of that.
3. Identify the deep-seated moral weakness and need that are the source of this action.

A second technique for creating a good moral need is to push a strength so far that it becomes a weakness. The technique works like this:

1. Identify a virtue in your character. Then make him so passionate about it that it becomes oppressive.
2. Come up with a value the character believes in. Then find the negative version of that value.

2. DESIRE

Once the weakness and need have been decided, you must give the hero desire. Desire is what your hero wants in the story, his particular goal.

A story doesn't become interesting to the audience until the desire comes into play. Think of the desire as the story track that the audience "rides along." Everyone gets on the "train" with the hero, and they all go after the goal together. Desire is the driving force in the story, the line from which everything else hangs.

Desire is intimately connected to need. In most stories, when the hero accomplishes his goal, he also fulfills his need. Let's look at a simple example from nature. A lion is hungry and needs food (a physical need). He sees a herd of antelope go by and spots a young one that he wants (desire). If he can catch the little antelope, he won't be hungry anymore. End of story.

One of the biggest mistakes a writer can make is to confuse need and desire or to think of them as a single step. They are in fact two unique story steps that form the beginning of your story, so you have to be clear about the function of each.

Need has to do with overcoming a weakness *within* the character. A hero with a need is always paralyzed in some way at the beginning of the story by his weakness. Desire is a goal *outside* the character. Once the hero comes up with his desire, he is moving in a particular direction and taking actions to reach his goal.

Need and desire also have different functions in relation to the audience. Need lets the audience see how the hero must change to have a better life. It is the key to the whole story, but it remains hidden, under the surface. Desire gives the audience something to want along with the hero, something they can all be moving toward through the various twists and turns—and even digressions—of the story. Desire is on the surface and is what the audience *thinks* the story is about. This can be shown schematically as follows:

Desire   ● ▶

Surface   ───────────────────────────────

Need   ━━━━━━━━━━━━━━━━━━▶   Self-Revelation

Let's look at some story examples to see the crucial difference between need and desire.

SAVING PRIVATE RYAN

- **Need** Hero John Miller must do his duty in spite of his fear (psychological and moral).
- **Desire** He wants to find Private Ryan and bring him back alive.

THE FULL MONTY

- **Need** Each of the men in the group needs to regain his self-respect (psychological).
- **Desire** They want to make a lot of money by performing naked in front of a roomful of women.

THE VERDICT

- **Need**   The hero must regain his self-respect (psychological) and learn to act with justice toward others (moral).
- **Desire**   As in all courtroom dramas, he wants to win the case.

CHINATOWN

- **Need**   Jake must overcome his cocky arrogance and learn to trust others (psychological). He also has to stop using people for money and bring a murderer to justice because it is the right thing to do (moral).
- **Desire**   As in all detective stories, Jake's desire is to solve a mystery—in this case, to find out who killed Hollis and why.

KEY POINT: Your hero's true desire is what he wants in this story, *not what he wants in life.*

For example, the hero in *Saving Private Ryan* wants to stop fighting, go home, and be with his family. But that isn't what tracks this particular story. His goal in this story, requiring him to take a series of very specific actions, is to bring back Private Ryan.

SEVEN-STEPS TECHNIQUE: STARTING WITH DESIRE

Writers who know that the story doesn't galvanize the audience until the hero's desire kicks in sometimes get a little too smart for their own good. They think, "I'll just skip the weakness-and-need step and start with desire." They've just made a pact with the devil.

Opening with desire does give your story a quick start. But it also kills the payoff, the ending of the story. Weakness and need are the foundation of any story. They are what makes it possible for your hero to change at the end. They're what makes the story personal and meaningful. And they're what makes the audience care.

Don't skip that first step. Ever.

3. OPPONENT

Writers often mistakenly think of the opponent, also known as the antagonist, as the character who looks evil, sounds evil, or does evil things. This way of looking at the opponent will prevent you from ever writing a good story.

Instead you must see the opponent structurally, in terms of his function in the story. A true opponent not only wants to prevent the hero from achieving his desire but is *competing with the hero for the same goal.*

Notice that this way of defining the opponent organically links this step to your hero's desire. It is only by competing for the same goal that the hero and the opponent are forced to come into direct conflict and to do so again and again throughout the story. If you give your hero and opponent two separate goals, each one can get what he wants without coming into direct conflict. And then you have no story at all.

If you look at a number of good stories, it often appears, at first glance, that hero and opponent are not competing for the same goal. But look again. See if you can spot what they are really fighting about. For example, in a detective story, it appears that the hero wants to catch the killer and the opponent wants to get away. But they are really fighting over which version of reality everyone will believe.

The trick to creating an opponent who wants the same goal as the hero is to find the deepest level of conflict between them. Ask yourself "What is the most important thing they are fighting about?" That must be the focus of your story.

KEY POINT: *To find the right opponent, start with your hero's specific goal; whoever wants to keep him from getting it is an opponent.*

Note that writers often talk about having a hero whose opponent is himself. This is a mistake that will cause all kinds of structural problems. When we talk about a hero fighting himself, we are really referring to a weakness within the hero.

Let's look at some opponents.

THE GODFATHER

Michael's first opponent is Sollozzo. However, his main opponent is the more powerful Barzini, who is the hidden power behind Sollozzo and wants to bring the entire Corleone family down. Michael and Barzini compete over the survival of the Corleone family and who will control crime in New York.

STAR WARS

Luke's opponent is the ruthless Darth Vader, and each is competing over who will control the universe. Vader represents the evil forces of the tyrannical Empire. Luke represents the forces of good, comprised of the Jedi Knights and the democratic Republic.

CHINATOWN

Like any good detective story, *Chinatown* gives us a unique and tricky opponent who remains hidden until the very end of the story. Jake's opponent turns out to be the rich and powerful Noah Cross. Cross wants to control the future of Los Angeles with his water scheme. But he is not competing with Jake about that. Because *Chinatown* is a detective story, he and Jake are actually competing over whose version of the truth will be believed. Cross wants everyone to believe that Hollis drowned accidentally and that Evelyn's daughter is his granddaughter. Jake wants everyone to believe that Cross killed Hollis and raped his own daughter.

4. PLAN

Action is not possible without some plan, in life and in storytelling. The plan is the set of guidelines, or strategies, the hero will use to overcome the opponent and reach the goal.

Again notice that the plan is organically linked to both desire and the opponent. The plan should always be specifically focused toward defeating the opponent and reaching the goal. A hero may have a vague plan. Or in certain genre stories like the caper or the war story, the plan is so complex that the characters may write it down so that the audience can see it.

CHINATOWN

Jake's plan is to question those who knew Hollis and track the physical evidence connected to Hollis's murder.

HAMLET

Hamlet's plan is to put on a play that mimics the murder of his father by the current king. He will then prove the king's guilt by the king's reaction to the play.

THE GODFATHER

Michael's first plan is to kill Sollozzo and his protector, the police captain. His second plan, near the end of the story, is to kill the heads of the other families in a single strike.

5. BATTLE

Throughout the middle of the story, the hero and opponent engage in a punch-counterpunch confrontation as each tries to win the goal. The conflict heats up. The battle is the final conflict between hero and opponent and determines which of the two characters wins the goal. The final battle may be a conflict of violence or a conflict of words.

THE ODYSSEY

Odysseus slays the suitors who have tormented his wife and destroyed his home.

CHINATOWN

A cop kills Evelyn, and Noah gets away with Evelyn's daughter while Jake walks off in despair.

THE VERDICT

Frank defeats opposing counsel by using brilliant lawyering and persuasive words in the courtroom.

6. SELF-REVELATION

The battle is an intense and painful experience for the hero. This crucible of battle causes the hero to have a major revelation about who he really is. Much of the quality of your story is based on the quality of this self-revelation. For a good self-revelation, you must first be aware that this step, like need, comes in two forms, psychological and moral.

In a psychological self-revelation, the hero strips away the facade he has lived behind and sees himself honestly for the first time. This stripping away of the facade is not passive or easy. Rather, it is the most active, the most difficult, and the most courageous act the hero performs in the entire story.

Don't have your hero come right out and say what he learned. This is obvious and preachy and will turn off your audience. Instead you want to suggest your hero's insight by the actions he takes leading up to the self-revelation.

BIG
Josh realizes he has to leave his girlfriend and life at the toy company and go back to being a kid if he is to have a good and loving life as an adult.

CASABLANCA
Rick sheds his cynicism, regains his idealism, and sacrifices his love for Ilsa so he can become a freedom fighter.

CHINATOWN
Jake's self-revelation is a negative one. After Evelyn's death, he mumbles, "As little as possible." He seems to believe that his life is not only useless but also destructive. Once again, he has hurt someone he loves.

DANCES WITH WOLVES
Dunbar finds a new reason to live and a new way of being a man because of his new wife and his extended Lakota Sioux family. Ironically, the Lakota way of life is almost at an end, so Dunbar's self-revelation is both positive and negative.

If you have given your hero a moral need, his self-revelation should be moral as well. The hero doesn't just see himself in a new light; he has an insight about the proper way to act toward others. In effect, the hero realizes that he has been wrong, that he has hurt others, and that he must change. He then proves he has changed by taking new moral action.

TOOTSIE

Michael realizes what it really means to be a man—"I was a better man with you as a woman than I ever was with a woman as a man. I just gotta learn to do it without the dress"—and he apologizes for hurting the woman he loves. Notice that even though the hero comes right out and says what he learned, he says it in such a clever and funny way that it avoids sermonizing.

ADVENTURES OF HUCKLEBERRY FINN

Huck realizes he has been wrong in thinking of Jim as less than human and declares that he would rather go to hell than tell Jim's owner of his whereabouts.

Structurally, the step with which self-revelation is most closely connected is need. These two steps communicate the character change of your hero (we'll explore this in more detail in the next chapter). Need is the beginning of the hero's character change. Self-revelation is the endpoint of that change. Need is the mark of the hero's immaturity at the beginning of the story. It is what is missing, what is holding him back. Self-revelation is the moment when the hero grows as a human being (unless the knowledge is so painful it destroys him). It is what he learns, what he gains, what allows him to live a better life in the future.

7. NEW EQUILIBRIUM

At the new equilibrium, everything returns to normal, and all desire is gone. Except there is now one major difference. The hero has moved to a higher or lower level as a result of going through his crucible. A fundamental and permanent change has occurred in the hero. If the self-revelation is positive—the hero realizes who he truly is and learns how to live properly in the world—he moves to a higher level. If the hero has a negative revelation—learning he has committed a terrible crime that expresses a corrupt personal flaw—or is incapable of having a self-revelation, the hero falls or is destroyed.

Let's look at some examples in which the hero rises.

DIE HARD

John has defeated the criminals, saved his wife, and reaffirmed their love.

PRETTY WOMAN

Vivian has left the world of prostitution behind and is with the man she loves (who, fortunately, is a billionaire).

THE SILENCE OF THE LAMBS

Clarice has brought Buffalo Bill to justice, has become an excellent FBI agent, and has apparently conquered her terrifying nightmares.

The following document the fall of the hero.

OEDIPUS THE KING

Oedipus gouges out his eyes upon learning that he has killed his father and slept with his mother.

THE CONVERSATION

The hero discovers he has contributed to someone's murder and ends up a shell-shocked man desperately tearing up his apartment to find a listening device.

VERTIGO

The hero drags the woman he loves to the top of a tower to get her to confess to a murder and then looks down in horror when the woman, overcome by guilt, accidentally falls to her death.

How to Use the Seven Steps—Writing Exercise 2

You've seen what the seven major steps of story structure mean. Here's how to use them in your story.

- **Story Events**   Write down some story events, describing each in a single sentence.

The seven steps are not imposed from the outside; they are embedded in the story idea itself. That's why the first thing you need to do to figure out the seven steps is to list some of the events that might be in your story.

Usually, when you get an idea for a story, certain events immediately pop into your mind. "This could happen, and this could happen, and this could happen." Story events are usually actions taken by your hero or opponent.

These initial thoughts about story events are extremely valuable, even if none of them ends up in the final story. Write down each event in one sentence. The point here is not to be detailed but to get down the basic idea of what happens in each event.

You should write down a minimum of five story events, but ten to fifteen would be even better. The more events you list, the easier it is to see the story and find the seven steps.

- **Order of Events**   Put the story events in some rough order, from beginning to end. Recognize that this will probably not be your final order. What's important is to get a look at how the story might develop from beginning to end.
- **Seven Steps**   Study the story events, and identify the seven structure steps.

KEY POINT: Start by determining the self-revelation, at the end of the story; then go back to the beginning and figure out your hero's need and desire.

This technique of starting at the end and going back to the beginning is one we will use again and again as we figure out character, plot, and theme. It's one of the best techniques in fiction writing because it guarantees that your hero and your story are always heading toward the true endpoint of the structural journey, which is the self-revelation.

■ **Psychological and Moral Self-Revelation**   When figuring out the self-revelation, try to give your hero both a psychological and a moral revelation.

Be specific about what your hero learns. And be flexible and ready to change what you have written as you figure out the other six steps and as you continue through the entire writing process. Figuring out the seven steps, as well as many of the other parts of your story, is much like doing a crossword puzzle. Some parts will come easily, others only with great difficulty. Use the parts that come easily to figure out the tough parts, and be willing to go back and change what you first wrote when later material gives you a new take on your story.

■ **Psychological and Moral Weakness and Need**   After figuring out the self-revelation, go back to the beginning of the story. Try to give your hero both a psychological and a moral weakness and need.

Remember the key difference. A psychological weakness or need affects just the hero. A moral weakness or need affects others.

Come up with not one but many weaknesses for your hero. These should be serious flaws, so deep and dangerous that they are ruining your hero's life or have the real possibility of doing so.

■ **Problem**   What is the problem, or crisis, your hero faces at the beginning of the story? Try to make it an outgrowth of your hero's weakness.

■ **Desire**   Be very specific when giving your hero a desire.

Make sure your hero's goal is one that will lead him to the end of the story and force him to take a number of actions to accomplish it.

- **Opponent**   Create an opponent who wants the same goal as the hero and who is exceptionally good at attacking your hero's greatest weakness.

You could create hundreds of opponents for your hero. The question is, who's the best one? Start by going back to that crucial question: What is the deepest conflict the hero and opponent are fighting about? You want your main opponent to be just as obsessed with winning the goal as the hero. You want to give your opponent a special ability to attack your hero's greatest weakness, and to do so incessantly while he tries to win the goal.

- **Plan**   Create a plan that requires the hero to take a number of actions but also to adjust when the initial plan doesn't work.

The plan generally shapes the rest of the story. So it must involve many steps. Otherwise you will have a very short story. The plan must also be unique and complex enough that the hero will have to adjust when it fails.

- **Battle**   Come up with the battle and the new equilibrium.

The battle should involve the hero and the main opponent, and it should decide once and for all who wins the goal. Decide whether it will be a battle of action and violence or a battle of words. Whatever kind of battle you choose, make sure it is an intense experience that puts your hero to the ultimate test.

Let's look at a seven-step breakdown from a single story, *The Godfather*, so that you can see what such a breakdown might look like for your own story.

THE GODFATHER
(novel by Mario Puzo, screenplay by Mario Puzo and Francis Ford Coppola, 1972)
- **Hero**   Michael Corleone.
- **Weaknesses**   Michael is young, inexperienced, untested, and overconfident.

- **Psychological Need**   Michael must overcome his sense of superiority and self-righteousness.
- **Moral Need**   He needs to avoid becoming ruthless like the other Mafia bosses while still protecting his family.
- **Problem**   Rival gang members shoot Michael's father, the head of the family.
- **Desire**   He wants to take revenge on the men who shot his father and thereby protect his family.
- **Opponent**   Michael's first opponent is Sollozzo. However, his true opponent is the more powerful Barzini, who is the hidden power behind Sollozzo and wants to bring the entire Corleone family down. Michael and Barzini compete over the survival of the Corleone family and who will control crime in New York.
- **Plan**   Michael's first plan is to kill Sollozzo and his protector, the police captain. His second plan is to kill the heads of the other families in a single strike.
- **Battle**   The final battle is a crosscut between Michael's appearance at his nephew's baptism and the killing of the heads of the five Mafia families. At the baptism, Michael says that he believes in God. Clemenza fires a shotgun into some men getting off an elevator. Moe Green is shot in the eye. Michael, following the liturgy of the baptism, renounces Satan. Another gunman shoots one of the heads of the families in a revolving door. Barzini is shot. Tom sends Tessio off to be murdered. Michael has Carlo strangled.
- **Psychological Self-Revelation**   There is none. Michael still believes that his sense of superiority and self-righteousness is justified.
- **Moral Self-Revelation**   There is none. Michael has become a ruthless killer. The writers use an advanced story structure technique by giving the moral self-revelation to the hero's wife, Kay, who sees what he has become as the door slams in her face.
- **New Equilibrium**   Michael has killed his enemies and "risen" to the position of Godfather. But morally, he has fallen and become the "devil." This man who once wanted nothing to do with the violence and crime of his family is now its leader and will kill anyone who betrays him or gets in his way.

CHAPTER 4

Character

*T*OOTSIE WAS A HUGE HIT because its main character, played by Dustin Hoffman, dressed up as a woman. Right? Wrong. What made that character funny, and what made the entire story work, was the *web* of characters that helped define the hero and *allowed* him to be funny. Look below the glossy surface of Dustin Hoffman in a dress and you will see that each character in that story is a unique version of the hero's central moral problem, which is how men mistreat women.

Most writers come at character all wrong. They start by listing all the traits of the hero, tell a story about him, and then somehow make him change at the end. That won't work, no matter how hard you try.

We're going to work through a different process that I think you will find much more useful. These are the steps:

1. We'll begin not by focusing on your main character but by looking at *all* your characters together as part of an interconnected web. We'll distinguish them by comparing each to the others according to story function and archetype.
2. Next we'll individualize each character based on theme and opposition.

3. Then we'll concentrate on the hero, "building" him step-by-step so that we end up with a multilayered, complex person that the audience cares about.

4. We'll create the opponent in detail, since this is the most important character after your hero and, in many ways, is the key to defining your hero.

5. We'll end by working through the character techniques for building conflict over the course of the story.

CHARACTER WEB

The single biggest mistake writers make when creating characters is that they think of the hero and all other characters as separate individuals. Their hero is alone, in a vacuum, unconnected to others. The result is not only a weak hero but also cardboard opponents and minor characters who are even weaker.

This great mistake is exacerbated in scriptwriting because of the huge emphasis placed on the high-concept premise. In these stories, the hero seems to be the only person who matters. But ironically, this intense spotlight on the hero, instead of defining him more clearly, only makes him seem like a one-note marketing tool.

To create great characters, think of all your characters as part of a web in which each helps define the others. To put it another way, a character is often defined by who he is not.

KEY POINT: *The most important step in creating your hero, as well as all other characters, is to connect and compare each to the others.*

Each time you compare a character to your hero, you force yourself to distinguish the hero in new ways. You also start to see the secondary characters as complete human beings, as complex and as valuable as your hero.

All characters connect and define each other in four major ways: by story function, archetype, theme, and opposition.

Character Web by Function in the Story

Every character must serve the purpose of the story, which is found in the story's designing principle (see Chapter 2, on premise). Every character has a specially designed role, or function, to play to help the story fulfill that purpose. Theater director Peter Brook, in speaking about actors, also makes a useful point for writers creating characters:

> [Brecht] pointed out that every actor has to serve the action of the play. . . . When [the actor] sees himself in relation to the wholeness of the play he will see that not only is too much characterizing (petty details) often opposed to the play's needs but also that many unnecessary characteristics can actually work against him and make his own appearance less striking.[1]

Even though the audience is most interested in how the hero has changed, you can't show them that change unless every character, including the hero, plays his assigned part on the team. Let's look at the story function of the major kinds of characters in fiction.

Hero

The most important character is the main character, or hero. This is the person who has the central problem and who drives the action in an attempt to solve the problem. The hero decides to go after a goal (desire) but possesses certain weaknesses and needs that hold him back from success.

All other characters in a story represent an opposition, an alliance with the hero, or some combination of the two. Indeed, the twists and turns of the story are largely the product of the ebb and flow of opposition and friendship between various characters and the hero.

■ **Hero in *Hamlet***   Hamlet

Opponent

The opponent is the character who most wants to keep the hero from achieving his desire. The opponent should not merely be a block to the hero. That is mechanical.

Remember, the opponent should want the same thing as the hero. That means that the hero and the opponent must come into direct conflict throughout the story. Often this doesn't seem to be the case. That's why you must always look for the deepest conflict that your hero and opponent are fighting over.

The relationship between the hero and the opponent is the single most important relationship in the story. In working out the struggle between these two characters, the larger issues and themes of the story unfold.

By the way, don't think of the opponent as someone the hero hates. He may be, or he may not be. The opponent is simply the person on the other side. He can be a nicer person than the hero, more moral, or even the hero's lover or friend.

- **Main Opponent in** *Hamlet*   King Claudius
- **Second Opponent**   Queen Gertrude
- **Third Opponent**   Polonius, the king's adviser

Ally

The ally is the hero's helper. The ally also serves as a sounding board, allowing the audience to hear the values and feelings of the lead character. Usually, the ally's goal is the same as the hero's, but occasionally, the ally has a goal of his own.

- **Ally in** *Hamlet*   Horatio

Fake-Ally Opponent

The fake-ally opponent is a character who appears to be the hero's friend but is actually an opponent. Having this character is one of the main ways you add power to the opposition and twists to the plot.

The fake-ally opponent is invariably one of the most complex and most fascinating characters in a story because he is usually torn by a dilemma. While pretending to be an ally of the hero, the fake-ally opponent comes to actually feel like an ally. So while working to defeat the hero, the fake-ally opponent often ends up helping the hero win.

- **Fake-Ally Opponents in** *Hamlet*   Ophelia, Rosencrantz, Guildenstern

Fake-Opponent Ally

This character appears to be fighting the hero but is actually the hero's friend. The fake-opponent ally is not as common in storytelling as the fake-ally opponent, because he is not as useful to the writer. Plot, as we will see in Chapter 8, comes from opposition, especially opposition that is hidden under the surface. An ally, even one who appears at first to be an opponent, cannot give you the conflict and surprises of an opponent.

■ **Fake-Opponent Ally in** *Hamlet*   None

Subplot Character

The subplot character is one of the most misunderstood in fiction. Most writers think of this character as the lead in the second story line—for example, as the love interest in a detective story. But that is not a true subplot character.

The subplot character has a very precise function in a story, and again it involves the comparative method. The subplot is used to contrast how the hero and a second character deal with the same problem in slightly different ways. Through comparison, the subplot character highlights traits and dilemmas of the main character.

Let's look more closely at *Hamlet* to see how you might create a true subplot character. We might say that Hamlet's problem, reduced to one line, is to take revenge on the man who killed his father. Similarly, Laertes' problem is to take revenge on the man who killed his father. The contrast focuses on the fact that one killing is premeditated murder and the other is an impetuous, misguided mistake.

KEY POINT: *The subplot character is usually not the ally.*

The subplot character, like the ally and the opponent, provides another opportunity to define the hero through comparison and advance the plot. The ally helps the hero reach the main goal. The subplot character tracks a line parallel to the hero, with a different result.

■ **Subplot Character in** *Hamlet*   Laertes, son of Polonius

Let's break down a couple of stories so you can see how characters contrast through function.

The Silence of the Lambs
(novel by Thomas Harris, screenplay by Ted Tally, 1991)

This is a story about an FBI trainee named Clarice who is searching for a serial killer known as Buffalo Bill. At the suggestion of her boss, Jack, she seeks the help of another serial killer already in prison, the infamous Hannibal "The Cannibal" Lecter. He is initially hostile to her, but ends up giving her far better training than she receives at the FBI.

- **Hero** Clarice Starling
- **Main Opponent** Buffalo Bill, the serial killer
- **Second Opponent** Dr. Chilton, the warden
- **Fake-Ally Opponent** None
- **Ally** Jack, her boss at the FBI
- **Fake-Opponent Ally** Hannibal Lecter
- **Subplot Character** None

American Beauty
(by Alan Ball, 1999)

American Beauty is a comedy-drama set in suburbia, so Lester's main opposition is within the family, with his wife, Carolyn, and his daughter, Jane, both of whom dislike him. He soon becomes infatuated with his daughter's friend Angela. But because he's married and she's a teenager, she becomes another opponent. Living next door to Lester is the rigid and conservative Colonel Frank Fitts, who disapproves of Lester's lifestyle. Brad is Lester's coworker who tries to fire him.

After Lester blackmails his company into giving him a nice severance package, he begins to live life as he pleases and gains an ally in Ricky Fitts, the boy next door, who sells him pot. Ricky and his father, Frank, are also subplot characters. Lester's central problem is figuring out how to live a meaningful life, one where he can express his deepest desires within a highly conformist society that values appearance and money. Ricky responds to his deadening, militaristic household by selling pot and spying on others with his video camera. Frank represses his homosexual desires by exerting an iron discipline over himself and his family.

- **Hero**   Lester
- **Main Opponent**   Carolyn, his wife
- **Second Opponent**   Jane, his daughter
- **Third Opponent**   Angela, Jane's pretty friend
- **Fourth Opponent**   Colonel Frank Fitts
- **Fifth Opponent**   Brad, his coworker
- **Ally**   Ricky Fitts
- **Fake-Ally Opponent**   None
- **Fake-Opponent Ally**   None
- **Subplot Characters**   Frank, Ricky

CHARACTER TECHNIQUE: TWO MAIN CHARACTERS

There are two popular genres, or story forms, that seem to have two main characters, the love story and the buddy picture. The buddy picture is actually a combination of three genres: action, love, and comedy. Let's see how the character web in these two forms actually works, based on the function that each character plays in the story.

Love Stories

Having to create two equally well-defined characters makes certain requirements for the character web of your story. The love story is designed to show the audience the value of a community between two equals. The central concept of love stories is quite profound. Love stories say that a person does not become a true individual by being alone. A person becomes a unique and authentic individual only by entering into a community of two. It is through the love of the other that each person grows and becomes his or her deepest self.

Expressing this profound idea with the right character web is no easy matter. If you try to write a love story with two main characters, you will have two spines, two desire lines, two tracks the story is trying to ride. So you have to make sure that one character is a little more central than the other. You must detail the need of *both* characters at the beginning of the story, but you should give one of the characters the main desire line. Most writers give that line to the man, because in our culture the man is supposed to pursue the woman. But one of the best ways to set your love story apart is to give the woman the driving line, as in *Moonstruck, Broadcast News,* and *Gone with the Wind.*

When you give one character the desire line, you automatically make him or her the more powerful character. In terms of story function, this means that the lover, the desired one, is actually the main opponent, not the second hero. You typically fill out the character web with one or more outside opponents, such as family members who oppose the union. You may also have other suitors for the hero or the lover so that you can compare different versions of a desirable man or woman.

THE PHILADELPHIA STORY
(play by Philip Barry, screenplay by Donald Ogden Stewart, 1940)
- **Hero**   Tracy Lord
- **Main Opponent**   Dexter, her ex-husband
- **Second Opponent**   Mike, the reporter
- **Third Opponent**   George, her stuffy, social-climbing fiancé
- **Fake-Ally Opponent**   Dinah, her sister
- **Ally**   Her mother
- **Fake-Opponent Ally**   Her father
- **Subplot Character**   Liz, the photographer

TOOTSIE
(by Larry Gelbart and Murray Schisgal, story by Don McGuire and Larry Gelbart, 1982)
- **Hero**   Michael
- **Main Opponent**   Julie
- **Second Opponent**   Ron, the director
- **Third Opponent**   John, the TV doctor
- **Fourth Opponent**   Les, Julie's father
- **Fake-Ally Opponent**   Sandy

- **Allies** George, Michael's agent; Jeff, Michael's roommate
- **Fake-Opponent Ally** None
- **Subplot Characters** Ron, Sandy

Buddy Stories

The strategy of using the buddy relationship as the foundation of the character web is as old as the story of Gilgamesh and his great friend Enkidu. We see a more unequal but highly informative partnership with Don Quixote and Sancho Panza, the dreamer and the realist, the master and the servant.

The buddy strategy allows you essentially to cut the hero into two parts, showing two different approaches to life and two sets of talents. These two characters are "married" into a team in such a way that the audience can see their differences but also see how these differences actually help them work well together, so that the whole becomes greater than the sum of the parts.

As in the love story, one of the buddies should be more central than the other. Usually it's the thinker, the schemer, or the strategist of the two, because this character comes up with the plan and starts them off on the desire line. The buddy is a kind of double of the hero, similar in important ways but also different.

Structurally, the buddy is both the first opponent and the first ally of the hero. He is not the second hero. Keep in mind that this first opposition between the two buddies is almost never serious or tragic. It usually takes the form of good-natured bickering.

Usually, you fill out the character web with at least one outside, dangerous, ongoing opponent. And because most buddy stories use a mythic journey, the buddies encounter a number of secondary opponents on the road. These characters are usually strangers to the buddies, and they are dispatched in quick succession. Each of these opponents should represent a negative aspect of the society that hates the buddies or wants to break them up. This technique is a great way of defining secondary characters quickly and distinguishing one from another. It also helps broaden and deepen the buddy form because you define various aspects of the society in relation to the two leads.

One of the most important elements of the buddy web has to do with the fundamental conflict between the friends. There is a snag in the relationship that keeps interfering. This allows an ongoing opposition between the two leads in a traveling story where most of the other opponents are strangers who quickly come and go.

BUTCH CASSIDY AND THE SUNDANCE KID
(by William Goldman, 1969)

- **Hero**   Butch
- **Main Opponent**   Sundance
- **Second Opponent**   Railroad boss E. H. Harriman (who never appears) and his hired guns, the all-star posse, led by Joe Lafors
- **Third Opponent**   Bolivian cops and army
- **Fake-Ally Opponent**   Harvey, who challenges Butch's leadership of the gang
- **Ally**   Etta, Sundance's girlfriend
- **Fake-Opponent Ally**   Sheriff Ray
- **Subplot Character**   None

CHARACTER TECHNIQUE: MULTIPLE HEROES AND NARRATIVE DRIVE

Although all the popular genres have a single main character, there are some nongenre stories that have multiple heroes. You'll recall that in Chapter 1, we talked about how stories move, with the extreme opposites being linear action and simultaneous action. Having a number of heroes is the main way you create a sense of simultaneous story movement. Instead of tracking the development of a single character (linear), the story compares what many heroes are doing at about the same time. The risk is that you show so many characters at the same time that the story is no longer a story; it has no forward narrative drive. Even the most simultaneous story must have some linear quality, sequencing events in time, one after another.

To write a successful multihero story, you must put each main character through all seven steps—weakness and need, desire, opponent, plan, battle, self-revelation, and new equilibrium. Otherwise the character is not a main character; the audience has not seen him move through the minimal stages of development.

Notice that having lots of heroes automatically reduces narrative drive. The more characters you must lay out in detail, the more you risk having your story literally come to a halt.

These are some of the techniques you can use to add narrative drive to a multihero story:

- Have one character emerge over the course of the story as more central than the rest.
- Give all the characters the same desire line.
- Make the hero of one story line the opponent in another story line.
- Connect the characters by making them all examples of a single subject or theme.
- Use a cliffhanger at the end of one line to trigger a jump to another line.
- Funnel the characters from many locations into one.
- Reduce the time. For example, the story may take place over one day or one night.
- Show the same holiday or group event at least three times over the course of the story to indicate forward drive and change.
- Have characters occasionally meet by coincidence.

Examples of multihero stories that use one or more of these techniques are *American Graffiti, Hannah and Her Sisters, L.A. Confidential, Pulp Fiction, The Canterbury Tales, La Ronde, Nashville, Crash,* and *Smiles of a Summer Night.*

CHARACTER TECHNIQUE: CUTTING EXTRANEOUS CHARACTERS

Extraneous characters are one of the primary causes of episodic, inorganic stories. The first question you must ask yourself when creating any character is "Does this character serve an important function in the overall story?" If he doesn't—if he only provides texture or color—you should consider cutting him entirely. His limited value probably won't justify the time he takes up in the story line.

CHARACTER WEB BY ARCHETYPE

A second way that characters connect and contrast in a story is through archetype. Archetypes are fundamental psychological patterns within a person; they are roles a person may play in society, essential ways of interacting with others. Because they are basic to all human beings, they cross cultural boundaries and have universal appeal.

Using archetypes as a basis for your characters can give them the appearance of weight very quickly, because each type expresses a fundamental pattern that the audience recognizes, and this same pattern is reflected both within the character and through interaction in the larger society.

An archetype resonates deeply with an audience and creates very strong feelings in response. But it is a blunt tool in the writer's repertoire. Unless you give the archetype detail, it can become a stereotype.

KEY POINT: Always make the archetype specific and individual to your unique character.

Starting with the psychologist Carl Jung, many writers have spoken about what the different archetypes mean and how they connect. For fiction writers, probably the key concept of an archetype is the notion of a shadow. The shadow is the negative tendency of the archetype, a psychological trap that a person can fall into when playing that role or living out that psychology.

We need to translate each major archetype and its shadow into practical techniques that you can use in creating a story. This involves thinking of the various archetypes in terms of both the beneficial role and the probable weaknesses that each might have in a story.

King or Father

- **Strength**   Leads his family or his people with wisdom, foresight, and resolve so that they can succeed and grow.
- **Inherent Weaknesses**   Can force his wife, children, or people to act according to a strict and oppressive set of rules, can remove himself

entirely from the emotional realm of his family and kingdom, or may insist that his family and people live solely for his pleasure and benefit.

- **Examples** King Arthur, Zeus, *The Tempest*, *The Godfather*, Rick in *Casablanca*, *King Lear*, *Hamlet*, Aragorn and Sauron in *The Lord of the Rings*, Agamemnon in the *Iliad*, *Citizen Kane*, *Star Wars*, Stanley in *A Streetcar Named Desire*, *American Beauty*, Willy Loman in *Death of a Salesman*, *Fort Apache*, *Meet Me in St. Louis*, *Mary Poppins*, *Tootsie*, *The Philadelphia Story*, *Othello*, *Red River*, *Howards End*, *Chinatown*.

Queen or Mother

- **Strength** Provides the care and protective shell within which the child or the people can grow.
- **Inherent Weaknesses** Can be protective or controlling to the point of tyranny, or can use guilt and shame to hold the child close and guarantee her own comfort.
- **Examples** *Hamlet*, *Macbeth*, Hera, Stella in *A Streetcar Named Desire*, *Elizabeth*, *American Beauty*, *The Lion in Winter*, *The Glass Menagerie*, *Long Day's Journey into Night*, and *Adam's Rib*.

Wise Old Man, Wise Old Woman, Mentor, or Teacher

- **Strength** Passes on knowledge and wisdom so that people can live better lives and society can improve.
- **Inherent Weaknesses** Can force students to think a certain way or speak for the glory of himself rather than the glory of his ideas.
- **Examples** Yoda in *Star Wars*, Hannibal Lecter in *The Silence of the Lambs*, *The Matrix*, Gandalf and Saruman in *The Lord of the Rings*, *Wuthering Heights*, Polonius in *Hamlet*, Homais in *Madame Bovary*, Miss Havisham in *Great Expectations*, Mr. Macawber in *David Copperfield*, and the *Iliad*.

Warrior

- **Strength** The practical enforcer of what is right.
- **Inherent Weaknesses** Can live according to the harsh motto of "kill

or be killed"; may believe that whatever is weak must be destroyed and so become the enforcer of what is wrong.

- **Examples**   Achilles and Hector in the *Iliad*; Luke Skywalker and Han Solo in *Star Wars*; *Seven Samurai*; King Arthur; Thor; Ares; Theseus; *Gilgamesh*; Aragorn, Legolas, and Gimli in *The Lord of the Rings*; *Patton*; *Die Hard*; Sonny in *The Godfather*; *A Streetcar Named Desire*; *The Great Santini*; *Shane*; *Platoon*; Sundance in *Butch Cassidy and the Sundance Kid*; *The Terminator*; and *Aliens*.

Magician or Shaman

- **Strength**   Can make visible the deeper reality behind the senses and can balance and control the larger or hidden forces of the natural world.
- **Inherent Weakness**   Can manipulate the deeper reality to enslave others and destroy the natural order.
- **Examples**   *Macbeth*, Harry Potter books, *Phantom of the Opera*, Merlin, *Star Wars*, *Chinatown*, *Vertigo*, Gandalf and Saruman in *The Lord of the Rings*, *A Connecticut Yankee in King Arthur's Court*, *The Conversation*, and detectives like Sherlock Holmes, Hercule Poirot, and Nick Charles in *The Thin Man*.

Trickster

The trickster is a lower form of the magician archetype and is extremely popular in modern storytelling.

- **Strength**   Uses confidence, trickery, and a way with words to get what he wants.
- **Inherent Weakness**   May become a complete liar who looks out only for himself.
- **Examples**   Odysseus in the *Odyssey*, *Men in Black*, *Beverly Hills Cop*, *Crocodile Dundee*, *Volpone*, Loki in Norse mythology, Iago in *Othello*, Indiana Jones, *Home Alone*, *Catch Me If You Can*, Hannibal Lecter in *The Silence of the Lambs*, *Brer Rabbit*, Butch in *Butch Cassidy and the Sundance Kid*, Sgt. Bilko on *The Phil Silvers Show*, Michael in *Tootsie*,

American Beauty, Verbal in *The Usual Suspects*, *Oliver Twist*, *Vanity Fair*, *Tom Sawyer*, and *Adventures of Huckleberry Finn*.

Artist or Clown

- **Strengths** Defines excellence for a people or, negatively, shows them what doesn't work; shows them beauty and a vision of the future or what appears to be beautiful but is in fact ugly or foolish.
- **Inherent Weaknesses** Can be the ultimate fascist insisting on perfection, may create a special world where all can be controlled, or simply tears everything down so that nothing has value.
- **Examples** Stephen in *Ulysses* and *A Portrait of the Artist as a Young Man*, Achilles in the *Iliad*, *Pygmalion*, *Frankenstein*, *King Lear*, *Hamlet*, the master swordsman in *Seven Samurai*, Michael in *Tootsie*, Blanche in *A Streetcar Named Desire*, Verbal in *The Usual Suspects*, Holden Caulfield in *The Catcher in the Rye*, *The Philadelphia Story*, and *David Copperfield*.

Lover

- **Strength** Provides the care, understanding, and sensuality that can make someone a complete and happy person.
- **Inherent Weaknesses** Can lose himself in the other or force the other to stand in his shadow.
- **Examples** Paris in the *Iliad*, Heathcliff and Cathy in *Wuthering Heights*, Aphrodite, *Romeo and Juliet*, Etta in *Butch Cassidy and the Sundance Kid*, *The Philadelphia Story*, *Hamlet*, *The English Patient*, Kay in *The Godfather*, *Camille*, *Moulin Rouge*, *Tootsie*, Rick and Ilsa in *Casablanca*, *Howards End*, and *Madame Bovary*.

Rebel

- **Strength** Has the courage to stand out from the crowd and act against a system that is enslaving people.
- **Inherent Weakness** Often cannot or does not provide a better alternative, so ends up only destroying the system or the society.
- **Examples** Prometheus, Loki, Heathcliff in *Wuthering Heights*, *American*

Beauty, Holden Caulfield in *The Catcher in the Rye*, Achilles in the *Iliad*, *Hamlet*, Rick in *Casablanca*, *Howards End*, *Madame Bovary*, *Rebel Without a Cause*, *Crime and Punishment*, *Notes from the Underground*, and *Reds*.

Here is a simple but effective character web emphasizing contrasting archetypes:

STAR WARS
(by George Lucas, 1977)

Luke (+ R2D2 + C3PO) (prince-warrior-magician)	Darth Vader (king-warrior-magician)
Han Solo (+ Chewbacca) (rebel-warrior)	Princess Leia (princess)

INDIVIDUALIZING CHARACTERS IN THE WEB

Once you have set your essential characters in opposition within the character web, the next step in the process is to make these character functions and archetypes into real individuals. But again, you don't create these unique individuals separately, out of whole cloth, with all of them just happening to coexist within the same story.

You create a unique hero, opponent, and minor characters by comparing them, but this time primarily through theme and opposition. We'll look at theme in detail in Chapter 5, "Moral Argument." But we need to look at a few of the key concepts of theme now.

Theme is your view of the proper way to act in the world, expressed through your characters as they take action in the plot. Theme is not subject matter, such as "racism" or "freedom." Theme is your moral vision, your view of how to live well or badly, and it's unique for each story you write.

KEY POINT: You begin individuating your characters by finding the moral problem at the heart of the premise. You then play out the various possibilities of the moral problem in the body of the story.

You play out these various possibilities through the opposition. Specifically, you create a group of opponents (and allies) who force the hero to deal with the central moral problem. And each opponent is a variation on the theme; each deals with the same moral problem in a different way.

Let's look at how to execute this crucial technique.

1. Begin by writing down what you think is the central moral problem of your story. If you worked through the techniques of the premise, you already know this.

2. Compare your hero and all other characters on these parameters:
   - weaknesses
   - need—both psychological and moral
   - desire
   - values
   - power, status, and ability
   - how each faces the central moral problem in the story

3. When making these comparisons, start with the most important relationship in any story, that between the hero and the main opponent. In many ways, this opponent is the key to creating the story, because not only is he the most effective way of defining the hero, but he also shows you the secrets to creating a great character web.

4. After comparing the hero to the main opponent, compare the hero to the other opponents and then to the allies. Finally, compare the opponents and allies to one another.

Remember that each character should show us a different approach to the hero's central moral problem (variations on a theme).

Let's look at some examples to see how this technique works.

TOOTSIE
(by Larry Gelbart and Murray Schisgal, story by Don McGuire and Larry Gelbart, 1982)

Tootsie is a wonderful story to start with because it shows how to begin with a high-concept premise and create a story organically. *Tootsie* is a classic example of what is known as a switch comedy. This is a premise technique in which the hero suddenly discovers he has somehow switched into being something or someone else. Hundreds of switch comedies have been written, going at least as far back as Mark Twain, who was a master of the technique.

The vast majority of switch comedies fail miserably. That's because most writers don't know the great weakness of the high-concept premise: it gives you only two or three scenes. The writers of *Tootsie*, however, know the craft of storytelling, especially how to create a strong character web and how to individuate each character by comparison. Like all high-concept stories, *Tootsie* has the two or three funny scenes at the switch when Dustin Hoffman's character, Michael, first dresses as a woman, reads for the part, and triumphantly visits his agent at the restaurant.

But the *Tootsie* writers do far more than create three funny scenes. Working through the writing process, they start by giving Michael a central moral problem, which is how a man treats a woman. The hero's moral need is to learn how to act properly toward women, especially the woman he falls in love with. The writers then create a number of opponents, each a variation on how men treat women or how women allow themselves to be treated by men. For example:

- Ron, the director, lies to Julie and cheats on her and then justifies it by saying that the truth would hurt Julie even more.
- Julie, the actress Michael falls for, is beautiful and talented but allows men, especially Ron, to abuse her and push her around.
- John, the actor who plays the doctor on the show, is a lecher who takes advantage of his stardom and position on the show to force himself on the actresses who work there.
- Sandy, Michael's friend, has such low regard for herself that when he lies to her and abuses her, she apologizes for it.
- Les, Julie's father, falls in love with Michael (disguised as Dorothy), and treats her with the utmost respect while courting her with dancing and flowers.
- Rita Marshall, the producer, is a woman who has hidden her femininity and her concern for other women in order to gain a position of power.
- Michael, when disguised as Dorothy, helps the women on the show

stand up to the men and get the respect and love they deserve. But when Michael is dressed as a man, he comes on to every woman at a party, pretends to be interested in Sandy romantically, and schemes to get Julie away from Ron.

GREAT EXPECTATIONS
(by Charles Dickens, 1861)

Dickens is a master storyteller famous for his character webs. One of his most instructive is *Great Expectations*, which in many ways is a more advanced web than most.

The distinguishing feature in the *Great Expectations* web is how Dickens sets up double pairs of characters: Magwitch and Pip, Miss Havisham and Estella. Each pair has fundamentally the same relationship—mentor to student—but the relationships differ in crucial ways. Magwitch, the criminal in absentia, secretly gives Pip money and freedom but no sense of responsibility. At the opposite extreme, Miss Havisham's iron control of Estella and her bitterness at what a man has done to her turn the girl into a woman too cold to love.

VANITY FAIR
(by William Makepeace Thackeray, 1847)

Thackeray called *Vanity Fair* a "novel without a hero," by which he meant a heroic character worthy of emulation. All the characters are variants of predatory animals climbing over the backs of others for money, power, and status. This makes the entire character web in *Vanity Fair* unique. Notice that Thackeray's choice of a character web is one of the main ways he expresses his moral vision and makes his vision original.

Within the web, the main contrast in character is between Becky and Amelia. Each takes a radically different approach to how a woman finds a man. Amelia is immoral by being obtuse, while Becky is immoral by being a master schemer.

TOM JONES
(by Henry Fielding, 1749)

You can see the huge effect that a writer's choice of character web has on the hero in a story like *Tom Jones*. This "picaresque" comic novel has a large number of characters. Such a big social fabric means the story has a lot of simultaneous action, with little specific depth. When this approach is applied to comedy, truth of character is found in seeing so many characters acting foolishly or badly.

This includes the hero. By making Tom a foolish innocent and basing the plot on misinformation about who Tom really is, Fielding is limited in how much self-revelation and character depth he can give Tom. Tom still plays out a central moral problem, having to do with fidelity to his one great love, but he has only limited accountability.

CREATING YOUR HERO

Creating a main character on the page that has the appearance of a complete human being is complex and requires a number of steps. Like a master painter, you must build this character in layers. Happily, you have a much better chance of getting it right by starting with the larger character web. Whatever character web you construct will have a huge effect on the hero that emerges, and it will serve as a valuable guide for you as you detail this character.

Creating Your Hero, Step 1: Meeting the Requirements of a Great Hero

The first step in building your hero is to make sure he meets the requirements that any hero in any story must meet. These requirements all have to do with the main character's function: he is driving the entire story.

1. Make your lead character constantly fascinating.

Any character who is going to drive the story has to grab and hold the audience's attention at all times. There must be no dead time, no treading water, no padding in the story (and no more metaphors to hammer home the point). Whenever your lead character gets boring, the story stops.

One of the best ways to grab and hold the audience's attention is to make the character mysterious. Show the audience that the character is hiding something. This forces the passive audience member to reach out and actively participate in your story. He says to himself, "That character is hiding something, and I want to find out what it is."

2. Make the audience identify with the character, but not too much.

"Identify" is a term that many people toss around but few define. We say that the audience should identify with the hero so that they will be emotionally attached to the character. But what does this really mean?

People who think you create a character by adding traits also think that audiences identify with such characteristics as background, job, dress, income, race, and sex. Nothing could be further from the truth. If audiences identified with specific characteristics, no one would identify with anyone, because each character would have too many traits the audience member doesn't share.

Audiences identify with a character based on two elements: his desire and the moral problem he faces—in short, desire and need, the first two of the all-important seven structure steps. Desire drives the story because the audience wants the hero to be successful. The moral problem is the deeper struggle of how to live properly with others and is what the audience wants the hero to solve.

Be aware that the audience should not identify too much with the character, or they will not be able to step back and see how the hero changes and grows. Again, Peter Brook's admonition to the actor is also excellent advice to the writer:

> When [the actor] sees himself in relation to the wholeness of the play . . . he will look at [his character's] sympathetic and unsympathetic features from a different viewpoint, and in the end will make different decisions from those he made when he thought "identifying" with the character was all that mattered.[2]

In Chapter 8, "Plot," we'll look at how you distance the audience from the hero at the appropriate time in the story.

3. Make the audience empathize with your hero, not sympathize.

Everyone talks about the need to make your hero likable. Having a likable (sympathetic) hero can be valuable because the audience wants the hero to reach his goal. In effect, the audience participates in telling the story.

But some of the most powerful heroes in stories are not likable at all. Yet we are still fascinated by them. And even in a story with an initially likable hero, this character often begins to act immorally—to do unlikable things—as he begins to lose to the opponent. Yet the audience doesn't get up in the middle of the story and walk out.

KEY POINT: What's really important is that audiences understand the character but not necessarily like everything he does.

To empathize with someone means to care about and understand him. That's why the trick to keeping the audience's interest in a character, even when the character is not likable or is taking immoral actions, is to show the audience the hero's motive.

KEY POINT: Always show why *your hero acts as he does.*

If you show the audience why the character chooses to do what he does, they understand the cause of the action (empathy) without necessarily approving of the action itself (sympathy).

Showing the hero's motive to the audience doesn't mean showing it to the hero. Often the hero is initially wrong about his true reason for going after the goal and does not discover his real motive until the end of the story, at the self-revelation.

4. Give your hero a moral as well as a psychological need.

The most powerful characters always have both a moral need and a psychological need. Remember the difference: a psychological need only affects the hero; a moral need has to do with learning to act properly toward others. By giving your hero a moral as well as a psychological need, you increase the effect the character has in the story and therefore increase the story's emotional power.

Creating Your Hero, Step 2: Character Change

Character change, also known as character arc, character development, or range of change, refers to the development of a character over the course of the story. It may be the most difficult but also the most important step in the entire writing process.

"Character development" is another one of those buzz words, like "identifying" with a character, that everyone talks about but few understand. Let's return for a moment to the standard approach to creating character. That's where you imagine a lone person, and you try to list as many traits about him as you can. You tell a story about him, and then you make him change at the end. This is what I call the "light switch school" of character change. Just flip the switch in the last scene, and boom, the character has "changed." This technique does not work. Let's explore a different way.

The Self Expressed as a Character

Before we can talk about true character change and how to create it, we first have to get some idea of what the self is, since that is what is changing. And to do that, we have to ask, What is the purpose of the self in storytelling?

A character is a fictional self, created to show simultaneously how each human being is totally unique in an unlimited number of ways but at the same time always and forever human, with features we all share. This fictional self is then shown in action, in space and over time, and compared to others, to show how a person can live well or badly and how a person can grow over his lifetime.

Not surprisingly, there is no monolithic concept of self in the history of stories. Here are some of the most important ways of looking at the self:

- A single unit of personality, governed internally with an iron hand. This self is cleanly separated from others but is searching for its "destiny." This is what the self was born to do, based on its deepest capabilities. This sense of self is common in myth stories, which typically have a warrior hero.
- A single unit comprised of many often conflicting needs and desires. The self has a strong urge to connect with others and sometimes even subsume another. This concept of self is found in a vast array of stories, especially in the work of modern dramatists like Ibsen, Chekhov, Strindberg, O'Neill, and Williams.

- A series of roles that the person plays, depending on what society demands at the time. Twain may be the most famous proponent of this view. He created his switch comedies *A Connecticut Yankee in King Arthur's Court* and *The Prince and the Pauper* to show that a person is largely determined by his position in society. But even in *Adventures of Huckleberry Finn* and *Tom Sawyer*, Twain emphasizes the power of the roles we play and how we usually turn out to be what society tells us we are.

- A loose collection of images, so unstable, porous, malleable, weak, and lacking in integrity that it can shift its shape to something entirely different. Kafka, Borges, and Faulkner are the major writers who express this loose sense of self. In popular fiction, we see this self in horror stories, especially ones about vampires, cat people, and wolf men.

Although these various notions of self have some important differences, the purpose of character change and the techniques for accomplishing it are pretty much the same for all of them.

KEY POINT: Character change doesn't happen at the end of the story; it happens at the beginning. More precisely, it is made possible at the beginning by how you set it up.

KEY POINT: Don't think of your main character as a fixed, complete person whom you then tell a story about. You must think of your hero as a range of change, a range of possibilities, from the very beginning. You have to determine the range of change of the hero at the start of the writing process, or change will be impossible for the hero at the end of the story.

I cannot overstate the importance of this technique. If you master the range of change, you will win the "game" of storytelling. If not, you will rewrite and rewrite and still never get it right.

A simple rule of thumb in fiction is this: the smaller the range, the less interesting the story; the bigger the range, the more interesting but the riskier the story, because characters don't change much in the limited time they appear in most stories.

But what exactly is this "range of change"? It is the range of possibilities of who the character can be, defined by his understanding of himself. Character change is the moment when the hero finally becomes who he will ultimately be. In other words, the main character doesn't suddenly flip to being someone else (except in rare instances). The main character completes a process, which has been occurring throughout the story, of becoming who he is in a deeper and more focused way.

This process of the hero becoming who he is more deeply can seem hopelessly ethereal, which is why it is often misunderstood. So let me be very detailed here: you can show a character going through many changes in a story, but not all of them represent character change.

For example, you may show a character who starts poor and ends up rich. Or he may begin as a peasant and end up a king. Or he may have a drinking problem and learn how to stay sober. These are all changes. They're just not character changes.

KEY POINT: *True character change involves a challenging and changing of basic beliefs, leading to new moral action by the hero.*

A character's self-knowledge is made up of his beliefs, about the world and about himself. They are his beliefs about what makes a good life and about what he will do to get what he wants. In a good story, as the hero goes after a goal, he is forced to challenge his most deep-seated beliefs. In the cauldron of crisis, he sees what he really believes, decides what he will act on, and then takes moral action to prove it.

Just as writers have expressed different senses of self, so have they used different strategies to express character change. I mentioned in Chapter 1 that a story "walks" on two "legs," acting and learning. Generally, in the long history of storytelling, there has been a move from almost total emphasis on acting—in the myth form, where the audience learns simply by modeling themselves on the hero's actions—to a heavy emphasis on learning, in which the audience's concern is to figure out what is happening, who these people really are, and what events really transpired, before achieving full understanding of how to live a good life.

We see these "learning" stories from authors like Joyce, Woolf, Faulkner, Godard, Stoppard, Frayn, and Ayckbourn, and in films as varied as *Last Year at Marienbad*, *Blow-Up*, *The Conformist*, *Memento*, *The Conversation*, and *The Usual Suspects*.

Character change in learning stories is not simply a matter of watching a character gain some new nugget of understanding of himself at the end of the story. The audience must actually participate in the character change and become various characters throughout the storytelling process, not only by experiencing the characters' different points of view but also by having to figure out whose point of view the audience is seeing.

Clearly, the possibilities of character change are limitless. Your hero's development depends on what beliefs he starts with, how he challenges them, and how they have changed by the end of the story. This is one of the ways that you make the story uniquely yours.

But certain kinds of character change are more common than others. Let's look at some of them, not because you have to use one of them in your story, but because understanding them will help you master this all-important technique in your own writing.

1. **Child to Adult**   Also known as the coming-of-age story, this change has nothing to do with a child physically becoming an adult, of course. You may think this is obvious, but many writers make the mistake in a coming-of-age story of defining character development as someone having his first sexual experience. Although this experience may be tragic or amusing, it has nothing to do with character change.

   A true coming-of-age story shows a young person challenging and changing basic beliefs and then taking new moral action. You can see this particular change in stories like *The Catcher in the Rye*, *Adventures of Huckleberry Finn*, *David Copperfield*, *The Sixth Sense*, *Big*, *Good Will Hunting*, *Forrest Gump*, *Scent of a Woman*, *Stand by Me*, *Mr. Smith Goes to Washington*, and *Tristram Shandy* (which is not only the first coming-of-age novel but the first anti-coming-of-age novel as well!).

2. **Adult to Leader**   In this change, a character goes from being concerned only with finding the right path for himself to realizing

that he must help others find the right path as well. You see this change in *The Matrix*, *Saving Private Ryan*, *Elizabeth*, *Braveheart*, *Forrest Gump*, *Schindler's List*, *The Lion King*, *The Grapes of Wrath*, *Dances with Wolves*, and *Hamlet*.

3. **Cynic to Participant**   This development is really a specialized form of going from adult to leader. Here the character begins as someone who sees value only in himself. He has pulled away from the larger society and is interested in pleasure, personal freedom, and money. By the end of the story, the hero has learned the value of making the larger world right and has rejoined society as a leader. Stories like *Casablanca* and the Han Solo character in *Star Wars* show this change.

4. **Leader to Tyrant**   Not all character change is positive. In leader-to-tyrant stories, the character moves from helping a few others find the right path to forcing others to follow his path. A lot of actors are afraid to play this change because they think it makes them look bad. But it usually makes for great drama. You can see it in *L.A. Confidential*, *A Few Good Men*, *Howards End*, *Red River*, *The Godfather*, and *Macbeth*.

5. **Leader to Visionary**   In this change, a character goes from helping a few others find the right path to seeing how an entire society should change and live in the future. We see this in the great religious stories and in some creation myths.

Writers often use the Moses story structure when depicting this change. For example, *Close Encounters of the Third Kind* has an everyman, Roy, who has a vision of a mountain. He climbs to the top of the mountain, and there he sees the future of the universe in the form of a giant spaceship.

Beware of a big problem you must overcome if you want to show a character becoming a visionary. *You* must come up with the vision. Most writers who try to tell this story get to the end and are shocked to realize they don't have a vision of how the entire society should act differently in the future. So at the moment of final revelation, they have the character see a white light or beautiful images of nature.

This doesn't work. The character's vision must be a detailed *moral* vision. Moses' Ten Commandments are ten moral laws. Jesus' Sermon on the Mount is a series of moral laws. Make sure yours are too, or don't write this type of story.

6. **Metamorphosis**   In horror, fantasy, fairy tale, and certain intense psychological dramas, the character may undergo metamorphosis, or extreme character change. Here the character actually becomes another person, animal, or thing.

This is radical and costly change, and it implies a self that is initially weak, fractured, or devastated. At its best, this development shows an act of extreme empathy. At its worst, it marks the complete destruction of the old self and entrapment in the new.

In horror stories like *The Wolf Man*, *Wolfen*, and *The Fly*, the human's change into an animal marks his complete surrender to sexual passion and predatory behavior. We watch the devolutionary process as man returns to his animal roots.

On rare occasions in stories, a character may change from beast to human. Arguably King Kong is such a character, when he seems to fall in love with Fay Wray's character and dies to be with her. "It was beauty killed the beast," says the far more predatory producer. The Feral Kid in *The Road Warrior* is a grunting animal child who not only learns to be human by watching Mad Max but ends as leader of his tribe. In *Gilgamesh*, the animal man, Enkidu, becomes human when he is tricked into sleeping with a woman.

In Kafka's *Metamorphosis*, in what might be called a "switch tragedy," traveling salesman Gregor Samsa wakes up one morning to find he has turned into a bug. This is a rare example of the character change happening at the beginning of the story, with the rest of the tale given over to the experience of being a bug (reportedly, it's the height of alienation).

Character change of this extreme sort necessarily involves the use of a symbol. Take a look at Chapter 7, "Symbol Web," to see the techniques for attaching a symbol to a character.

Creating Character Change in Your Story

Having looked at how character change works in storytelling, the question now becomes, how do you build this change for *your* story?

In Chapter 2, on premise, we explored the technique of going to the opposites of the basic action in the story to get a sense of the possible character change of your hero. You'll recall that *The Godfather* works like this:

■ **Premise** The youngest son of a Mafia family takes revenge on the men who shot his father and becomes the new Godfather.

   W—weaknesses at the beginning: unconcerned, afraid, mainstream, legitimate, separated from the family

   A—basic action: takes revenge

   C—changed person: tyrannical, absolute ruler of the family

Then in Chapter 3, we talked about how you set up the seven main structural steps of your story so that the character drives the plot and experiences deep change at the same time. Here I want to focus in much greater detail on the techniques for creating the character change that will serve as the foundation for your story.

When I asked earlier how you build this change, I used the word "build" purposely, because this is where you literally set the frame of your story.

KEY POINT: Always begin at the end of the change, with the self-revelation; then go back and determine the starting point of the change, which is the hero's need and desire; then figure out the steps of development in between.

This is one of the most valuable techniques in all of fiction writing. Use it, and you will see your storytelling ability improve dramatically. The reason you start at the endpoint is that every story is a *journey of learning* that your hero takes (which may or may not be accompanied by a physical journey). As with any journey, before you can take your first step, you have to know the endpoint of where you're going. Otherwise, you walk in circles or wander aimlessly.

By starting with the self-revelation, the end of the character change, you know that every step your character takes will lead to that end. There will be no padding, nothing extraneous. This is the only way to make the story *organic* (internally logical), to guarantee that every step on the journey is necessarily connected to every other step and that the journey builds to a crescendo.

Some writers are afraid of this technique because they think it constricts them or forces them to write schematically. In fact, this technique gives you greater freedom because you always have a safety net. No matter where you are in the story, you know your eventual destination. So you can take chances and try out story events that may appear on the surface to be off the path but are actually taking you in a more creative way to where you need to go.

Remember, the self-revelation is made possible at the beginning of the story. This means that a good self-revelation has two parts: the revelation itself and the setup.

The *moment of revelation* should have these qualities:

- It should be sudden, so that it has maximum dramatic force for the hero and the audience.
- It should create a burst of emotion for the audience as they share the realization with the hero.
- It should be *new* information for the hero: he must see, for the first time, that he has been living a lie about himself and that he has hurt others.
- It should trigger the hero to take new moral action immediately, proving that the revelation is real and has profoundly changed him.

The *setup* to the revelation should have these qualities:

- The hero must be a thinking person, someone who is capable of seeing the truth and knowing right action.
- The hero must be hiding something from himself.
- This lie or delusion must be hurting the hero in a very real way.

You may notice what appears to be a contradiction: a thinking person who is lying to himself. But even though this may be a contradiction, it is real. We all suffer from it. One of the powers of storytelling is showing us how a human being who is so capable of brilliant and creative thought is also capable of intricate and enslaving delusion.

CHARACTER TECHNIQUE: DOUBLE REVERSAL

The standard way of expressing character change is to give the hero a need and a self-revelation. He challenges and changes his basic beliefs and then takes new moral action. Because the audience identifies with the hero, they learn when he learns.

But a problem arises: How do you show your own moral vision of right and wrong action as distinct from the hero's? These visions are not necessarily the same. Also, you may wish to express the character change with more complexity and emotional impact than the standard method allows.

An advanced technique for showing character change in a story is a unique kind of self-revelation, what I call the "double reversal." In this technique, you give the opponent, as well as the hero, a self-revelation. Each learns from the other, and the audience receives two insights about how to act and live in the world instead of one.

There are a couple of advantages to using the double reversal over the standard single self-revelation. First, by using the comparative method, you can show the audience the right way of acting and being that is both subtler and clearer than a single revelation. Think of it as the difference between stereo and mono sound. Second, the audience is not so locked onto the hero. They can more easily step back and see the bigger picture, the larger ramifications of the story.

To create a double reversal, take these steps.

1. Give both the hero and the main opponent a weakness and a need (the weaknesses and needs of the hero and the opponent do not have to be the same or even similar).
2. Make the opponent human. That means that he must be capable of learning and changing.
3. During or just after the battle, give the opponent as well as the hero a self-revelation.
4. Connect the two self-revelations. The hero should learn something from the opponent, and the opponent should learn something from the hero.
5. Your moral vision is the best of what both characters learn.

The double reversal is a powerful technique, but it is not common. That's because most writers don't create opponents who are capable of a self-revelation. If your opponent is evil, innately and completely bad, he will not discover how wrong he has been at the end of the story. For example, an opponent who reaches into people's chests and rips their heart out for dinner is not going to realize he needs to change.

Not surprisingly, you see the greatest use of the double reversal in love stories, which are designed so that the hero and the lover (the main opponent) learn from each other. You can see examples of double reversal in films like *Kramer vs. Kramer*; *Adam's Rib*; *Pride and Prejudice*; *Casablanca*; *Pretty Woman*; *sex, lies, and videotape*; *Scent of a Woman*; and *The Music Man*.

Once you have figured out your hero's self-revelation, you go back to the need. One of the benefits of creating the self-revelation first is that it automatically tells you your hero's need. If the self-revelation is what the hero learns, the need is what the hero doesn't yet know but must learn to have a better life. Your hero needs to see through the great delusion he is living under to overcome the great weakness that is crippling his life.

Creating Your Hero, Step 3: Desire

The third step in creating a strong hero is to create the desire line. Chapter 3 described this step as the spine of the story. Keep in mind three rules for a strong desire line:

1. You want only one desire line that builds steadily in importance and intensity. If you have more than one desire line, the story will fall apart. It will literally go in two or three directions at once, leaving it with no narrative drive and leaving the audience confused. In good stories, the hero has a single overriding goal that he pursues with greater and greater intensity. The story moves faster and faster, and the narrative drive becomes overwhelming.

2. The desire should be specific—and the more specific, the better. To make sure your desire line is specific enough, ask yourself if there is a specific moment in the story when the audience knows whether your hero has accomplished his goal or not. In *Top Gun*, I know when the hero succeeds or fails in winning the Top Gun award because the head of the flight school hands it to someone else. In *Flashdance*, I know when the hero succeeds or fails in reaching her desire of getting into the ballet school because she gets a letter telling her she got in.

    Sometimes a writer will say something like "My hero's desire is to become independent." Applying the rule of the specific moment, when does someone become independent in life? When he leaves home for the first time? When he gets married? When he gets divorced? There is no specific moment when someone becomes independent. Dependence or independence has more to do with need and makes a very poor desire.

3. The desire should be accomplished—if at all—near the end of the story. If the hero reaches the goal in the middle of the story, you must either end the story right there or create a new desire line, in which case you have stuck two stories together. By extending the hero's desire line almost to the end, you make your story a single unit and ensure that it has tremendous narrative drive.

The desire line in each of the following films meets all three criteria:

- *Saving Private Ryan*: to find Private Ryan and bring him back alive
- *The Full Monty*: to make a lot of money by performing naked in front of a roomful of women
- *The Verdict*: to win the case
- *Chinatown*: to solve the mystery of who killed Hollis
- *The Godfather*: to take revenge on the men who shot Vito Corleone

Creating Your Hero, Step 4: The Opponent

I'm not exaggerating when I say that the trick to defining your hero and figuring out your story is to figure out your opponent. Of all the connections in the character web, the most important is the relationship between hero and main opponent. This relationship determines how the entire drama builds.

That's why, as a writer, you should love this character, because he will help you in countless ways. Structurally the opponent always holds the key, because your hero learns *through* his opponent. It is only because the opponent is attacking the hero's great weakness that the hero is forced to deal with it and grow.

KEY POINT: *The main character is only as good as the person he fights.*

To see how important this principle is, think of your hero and opponent as tennis players. If the hero is the best player in the world but the opponent is a weekend hacker, the hero will hit a few shots, the opponent will stumble around, and the audience will be bored. But if the opponent is the second-best player in the world, the hero will be forced to hit his best shots, the opponent will hit back some spectacular shots of his own, they'll run each other all over the court, and the audience will go wild.

That's exactly how good storytelling works. The hero and the opponent drive each other to greatness.

The story drama unfolds once you have set the relationship between hero and main opponent. If you get this relationship right, the story will almost certainly work. If you get this relationship wrong, the story will most definitely fail. So let's look at the elements that you need to create a great opponent.

1. Make the opponent necessary.

The single most important element of a great opponent is that he be necessary to the hero. This has a very specific structural meaning. The main opponent is the one person in the world best able to attack the great weakness of the hero. And he should attack it relentlessly. The necessary opponent either forces the hero to overcome his weakness or destroys him. Put another way, the necessary opponent makes it possible for the hero to grow.

2. Make him human.

A human opponent is not just a person as opposed to an animal, an object, or a phenomenon. A human opponent is as complex and as valuable as the hero.

Structurally, this means that a human opponent is always some form of double of the hero. Certain writers have used the concept of the double (also known as a doppelgänger) when determining the specific characteristics of the opponent, who is extremely similar to the hero. But it is really a much larger technique, one of the major principles to use for creating any hero and opponent pair. The concept of the double provides a number of ways that the hero and the opponent should compare with, contrast with, and help define each other:

■ The opponent-double has certain weaknesses that are causing him to act wrongly toward others or act in ways that prevent the opponent from having a better life.

■ Like the hero, the opponent-double has a need, based on those weaknesses.

■ The opponent-double must want something, preferably the same goal as the hero.

■ The opponent-double should be of great power, status, or ability, to put ultimate pressure on the hero, set up a final battle, and drive the hero to larger success (or failure).

3. Give him values that oppose the values of the hero.

The actions of the hero and the opponent are based on a set of beliefs, or values. These values represent each character's view of what makes life good.

In the best stories, the values of the opponent come into conflict with the values of the hero. Through that conflict, the audience sees which way of life is superior. Much of the power of the story rests on the quality of this opposition.

4. Give the opponent a strong but flawed moral argument.

An evil opponent is someone who is inherently bad and therefore mechanical and uninteresting. In most real conflict, there is no clear sense of good and evil, right and wrong. In a well-drawn story, both hero and opponent believe that they have chosen the correct path, and both have reasons for believing so. They are also both misguided, though in different ways.

The opponent attempts to justify his actions morally, just as the hero does. A good writer details the moral argument of the opponent, making sure it is powerful and compelling, but ultimately wrong (I'll discuss how in the next chapter, "Moral Argument").

5. Give him certain similarities to the hero.

The contrast between hero and opponent is powerful only when both characters have strong similarities. Each then presents a slightly different approach to the same dilemma. And it is in the similarities that crucial and instructive differences become most clear.

By giving the hero and the opponent certain similarities, you also keep the hero from being perfectly good and the opponent from being completely evil. Never think of the hero and opponent as extreme opposites. Rather, they are two possibilities within a range of possibilities. The argument between hero and opponent is not between good and evil but between two characters who have weaknesses and needs.

6. Keep him in the same place as the hero.

This runs counter to common sense. When two people don't like each other, they tend to go in opposite directions. But if this happens in your story, you will have great difficulty building conflict. The trick is to find a natural reason for the hero and opponent to stay in the same place during the course of the story.

A textbook example of how an opponent works on a hero is the Hannibal Lecter character in *The Silence of the Lambs*. Ironically, in this film, Lecter is not a true opponent. He is the fake-opponent ally, a character who appears to be Clarice's opponent but is really her greatest friend. I like to think of Lecter as Yoda from hell; the training he gives Clarice, though brutal, is far more valuable than anything she learns at the FBI Academy.

But in their first meeting, Lecter shows us, in miniature, how an opponent relentlessly attacks the hero's weaknesses until she fixes them or falls. Clarice visits Lecter in his cell to get some insights about the serial killer Buffalo Bill. After a promising start, she overplays her hand and insults Lecter's intelligence. He goes on the attack.

LECTER: Oh, Agent Starling, you think you can dissect me with this blunt little tool?

CLARICE: No, I thought that your knowledge . . .

LECTER: You're so ambitious, aren't you? You know what you look like to me with your good bag and your cheap shoes. You look like a rube. A well-scrubbed, hustling rube. With a little taste. Good nutrition's given you some length of bone, but you're not more than one generation from poor white trash. Are you, Agent Starling? And that accent you've tried so desperately to shed, pure West Virginia. Who's your father, dear, is he a coal miner? Does he stink of the lamp? And oh how quickly the boys found you. All those tedious, sticky fumblings in the back seats of cars. While you could only dream of getting out, getting anywhere, getting all the way to the FBI.

Let's look at some examples of opponents in storytelling, noting that each is not so much a separate individual as the one best opponent for that hero.

OTHELLO
(by William Shakespeare, 1604)

Othello is a warrior-king, always going straight through the front door, all force with no guile. A lesser writer, believing the conventional wisdom that "drama is conflict," would have created another warrior-king to oppose him. There would have been lots of conflict but not much of a story.

Shakespeare understood the concept of the necessary opponent. Starting with Othello's great weakness, his insecurity about his marriage, Shakespeare created Iago. Iago isn't much of a warrior. He doesn't attack well from the front. But he is a master of attacking from behind, using words, innuendo, intrigue, and manipulation to get what he wants. Iago is Othello's necessary opponent. He sees Othello's great weakness and attacks it brilliantly and ruthlessly until he brings the great warrior-king down.

CHINATOWN
(by Robert Towne, 1974)

Jake Gittes is a simple detective who is overconfident and too idealistic, believing he can bring justice by discovering the truth. He also has a weakness for money and the finer things in life. His opponent, Noah Cross, is one of the richest, most powerful men in Los Angeles. He outsmarts Jake and then uses his wealth and power to bury Jake's truth and get away with murder.

PRIDE AND PREJUDICE
(by Jane Austen, 1813)

Elizabeth Bennet is a smart, charming young woman who is too pleased with her own intelligence and too quick to judge others. Her opponent is Mr. Darcy, who is guilty of extreme pride and a disdain for the lower classes. But it is because of Darcy's pride and prejudice and his efforts to overcome them for her that Elizabeth finally becomes aware of the pride and prejudice in herself.

STAR WARS
(by George Lucas, 1977)

Luke Skywalker is an impetuous, naive young man with a desire to do good and a tremendous but untrained ability in the use of the Force. Darth Vader is a grand master of the Force. He can outthink and outfight Luke, and he uses his knowledge of his son and of the Force to try to lure Luke to the "dark side."

CRIME AND PUNISHMENT
(by Fyodor Dostoyevsky, 1866)

Raskolnikov is a brilliant young man who commits a murder just to prove the philosophy that he is above the law and the common man. His opponent, Porfiry, is a petty bureaucrat, a lowly police detective. But this common man of the law is smarter than Raskolnikov and, more important, wiser. He shows Raskolnikov the error of his philosophy and gets him to confess by showing him that true greatness comes from self-revelation, responsibility, and suffering.

BASIC INSTINCT
(by Joe Eszterhas, 1992)

Nick is a sharp, tough police detective who is guilty of using drugs and killing without sufficient cause. Catherine, who is just as smart, challenges him at every turn and uses Nick's weakness for sex and drugs to lure him into her lair.

A STREETCAR NAMED DESIRE
(by Tennessee Williams, 1947)

Blanche, a faded beauty with a fragile hold on reality, has lied and used sex to defend herself against her crumbling situation. Stanley is a brutal, competitive "top dog" who refuses to let Blanche get away with her tall tales. Thinking she is a lying whore who has tried to swindle him and fool his friend Mitch, he jams the "truth" in her face so relentlessly that she goes mad.

Vertigo
(novel by Pierre Boileau and Thomas Narcejac, screenplay by Alec Coppel and Samuel Taylor, 1958)

Scottie is a decent guy but is a bit naive and suffers from vertigo. His college friend, Gavin Elster, uses Scottie's weaknesses to concoct a plan to murder Elster's wife.

BUILDING CONFLICT

Once you set up a hero and an opponent competing for the same goal, you must build the conflict steadily until the final battle. Your purpose is to put constant pressure on your hero, because this is what will force him to change. The way you build conflict and put pressure on your hero depends primarily on how you distribute the attacks on the hero.

In average or simple stories, the hero comes into conflict with only one opponent. This standard opposition has the virtue of clarity, but it doesn't let you develop a deep or powerful sequence of conflicts, and it doesn't allow the audience to see a hero acting within a larger society.

KEY POINT: A simplistic opposition between two characters kills any chance at depth, complexity, or the reality of human life in your story. For that, you need a web of oppositions.

Four-Corner Opposition

Better stories go beyond a simple opposition between hero and main opponent and use a technique I call four-corner opposition. In this technique, you create a hero and a main opponent plus at least two secondary opponents. (You can have even more if the added opponents serve an important story function.) Think of each of the characters—hero and three opponents—as taking a corner of the box, meaning that each is as different from the others as possible.

Standard two-character opposition:

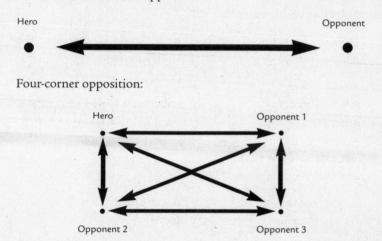

There are five rules to keep in mind to make best use of the key features of four-corner opposition.

1. Each opponent should use a different way of attacking the hero's great weakness.

Attacking the hero's weakness is the central purpose of the opponent. So the first way of distinguishing opponents from one another is to give each a unique way of attacking. Notice that this technique guarantees that all conflict is organically connected to the hero's great flaw. Four-corner opposition has the added benefit of representing a complete society in miniature, with each character personifying one of the basic pillars of that society.

In the following examples, the hero is in the upper left corner, as in the diagram, while his main opponent is opposite him, with the two secondary characters underneath. In parentheses is the archetype each embodies, if one exists. As you study the examples, notice that four-corner opposition is fundamental to any good story, regardless of the medium, genre, or time when it was written.

HAMLET
(by William Shakespeare, circa 1601)

Hamlet (rebel prince)	King Claudius (+ Rosencrantz + Guildenstern) (king)
Queen Gertrude (queen)	Polonius (+ Ophelia) (mentor) + (maiden)

THE USUAL SUSPECTS
(by Christopher McQuarrie, 1995)

Keaton (+ team) (trickster-warriors)	Agent Kujan (none)
Verbal (artist-trickster)	Keyser Soze (+ his representative) (warrior-king)

2. Try to place each character in conflict, not only with the hero but also with every other character.

Notice an immediate advantage four-corner opposition has over standard opposition. In four-corner opposition, the amount of conflict you can create and build in the story jumps exponentially. Not only do you place your hero in conflict with three characters instead of one, but you can also put the opponents in conflict with each other, as shown by the arrows in the four-corner opposition diagram. The result is intense conflict and a dense plot.

AMERICAN BEAUTY
(by Alan Ball, 1999)

Lester (+ Ricky) (deposed king–trickster)	Carolyn (+ real estate king) (queen-mother)
Jane (+ Angela) (princess-rebel + princess)	Col. Fitts (warrior)

WUTHERING HEIGHTS

(novel by Emily Brontë, 1847, screenplay by Charles MacArthur and Ben Hecht, 1939)

Cathy
(lover)

Heathcliff
(lover-rebel)

Hindley, her brother
(none)

Linton (+ Isabella, his sister)
(king)

3. Put the values of all four characters in conflict.

Great storytelling isn't just conflict between characters. It's conflict between characters *and their values.* When your hero experiences character change, he challenges and changes basic beliefs, leading to new moral action. A good opponent has a set of beliefs that come under assault as well. The beliefs of the hero have no meaning, and do not get expressed in the story, unless they come into conflict with the beliefs of at least one other character, preferably the opponent.

In the standard way of placing values in conflict, two characters, hero and single opponent, fight for the same goal. As they fight, their values—and their ways of life—come into conflict too.

Four-corner opposition of values allows you to create a story of potentially epic scope and yet keep its essential organic unity. For example, each character may express a unique system of values, a way of life that can come into conflict with three other major ways of life. Notice that the four-corner method of placing values in conflict provides tremendous texture and depth of theme to a story.

A story with four-corner opposition of values might look like this:

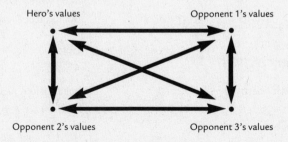

Hero's values   Opponent 1's values

Opponent 2's values   Opponent 3's values

KEY POINT: Be as detailed as possible when listing the values of each character.

Don't just come up with a single value for each character. Think of a *cluster* of values that each can believe in. The values in each cluster are unique but also related to one another.

KEY POINT: Look for the positive and negative versions of the same value.

Believing in something can be a strength, but it can also be the source of weakness. By identifying the negative as well as the positive side of the same value, you can see how each character is most likely to make a mistake while fighting for what he believes. Examples of positive and negative versions of the same value are determined and aggressive, honest and insensitive, and patriotic and domineering.

THE CHERRY ORCHARD
(by Anton Chekhov, 1904)

Madame Ranevsky (+ brother Gaev)   Lopakhin
(queen + lover)   (prince)   (businessman)

real love, beauty,   money, status,
the past   power, the future

              Varya
              (worker)

              hard work, family,
              marriage, practicality

Trofimov   Anya
(student + teacher)   (princess)

the truth, learning,   her mother, kindness,
compassion,   higher love
higher love

4. Push the characters to the corners.

When creating your four-corner opposition, pencil in each character—hero and three opponents—into one of four corners in a box, as in our diagrams. Then "push" each character to the corners. In other words, make each character as different as possible from the other three.

BUTCH CASSIDY AND THE SUNDANCE KID
(by William Goldman, 1969)

Butch (trickster)	Sundance (+ Etta) (warrior + lover)
Harvey (warrior)	E. H. Harriman + posse (Lafors) (king + warriors)

THE PHILADELPHIA STORY
(play by Philip Barry, screenplay by Donald Ogden Stewart, 1940)

Tracy (goddess)	Dexter (lover)
George, her fiancé (king)	Mike (+ Liz) (artist)

5. Extend the four-corner pattern to every level of the story.

Once you've determined the basic four-corner opposition, consider extending that pattern to other levels of the story. For example, you might set up a unique four-corner pattern of opposition within a society, an institution, a family, or even a single character. Especially in more epic stories, you will see a four-corner opposition on several levels.

Here are three stories that use four-corner opposition at two different levels of the story.

THE ILIAD
(by Homer)

Within the Greeks

Achilles
(warrior-artist-rebel)

Agamemnon
(king)

Odysseus
(trickster-warrior)

Ajax
(warrior)

Within the World

Achilles
(warrior-artist-rebel)

Hector
(warrior-prince)

Agamemnon
(king)

Paris (+ Helen)
(lover)

THE SEVEN SAMURAI
(by Akira Kurosawa & Shinobu Hashimoto & Hideo Oguni, 1954)

Within the Samurai

Lead samurai + others
(warrior-king)

master swordsman
(artist-warrior)

apprentice
(student)

Mifune samurai
(farmer-warrior)

Within the World

Lead samurai + team
(killer-king)

bandit samurai
(killers)

farmers
(growers)

Mifune samurai
(grower-killer)

THE GODFATHER
(novel by Mario Puzo, screenplay by Mario Puzo and Francis Ford Coppola, 1972)

Within the Family

Godfather (+ Tom) (king)	Sonny (warrior)
Fredo (then Kay) (lover)	Michael (trickster-warrior-king)

Within the World

Corleone family (king + warriors)	Sollozzo (warrior)
Barzini (king)	Carlo (+ Tessio + driver + bodyguards) (tricksters)

CREATING YOUR CHARACTERS—WRITING EXERCISE 3

- **Character Web by Story Function and Archetype** Create your character web. Start by listing all of your characters, and describe what function they play in the story (for example, hero, main opponent, ally, fake-ally opponent, subplot character). Write down next to each character the archetype, if any, that applies.
- **Central Moral Problem** List the central moral problem of the story.
- **Comparing the Characters** List and compare the following structure elements for all your characters.
  1. Weaknesses
  2. Need, both psychological and moral
  3. Desire
  4. Values
  5. Power, status, and ability
  6. How each faces the central moral problem

Begin the comparison between your hero and main opponent.

- **Variation on the Moral Problem** Make sure each character takes a different approach to the hero's central moral problem.
- **Requirements of a Hero** Now concentrate on fleshing out your hero. Begin by making sure you have incorporated the four requirements of any great hero:
  1. Make your lead character constantly fascinating.
  2. Make the audience identify with the character, but not too much.
  3. Make the audience empathize with your hero, not sympathize.
  4. Give your hero a moral as well as a psychological need.
- **Hero's Character Change** Determine your hero's character change. Write down the self-revelation first, and then go back to the need. Make sure the self-revelation actually solves the need. In other words, whatever lies or crutches the hero is living with in the beginning must be faced at the self-revelation and overcome.
- **Changed Beliefs** Write down the beliefs your hero challenges and changes over the course of your story.

- **Hero's Desire**   Clarify your hero's desire line. Is it a single, specific goal that extends throughout the story? When does the audience know whether the hero has accomplished the goal or not?
- **Opponents**   Detail your opponents. First describe how your main opponent and each of your lesser opponents attack the great weakness of your hero in a different way.
- **Opponents' Values**   List a few values for each opponent.

     How is each opponent a kind of double for the hero? Give each some level of power, status, and ability, and describe what similarities each shares with the hero.

     State in one line the moral problem of each character and how each character justifies the actions he takes to reach his goal.

- **Minor Character Variation on the Hero's Weakness and Moral Problem**   In what ways are any of the minor characters variations on the hero's unique weakness and moral problem?
- **Four-Corner Opposition**   Map out the four-corner opposition for your story. Put your hero and main opponent on the top line with at least two secondary opponents underneath. Label each character with his or her archetype, but only if it is appropriate. Many characters are not archetypes. Don't force it.

     Push the four major characters to the corners. That is, make sure each is as different from the other three as possible. The best way to ensure that is to focus on how the values of each differ.

Let's use *A Streetcar Named Desire* as an example of how to flesh out characters.

A STREETCAR NAMED DESIRE
(by Tennessee Williams, 1947)

- **Character Web by Story Function and Archetype**
  Hero: Blanche DuBois (artist)
  Main opponent: Stanley Kowalski (warrior-king)
  Fake-ally opponents: Mitch, Stanley's friend, and Stella Kowalski
       (mother), Blanche's sister
  Ally: None

Fake-opponent ally: None
Subplot character: None

- **Central Moral Problem**   Is someone ever justified in using lies and illusion to get love?

- **Comparing the Characters**

BLANCHE

Weaknesses: Beaten down, relies on her fading looks, has no true sense of self, often retreats into delusion when life is too hard, uses sex to get love, uses others to serve her and preserve the illusion that she's still a belle.

Psychological need: Blanche must learn to see the value that is in her heart and not in her looks. Also, she must stop looking for a man to save her.

Moral need: She must learn to tell the truth when seeking someone's love.

Desire: At first, Blanche wants a place to rest. But her main desire is to get Mitch to marry her so that she can feel safe.

STANLEY

Weaknesses: Mean-spirited, suspicious, quick-tempered, brutal.

Psychological need: Stanley needs to overcome the petty competitiveness that drives him to beat everyone else and prove what a big man he is.

Moral need: Stanley must overcome the base cruelty he shows toward anyone weaker than himself. He is a mean, selfish child who must deprive others of happiness.

Desire: Stanley wants Blanche out of his house and wants his life back the way it was. Then he wants to keep Mitch from marrying Blanche.

STELLA

Weaknesses: Naive, dependent on Stanley, simpleminded.

Psychological need: Stella needs to become her own person and see Stanley for what he really is.

Moral need: Stella must take responsibility for supporting Stanley's brutality.

Desire: She wants to see her sister marry Mitch and be happy.

MITCH

Weaknesses: Shy, weak, unable to think or act on his own.

Psychological need: Mitch needs to break away from Stanley and his
   mother and live his own life.

Moral need: He must treat Blanche as a human being, respecting her
   decency and the pain with which she has had to live her life.

Desire: At first, Mitch wants to marry Blanche. But when he learns of
   her past, he just wants her for sex.

■ **Variation on the Moral Problem**

Blanche: Blanche lies to herself and to others in order to get love.

Stanley: Stanley is so brutally honest when it comes to exposing the
   lies of others that he actually tears people apart. His belief that
   the world is harsh, competitive, and underhanded makes it more
   so than it really is. His aggressive, self-righteous view of the truth
   is far more destructive than Blanche's lies.

Stella: Stella is guilty of a sin of omission. She allows her sister to
   have her little delusions, but she cannot see the lies her own
   husband tells after he brutally attacks her sister.

Mitch: Mitch is taken in by Blanche's superficial lies and is therefore
   unable to see the deeper beauty that she possesses.

Blanche's Character Change:

> *Weaknesses: Loneliness, false* → *Change: Madness, despair,*
>   *hope, bravado, lies*   *broken spirit*

■ **Changed Beliefs**   Blanche moves beyond her belief that she must
fool a man by physical and verbal lies to get him to love her. But her
honesty and insight are wasted on the wrong man.

■ **Blanche's Desire**   Blanche wants Mitch to marry her. We know
that Blanche fails to achieve her desire when Mitch brutally turns
her down.

■ **Opponents' Attacks on the Hero's Weaknesses**

Stanley: Stanley is brutally aggressive in forcing Blanche to face the
   "truth" about herself.

Stella: Stella is largely unaware of her part in destroying her sister. Her

simplemindedness and love for Stanley prevent her from
protecting her sister's fragile state from her husband's attacks.
Stella refuses to believe that Stanley has raped her sister.

Mitch: Mitch is essentially decent, but he is weak and cowardly. When
he shows interest in Blanche but then backs away and even abuses
her, he dashes her last best hopes and hurts her deeply.

- **Characters' Values**
Blanche: Beauty, appearance, manners, refinement, kindness, Stella.
Stanley: Strength, power, women, sex, money, Stella, his male friends.
Stella: Stanley, her marriage, Blanche, sex, her baby.
Mitch: His mother, his friends, manners, Blanche.

- **Opponents' Similarities to the Hero**
Stanley: Blanche and Stanley are very different in many ways. But they
share a deeper understanding of the world that Stella does not
see. They are both smart in a scheming, tactical way and
recognize that ability in the other.

Stella: Stella shares Blanche's past, when they lived in the beautiful,
graceful, mannered world of old Southern aristocracy. Stella also
shares her sister's need for love and kindness.

Mitch: Mitch responds to Blanche's love of manners and courtship.
He appreciates her gentility and the last vestiges of her beauty.

- **Power, Status, and Ability**
Blanche: Blanche has lost all status. She desperately holds on to her
ability to please a man with her looks and charm.

Stanley: Stanley is the "top dog" in his circle of male friends. He is
also very capable of getting what he wants, especially from Stella.

Stella: Stella has no power or status except what is given to her by
Stanley. But she is very good at pleasing Stanley.

Mitch: Mitch has little status or power either within his group or in
the larger world. He is a born follower.

- **Moral Problem and Justification**
Blanche: Blanche feels that her lies have not hurt anyone and that this
is her only chance at happiness.

Stanley: He thinks Blanche is a lying whore who has swindled him.

He believes he is just looking out for his friend when he tells Mitch about Blanche's past.

Stella: Stella is not smart enough to see that she is part of a process that is destroying her sister.

Mitch: Mitch feels that a woman who has acted as a prostitute can be treated like one.

- **Minor Character Variation on the Hero's Weakness and Moral Problem**   Eunice and Steve are married and live upstairs. They argue over his infidelity. When she leaves, Steve chases after her and brings her back.

- **Four-Corner Opposition**

Blanche	Stanley
(artist)	(warrior-king)
Stella	Mitch
(mother)	(none)

CHAPTER 5

Moral Argument

ACCORDING TO HOLLYWOOD LORE, it was Samuel Goldwyn who said, "If you want to send a message, try Western Union." He was right about not sending a message in an obvious, preachy way. But stories with powerful themes, expressed properly, are not only more highly regarded but more popular as well.

A great story is not simply a sequence of events or surprises designed to entertain an audience. It is a sequence of actions, with moral implications and effects, designed to express a larger theme.

Theme may be the most misunderstood of all major aspects of storytelling. Most people think of theme as subject matter, in categories such as the moral, psychological, and social, citing examples such as death, good versus evil, redemption, class, corruption, responsibility, and love.

I don't refer to theme as subject matter. Theme is the author's view of how to act in the world. It is your moral vision. Whenever you present a character using means to reach an end, you are presenting a moral predicament, exploring the question of right action, and making a moral argument about how best to live. Your moral vision is totally original to you, and expressing it to an audience is one of the main purposes of telling the story.

Let's return to the body metaphor for story. A good story is a "living" system in which the parts work together to make an integrated whole. These parts are themselves systems, each—like character, plot, and theme—hanging together as a unit but also connecting in myriad ways to each of the other subsystems of the story body. We have compared character to the heart and the circulatory system of the story. Structure is the skeleton. Continuing the metaphor, we might say that theme is the brain of the story body, because it expresses the higher design. As the brain, it should lead the writing process, without becoming so dominant that it turns the story—a work of artistry—into a philosophical thesis.

How writers weave their moral vision into the story covers a wide range of possibilities, depending on the author and the story form. At one extreme are highly thematic forms like drama, allegory, irony, "serious literature," and religious stories. They place heavy emphasis on creating a complex moral vision, with dialogue that highlights the complexity and contradiction in the characters' moral situation.

At the other extreme are such popular story forms as adventure, myth, fantasy, and action stories. Here the moral vision is usually slight, with almost total emphasis on surprise, suspense, imagination, and the psychological and emotional states, rather than the moral difficulties, of the characters.

Regardless of story form, average writers express their moral vision almost solely through the dialogue, so that the "morals" overwhelm the story. Stories like these, such as *Guess Who's Coming to Dinner?* and *Gandhi,* get criticized for being "on the nose" and preachy. At their worst, overtly moralizing stories are ponderous, causing their audience to shrink back from the author's oppressive lecturing, clumsy narrative, and lack of technique.

You never want to create characters that sound like a mouthpiece for your ideas. Good writers express their moral vision slowly and subtly, primarily through the story structure and the way the hero deals with a particular situation. Your moral vision is communicated by how your hero pursues his goal while competing with one or more opponents and by what your hero learns, or fails to learn, over the course of his struggle.

In effect, you, as the author, are making a moral argument through what your characters do in the plot. How does this sort of moral argument, the argument of action, work in storytelling?

FINDING THE THEME LINE IN THE DESIGNING PRINCIPLE

The first step in making an argument of action is to condense your theme to a single line. The theme line is your view about right and wrong actions and what those actions do to a person's life. A theme line is not a highly nuanced expression of your moral vision. And written as only one line, it can seem heavy-handed. But it is still valuable because it forces you to focus all the moral elements of the story into a single moral idea.

The complex argument of action that you will eventually weave through the story begins, as always, with the seed, which is the designing principle. Just as the designing principle is the key to your premise line, so is it the key to your theme line.

The designing principle is what makes all the actions of the story organic. The trick to using the designing principle to figure out your theme line is to focus on the actions in the story strictly for their *moral* effects. In other words, how do the characters' actions hurt other people, and how, if at all, do the characters make things right?

The same techniques of designing principle that help you deepen your premise will open up your theme as well. Here are just a few.

Traveling

The traveling metaphor, or journey, is a perfect foundation for a moral line because you can embed an entire moral sequence into the line. Huck's trip down the Mississippi is also a trip into greater slavery. Marlow's trip up the river into the jungle is also a trip deeper into moral confusion and darkness. The journey from Manhattan Island to Skull Island in *King Kong* suggests the move from moral civilization to the most immoral state of nature. But the return to Manhattan shows the real theme line, that both islands are governed by the most cutthroat competition, with the island of humans being the more brutal.

Single Grand Symbol

A single grand symbol can also suggest a theme line or central moral element. A classic example of the single moral symbol is presented in *The Scarlet Letter*. The letter *A* that Hester Prynne must wear stands of course for her immoral act of adultery from which the story begins. But it also stands for the deeper immorality to which the story leads, that of the townspeople who hide their own sins and who attack true love with their laws of public conformity.

In *For Whom the Bell Tolls*, the single image of the tolling bell signifies death. But the phrase "for whom the bell tolls" refers to another line that is the real key to the designing principle of the story and the theme that comes out of it. That line, from John Donne's *Devotions upon Emergent Occasions*, is "No man is an island, entire of itself. . . . Any man's death diminishes me, because I am involved in Mankind. And therefore, never send to know for whom the bell tolls, it tolls for thee." The symbol of man, not as an island but as an individual in a community, organizes this story under one image, and it implies the probable theme line: in the face of death, the only thing that gives life meaning is sacrificing for the individuals you love.

Connecting Two Grand Symbols in a One-Line Process

Connecting two symbols gives you the same benefit as the journey: the symbols represent two poles in a moral sequence. When this technique is used, it usually signals a declining morality. But it could be rising. *Heart of Darkness* uses the technique of the two symbols but also adds the traveling metaphor to express its theme line. Implied in the two-symbol title are the dark heart and the center of the moral darkness, both of which suggest an investigation into what constitutes human depravity.

Other designing principles—units of time, use of a storyteller, a special way the story unfolds—can also help you clarify your theme line. Let's return to the designing principles of the stories we discussed in Chapter 2 to see the possible theme lines they produce.

Moses, in the Book of Exodus

- **Designing Principle** A man who does not know who he is struggles to lead his people to freedom and receives the new moral laws that will define him and his people.
- **Theme Line** A man who takes responsibility for his people is rewarded by a vision of how to live by the word of God.

Ulysses

- **Designing Principle** In a modern odyssey through the city, over the course of a single day, one man finds a father and the other man finds a son.
- **Theme Line** The true hero is the man who endures the slings and arrows of everyday life and shows compassion to another person in need.

Four Weddings and a Funeral

- **Designing Principle** A group of friends experiences four utopias (weddings) and a moment in hell (funeral) as they all look for their right partner in marriage.
- **Theme Line** When you find your one true love, you must commit to that person with your whole heart.

Harry Potter Books

- **Designing Principle** A magician prince learns to be a man and a king by attending a boarding school for sorcerers over the course of seven school years.
- **Theme Line** When you are blessed with great talent and power, you must become a leader and sacrifice for the good of others.

The Sting

- **Designing Principle** Tell the story of a sting in the form of a sting, and con both the opponent and the audience.
- **Theme Line** A little lying and cheating are OK if you bring down an evil man.

LONG DAY'S JOURNEY INTO NIGHT

- **Designing Principle**   As a family moves from day into night, its members are confronted with the sins and ghosts of their past.
- **Theme Line**   You must face the truth about yourself and others and forgive.

MEET ME IN ST. LOUIS

- **Designing Principle**   The growth of a family over the course of a year is shown by events in each of the four seasons.
- **Theme Line**   Sacrificing for the family is more important than striving for personal glory.

COPENHAGEN

- **Designing Principle**   Use the Heisenberg uncertainty principle to explore the ambiguous morality of the man who discovered it.
- **Theme Line**   Understanding why we act, and whether it is right, is always uncertain.

A CHRISTMAS CAROL

- **Designing Principle**   Trace the rebirth of a man by forcing him to view his past, his present, and his future over the course of one Christmas Eve.
- **Theme Line**   A person lives a much happier life when he gives to others.

IT'S A WONDERFUL LIFE

- **Designing Principle**   Express the power of the individual by showing what a town, and a nation, would be like if one man had never lived.
- **Theme Line**   A man's riches come not from the money he makes but from the friends and family he serves.

CITIZEN KANE

- **Designing Principle**   Use a number of storytellers to show that a man's life can never be known.
- **Theme Line**   A man who tries to force everyone to love him ends up alone.

SPLITTING THE THEME INTO OPPOSITIONS

The theme line is your moral argument focused into one sentence. Now you must express the theme line *dramatically*. That requires that you split it into a set of oppositions. You then attach these thematic oppositions to the hero and his opponents as they fight.

There are three main techniques you can use to break your theme line into dramatic oppositions: giving the hero a moral decision, making each character a variation on the theme, and placing the characters' values in conflict.

The Hero's Moral Decision

In the hero's moral development, the endpoints are your hero's moral need at the beginning of the story and his moral self-revelation, followed by his moral decision, at the end. This line is the moral frame of the story, and it tracks the fundamental moral lesson you want to express.

The classic strategy for dramatizing the hero's moral line is to give him a moral flaw at the beginning and then show how his desperation to beat the opponent brings out the worst in him. In short, he has to get worse before he gets better. Slowly but surely, he becomes aware that his central moral problem comes down to a choice between two ways of acting.

No matter how complex the actions of the characters over the course of the story, the final moral decision brings everything down to a choice between two. And it is final. So the moral decision is the narrow part of the funnel for your theme. The two options are the two most important moral actions your hero can take, so they provide you with the primary thematic opposition for the entire story.

This great decision usually comes just after the hero has his moral self-revelation, which shows him which choice to make. On rare occasion, the choice comes first, and the hero's self-revelation is a recognition that he made either the right or the wrong choice.

KEY POINT: *Since the endpoint of the hero's moral line is his final choice, you want to begin figuring out the moral oppositions using that choice.*

- *Casablanca*: When Rick's ex-love, Ilsa, returns to him, he can use two exit visas to escape with her to America. Rick chooses fighting the Nazis over his love for Ilsa.
- *The Maltese Falcon*: Detective Sam Spade discovers that Brigid O'Shaughnessy murdered his partner. When the police show up, Spade chooses justice over the woman he loves.
- *Sophie's Choice*: Sophie tells a young American writer about her past as a prisoner in the Auschwitz concentration camp. When she arrived, she had to choose between two negatives: Which child would she let the Nazis kill? (You could argue that this is not a true choice.)
- The *Iliad*: In a final showdown, Achilles kills Hector, the great warrior of the Trojans, and then drags Hector's body behind his chariot. Achilles lets Hector's father, Priam, take the body so that it can receive a proper burial.
- *Vertigo*: Scottie finds out that his lover, Madeleine, helped a man murder his wife. His moral decision at the end comes before his self-revelation. He decides not to forgive Madeleine and so is destroyed when he realizes that his wrong decision has killed the woman he loves.

Characters as Variations on a Theme

Once you have figured out the deepest moral opposition by looking at the hero's final moral choice, you detail this opposition through the character web by making each of the major characters a variation on the theme. Here is the sequence for making this technique work:

1. Look again at the final moral decision and your work on the premise line so you are clear about the central moral problem your hero must deal with in the story.
2. Make sure each of the major characters deals with the same moral problem, but in a different way.

3. Start by comparing the hero and the main opponent, since these characters personify the primary moral opposition you detail in the story. Then compare the hero to the other opponents.

4. Over the course of the story, each of the major characters should make a moral argument *in dialogue* justifying what they do to reach the goal. (Good moral argument is done primarily but not solely through structure. We'll discuss how to write moral dialogue in Chapter 10, "Scene Construction and Symphonic Dialogue.")

TOOTSIE
(by Larry Gelbart and Murray Schisgal, story by Don McGuire and Larry Gelbart, 1982)

Tootsie is the tale of an actor who disguises himself as a woman in order to get work on a TV show. But then he falls in love with an actress on the show, and various men are attracted to him as a woman.

The hero's central moral problem in the story is how a man treats a woman in love. Each opponent and ally is a variation of how men treat women or how women allow themselves to be treated by men.

L.A. CONFIDENTIAL
(novel by James Ellroy, screenplay by Brian Helgeland & Curtis Hanson, 1997)

In *L.A. Confidential*, three police detectives investigate a mass murder. All three are main characters, and each must deal with the central moral problem of administering justice. Bud is a cop who takes the law into his own hands, acting as judge, jury, and executioner. Jack has forgotten why he became a cop and arrests people for money. Ed wants to bring the guilty to justice, but he has become more interested in playing the political game of justice and rising to the top of the profession. All the other major characters exemplify a different version of the corruption of justice.

DANCES WITH WOLVES
(novel and screenplay by Michael Blake, 1990)

Dances with Wolves follows the exploits of an army officer in the American West during the late 1800s. Gradually he is drawn to take up the life of the Sioux Indians he thought were his enemy.

The hero's central moral problem is how he treats another race and culture and how he lives with animals and the land. Each opponent and ally takes a different approach to this problem.

The Characters' Values in Conflict

Using your character web, now place the values of each of the major characters in conflict as these people compete for the same goal.

1. Identify a set of values for your hero and each of the other major characters. Remember, values are deep-seated beliefs about what makes a good life.
2. Try to give a cluster of values to each character.
3. Make each set of values as different from the others as possible.
4. As your hero and his opponents fight over the goal, make sure their values come into direct conflict.

IT'S A WONDERFUL LIFE
(short story "The Greatest Gift" by Philip Van Doren Stern, screenplay by Frances Goodrich & Albert Hackett and Frank Capra, 1946)

Frustrated by living in a small town ruled by a tyrant, George Bailey is about to commit suicide until an angel shows him what the world would be like if he had never lived.

The hero and the opponent in this story compete over the town in which they live, based on the very different values each holds.

- George Bailey (Bedford Falls): Democracy, decency, kindness, hard work, the value of the common workingman
- Mr. Potter (Pottersville): One-man rule, money, power, survival of the fittest

THE CHERRY ORCHARD
(by Anton Chekhov, 1904)

In *The Cherry Orchard*, an aristocratic but poor family returns to their family estate, which is deep in debt, to try to save it.

These characters compete over who will control the estate. The focus of this competition is the value of the cherry orchard. Madame Ranevsky and her family value it for its immense beauty and its evocation of their past. Lopakhin values it only for its practical, monetary value; he wants to cut it down so he can build cottages he can rent.

- Madame Ranevsky: Real love, beauty, the past
- Lopakhin: Money, status, power, practicality, the future
- Varya: Hard work, family, marriage, practicality
- Trofimov: The truth, learning, compassion, higher love
- Anya: Her mother, kindness, higher love

FIELD OF DREAMS

(novel Shoeless Joe *by W. P. Kinsella, screenplay by Phil Alden Robinson, 1989)*
Field of Dreams is an American version of *The Cherry Orchard* in which the "orchard" wins. The competition in this story is over the value of the farmland that Ray has turned into a baseball diamond.

- Ray: Baseball, family, passion for your dreams
- Mark: Money, practical use of the land

With characters as variations on a theme and opposition of values, you may want to use the technique of four-corner opposition, explained in Chapter 4. In four-corner opposition, you have a hero and a main opponent and at least two secondary opponents. This gives even the most complex story an organic unity. Each of the four main characters can represent a fundamentally different approach to the same moral problem, and each can express an entire system of values, without the story collapsing into a complicated mess.

KEY POINT: Your moral argument will always be simplistic if you use a two-part opposition, like good versus evil. Only a web of moral oppositions (four-corner opposition is one such web) can give the audience a sense of the moral complexity of real life.

Notice that all three of these techniques guarantee that the theme is not imposed on the characters but rather is expressed through the characters. This ensures that the story doesn't come across as preachy. Notice also that the story has more depth because the opposition between the characters is not just based on plot, on people competing for a goal. Entire ways of living are at stake, so the emotional impact on the audience is huge.

THEME THROUGH STRUCTURE

Moral argument doesn't mean your hero and opponent appear in the first scene and engage in a verbal argument about morality. Moral argument in a story is an argument of action you make by showing your hero and opponent taking certain means to reach a goal. This is how you weave theme through the story structure instead of preaching to the audience in the dialogue.

In fact, one of the great principles of storytelling is that structure doesn't just carry content; it *is* content. And it is far more powerful content than what your characters say. Nowhere is this principle more accurately expressed than in theme.

In a good story, the story structure converges near the end at the same time that the theme expands in the mind of the audience. How does a converging story structure cause the theme to expand? A diagram of good structure and theme might look like this:

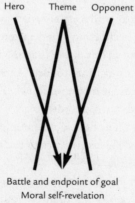

Hero   Theme   Opponent

Battle and endpoint of goal
Moral self-revelation
Moral decision

At the beginning of the story, you set the hero and opponent in opposition. But the conflict is not intense, and the audience doesn't yet know how the values of each come into conflict. So they have almost no sense of the theme of the story.

Throughout the middle of the story, the hero and the opponent come into increasing conflict, hence the converging structure. Through this conflict, a difference in values begins to emerge. So the theme starts to expand. Still, for most of a good story, the theme is largely hidden; it is quietly growing in the minds of the audience, and it will hit with full force at the end.

The convergent point of story structure is the battle, and right after that, the self-revelation and moral decision. In the battle, the audience sees not just which force but also which set of values is superior. The audience's understanding of the theme expands rapidly. At the self-revelation—especially if it's a moral self-revelation—the theme expands again. At the moral decision, it expands yet again. And because the theme has been expressed primarily through structure, it seems to emerge from the very soul of the audience, not to have been imposed on them like a tiresome sermon.

Let's look at how moral argument is expressed through structure over the course of the entire story, in detail, from beginning to end. We'll start with the basic strategy for expressing moral argument and then look at some variations.

Moral Argument: Basic Strategy

- **Values** The hero starts with a set of beliefs and values.
- **Moral Weakness** He is hurting others in some way at the beginning of the story. He is not evil but rather is acting from weakness or is unaware of the proper way to act toward others.
- **Moral Need** Based on his moral weakness, the hero must learn how to act properly toward others in order to grow and live a better life.
- **First Immoral Action** The hero almost immediately acts in some way that hurts others. This is evidence to the audience of the hero's basic moral flaw.
- **Desire** The hero comes up with a goal toward which all else is sacrificed. This goal leads him into direct conflict with an opponent who has a differing set of values but the same goal.
- **Drive** The hero and the opponent take a series of actions to reach the goal.

- **Immoral Actions**   During the early and middle parts of the story, the hero is usually losing to the opponent. He becomes desperate. As a result, he starts taking immoral actions to win.
  Criticism: Other characters criticize the hero for the means he is taking.
  Justification: The hero tries to justify his actions. He may see the deeper truth and right of the situation by the end of the story, but not now.
- **Attack by Ally**   The hero's closest friend makes a strong case that the hero's methods are wrong.
- **Obsessive Drive**   Galvanized by new revelations about how to win, the hero becomes obsessed with reaching the goal and will do almost anything to succeed.
- **Immoral Actions**   The hero's immoral actions intensify.
  Criticism: Attacks by other characters grow as well.
  Justification: The hero vehemently defends his actions.

As the story proceeds, the differing values and ways of living in the world represented by the hero and the opponent become clear through action and dialogue. There are four places at the end of a story where the theme explodes in the mind of the audience: the battle, self-revelation, moral decision, and a structure step we haven't discussed yet, the thematic revelation.

- **Battle**   The final conflict that decides the goal. Regardless of who wins, the audience learns which values and ideas are superior.
- **Final Action Against Opponent**   The hero may make one last action—moral or immoral—against the opponent just before or during the battle.
- **Moral Self-Revelation**   The crucible of the battle produces a self-revelation in the hero. The hero realizes that he has been wrong about himself and wrong toward others and realizes how to act properly toward others. Because the audience identifies with this character, the self-revelation drives the theme home with great power.
- **Moral Decision**   The hero chooses between two courses of action, thus proving his moral self-revelation.

■ **Thematic Revelation**   In great storytelling, the theme achieves its greatest impact on the audience at the thematic revelation. The thematic revelation is not limited to the hero. Instead, it is an insight the audience has about how people in general should act and live in the world. This insight breaks the bounds of these particular characters and affects the audience where they live. With a thematic revelation, the audience sees the "total design" of the story, the full ramifications of what it means, on a much greater scale than just a few characters.

Note that a balance of power between hero and main opponent is important not just in character and plot but also in the moral argument. If the hero is too strong or too good, the opponent does not test him sufficiently to create moral mistakes. If the opposition is too strong and the hero too simple and unaware, the opponent becomes a spider, weaving a web from which the hero cannot hope to escape. The hero becomes a victim, and the opponent is perceived as evil.

Henry James's *Portrait of a Lady*, though masterful in many ways, suffers from this imbalance of power, and the moral argument suffers with it. Isabel Archer is guilty of self-deception throughout, even when making her final moral decision to help Pansy, who can't be helped. This sweet but unaware woman faces a master schemer in Osmond, whose ability to weave the web is matched only by his willingness, even pleasure, in doing so.

MORAL ARGUMENT TECHNIQUE: BALANCE MORAL ARGUMENT WITH PLOT

The single biggest reason a story comes across as preachy is because there is an imbalance between moral argument and plot. You can express the moral argument through the story structure, sequence it perfectly, and highlight it with subtle moral dialogue. But if you don't have enough plot to support the moral argument, it will come crashing down as a sermonizing bore.

Plot, as you will see in Chapter 8, is an intricate choreography of actions by the hero and the opponents designed to surprise the audience. It is this element of surprise, of magic, that floats the moral sequence and gives it its punch.

Let's look at *The Verdict* as an example of the basic strategy of moral argument in a story.

THE VERDICT
(novel by Barry C. Reed, 1980; screenplay by David Mamet, 1982)

- **Hero's Beliefs and Values**   At first, Frank values alcohol, money, and expediency.
- **Moral Weakness**   Addicted to alcohol and with no self-respect or prospects for the future, Frank will do anything for money.
- **Moral Need**   To act with justice toward others instead of using them for money.
- **First Immoral Action**   Frank invades a funeral, pretending to be a friend of the dead man in order to get business.
- **Desire**   To win his legal case at trial and so collect the damages his clients need to start a new life.
- **Drive**   Frank takes a number of actions to get an expert doctor to testify for his side.
- **Immoral Action**   Frank reassures the victim's sister, Sally, and circles possible settlement amounts of $200,000 and $250,000 on paper. Frank intends to settle the case so that he can take one third of the money without doing anything.
  Criticism: None.
  Justification: Frank's an alcoholic who has lost all self-respect along with his sense of justice and morality. He figures, why not get the sure money now instead of gambling on winning at trial?
- **Attack by Ally**   The main attack by the ally is provided not by fellow attorney Mickey but by Frank's clients. When they learn he has turned down the settlement without consulting them, they accuse him of being incompetent and immoral.
  Justification: Frank tells them he will get them far more by fighting the case in court than by taking the offer. Although he defends himself based on money, the real reason he turns down the settlement is that he wants to see that justice is done.

- **Obsessive Drive**   He is determined to find the nurse who was in the operating room.
- **Immoral Action**   Frank tricks a woman into talking about the nurse, who won't testify for the other side.
  Criticism: None.
  Justification: Frank feels he must find the nurse in order to win his case.
- **Immoral Action**   Frank breaks open the woman's mailbox to find out the phone number of the nurse.
  Criticism: None. Frank does this in secret.
  Justification: This is Frank's only chance to win a case he knows is right.
- **Immoral Action**   Frank punches Laura, his girlfriend, when he finds out she was hired by the other side to feed them information about Frank's case.
  Criticism: Laura offers no criticism because she is so filled with guilt of her own.
  Justification: Frank loves this woman and feels she has betrayed him totally.
- **Battle**   Frank questions Dr. Towler about when the patient ate. The nurse, Kaitlin, testifies that the victim ate not at nine but one hour before admittance. She says that Dr. Towler failed to read the admittance form and told her to change the 1 to a 9 or he'd fire her. Opposing attorney Concannon reads precedent on the inadmittance of a copy. The judge agrees and also disallows the nurse's entire testimony.
- **Final Action Against Opponent**   Frank does nothing immoral during the trial. He simply presents his case in a strong and crafty way.
- **Moral Self-Revelation**   Fairly early in the story, Frank sees his client, the victim, who is in a vegetative state, and he knows he must act with justice or he is lost forever.
- **Moral Decision**   Frank risks his share of the money by refusing the bishop's settlement offer and by taking the case to trial so that justice can be done.
- **Thematic Revelation**   Only if we act with justice can our lives be saved.

The Verdict is a textbook example of how to use moral argument in a story, with one notable exception, and that exception is instructive. The hero has a strong moral self-revelation when he realizes what has been done to his client: two doctors put her into a coma, and he was willing to turn his back on her for money. He makes a moral decision when he then turns down the settlement money so that he can fight for justice at trial, even though he may never make a dime.

However, the self-revelation and decision occur only twenty-five minutes into the story. This diminishes the power of the moral argument because from that point on, the hero's moral jeopardy has been removed. The audience still enjoys the suspense of whether the hero will win the case or not. After all, Frank is a shaky lawyer with an addiction to alcohol. But they know that Frank has learned to act with justice and is doing so.

The moral argument is most powerful when it is most dramatic. That means, among other things, holding off the hero's moral self-revelation and decision until as close to the end of the story as possible. Keep the question "Will the hero do the right thing, and will he do it in time?" in the back of the audience's mind for as much of the story as you can.

THE ILIAD
(by Homer)

The moral argument of the *Iliad* uses the basic strategy of the hero's slow decline and then rise at the self-revelation. But the *Iliad* makes an important variation by working through this sequence twice.

The first sequence of decline and rise happens over the first three-quarters of the story. The hero, Achilles, starts off justified in his anger at his main opponent, Agamemnon, for taking the woman he has rightfully won. But his excessive pride (his moral weakness) has pushed him to act immorally, going too far in response, by withholding his services in battle. As a result, many of his fellow soldiers die.

Throughout the early and middle parts of the story, Achilles becomes even more unjustified in his anger and more selfish in his actions. Then, realizing his guilt when his friend Patroklos dies, he reconciles with Agamemnon and returns to the fight. This is his first self-revelation and moral decision.

The moral argument is repeated more intensely and in shorter form in the last quarter of the story: Achilles begins justified in his wrath at his second opponent, Hector, but then declines morally when his anger makes him desecrate Hector's body by dragging it around the camp. Finally, Hector's father, Priam, pleads for the return of his son's body. Achilles has a second, much deeper self-revelation about the need for compassion over vengeance, and he decides to let Priam take the body so it can receive a proper burial.

VARIANTS OF MORAL ARGUMENT

The basic strategy of moral argument has a number of variants, depending on the story form, the particular story, and the individual writer. You may find that more than one kind of moral argument is useful for your story, though, as we shall see, combining forms is risky.

1. Good Versus Bad

In this lowest variation of moral argument, the hero remains good and the opponent bad throughout. This approach is especially common in myth stories, action stories, and melodramas, which are simple moral tales with easily recognizable characters. The sequence goes like this:

- The hero has psychological weaknesses but is essentially good.
- His opponent is morally flawed and may even be evil (inherently immoral).
- In the competition for the goal, the hero makes mistakes but does not act immorally.
- The opponent, on the other hand, executes a number of immoral actions.
- The hero wins the goal simply because he is good. In effect, the two sides of the moral ledger are added up, and the good hero wins the "game" of life.

Examples of good-versus-bad moral argument are *The Matrix, City Slickers, Field of Dreams, Crocodile Dundee, Dances with Wolves, The Blues Brothers, Star Wars, Forrest Gump, My Darling Clementine, Places in the Heart, The Terminator, The Fugitive, Last of the Mohicans, Shane*, and *The Wizard of Oz*.

2. Tragedy

Tragedy takes the basic strategy of moral argument and twists it at the end-points. You give the hero a fatal character flaw at the beginning and a self-revelation that comes too late near the end. The sequence works like this:

- The community is in trouble.
- The hero has great potential but also a great flaw.
- The hero enters into deep conflict with a powerful or capable opponent.
- The hero is obsessed with winning and will perform a number of questionable or immoral acts to do so.
- The conflict and competition highlight the hero's flaw and show him getting worse.
- The hero gains a self-revelation, but it comes too late to avoid destruction.

The key to this strategy is heightening the sense of the hero's might-have-been and lost potential while also showing that the hero's actions are his responsibility. The sense of might-have-been is the single most important element for getting audience sympathy, while the fatal character flaw makes the hero responsible and keeps him from becoming a victim. The audience feels sadness at the lost potential, made more acute by the hero's having gained his great insight mere minutes after it could have saved him. But even though he has died or fallen, the audience is left with a deep sense of inspiration from the hero's moral as well as emotional success.

Notice also that this strategy represents a crucial shift from classic Greek drama. The fall of the hero is not the inevitable result of large impersonal forces but rather the consequence of the hero's own choices.

Classic tragedies include *Hamlet, King Lear, Othello, The Seven Samurai, The Bridge on the River Kwai, Nixon, The Thomas Crown Affair* (the original), *The Age of Innocence, Wuthering Heights, Vertigo, Amadeus, Le Morte d'Arthur, American Beauty, Touch of Evil,* and *Citizen Kane.*

WUTHERING HEIGHTS

(novel by Emily Brontë, 1847, screenplay by Charles MacArthur and Ben Hecht, 1939)

Wuthering Heights is a love story written as a classic tragedy. The moral argument follows a number of strands in which characters commit devastating acts on one another. And using the tragic strategy, the characters are all broken by a terrible sense of responsibility for what they've done.

Cathy, the hero, is not just a lovelorn girl passively acted on by a man. She is a woman who has a great love, a love that can only be "found in heaven," and she freely gives it up for a man of wealth and comfort. Initially, she is in love with Heathcliff and he with her, but she won't live with him as a poor beggar. She wants "dancing and singing in a pretty world."

When she returns from her stay at Edgar Linton's mansion, Heathcliff, her main opponent, criticizes her by demanding to know why she stayed so long. She defends herself by replying that she was having a wonderful time among human beings. She further hurts Heathcliff by ordering him to bathe so she won't be ashamed of him in front of a guest (Edgar).

Cathy immediately recovers from her moral fall in the next moment when Edgar asks Cathy how she can tolerate having Heathcliff under her roof. She flares in anger, saying Heathcliff was her friend long before Edgar was and telling him he must speak well of Heathcliff or leave. When Edgar goes, Cathy tears off her pretty clothes, runs to the crag where Heathcliff is waiting, and asks his forgiveness.

Brontë's moral argument through Cathy reaches its apex when Cathy tells her servant Nellie that she will marry Edgar while Heathcliff secretly listens in the next room. Now it is Nellie, the ally, who leads the criticism. She asks Cathy why she loves Edgar, and Cathy replies that it's because he's handsome and pleasant and will be rich someday. When Nellie asks about Heathcliff, Cathy says it would degrade her to marry him.

Brontë matches this strong moral argument in the dialogue with a brilliant and highly emotional plot beat. Devastated, Heathcliff leaves, but only Nellie can see that. In the next breath, Cathy flips and says she doesn't belong with Edgar. She dreamed that she was thrown out of heaven onto the heath, and she sobbed with joy. She says she only thinks of Heathcliff, but he seems to take pleasure in being cruel. Yet he is more herself than she is. Their souls are the same. In a stunning self-revelation, she says, "I *am* Heathcliff." When she discovers that Heathcliff was listening up to the point where she said it would degrade her to marry him, Cathy rushes out into the storm, screaming out her love. But it is too late.

At this point, Brontë makes a radical change in tragic moral argument: she essentially reverses heroes and gives Heathcliff the lead. Heathcliff returns and attacks ruthlessly, as a love made in heaven must when it has been scorned for something so pedestrian.

Heathcliff is a rebel who, like Achilles, is initially right in his revenge against injustice. Brontë uses the "return of the man" technique when Heathcliff comes back, Monte Cristo style, wealthy and sophisticated. The audience feels tremendous triumph in these scenes, and they don't even need to see how the character has made such a huge transformation. The man is back, finally armed as everyone has dreamed of being armed in a similar situation. The audience feels "It could be done—I could have done it," followed by "Now I will take my sweet revenge."

With the audience firmly on Heathcliff's side, Brontë reverses the moral argument by having Heathcliff go too far. Even losing such a love in so unjust a manner does not allow you to marry the sister and sister-in-law of your enemies just to pay them back. To see the innocent love that Edgar's sister, Isabella, has on her face as she walks into Heathcliff's trap is a heartbreaking moment. It is what great moral argument in storytelling is all about.

These moments between Cathy and Heathcliff are common-man versions of kings and queens at war. This is Lear raging on the moors. What makes the concept of the love made in heaven so believable is the ferocity of the immoral attacks that these two make on one another. This is pure savagery, and they do it *because* of the extreme love they have for each other.

At the end of the film adaptation, Heathcliff attacks Cathy one more time, and it is a justifiable attack, even though she is on her deathbed. He won't comfort her. His tears curse her. She begs him not to break her heart. But he says she broke it. "What right did you have to throw love away for the poor fancy thing you felt for him?" Nothing in the world could have separated them. You did that, he says, by wandering off like a greedy child. Cathy begs his forgiveness, and they kiss.

In the book, Heathcliff goes too far again, this time way beyond the pale, when he tries to destroy the Linton line. That's why this section was cut in the classic film, a work in many ways superior to the novel as a piece of storytelling. As Brontë wrote it, from this point of attack on, the organic story between Cathy and Heathcliff is essentially over, and Heathcliff's actions, though emotionally effective, are simply overkill.

KING LEAR
(by William Shakespeare, 1605)

In *King Lear*, Shakespeare gives a more nuanced moral argument than is found in most classic tragedy. The key to his technique is the creation of two "heroes": the main character, Lear, and the subplot character, Gloucester. Both Lear and Gloucester start with moral flaws, and both decline over the course of the story, gain moral self-revelations, and die. But we find no sense of the noble death that we see in, say, *Hamlet*. There is no feeling that order has been restored to the world, that all will be well again.

Instead Shakespeare points toward the basic immorality of humans and the amorality of the natural world. First, he has his two leads, Lear and Gloucester, make the same moral mistakes and die pitilessly. One king having a tragic fall is inspiring. Two shows a pattern of moral blindness that feels endemic to the human race.

Second, Shakespeare kills off Cordelia, the one morally good character in the play, and does so in an especially cruel way. It is true that Edgar, a good but initially foolish man, has defeated his bad brother and Lear's two nasty daughters. But in the overwhelming devastation, we are left with only a sliver of the value of living a good life. Edgar says, in the play's famous last line, "We that are young shall never see so much, nor live so long." In other words, in a world of immoral humans, one man's immense suffering has let him live deeply, but at tremendous cost. For later Shakespeare, that's about as much nobility as you can expect from the human race.

3. Pathos

Pathos is a moral argument that reduces the tragic hero to an everyman and appeals to the audience by showing the beauty of endurance, lost causes, and the doomed man. The main character doesn't get a self-revelation too late. He isn't capable of one. But he keeps fighting all the way to the end. The moral argument works like this:

- The hero has a set of beliefs and values that have atrophied. They are out-of-date or rigid.
- The hero has a moral need; he is not just a victim.
- His goal is beyond his grasp, but he doesn't know it.
- His opponent is far too powerful for him and may be a system or a set of forces that the hero cannot comprehend. This opposition is not evil. It is simply impersonal or uncaring and very powerful.
- The hero takes immoral steps to win and refuses to heed any warnings or criticism from his allies.
- The hero fails to win the goal. The opponent wins an overwhelming victory, but the audience senses that this was not a fair fight.
- The hero ends in despair: he is a broken man with no self-revelation and dies of heartbreak, or—and this is what his moral decision has been reduced to—he takes his own life.
- The audience feels a deep sense of injustice in the world and sadness at the death of the little man who had no idea what hit him. But they also feel a deep admiration for the beautiful failure, the good fight, and the hero's refusal to admit defeat.

The moral argument of pathos is found in *Don Quixote*, *A Streetcar Named Desire*, many Japanese films such as *Ikiru (To Live)*, *Death of a Salesman*, *Hedda Gabler*, *The Conversation*, *McCabe and Mrs. Miller*, *Falling Down*, *M*, *The Apu Trilogy*, *Madame Bovary*, *The Magnificent Ambersons*, *The Cherry Orchard*, *Dog Day Afternoon*, and *Cinema Paradiso*.

4. Satire and Irony

Satire and irony are not the same, but they commonly go together. Satire is the comedy of *beliefs*, especially those on which an entire society is based. Irony is a form of story *logic* in which a character gets the opposite of what he wants and takes action to get. When it's used over an entire story and not just for a moment, irony is a grand pattern that connects all actions in the story and expresses a philosophy of how the world works.

Irony also has a bemused tone that encourages the audience to laugh at the relative incompetence of the characters.

In the satiric-ironic form, you make the moral argument by constantly setting up a contrast between a character who thinks he is being moral—supporting the beliefs of the society—and the effects of those actions and beliefs, which are decidedly immoral. The main steps of the satiric-ironic argument go like this:

- The hero lives within a clearly defined social system. Typically, at least one character explains in part or in whole the values on which the system is based.
- The hero believes strongly in the system and is determined to rise to the top. He decides to pursue a goal having to do with ambition or romance.
- An opponent who also believes strongly in the system and its values goes after the same goal.
- As the characters compete for the goal, their beliefs lead them to take silly and destructive actions.
- The argument of action in the middle of the story comes from a sequence of juxtapositions between characters who insist they are acting morally, expressing the highest ideals of the society, and the disastrous results.
- In the battle, the pretentiousness and hypocrisy on both sides is exposed.
- The hero has a self-revelation that usually involves questioning the value of the system's beliefs.
- The hero, or a second character, often undercuts the self-revelation, showing that the self-revelation hasn't really been learned.
- The hero takes moral action that is right personally but usually has no effect on the foolishness or destructiveness of the system.
- There is a marriage of friendship or love, suggesting that the couple will form a better microcosm of their own but have little effect on the larger society.

The satiric-ironic argument is used in *Pride and Prejudice*, *Emma* (and its modern version, *Clueless*), *American Beauty*, *Wedding Crashers*, *Madame*

Bovary, The Cherry Orchard, The Graduate, M*A*S*H, Tom Jones, Waiting for Guffman, The Player, Being John Malkovich, Down and Out in Beverly Hills, The Prince and the Pauper (and its modern version, *Trading Places*), *La Cage aux Folles, The Importance of Being Earnest, Private Benjamin, Dog Day Afternoon, Victor/Victoria, Shampoo, Bob and Carol and Ted and Alice,* and *Lost in America.*

EMMA
(by Jane Austen, 1816)

Jane Austen is the master of the satiric-ironic moral argument, and *Emma* is probably her finest achievement. Here is the moral sequence of this classic satire:

- Emma is a headstrong, self-righteous, insensitive, and socially blind young woman constantly trying to be a matchmaker.
- Her first goal is to get Harriet, who is an orphan, married.
- Believing in the class system but also self-deceptive in thinking Harriet is of finer background than she appears, Emma convinces her to turn down a marriage proposal from farmer Robert Martin.
- She also convinces Harriet that the higher-born rector, Mr. Elton, should be her husband. In the process, Emma unwittingly leads Mr. Elton to believe that it is she, Emma, not Harriet, who is interested in him.
- The result of these well-intentioned but immoral actions is that Harriet loses the offer of a good man and that Mr. Elton proposes his undying love to Emma. He is then crushed to find out that Emma does not share his love in the least.
- At a ball, Mr. Elton, now married to someone else, embarrasses Harriet by refusing to dance with her. But she is saved when Mr. Knightley steps in to be her partner.
- Frank, a visitor to the county, saves Harriet from some unpleasant characters on the road. Emma wrongly believes Frank is Harriet's new love interest, even though he is quite superior to her in social position.
- At an outdoor party, Emma flirts with Frank, even though she is not interested in him and it clearly upsets another visitor to the social group, the beautiful Jane.

- Emma also humiliates the prattling but kindly Miss Bates in front of everyone. Mr. Knightley takes Emma aside and criticizes her for her insensitivity.

- When she learns that it is Mr. Knightley, not Frank, that Harriet has set her sights on, Emma is shocked into the realization that she is in love with Mr. Knightley. Furthermore, she realizes that she has been a meddling, overbearing, clueless woman and is sorry she kept Harriet from marrying Robert Martin in the first place.

- Mr. Knightley confesses his love for Emma and agrees to move into Emma's house so she can continue to take care of her father. In the novel (but not the film), the classic marriage at the end of the comedy, and Emma's great self-revelation, are undercut by the fact that she is able to marry Mr. Knightley only because her father is afraid of chicken theft and wants a younger man around the house.

In this story, the main satiric-ironic argument is carried by Emma's efforts to find Harriet a suitable mate. Through it, Austen lays out a system based on strict class differences and women's total dependence on men. Her hero, Emma, supports the system, but she is also self-deceptive and foolish. Austen slightly undercuts the system still further by making the farmer, who Emma believes is below Harriet's station, a good and worthy man.

The moral argument proceeds with a series of bad effects from Emma's matchmaking perceptions and actions. Austen focuses this argument using two parallel scenes of social slight and immorality. The first is when Harriet is embarrassed by Mr. Elton's refusal to dance, followed by Mr. Knightley coming to her rescue. The second is when Emma is painfully cutting to Miss Bates at a picnic, and again Mr. Knightley is the moral correction, upbraiding Emma for her insensitivity.

Notice that Austen makes the case in these crucial scenes for a deeper morality, based not on one's social position but on what is kind and decent, one human being to another. Notice also that Austen avoids sermonizing by making these moments emotionally powerful in the story. It hurts to see Harriet snubbed and Miss Bates humiliated in public. And it feels good when Mr. Knightley does the right thing, saving a defenseless young woman and calling our hero to task for her cruelty.

The marriage between Emma and Mr. Knightley is a reaffirmation of the system, in that both are of relatively high and equal standing. That system, and the values it is based on, will not change at the end of this satire. But their union does subtly undercut the system. Emma and Mr. Knightley come together not because they are of the right class but because Emma has matured and become a better person and Mr. Knightley is a man of high character, regardless of class.

5. Black Comedy

Black comedy is the comedy of the logic—or more exactly, the illogic—of a system. This advanced and difficult form of storytelling is designed to show that destruction is the result not so much of individual choice (like tragedy) but of individuals caught in a system that is innately destructive. The key feature of this moral argument is that you withhold the self-revelation from the hero to give it more strongly to the audience. This is how the black comedy moral argument works:

- Many characters exist in an organization. Someone explains the rules and logic by which the system operates in great detail.
- Many of these characters, including the hero, go after a negative goal that involves killing someone or destroying something.
- Each believes strongly in the goal and thinks what he is doing makes complete sense. In fact, it is totally illogical.
- The opponents, also within the system, compete for the same goal and also give detailed but insane justifications.
- One sane person, usually the ally, continually points out that none of this makes any sense and action will lead to disaster. He functions as a chorus, but no one listens to him.
- All the characters, including the nominal hero, use extreme, sometimes even murderous, methods to reach the goal.
- The actions of the characters lead to death and destruction for almost all.
- The battle is intense and destructive, with everyone still thinking he is right. The consequences are death and madness.

■ No one, including the hero, has a self-revelation. But it is so obvious that the hero *should* have had a self-revelation that the audience has it instead.

■ The remaining characters are horribly maimed by the struggle but immediately resume their efforts to reach the goal.

■ Slightly more positive black comedies end with the sane person watching in horror and either leaving the system or trying to change it.

This tricky form is easy to screw up. For the moral argument in black comedy to work, you must first make sure your hero is likable. Otherwise the comedy becomes an abstraction, an intellectual essay, as your audience backs away from the characters and feels morally superior to them. You want the audience to get sucked in so that they suddenly discover that they *are* these characters in some fundamental way and not above them.

Besides a likable hero, the best way to pull the audience emotionally into a black comedy is to have your hero speak passionately about the logic of his goal. Writers who want to add some hope to the bleakness of the form give the lone sane person an alternative to the madness, worked out in detail.

Stories using the black comedy argument are *Goodfellas*, *Network*, *Wag the Dog*, *After Hours*, *Dr. Strangelove*, *Catch-22*, *The Positively True Adventures of the Alleged Texas Cheerleader-Murdering Mom*, *Brazil*, and *Prizzi's Honor*.

COMBINING MORAL ARGUMENTS

Though unique forms, the various moral arguments are not mutually exclusive. Indeed, an excellent technique used by advanced storytellers is to combine some of these forms in one story. James Joyce's *Ulysses* starts with the simple good-versus-bad argument found in most myths and deepens it with the far more complex satiric-ironic approach. *The Cherry Orchard* is a combination of pathos and satire-irony.

The attempt to mix tragedy with elements of black comedy and satire or irony in *American Beauty* shows how difficult it is to combine these forms. Though brilliant in many ways, the story never quite reaches its full potential as tragedy, black comedy, or satire. The major moral arguments are unique variants for a reason. They work in different ways and have quite different emotional effects on the audience. Putting them together in a seamless way requires extraordinary mastery of technique.

Other examples of mixed moral arguments include *Madame Bovary*, *Adventures of Huckleberry Finn*, and *Dog Day Afternoon*.

THE UNIQUE MORAL VISION

At the most advanced level of moral argument in storytelling is the writer who creates a unique moral vision. For example, Nathaniel Hawthorne in *The Scarlet Letter* sets up a three-person character opposition that makes the case for a natural morality based on real love. Joyce in *Ulysses* creates a natural religion and an everyday heroism by sending a "father" and a "son" on a day trip through Dublin. This is big-picture moral argument, but it is not moral argument alone. The expertise, the craft, of these writers shows itself in webs of character, plot, story world, and symbol that are as broad and as detailed as their moral arguments.

A unique moral vision is also present in a few blockbuster films. If you think these films are huge hits primarily because of their visual special effects, you are mistaken. In *Star Wars*, George Lucas creates a modern-day amalgam of Eastern and Western morality, combining a Western hero with a Zen-like knighthood and a morality known as the Force. Obviously, this is a much less advanced moral argument than *The Scarlet Letter* or *Ulysses*. But the attempt is made, and its brevity has helped give the *Star Wars* films universal appeal. As simplistic as it is, "May the Force be with you" has been, for many in the audience, a creed they could live by.

Similarly, *The Godfather* not only portrays the world of the Mafia in 1940s America but also lays out a moral system based on modern business and modern warfare. Taglines like "I'm gonna make him an offer he can't refuse," "It's not personal, it's business," and "Keep your friends close and your enemies closer" are the catechism for the modern American version of Machiavelli's *Prince*. Like *Star Wars*, *The Godfather* is dealing in moral shorthand. But you should not forget that the attempt to lay out a moral system in the story—with at least some success—is a major source of the appeal of these stories.

MORAL ARGUMENT IN DIALOGUE

Story structure is the main way that you make your moral argument in a good story. But it isn't the only way. You also need to use dialogue. When you let structure do the heavy lifting to make the moral case, you free up the dialogue to do what it does best, which is provide subtlety and emotional force.

I will explain in detail how to write moral dialogue in Chapter 10, "Scene Construction and Symphonic Dialogue." For now, let's look at the best places to use it in the story.

The most common place to use dialogue to express moral argument is when an ally criticizes the hero for taking an immoral action while trying to win the goal. The ally contends that the hero's actions are wrong. The hero, who hasn't yet had a self-revelation, defends his actions.

A second way that moral argument comes out in dialogue is in a conflict between the hero and the opponent. This can happen anywhere over the course of the story but is most likely during a battle scene. A classic example of a moral argument in a battle scene occurs between Fast Eddie and his ex-manager, Bert, in *The Hustler*. In *It's a Wonderful Life*, a great moral argument between hero and opponent occurs much earlier in the story when George stops Potter from getting rid of his father's Building and Loan. The great advantage of an early moral argument between hero and opponent is that it gives the audience a clue about what values are really at stake, and that allows the drama to build.

A third place to use moral dialogue, and a mark of really good writing, is a scene in which the main opponent gives a moral justification for his actions, even though he is wrong. Why is moral dialogue from the opponent so crucial to making your overall moral argument?

A purely evil opponent is someone who is inherently bad and therefore mechanical and uninteresting. In most real conflict, there is no clear good and evil, right and wrong. In a good story, both hero and opponent believe that they are right, and both have reasons for believing so. They are also both wrong, though in different ways.

By giving your opponent a strong (though wrong) justification, you avoid the simplistic good-hero-versus-evil-opponent pattern and give depth to the opponent. And because the hero is only as good as the person he fights, you give depth to your hero as well.

You can see an excellent example of the opponent's moral argument in *The Verdict*, where opposing attorney Concannon explains to the woman he hired to spy on Frank, "We're paid to win." In the battle scene in *A Few Good Men*, Colonel Jessup justifies ordering the killing of a Marine by saying that he is the last bastion against the barbarians coming over the gate. In *Shadow of a Doubt*, brilliantly written by Thornton Wilder, Uncle Charlie, a serial killer, makes a chilling justification for killing widows by referring to them as fat animals "drinking the money, eating the money. . . . And what happens to animals when they get too fat and too old?"

The key to good moral dialogue by the opponent is not to set him up as a straw man, an opponent who appears formidable but is really hollow. Never give your opponent an obviously weak argument. Give him the best, most compelling argument you can. Make sure he is right about some things. But also make sure there is a fatal flaw in his logic.

OUTLINING THE MORAL ARGUMENT—WRITING EXERCISE 4

- **Designing Principle**   Start by turning the designing principle of your story into a theme line. The theme line is your view about right and wrong action, in *this* story, stated in one sentence. As you look again at the designing principle, focus on its key actions and their moral effects.
- **Theme Line Techniques**   Look for any techniques, like symbols, that can condense your moral statement to one line or can encapsulate the unique structure you will give to your story.
- **Moral Choice**   Write down the key choice the hero must make near the end of the story.
- **Moral Problem**   After reviewing your work on premise, state in one line the central moral problem your hero will confront throughout the story.
- **Characters as Variations on a Theme**   Starting with the hero and the main opponent, describe how each major character approaches the central moral problem of the story in a different way.
- **Values in Conflict**   List the key values of each of the major characters, and explain how those values will come into conflict as each character tries to reach the goal.

MORAL ARGUMENT

Detail the moral argument you will make through the structure of the story, using the following sequence.

- **Hero's Beliefs and Values**   Restate your hero's essential beliefs and values.
- **Moral Weakness**   What is your hero's main weakness when it comes to acting toward others?
- **Moral Need**   What must your hero learn by the end of the story about the right way to act and live in the world?
- **First Immoral Action**   Describe the first action your hero takes that hurts someone else in the story. Make sure it is an outgrowth of your hero's great moral weakness.

- **Desire**   Restate your hero's specific goal.
- **Drive**   List the actions your hero will take to win that goal.
- **Immoral Actions**   In what way, if any, are these actions immoral?
  Criticism: For any immoral action, describe the criticism, if any, that the hero receives.
  Justification: How does the hero justify each immoral action?
- **Attack by Ally**   Explain in detail the main moral attack that the ally makes against the hero. Again, write down how the hero justifies himself.
- **Obsessive Drive**   Describe when and how your hero becomes obsessed with winning. Put another way, is there a moment when your hero decides to do almost anything to win?
- **Immoral Actions**   While obsessed with winning, what immoral steps does your hero take?
  Criticism: Describe the criticism, if any, that the hero faces for these actions.
  Justification: Explain how the hero justifies his methods.
- **Battle**   During the final battle, how do you express which values, the hero's or the opponent's, are superior in this fight?
- **Final Action Against Opponent**   Does your hero take a final action against the opponent, whether moral or immoral, before or during the battle?
- **Moral Self-Revelation**   What, if anything, does your hero learn morally at the end of the story? Be sure that this insight is about how to act properly toward others.
- **Moral Decision**   Does the hero make a decision between two courses of action near the end of the story?
- **Thematic Revelation**   Can you think of a story event in which you express your vision of how human beings should act in some other way than through the self-revelation of your hero?

Let's take a look at the film *Casablanca* to see how moral argument works.

CASABLANCA

(play Everybody Comes to Rick's *by Murray Burnett and Joan Alison, screenplay by Julius J. Epstein, Philip G. Epstein, and Howard Koch, 1942)*

- **Designing Principle**   A former freedom fighter drops out of society over a lost love but is then inspired to get back into the fight when his love returns.
- **Theme Line**   Even a great love between two people may have to be sacrificed in the fight against oppression.
- **Moral Choice**   Rick must choose between being with the woman he loves and fighting worldwide dictatorship.
- **Moral Problem**   How do you balance your personal desires against sacrifices for the larger good of society?
- **Characters as Variations on a Theme**

  Rick: For most of the story, Rick cares only about himself and nothing about the troubles of the world.

  Ilsa: Ilsa tries to do the right thing, but ultimately love is too strong for her.

  Laszlo: Laszlo will sacrifice anything, including his love, to lead the fight against fascism.

  Renault: Renault is a complete opportunist, concerned only with his own pleasure and money.
- **Values in Conflict**

  Rick: Self, honesty, his friends.

  Ilsa: Loyalty to her husband, love for Rick, fighting Nazi takeover.

  Laszlo: Fighting Nazi takeover, love for Ilsa, love for mankind.

  Renault: Women, money, power.

MORAL ARGUMENT

- **Rick's Beliefs and Values**   Self, honesty, his friends.
- **Moral Weaknesses**   Cynical, selfish, cruel.
- **Moral Need**   To stop looking out for himself at the expense of others. To return to society and become a leader in the fight against fascism.
- **First Immoral Action**   Rick accepts the letters of transit from Ugarte, even though he suspects they came from the murdered couriers.

- **Second Immoral Action**   Rick refuses to help Ugarte escape from the police.

  Criticism: A man tells Rick that he hopes someone else is around if the Germans come for him.

  Justification: Rick tells the man that he sticks his neck out for nobody.

- **Desire**   Rick wants Ilsa.

- **Drive**   Rick attacks Ilsa many times while also trying to lure her back. He also takes a number of steps to preserve the letters of transit, either to sell them or to use them for himself.

- **Immoral Action**   When Ilsa returns after the club closes, Rick refuses to listen to her and calls her a tramp.

  Criticism: Ilsa voices no criticism, but she does give Rick a stricken look as she leaves.

  Justification: Rick offers no justification for his abuse.

- **Attack by Ally**   Rick's first opponent, Ilsa, makes the main moral attack against him and his methods over the course of the story. However, his friend, the bartender Sam, does urge him to quit dwelling on his lost love. Rick's classic response: "If she can stand it, I can. Play it [our song]."

- **Immoral Action**   In the marketplace, Rick propositions Ilsa and tells her she'll lie to Laszlo and come to him.

  Criticism: Ilsa accuses Rick of not being the man she knew in Paris and tells Rick she was married to Laszlo before she met him.

  Justification: Rick offers no justification for what he said except that he was drunk the night before.

- **Obsessive Drive**   Rick is initially driven to hurt Ilsa because of the pain she caused him. It is not until later in the story that he becomes obsessively driven to help her and Laszlo escape.

- **Immoral Action**   Rick rejects Laszlo's offers for the letters and tells him to ask Ilsa why.

  Criticism: None.

  Justification: Rick wants to hurt Ilsa.

- **Immoral Action**   Rick turns down Ilsa's request for the letters.

  Criticism: Ilsa says this cause is more important than personal feelings and it is Rick's fight too. If Rick doesn't give her the letters, Victor Laszlo will die in Casablanca.

Justification: Rick says he only looks out for himself now.

- **Immoral Action**   Rick tells Ilsa he will help Laszlo escape, alone. This final lie to Ilsa—that the two of them will leave together—is actually the start of a noble action, saving Laszlo and Ilsa.

  Criticism: Renault says he would do the same thing in Rick's place. Considering Renault's character, this is not a compliment.

  Justification: Rick offers no justification. He must fool Renault into thinking he plans to leave with Ilsa.

- **Battle**   Rick has Renault call ahead to the airport, but Renault actually calls Major Strasser. At the airport, Rick holds a gun on Renault and tells Ilsa she must leave with Laszlo. Rick tells Laszlo that Ilsa has been faithful. Laszlo and Ilsa get on the plane. Strasser arrives and tries to stop the plane, but Rick shoots him.

- **Final Action Against Opponent**   Rick takes no final immoral action. Although he shoots Strasser, within the world situation, he is justified in the killing.

- **Moral Self-Revelation**   Rick realizes that his love for Ilsa is not as important as helping Laszlo fight Nazi domination.

- **Moral Decision**   Rick gives Laszlo the letters, makes Ilsa leave with him, and tells Laszlo that Ilsa loves him. He then goes off to join the Free French.

- **Thematic Revelation**   Renault's surprise flip at the end, where he decides to join Rick in the fight (a classic double reversal), produces the thematic revelation: in the battle against fascism, everyone must play a part.

CHAPTER 6

Story World

ULYSSES and the Harry Potter novels exemplify one of the keys to great storytelling. On the surface, they couldn't be more different. *Ulysses* is a complex, adult, extremely challenging story, often considered the greatest novel of the twentieth century. The Harry Potter books are fun fantasy stories for children. Yet both writers know that creating a unique world for the story—and organically connecting it to the characters—is as essential to great storytelling as character, plot, theme, and dialogue.

The statement "Film is a visual medium" is extremely misleading. While it is true that movies let us see a story on a screen and witness incredible visual effects not possible in any other medium, the "visual" that really affects the audience is the *world* of the story: a complex and detailed web in which each element has story meaning and is in some way a physical expression of the character web and especially of the hero. This key principle is true not only in film but in *every story medium*.

Notice that in this area, storytelling expresses real life by being the reverse of real life. In real life, we are born into a world that already exists, and we must adapt to it. But in good stories, the characters come first, and the writer designs the world to be an infinitely detailed manifestation of those characters.

T. S. Eliot called this the "objective correlative." Whatever fancy name you want to give it, the world of your story is where you begin to add the rich texture that is one of the marks of great storytelling. A great story is like a tapestry in which many lines have been woven and coordinated to produce a powerful effect. The world of the story provides many of these threads. Certainly, you can tell a story without adding the texture of the story world. But it's a big loss.

Notice that the physical story world acts as a "condenser-expander" for the storyteller. You have very little time to create a massive amount of material: characters, plot, symbols, moral argument, and dialogue. So you need techniques that can allow you to condense meaning into the limited space and time you have. The more meaning you condense in the story, the more the story expands in the minds of the audience, with the story elements mentally ricocheting against one another in almost infinite ways.

Gaston Bachelard, in his classic book *The Poetics of Space*, explains "the drama that attaches to the dwellings of men."[1] Meaning is embedded in all kinds of forms and spaces, from shells to drawers to houses. His main point is crucial for the storyteller: "Two kinds of space, intimate space and exterior space, keep encouraging each other . . . in their growth."[2] Notice that Bachelard is talking about organic storytelling: when you create the right world for your story, you plant certain seeds in the hearts and minds of your audience that grow and move them deeply.

To sum up this part of the writing process: you start with a simple story line (the seven steps) and a set of characters. You then create the exterior forms and spaces that express these story elements, and these forms and spaces have the desired effect in the hearts and minds of your audience.

The meaning we take from physical forms and spaces seems to be deeper than culture and learning; it seems to be part of the human psyche. This is why it has profound effects on the audience. So the elements of the story world become another set of tools and techniques you can use to tell your story.

The process of translating the story line into a physical story world, which then elicits certain emotions in the audience, is a difficult one. That's because you are really speaking two languages—one of words, the other of images—and matching them exactly over the course of the story.

How are you going to apply these techniques to your story? The sequence for creating your story world goes like this (the first three steps have to do with creating the story space, the last two with the world over time):

1. We'll begin once again with the designing principle, since this is what holds everything together. The designing principle will tell you how to define the overall arena in which your story will occur.
2. Then we'll divide the arena into visual oppositions, based on how your characters oppose one another.
3. Then we'll detail the world using three of the four major building blocks—natural settings, artificial spaces, and technology—that make up the story world, with an emphasis on what these spaces and forms inherently or typically mean to an audience.
4. Next, we'll connect the story world to your hero's overall development and apply the fourth major building block of the story world, time.
5. Finally, we'll track the detailed development of the story world through the story structure by creating a visual seven steps.

FINDING THE STORY WORLD IN THE DESIGNING PRINCIPLE

Since the world is part of an organic story, you should start by going back to the nucleus of the story, which is the designing principle. Just as premise, characters, and theme take their shape from the designing principle, so does the story world.

For many reasons, finding the world in the designing principle is more difficult than finding the premise, characters, and theme. As I mentioned before, story and "visuals" are really two different languages. But languages can be learned. The deeper problem is that the designing principle and the story world work in opposite ways.

The designing principle typically describes *linear* story movement, like a single main character who develops. The story world is everything *surrounding* the characters all at once. In other words, it represents *simultaneous* elements and actions.

To connect them, you take the rough sequence of the story line, found in the designing principle, and expand it three-dimensionally to make the story world. Again, start simply. Look at the designing principle, and see if you can come up with a single visual idea that expresses the line of the story.

For practice, let's return one more time to the designing principles of the stories we discussed in Chapter 2 on premise, this time to describe the story world in one line.

MOSES, IN THE BOOK OF EXODUS
- **Designing Principle**   A man who does not know who he is struggles to lead his people to freedom and receives the new moral laws that will define him and his people.
- **Theme Line**   A man who takes responsibility for his people is rewarded by a vision of how to live by the word of God.
- **Story World**   A journey from an enslaving city through a wilderness to a mountaintop.

ULYSSES
- **Designing Principle**   In a modern odyssey through the city, over the course of a single day, one man finds a father and the other man finds a son.
- **Theme Line**   The true hero is the man who endures the slings and arrows of everyday life and shows compassion to another person in need.
- **Story World**   A city over the course of twenty-four hours, with each of its parts being a modern version of a mythical obstacle.

FOUR WEDDINGS AND A FUNERAL
- **Designing Principle**   A group of friends experiences four utopias (weddings) and a moment in hell (funeral) as they all look for their right partner in marriage.
- **Theme Line**   When you find your one true love, you must commit to that person with your whole heart.
- **Story World**   The utopian world and rituals of weddings.

HARRY POTTER BOOKS

- **Designing Principle**   A magician prince learns to be a man and a king by attending a boarding school for sorcerers over the course of seven school years.
- **Theme Line**   When you are blessed with great talent and power, you must become a leader and sacrifice for the good of others.
- **Story World**   A school for wizards in a giant magical medieval castle.

THE STING

- **Designing Principle**   Tell the story of a sting in the form of a sting, and con both the opponent and the audience.
- **Theme Line**   A little lying and cheating are OK if you bring down an evil man.
- **Story World**   A fake place of business in a run-down Depression-era city.

LONG DAY'S JOURNEY INTO NIGHT

- **Designing Principle**   As a family moves from day into night, its members are confronted with the sins and ghosts of their past.
- **Theme Line**   You must face the truth about yourself and others and forgive.
- **Story World**   The dark house, full of crannies where family secrets can be hidden away.

MEET ME IN ST. LOUIS

- **Designing Principle**   The growth of a family over the course of a year is shown by events in each of the four seasons.
- **Theme Line**   Sacrificing for the family is more important than striving for personal glory.
- **Story World**   The grand house that changes its nature with each season and with each change of the family that lives in it.

COPENHAGEN

- **Designing Principle**   Use the Heisenberg uncertainty principle to explore the ambiguous morality of the man who discovered it.
- **Theme Line**   Understanding why we act, and whether it is right, is always uncertain.
- **Story World**   The house in the form of a courtroom.

A Christmas Carol

- **Designing Principle** Trace the rebirth of a man by forcing him to view his past, his present, and his future over the course of one Christmas Eve.
- **Theme Line** A person lives a much happier life when he gives to others.
- **Story World** A nineteenth-century London countinghouse and three different homes—rich, middle-class, and poor—glimpsed in the past, present, and future.

It's a Wonderful Life

- **Designing Principle** Express the power of the individual by showing what a town, and a nation, would be like if one man had never lived.
- **Theme Line** A man's riches come not from the money he makes but from the friends and family he serves.
- **Story World** Two different versions of the same small town in America.

Citizen Kane

- **Designing Principle** Use a number of storytellers to show that a man's life can never be known.
- **Theme Line** A man who tries to force everyone to love him ends up alone.
- **Story World** The mansion and separate "kingdom" of a titan of America.

THE ARENA OF THE STORY

Once you have the designing principle and a one-line description of the story world, you must find a single arena that marks the physical boundaries of that world. The arena is the basic space of drama. It is a single, unified place surrounded by some kind of wall. Everything inside the arena is part of the story. Everything outside the arena is not.

Many writers, especially novelists and screenwriters, mistakenly believe that since you can go anywhere, you should. This is a serious mistake, because if you break the single arena of your story, the drama will literally dissipate. Having too many arenas results in fragmented, inorganic stories.

The single arena is easiest to maintain in theater because you have the natural advantage of the stage frame, edged by the curtain. Movies and novels expand the arena, but that just makes a unified place even more essential for building the drama.

Creating the Arena

I'm not suggesting that you adhere to the rigid "Aristotelian unity of place" that says all action should occur in a single location. There are four major ways of creating the single arena without destroying the variety of place and action necessary for a good story.

1. Create a large umbrella and then crosscut and condense.

In this approach, you describe the largest scope of the story somewhere near the beginning. In effect, you start with the big world and the wall that divides it from everything else. Then you focus on the smaller worlds within the arena as the story progresses.

This large umbrella could be as big as the flat plain of the West, a city, outer space, or the ocean, or it could be as small as a small town, a house, or a bar.

This technique can be found in *Casablanca, Alien, Spider-Man, L.A. Confidential, The Matrix, Death of a Salesman, A Streetcar Named Desire, Mary Poppins, Groundhog Day, Sunset Boulevard, Nashville, Blood Simple, Meet Me in St. Louis, The Great Gatsby, Shane, Star Wars*, and *It's a Wonderful Life*.

2. Send the hero on a journey through generally the same area, but one that develops along a single line.

This approach appears to destroy the single arena, and when not done properly, it does. One reason many journey stories feel fragmented is that the hero travels to a number of very different, unconnected places, and each place feels like a separate episode.

You can create the sense of a single arena if the area the character travels through remains fundamentally the same, like a desert, an ocean, a river, or a jungle. But even here, try to make the journey a single recognizable line and show a simple development of the area from beginning to end. This gives the area the appearance of unity.

We see the single-line journey in *Titanic*, *The Wild Bunch*, *The Blues Brothers*, Jacques Tati's *Traffic*, and *The African Queen*.

3. Send the hero on a circular journey through generally the same area.

This approach works in much the same way as the second one, except that the hero returns home at the end. You don't get the benefit of the single line to give the audience a sense of a unified, directed path. But by going from home to home, ending back at the beginning, you highlight the change in the character in contrast to the world, which has remained the same.

The circular journey is the foundation for *The Wizard of Oz*, *Ulysses*, *Finding Nemo*, *King Kong*, *Don Quixote*, *Big*, *Heart of Darkness*, *Beau Geste*, *Swept Away*, *Deliverance*, *Adventures of Huckleberry Finn*, *Field of Dreams*, and *Alice in Wonderland*.

4. Make the hero a fish out of water.

Start the hero in one arena. Spend enough time there to show whatever talents he has that are unique to that world. Then jump the character to a second world—without traveling—and show how the talents the hero used in the first world, while seeming to be out of place, work equally well in the second.

This approach is found in *Beverly Hills Cop*, *Crocodile Dundee*, *Black Rain*, and to a lesser but still important extent in *Witness* and *Dances with Wolves*.

Strictly speaking, fish-out-of-water stories take place in two distinct arenas, not one. Consequently, they often feel like two-part stories. What holds them together is that the hero uses the same talents in both places, so the audience comes to feel that while both arenas are superficially quite different, they are in a deeper sense the same.

One of the keys to using the fish-out-of-water technique is to avoid staying too long in the first arena. The first arena is the jumping-off point for the main story, which takes place in the second arena. The first arena has fulfilled its function as soon as you show the hero's talents in that world.

Oppositions Within the Arena

You don't create characters to fill a story world, no matter how fabulous that world may be. You create a story world to express and manifest your characters, especially your hero.

Just as you define the character web by dramatizing the oppositions among the characters, so do you define the story world within your single arena by dramatizing the *visual oppositions*. You do that by going back to the oppositions among the characters and the values they hold.

Return to your character web, and look for all the ways the characters fight with each other. Look especially at the conflict of values, because values are what the main characters are really fighting about. From these oppositions, you will start to see visual oppositions emerge in the physical world as well.

Tease out the visual oppositions, and figure out what the three or four central ones might be. Let's look at some examples in stories and see how they come out of the character oppositions.

It's a Wonderful Life
(short story "The Greatest Gift" by Philip Van Doren Stern, screenplay by Frances Goodrich & Albert Hackett and Frank Capra, 1946)

It's a Wonderful Life is structured so that the audience can see two different versions of the same town. Notice that this huge element of the story world, a town, is a direct expression of the fundamental character opposition between George Bailey and Mr. Potter. And each version of the town is a physical manifestation of the *values* of these two men. Pottersville is what you get with one-man rule and unchecked greed. Bedford Falls is what you get with democracy, decency, and kindness.

Sunset Boulevard
(by Charles Brackett & Billy Wilder & D. M. Marshman, Jr., 1950)

The central opposition in *Sunset Boulevard* is between struggling screenwriter Joe Gillis, who still has a belief in doing good work beneath that money-grubbing veneer, and rich, aging movie star Norma Desmond. The visual oppositions come from Joe's cramped apartment versus Norma's run-down mansion; sunny, modern, wide-open Los Angeles versus a dark Gothic house; young versus old; struggling outsiders trying to break in versus the grand and secure but ruthless movie studio; and the common-man entertainment workers versus Hollywood movie star royalty.

THE GREAT GATSBY

(by F. Scott Fitzgerald, 1925)

In *The Great Gatsby*, the primary oppositions are between Gatsby and Tom, Gatsby and Daisy, Gatsby and Nick, and Nick and Tom (notice the four-corner opposition). Each of these characters is some version of an ordinary midwesterner who has come east to make money. So the first story world opposition is between the flat plains of the Midwest and the tall towers and elegant mansions of the East. Tom is "new money," but he is older money than Gatsby, so there is an opposition within the riches of Long Island between the more established East Egg, where Tom and Daisy live, and the still wealthy but more nouveau West Egg, where Gatsby lives. Indeed, Tom and Daisy's mansion is depicted as opulent but conservative, while Gatsby's mansion and his use of it are portrayed as the epitome of garish bad taste.

Gatsby has gained his extreme wealth illegally, as a bootlegger, while Nick is a struggling, honest bond trader. So Nick rents Gatsby's little guest cottage, where he can gaze on the fake community of Gatsby's parties. Tom is a brute and a bully who is cheating on his wife, so Fitzgerald contrasts Tom's mansion with the gas station of Tom's mistress. Fitzgerald adds another contrast of subworlds when he depicts the city of ashes, the hidden detritus of the great capitalist, mechanistic engine represented by New York City and Long Island. In a final thematic burst, Fitzgerald compares the city of New York, the height of American "civilization," with New York before it was developed, when it was full of promise, the "great green breast of the New World."

KING KONG

(by James Creelman and Ruth Rose, 1931)

King Kong sets up its primary opposition between the showman-producer, Carl Denham, and the giant prehistoric beast, Kong. So the main opposition within the story world is the island of New York, the man-made and overly civilized but extremely harsh world where image-maker Denham is "king," versus Skull Island, the extremely harsh state of nature where Kong, master of physical force, is king. Within this main visual opposition is a three-part contrast of subworlds between the city dwellers, the villagers of Skull Island, and the prehistoric beasts of the jungle, all of whom are involved in a different form of the struggle to survive.

DANCES WITH WOLVES
(novel and screenplay by Michael Blake, 1990)

Dances with Wolves shifts the central opposition of characters and values over the course of the story, and so the main visual oppositions shift as well. At first, the hero, John Dunbar, wants to participate in building the American frontier before it vanishes. So the first opposition of the story world is between the Civil War America of the East, where the nation has been corrupted through slavery, and the broad empty plains of the Western wilderness, where America's promise is still fresh. Within the world of the Western plains, the apparent conflict of values is between the white soldier, Dunbar, who believes in building the American nation, and the Lakota Sioux, who appear to be savages bent on its destruction.

But writer Michael Blake uses his depiction of the subworlds to undercut this *apparent* opposition of values. Dunbar's cavalry outpost is an empty mud hole, devoid of life, an ugly gash on the land. The Sioux village is a little utopia, a cluster of tepees by the river, with horses grazing and children playing. As the story progresses, Blake shows that the deeper opposition of values is between an American expansionist world that treats animals and Indians as objects to be destroyed versus an Indian world that lives with nature and treats each human being according to the quality of their heart.

L.A. CONFIDENTIAL
(novel by James Ellroy, screenplay by Brian Helgeland & Curtis Hanson, 1997)

In *L.A. Confidential*, the main character opposition appears to be between cops and killers. In fact, it is between police detectives who believe in different versions of justice and a murderous police captain and a corrupt district attorney. That's why the first visual opposition, done in voice-over, is between Los Angeles as an apparent utopia and Los Angeles as a racist, corrupt, oppressive city. This essential opposition is then divided further as the three lead cops are introduced: Bud White, the real cop who believes in vigilante justice; Jack Vincennes, the smooth cop who makes extra money as a technical adviser on a TV cop show and who arrests people for money; and Ed Exley, the smart cop who knows how to play the political game of justice to further his own ambitions. The investigation plays out this opposition of characters and values through various sub-worlds by contrasting locations of the rich, white, corrupt Los Angeles that actually commits the crime and the poor black Los Angeles that is blamed for it.

DETAILING THE STORY WORLD

You detail the visual oppositions and the story world itself by combining three major elements: the land (natural settings), the people (man-made spaces), and technology (tools). A fourth element, time, is the way your unique world develops over the course of the story, which we'll discuss later. Let's begin by looking at the natural settings.

Natural Settings

Never select the natural settings for your story by happenstance. Each setting carries a multitude of meanings for an audience. As Bachelard says, "A psychologist of the imagination . . . comes to realize that the cosmos molds mankind, that it can transform a man of the hills into a man of islands and rivers, and that the house remodels man."[3] You need to know some of the possible meanings of the various natural settings, such as hills, islands, and rivers, so that you can determine if one best expresses your story line, characters, and theme.

Ocean

For the human imagination, the ocean divides into two distinct places, the surface and the deep. The surface is the ultimate two-dimensional landscape, the flat table as far as the eye can see. This makes the ocean surface seem abstract while also being totally natural. This abstract flat surface, like a huge chessboard, intensifies the sense of the *contest*, a game of life and death played out on the grandest scale.

The ocean deep is the ultimate three-dimensional landscape where all creatures are weightless and thus live at every level. This weightless, floating quality is a common element when the human mind imagines a utopia, which is why the ocean deep has often been the place of utopian dreamworlds.

But the ocean deep is also a terrifying graveyard, a great, impersonal force quietly grabbing anyone or anything on the surface and pulling it down to the infinite black depths. The ocean is the vast cavern where ancient worlds, prehistoric creatures, past secrets, and old treasure are swallowed up and lie waiting to be discovered.

Ocean stories include *Moby-Dick*; *Titanic*; *Finding Nemo*; *20,000 Leagues Under the Sea*; *The Little Mermaid*; *Atlantis*; *The Sea Wolf*; *Master and Commander*; *Run Silent, Run Deep*; *Mutiny on the Bounty*; *The Hunt for Red October*; *Jaws*; and *Yellow Submarine*.

Outer Space

Outer space is the ocean of "out there," an infinite black nothingness that hides an unlimited diversity of other worlds. Like the ocean deep, it is three-dimensional. Like the ocean surface, outer space feels both abstract and natural. Everything moves through blackness, so each thing, though a unique individual, is also highlighted in its most essential quality. There is the "spaceship," the "human being," the "robot," the "alien." Science fiction stories often use the myth form, not only because myth is about the journey but also because myth is the story form that explores the most fundamental human distinctions.

Because outer space holds the promise of unlimited diversity of other worlds, it is a place of unending adventure. Adventure stories are always about a sense of discovery, of the new, of the amazing, and this can be both exciting and terrifying. At this point in the history of humans on earth and the development of stories, outer space is the only natural setting where this sense of unlimited adventure is still possible. (The ocean is largely unexplored territory as well. But because we can't imagine a real community living there, the ocean is the site of a human world only in fantasy.)

Outer space is the realm of science fiction stories such as *2001: A Space Odyssey, Dune,* the *Star Wars* movies, *Blade Runner, Apollo 13, Forbidden Planet,* many of the *Twilight Zone* stories, the *Star Trek* movies and television shows, and the *Alien* films.

Forest

The central story quality of the forest is that it is a natural cathedral. The tall trees, with their leaves hanging over us and protecting us, seem like the oldest wise men assuring us that whatever the circumstances, it will resolve as time moves on. It is the place where contemplative people go and to which lovers sneak away.

But this intense inward gaze of the forest also has a sense of foreboding. The forest is where people get lost. It's the hiding place of ghosts and past lives. It is where hunters stalk their prey, and their prey is often human. The forest is tamer than the jungle; the jungle will kill anything in it at any moment. The forest, when it does its frightening work, causes mental loss first. It is slower than the jungle but still deadly.

We see the forest used in many fairy tales, as well as *The Legend of Sleepy Hollow, The Lord of the Rings,* the Harry Potter books, *Return of the Jedi, Shrek, Excalibur, As You Like It, A Midsummer Night's Dream, Song of Solomon, The Wizard of Oz, McCabe and Mrs. Miller, The Wolf Man, The Blair Witch Project,* and *Miller's Crossing.*

Jungle

The jungle is the state of nature. Its primary effect on the imagination is the feeling of suffocation. Everything about it is grabbing you. The jungle gives audiences the strongest sense of the power of nature over man. In that environment, man is reduced to beast.

Ironically, such a primal place is also one of the two natural settings that express the theory of evolution, the modern theory of change.

The jungle world is found in the *Star Wars* movies; the *Tarzan* stories, including *Greystoke; King Kong; The African Queen; Jurassic Park* and *The Lost World; The Emerald Forest; Aguirre: The Wrath of God; Mosquito Coast; Fitzcarraldo; The Poisonwood Bible; Heart of Darkness;* and *Apocalypse Now.*

Desert and Ice

Desert and ice are the places of dying and death, at all times. Even stories have a hard time growing there. Desert and ice seem completely impersonal in their brutality.

When something valuable comes out of these places, it is because the strong-willed have gone there to be toughened and grow through isolation. A rare example of the ice world portrayed as a utopia is found in Mark Helprin's novel *Winter's Tale*. Helprin presents a village whose sense of community is actually heightened when winter shuts it off from the rest of the world and freezes the lake, on which the villagers enjoy every kind of winter fun.

Desert or ice worlds are prominent in the *Star Wars* movies, *Fargo*, *Lawrence of Arabia*, *Beau Geste*, *Dune*, *The Ballad of Cable Hogue*, *My Darling Clementine*, *She Wore a Yellow Ribbon*, *Once upon a Time in the West*, *The Wild Bunch*, *The Sheltering Sky*, *The Gold Rush*, and *The Call of the Wild*.

Island

The island is an ideal setting for creating a story in a social context. Like the ocean and outer space, the island is both highly abstract and completely natural. It is a miniature of the earth, a small piece of land surrounded by water. The island is, by definition, a separated place. This is why, in stories, it is the laboratory of man, a solitary paradise or hell, the place where a special world can be built and where new forms of living can be created and tested.

The separate, abstract quality of the island is why it is often used to depict a utopia or dystopia. And even more than the jungle, the island is the classic setting for showing the workings of evolution.

Stories that use the island as a central setting include *Robinson Crusoe*, *The Tempest*, *Gulliver's Travels*, *The Incredibles*, *King Kong*, *Treasure Island*, *The Mysterious Island*, *The Island of Dr. Moreau*, *Lord of the Flies*, *Swept Away*, *Jurassic Park* and *The Lost World*, *Cast Away*, the television show *Lost*, and arguably the greatest use of the island in story history, *Gilligan's Island*.

In many ways, the island has the most complex story possibilities of any natural setting. Let's take a closer look at how to get the most out of the island world in your story. Notice that the best way to express the inherent meaning of this natural setting is through the story structure:

- Take time in the beginning to set up the normal society and the characters' place within it. (need)
- Send the characters to an island. (desire)
- Create a new society based on different rules and values. (desire)
- Make the relationship between the characters very different from what it was in the original society. (plan)
- Through conflict, show what works and what doesn't. (opponent)
- Show characters experimenting with something new when things don't work. (revelation or self-revelation)

Mountain

This highest of all places translates, in human terms, into the land of greatness. This is where the strong go to prove themselves—usually through seclusion, meditation, a lack of comfort, and direct confrontation with nature in the extreme. The mountaintop is the world of the natural philosopher, the great thinker who must understand the forces of nature so he can live with them and sometimes control them.

Structurally, the mountain, the high place, is most associated with the reveal, the most mental of the twenty-two story structure steps (see Chapter 8, "Plot"). Revelations in stories are moments of discovery, and they are the keys to turning the plot and kicking it to a "higher," more intense level. Again, the mountain setting makes a one-to-one connection between space and person, in this case, height and insight.

This one-to-one connection of space to person is found in the negative expression of the mountain as well. It is often depicted as the site of hierarchy, privilege, and tyranny, typically of an aristocrat who lords it over the common people down below.

KEY POINT: The mountain is usually set in opposition to the plain.

The mountain and the plain are the only two major natural settings that visually stand in contrast to one another, so storytellers often use the comparative method to highlight the essential and opposing qualities of each.

The mountain world is important in the Moses story, Greek myths of the gods on Mount Olympus, many fairy tales, *The Magic Mountain*, *Lost Horizon*, *Brokeback Mountain*, *Batman Begins*, *The Snows of Kilimanjaro*, *A Farewell to Arms*, *The Deer Hunter*, *Last of the Mohicans*, *Dances with Wolves*, *Shane*, *The Shining*, and a number of other horror stories.

Plain

The flat table of the plain is wide open and accessible to all. In contrast to the jungle, which presses in, the plain is totally free. This is why, in stories, it is the place of equality, freedom, and the rights of the common man. But this freedom is not without cost and conflict. Like the surface of the ocean, the extreme flatness of the plain becomes abstract, highlighting the sense of contest or life-and-death struggle that will be played out in this arena.

Negatively, the plain is often depicted as the place where the mediocre make their lives. In contrast to the few great ones living up on the mountaintop, the many average ones live as part of a herd down below. They do not think for themselves, so they are easily led, usually in ways that are destructive to them.

We see the plain depicted in most Westerns, including *Shane* and *The Big Country*, *Days of Heaven*, *Dances with Wolves*, *In Cold Blood*, *Lost Horizon*, *The Snows of Kilimanjaro*, *A Farewell to Arms*, *Blood Simple*, and *Field of Dreams*.

River

The river is a uniquely powerful natural setting, maybe the greatest one of all when it comes to storytelling. The river is a path, which makes it a perfect physical manifestation for myth stories that rely on the journey for their structure.

But the river is more than a path. It is the road *into* or *out of* somewhere. This intensifies the sense that the path is a developing, organic line, not just a series of episodes. For example, in *Heart of Darkness*, the hero goes up the river, ever deeper into the jungle. The line of human development attached to this path is one from civilization to barbaric hell.

In *The African Queen*, the hero reverses that trip and that process by going down the river, out of the jungle. His development begins in a hellish landscape of death, isolation, and madness and moves toward the human world of commitment and love.

The river as the place of physical, moral, and emotional passage is found in *Adventures of Huckleberry Finn*; *Deliverance*; *Heart of Darkness* and its adaptation, *Apocalypse Now*; *A River Runs Through It*; and *The African Queen*.

A note of caution: beware of visual clichés. It's easy to fall into the trap of using natural settings in a formulaic way. "My hero is getting a big revelation? I'll send him to the mountaintop." Make sure any natural setting you use is fundamental to the story. And above all, use it in an original way.

Weather

Weather, like natural settings, can provide a powerful physical representation of the inner experience of the character or evoke strong feelings in the audience. Here are the classic correlations between weather and emotion:

- Lightning and thunder: Passion, terror, death
- Rain: Sadness, loneliness, boredom, coziness
- Wind: Destruction, desolation
- Fog: Obfuscation, mystery
- Sun: Happiness, fun, freedom, but also corruption hidden below a pleasant exterior
- Snow: Sleep, serenity, quiet inexorable death

Again, avoid simply repeating these classic correlations and instead try to use weather in surprising and ironic ways.

Man-made Spaces

Man-made spaces are even more valuable to you as a writer than natural settings, because they solve one of the most difficult problems a writer faces: How do you express a society? All man-made spaces in stories are a form of condenser-expander. Each is a physical expression, in microcosm, of the hero and the society in which he lives.

The problem for the writer is to express that society on paper in such a way that the audience can understand the deepest relationship between the hero and other people. The following are some of the major man-made spaces that can help you do that.

The House

For the storyteller, man-made spaces begin with the house. The house is a person's first enclosure. Its unique physical elements shape the growth of the person's mind and the mind's well-being in the present. The house is also the home of the family, which is the central unit of social life and the central unit of drama. So all fiction writers must strongly consider what place a house may play in their story.

The house is unsurpassed as a place of intimacy, for your characters and your audience. But it is filled with visual oppositions that you must know in order to express the house to its fullest dramatic potential.

Safety Versus Adventure

The house is, first and foremost, the great protector. "In every dwelling, even the richest, the first task . . . is to find the original shell."[4] Put another way, "Always in our daydreams, the house is a large cradle. . . . Life begins well, it begins enclosed, protected, all warm in the bosom of the house."[5]

The house may begin as the shell, cradle, or nest of the human being. But that protective cocoon is also what makes its opposite possible: the house is the strong foundation from which we go out and take on the world. "[The] house breathes. First it is a coat of armor, then it extends *ad infinitum*, which amounts to saying that we live in it in alternate security and adventure. It is both cell and world."[6] Often in stories, the first step of adventure, the longing for it, happens at the window. A character looks out through the eyes of the house, maybe even hears a train whistle calling, and dreams of going.

Ground Versus Sky

A second opposition embedded in the house is that between ground and sky. The house has deep roots. It hunkers down. It tells the world and its inhabitants that it is solid and can be trusted.

But a house also extends skyward. Like a tiny but proud cathedral, it wishes to generate the "highest" and the best in its inhabitants. "All strongly terrestrial beings—and a house is strongly terrestrial—are nevertheless subject to the attractions of an aerial, celestial world. The well-rooted house likes to have a branch that is sensitive to the wind, or an attic that can hear the rustle of leaves."[7]

The Warm House

The warm house in storytelling is big (though usually not a mansion), with enough rooms, corners, and cubbyholes for each inhabitant's uniqueness to thrive. Notice that the warm house has within it two additional opposing elements: the safety and coziness of the shell and the diversity that is only possible within the large.

Writers often intensify the warmth of the big, diverse house by using the technique known as the "buzzing household." This is the Pieter Brueghel technique (especially in paintings like *The Hunters in the Snow* and *Winter Landscape with a Bird Trap*) applied to the house. In the buzzing household, all the different individuals of an extended family are busy in their own pocket of activity. Individuals and small groups may combine for a special moment and then go on their merry way. This is the perfect community at the level of the household. Each person is both an individual and part of a nurturing family, and even when everyone is in different parts of the house, the audience can sense a gentle spirit that connects them.

The big, diverse house and the buzzing household are found in such stories as *You Can't Take It with You*, *Meet Me in St. Louis*, *Life with Father*, *The Cider House Rules*, *Pride and Prejudice*, *The Magnificent Ambersons*, *The Royal Tenenbaums*, *Steel Magnolias*, *It's a Wonderful Life*, TV's *Waltons*, *David Copperfield*, *How Green Was My Valley*, *Mary Poppins*, and *Yellow Submarine*.

Part of the power of the warm house is that it appeals to the audience's sense of their own childhood, either real or imagined. Everyone's house was big and cozy when they were very young, and if they soon discovered that they lived in a hovel, they can still look at the big, warm house and see what they wished their childhood had been. That's why the warm house is so often used in connection with memory stories, like Jean Shepherd's *Christmas Story*, and why American storytellers so often use ramshackle Victorian places, with their many snug gables and corners from a bygone era.

The bar is a version of the house in storytelling, and it too can be warm or terrifying. In the television show *Cheers,* the bar is a utopia, a community where "everybody knows your name." The regulars are always in the same spot, always making the same mistakes, and always in the same quirky relation to one another. This bar is also a warm place because nobody *has* to change.

CASABLANCA

(play Everybody Comes to Rick's *by Murray Burnett and Joan Alison, screenplay by Julius J. Epstein, Philip G. Epstein, and Howard Koch, 1942)*

The story world is as important to the success of *Casablanca* as it is to the most advanced fantasy, myth, or science fiction story. And it is all focused on the bar, Rick's Café Américain.

What makes the bar in *Casablanca* unique as a story world, and incredibly powerful for the audience, is that it is both a dystopia and a utopia. This bar is where the king of the underworld makes his home.

Rick's Café Américain is a dystopia because everyone wants to escape Casablanca, and this is where they pass the time, waiting, waiting, always waiting to get out. There is no exit here. It is also a dystopia because it is all about money grubbing and bribery, a perfect expression of the hero's cynicism, selfishness, and despair.

But this bar is at the same time a fabulous utopia. Rick is the master here, the king in his lair, and all of his courtiers pay their respects. The café is a big, warm house with lots of nooks and corners and all sorts of characters to fill them. Each character not only knows his place but also enjoys it. There's Carl the waiter and Sascha the bartender; Abdul the bouncer; Emil, who manages the casino; and Rick's sidekick, Sam, master of song. Over in that booth is Berger, the nerdy Norwegian underground fighter, just waiting to follow Laszlo's command. There's even the perfect hiding place for the letters of transit, under the lid of Sam's piano.

In a land of contradictions, this warm house is the home of cool, the origin of hip, embodied in King Rick, impeccably dressed in his white tuxedo jacket, a man who is always suave and witty, even under threat from Nazi killers. But this is a world that lives at night, and the king is dark and brooding too. He refers to two murdered couriers as the "honored dead." This king is Hades.

By creating a sealed world that is both dystopia and utopia, the writers of *Casablanca* in effect create a Mobius strip story world that never stops. Forever in time, Rick's Café Américain is open every night. Refugees still gather there; the captain still gambles and enjoys the women; the Germans still make their arrogant appearance. It is one of those timeless places that make great stories, and it continues to exist because it is a cozy lair where everyone enjoys their role.

Far from being the place where everyone wants an exit visa, Rick's bar in far-off Casablanca is the perfect community where no one in the audience ever wants to leave.

The Terrifying House

Opposite the warm house, the terrifying house is usually a house that has gone over the line from cocoon to prison. In the best stories of this kind, the house is terrifying because it is an outgrowth of the great weakness and need of the character. This house is the hero's biggest fear made manifest. In the extreme, the character's mind has rotted in some way, and the house too is in ruins. But it is no less powerful a prison.

In *Great Expectations*, Miss Havisham is a slave in her own run-down mansion because she has chosen to martyr herself on the altar of unrequited love. Her mind has grown sick with bitterness; her house is a perfect picture of her mind. In *Wuthering Heights*, the house is a horrible prison because Cathy gave up true love there and because Heathcliff's bitterness has made him commit awful acts against its inhabitants in her name.

Horror stories place such strong emphasis on the haunted house that it is one of the unique story beats of the form. Structurally, the terrifying or haunted house represents the power the past holds over the present. The house itself becomes a weapon of revenge for the sins committed by the fathers and mothers. In such stories, the house doesn't have to be a decrepit, creaking mansion with slamming doors, moving walls, and secret, dark passageways. It can be the simple, suburban houses of *Poltergeist* and *A Nightmare on Elm Street* or the grand hotel on the mountaintop in *The Shining*. On this mountaintop, the seclusion and the hotel's past sins don't lead the hero to think great thoughts; they drive him mad.

When the terrifying house is a grand Gothic hulk, an aristocratic family often inhabits it. The inhabitants have lived off the work of others, who typically dwell in the valley below, simply because of their birth. The house is either too empty for its size, which implies that there is no life in the structure, or it is stuffed with expensive but out-of-date furnishings that oppress by their sheer numbers. In these stories, the house feeds on its parasitic inhabitants just as they feed on others. Eventually, the family falls and, when the story is taken to the extreme, the house burns, devours them, or collapses on them. Examples are "The Fall of the House of Usher" and other stories by Poe, *Rebecca*, *Jane Eyre*, *Dracula*, *The Innocents*, *The Amityville Horror*, *Sunset Boulevard*, *Frankenstein*, *Long Day's Journey into Night*, and stories by Chekhov and Strindberg.

In more modern stories, the terrifying house is a prison because it is not big and diverse. It is small and cramped, with thin walls or no walls at all. The family is jammed in, so there is no community, no separate, cozy corners where each person has the space to become who he uniquely should be. In these houses, the family, as the basic unit of drama, is the unit of never-ending conflict. The house is terrifying because it is a pressure cooker, and with no escape for its members, the pressure cooker explodes. Examples are *Death of a Salesman*, *American Beauty*, *A Streetcar Named Desire*, *Who's Afraid of Virginia Woolf?*, *Long Day's Journey into Night*, *The Glass Menagerie*, *Carrie*, *Psycho*, and *The Sixth Sense*.

Cellar Versus Attic

Inside the house, the central opposition is between cellar and attic. The cellar is underground. It is the graveyard of the house, where the dead bodies, the dark past, and the terrible family secrets are buried. But they are not buried there for long. They are waiting to come back, and when they finally do make it back to the living room or the bedroom, they usually destroy the family. The skeletons in the basement can be shocking, as in *Psycho*, or darkly funny, as in *Arsenic and Old Lace*.

The cellar is also where plots are hatched. Plots come from the darkest part of the house and the darkest part of the mind. The cellar is the natural workplace of the criminal and the revolutionary. This technique is used in *Notes from the Underground*, *The Lavender Hill Mob*, *The Silence of the Lambs*, and *M*.

The attic is a cramped half-room, but it is at the top of the structure, where the house meets the sky. When it is inhabited, the attic is the place where great thoughts and art are created, as yet unknown to the world (*Moulin Rouge*). The attic also has the benefit of height and perspective. Attic inhabitants can look out their tiny window and see a Brueghel-like scene of community in the street below.

The attic, like the cellar, is a place where things are hidden away. Because the attic is the "head" of the house, these hidden things, when they are terrifying, have to do with madness (*Jane Eyre*, *Gaslight*). But more often the hidden things are positive, like treasures and memories. A character discovers an old chest in the attic that opens a window into who that character was or the character's forebears.

The Road

In the man-made spaces of storytelling, the opposite of the house is the road. The house calls us to nestle, to live in a timeless moment, to get comfortable, to make ourselves at home. The road is the call to go out, explore, and become someone new. The house is the simultaneous story, everything happening at once. The road is the linear story, one thing happening along a line of development.

George Sand wrote, "What is more beautiful than a road? It is the symbol and the image of an active, varied life."[8] The road is always tenuous. It is a single, slim line, the barest mark of man surrounded by rough, impersonal wilderness. So the road requires courage. But it offers almost infinite vistas of who the traveler can become. The road, no matter how thin, promises a destination that is worth reaching.

Myth stories center on this fundamental opposition between house and road. The classic myth story begins at home. The hero goes on a journey, encountering many opponents who test him, only to return home having learned what was already deep within. In these myth stories, the home at the beginning is not well used. The hero has not created his unique self in that safe place, or he has felt enslaved. The road forces him to test his abilities. But in myth, he will not become someone new on the road. He must return home, this time to realize who he always was, but in a deeper way.

STORY WORLD TECHNIQUE: THE VEHICLE

A major reason journey stories feel fragmented, besides having too many arenas, is that the hero encounters a number of opponents in succession on the road. That's why one of the keys to making the journey story work is the vehicle in which the hero travels. A simple rule of thumb is this: the bigger the vehicle, the more unified the arena. The bigger the vehicle, the easier it is to bring opponents along for the ride. These are the *ongoing* opponents, and with the hero, they create the single arena within the vehicle.

Traveling stories that use large vehicles include *Titanic* and *Ship of Fools* (ship), *Murder on the Orient Express* and *Twentieth Century* (train), and *Almost Famous* (bus).

The City

The biggest man-made microcosm is the city. It is so big that it breaks the bounds of microcosm and becomes overwhelming. The city is thousands of buildings, millions of people. And yet it is a unique experience of human life, which you must somehow convey in story terms.

To codify the vast scope of the city, storytellers shrink the city down to a smaller microcosm. One of the most popular is the institution. An institution is an organization with a unique function, boundaries, set of rules, hierarchy of power, and system of operation. The institution metaphor turns the city into a highly organized military operation where vast numbers of people are defined and relate to one another strictly by their function in the whole.

Typically, a writer portraying the city as an institution creates a single large building with many levels and rooms, including one immense room with hundreds of desks in perfect rows. The city as institution is found in *The Hospital, American Beauty, Network, Double Indemnity, The Incredibles,* and *The Matrix.*

STORY WORLD TECHNIQUE: COMBINING NATURAL SETTINGS WITH THE CITY

Fantasy uses an opposite approach from the institution to find a metaphor for the city. Instead of locking the city down to a regulated organization, fantasy opens the city up by imagining it as a kind of natural setting, like a mountain or a jungle. One advantage of this technique is that it makes the overwhelming city a single unit, with special traits the audience can recognize. But more important, it hints at the tremendous potential of the city, for both good and bad.

City as Mountain

The mountaintop is a common natural metaphor for the city, especially an extremely vertical city like New York. The highest towers, the apex of the mountain, are home to the most powerful and wealthiest. The middle classes live in the middle towers, while the poor crawl about in the low-lying tenements at the mountain's base. Highly stylized crime fantasies such as the *Batman* stories often use the mountain metaphor.

City as Ocean

A more powerful natural metaphor for the city than the classic but predictable mountain is the ocean. With this metaphor, the writer usually begins on the rooftops, which are gabled so that the audience has the impression of floating on the waves. Then the story "dips" below the surface to pick up various strands, or characters, who live at different levels of this three-dimensional world and are typically unaware of the others "swimming" in this sea. Films as different as *Beneath the Rooftops of Paris*, *Wings of Desire*, and *Yellow Submarine* use this ocean metaphor to great advantage.

The city as ocean is also the key metaphor when you want to portray the city in its most positive light, as a playground where individuals can live with freedom, style, and love. In fantasy stories, the main way to do that is to make the city dwellers literally float. Not only does this give them the power to fly, but also, when characters float, ceilings become floors, nothing is locked down, and people can experience the ultimate freedom that comes from imagining things together. This floating is a metaphor for the potential that is hidden within the mundane city; when you approach the predictable world in a new way, suddenly everything becomes possible.

In nonfantasy movies that treat the city as an ocean, the effect of floating is created with the eye of the camera. For example, in the beginning of *Beneath the Rooftops of Paris*, the camera glides along the gabled rooftops, then dips down below the "ocean's" surface and into an open window. After watching some characters for a while, it "swims" out of the window and into another window, where it picks up another set of characters. All of this is part of the story structure, created by the writer and intended to evoke the feeling of an extended community within the vast ocean of the city.

MARY POPPINS
(books by P. L. Travers, screenplay by Bill Walsh and Don Da Gradi, 1964)
Mary Poppins is a story based on the metaphor of city as ocean. Mary floats down from the sky to begin her stay with the Banks household. In the house next door, a ship captain stands on the roof (deck of his "ship"), along with his first mate. From Mary, the children learn that you can float if you love to laugh the day away. And Bert and the chimney sweeps dance on the rooftops, which he calls the "sea of enchantment." With bursting energy, they prance on the waves (the gables) and defy gravity until the captain fires a shot from his cannon and the sweeps all disappear under the ocean's surface until it is time to dance once more.

City as Jungle
City as jungle is the opposite of the city as ocean. Here the three-dimensional quality of the city is not liberating but rather the source of death—enemies lurk all around, and a fatal attack comes from any direction in an instant. This kind of city is typically closely packed, steaming and wet, with the residents portrayed as animals who differ only in the way they kill. Many detective and cop stories have used this metaphor, to such a degree that it long ago became a cliché. Stories that have used the city-as-jungle metaphor in more original ways are *Pepe Le Moko* (the Casbah of Algiers), *Spider-Man* (New York), *Batman Begins* (Gotham), *The Jungle* (Chicago), *Blade Runner* (Los Angeles), *M* (Berlin), and *King Kong* (New York).

City as Forest

City as forest is the positive version of the city as jungle. In this technique, the buildings are a scaled-down version of the city, more human, as though people were living in trees. This city looks and feels like a neighborhood or a town in the midst of impersonal towers. When the city is portrayed as a forest, it is usually a utopian vision in which people enjoy the benefits of teeming urban life while living in the coziness of a tree house. We see this technique in films such as *You Can't Take It with You* and *Ghostbusters*.

GHOSTBUSTERS
(by Dan Aykroyd and Harold Ramis, 1984)

Ghostbusters is a boys' adventure story set in New York. The three "musketeers" start off as professors at a warm, townlike university. They work in paranormal studies, which allows them to do all kinds of loony experiments with pretty girls. They create a business where they get paid large sums of money for dressing up in cool uniforms, driving a souped-up ambulance, shooting great gadgets, and living in a firehouse. The firehouse is the ultimate tree house for boys. These boys live in a dorm together, where they dream of sexy girls, and when they have a job, they get to slide down the "tree trunk" or the "beanpole" and take a wild ride. All kinds of floating are going on in this city.

Miniatures

A miniature is a society shrunk down. Miniatures are chaos theory applied to storytelling; they show the audience *levels of order*. The order of the larger world, which is too difficult to grasp because we can't see it as a whole, is suddenly clarified when made small.

All man-made spaces in a story are some form of miniature. The only difference is the scale. A miniature is one of the fundamental techniques of the story world because it is such a good condenser-expander. By its very nature, it doesn't show one thing after another in succession. It shows many things at once in all the complexity of their relationships.

A miniature has three main uses in a story:

1. It lets the audience see the world of the story as a whole.
2. It allows the author to express various aspects, or facets, of a character.
3. It shows the exercise of power, often of tyranny.

Ray and Charles Eames's classic documentary film *The Powers of Ten* shows how miniatures work in a story. From a yard up, we see a couple lying on the grass having a picnic. A split second later, we see the same couple from ten yards up, then a hundred, then a thousand, ten thousand, and so on. The perspective increases by powers of ten until we see vast reaches of outer space from an incomprehensible height. The perspective quickly telescopes back down to the couple on the grass and then reverses the powers of ten, delving ever deeper into the microscopic world of cells, molecules, and atoms. Each perspective shows a complete subworld, an order of things that explains, in a nutshell, how that world works.

Miniatures provide this same function in stories. But what they show is not simply a factual sense of how the pieces of the story world fit together. They show what matters. "Values become condensed and enriched in miniature."[9]

Citizen Kane

(by Herman J. Mankiewicz and Orson Welles, 1941)

Citizen Kane is a story built on miniatures. In the opening sequence, Kane, on his deathbed, drops and shatters a glass-ball paperweight that depicts a wooden cabin in the snow. This is a miniature of Kane's childhood, which he lost. Next comes a newsreel about Kane, which is his life story in miniature, but told from a distant, pseudohistorical perspective. The newsreel introduces Kane's estate, Xanadu, which is a miniature of the entire world re-created behind walls for Kane's personal pleasure and dominance. Each miniature gives the audience a highly value-laden picture of this rich, lonely, and often tyrannical man. At the same time, the use of so many miniatures suggests one of the themes of the story: we can never know another person, no matter how many perspectives and storytellers we use.

The Shining

(novel by Stephen King, screenplay by Stanley Kubrick and Diane Johnson, 1980)

In *The Shining*, Jack Torrance, while procrastinating writing, views in miniature the huge garden labyrinth behind the hotel. Gazing down at it from directly overhead, taking the "God perspective," he sees the tiny figures of his wife and son walking. This miniature is a foreshadowing (a kind of miniature of time) of his attempt to murder his son in the real garden at the end of the story.

Big to Small, Small to Big

Changing the physical size of a character is a great way of calling attention to the relationship between character and story world. In effect, you cause a revolutionary shift in the minds of the audience, forcing them to rethink both the character and the world in a radically new way. The audience is suddenly confronted by the underlying principles, or abstractions, of what they once took for granted; the very foundations of the world are now totally different.

One of the main reasons the fantasy genre exists is to allow us to see things as though for the first time. Making a character tiny does that better than any other story technique. Whenever a character shrinks, he regresses to a small child. Negatively, he experiences a sudden loss of power and may even be terrified by his now massive and domineering surroundings. Positively, the character and the audience have the amazing feeling of seeing the world anew. "The man with the magnifying glass is . . . youth recaptured. It gives him back the enlarging gaze of the child. . . . Thus the minuscule, the narrow gate, opens up an entire world."[10]

It is at the shift moment that the underlying principles of the world jump out at the audience, and yet the world remains intensely real. Suddenly, the mundane is sublime. In *Honey, I Shrunk the Kids*, the backyard lawn becomes a terrifying jungle. In *Fantastic Voyage*, the human body becomes a monstrous but beautiful inner space. In *Alice in Wonderland*, Alice's tears become an ocean in which she almost drowns. In *King Kong*, the subway train is a giant snake to Kong, and the Empire State Building is the tallest tree he has ever known.

The main value in making a character small is that he immediately becomes more heroic. Jack climbs a bean stalk to battle a giant, and he must use his brain, not his brawn, to win this fight. So too must Odysseus, who defeats the Cyclops by clinging to the underbelly of a sheep and telling the Cyclops that the one who blinded him is named Noman.

Other examples of stories of tiny characters or of characters becoming small include *Gulliver's Travels*, *Stuart Little*, *Thumbelina*, *The Borrowers*, *Tom Thumb*, *Ben and Me*, and *The Incredible Shrinking Man*.

Getting big is always less interesting in a story than getting small because it removes the possibility of subtlety and plot. The monstrously large character becomes the proverbial bull in the china shop. Everything is straight-line dominance. That's why Alice is a giant in Wonderland only near the beginning of the story, when she fills the house to overflowing. The wonder of Wonderland would quickly be wiped out if Alice were to clomp through it as the fifty-foot woman. That's also why the best part of Gulliver's trip to Lilliput is the early part when he is still enslaved by the six-inch Lilliputians. When Gulliver, as a giant, towers over the warring factions, he makes the abstract point that conflict between nations is absurd. But the story has essentially stopped. Nothing can happen unless Gulliver lets it happen.

A wonderful fantasy story, *Big* is an apparent exception to the rule that getting big is less interesting than getting small. But *Big* is not the story of a man who becomes a giant among little people. *Big* puts a twist on the tale of a man getting small by having a boy wake up as a man. The charm of the story is in seeing the Tom Hanks character, physically an adult, behaving with the personality, mind, and enthusiasm of a boy.

Passageways Between Worlds

Anytime you set up at least two subworlds in your story arena, you give yourself the possibility of using a great technique, the passageway between worlds. A passageway is normally used in a story only when two subworlds are extremely different. We see this most often in the fantasy genre when the character must pass from the mundane world to the fantastic. Some of the classic passageways are the rabbit hole, the keyhole, and the mirror (*Alice in Wonderland, Through the Looking-Glass*), the cyclone (*The Wizard of Oz*), the wardrobe closet (*The Chronicles of Narnia: The Lion, the Witch and the Wardrobe*), the painting and the chimney (*Mary Poppins*), the computer screen (*Tron*), and the television set (*Pleasantville, Poltergeist*).

A passageway has two main uses in a story. First, it literally gets your character from one place to another. Second, and more important, it is a kind of decompression chamber, allowing your audience to make the transition from the realistic to the fantastic. It tells the audience that the rules of the story world are about to change in a big way. The passageway says, "Loosen up; don't apply your normal concept of reality to what you are about to see." This is essential in a highly symbolic, allegorical form like fantasy, whose underlying themes explore the importance of looking at life from new perspectives and finding possibilities in even the most ordinary things.

Ideally, you want your character to move through the passageway slowly. A passageway is a special world unto itself; it should be filled with things and inhabitants that are both strange and organic to your story. Let your character linger there. Your audience will love you for it. The passageway to another world is one of the most popular of all story techniques. Come up with a unique one, and your story is halfway there.

Technology (Tools)

Tools are extensions of the human form, taking a simple capability and magnifying its power. They are a fundamental way that characters connect to the world. Any tool a character uses becomes part of his identity, showing not only how his own power has been magnified but also how well he is able to manipulate the world and maneuver through it.

Technology is most useful in genres that place the most emphasis on the story world, such as science fiction and fantasy, and in highly ambitious stories that place the hero within a larger social system. Because you, the writer, create the world in science fiction, the specific technology you invent highlights those elements of mankind that most trouble you. And because all great science fiction is about the writer's view of universal evolution, the relationship of humans to technology is always central. In fantasy, a tool such as a magic wand is a symbol of a character's self-mastery and indicates whether he uses his knowledge for good or evil.

In stories where characters are trapped in a system, tools let you show how the system exercises its power. This is especially true in modernization stories, where an entire society shifts to a more complex and technologically advanced stage. For example, *The Magnificent Ambersons* shows the effects of the rise of the automobile. In *Cinema Paradiso*, the movie house is torn down to make way for a parking lot. In the classic anti-Western *The Wild Bunch*, set in the last days of the American frontier, the aging cowboys encounter their first automobile and machine gun. *Butch Cassidy and the Sundance Kid*, another great anti-Western, has a terrific scene in which an enterprising bicycle salesman makes his pitch to people reluctant to join a posse.

Even in story forms that do not explore the larger world, tools can be helpful. For example, action stories place tremendous emphasis on the hero's ability to turn everyday objects into weapons or use them to gain superiority over the enemy. In drama, the tools of daily life are so common as to be practically invisible. But even here, technology (and sometimes the lack thereof) helps define a character and his place in the world. In *Death of a Salesman*, Willy Loman brings home $70 in commission, but he owes $16 on the refrigerator. His son Happy gives him $50 at Christmas, but fixing the hot water heater costs $97, and he's been putting off that motor job on the car. Willy is always "getting stuck on the machine."

CONNECTING THE WORLD TO THE HERO'S OVERALL DEVELOPMENT

The first step to building your story world is identifying the key visual oppositions based on characters and values. The second step is looking at the endpoints of your hero's development.

This is similar to the process we used when creating characters. There we began by sketching out the character web, since each character, through contrast and similarity, helps define the others. Then, focusing on the hero, we looked first at his overall range of change, starting at the endpoint (self-revelation), going back to the beginning (weakness and need, desire), and then creating the structure steps in between. We did that because every story is a journey of learning that the hero goes through, and as writers, we have to know the end of that journey before we can take any steps.

You need to match that process exactly when detailing the story world. We've already examined some of the major visual oppositions in the world by looking at the character web. Now we have to focus on the hero's overall change to see what the world will be like at the beginning and end of the story.

In the vast majority of stories, the hero's overall change moves from slavery to freedom. If that's true in your story, the visual world will probably move from slavery to freedom as well. Here's how the overall move-ment of character and world match up.

A *character* is enslaved primarily because of his psychological and moral weaknesses. A *world* is enslaving (or freeing) based on the relationship of the three major elements—land (natural settings), people (man-made spaces), and technology (tools)—and how they affect your hero. The unique way you combine these elements defines the nature of the story world.

■ Beginning (slavery): If the land, people, and technology are out of balance, everyone is out for himself, each is reduced to an animal clawing for scarce resources or a cog working for the greater good of a machine. This is a world of slavery and, taken to its extreme, a dystopia, or hell on earth.

■ Endpoint (freedom): If the land, people, and technology are in balance (as you define it), you have a *community*, where individuals can grow in their own way, supported by others. This is a world of freedom and, taken to the extreme, a utopia, or heaven on earth.

Besides slavery and dystopia, freedom and utopia, there is one other kind of world you can create for the beginning or end of your story: the apparent utopia. This world appears to be perfect, but the perfection is only skin deep. Below the surface, the world is actually corrupt, rotten, and enslaving. Everyone is desperate to put on a good face to hide a psychological or moral disaster. This technique is used in the opening of *L.A. Confidential* and *Blue Velvet*.

The point of creating these different kinds of worlds is to connect them to your hero. In the vast majority of stories, there is a one-to-one connection between hero and world. For example, an enslaved hero lives in a world of slavery. A free hero lives in and, in getting free, often creates a free world.

KEY POINT: In most stories you write, the world is a physical expression of who your hero is and how he develops.

In this technique, the world helps define your main character through the structure of the story. It shows his needs, his values, his desires (both good and bad), and the obstacles he faces. And since in the vast majority of stories your hero begins the story enslaved in some way, you must focus on slavery.

KEY POINT: *Always ask yourself, how is the world of slavery an expression of my hero's great weakness? The world should embody, highlight, or accentuate your hero's weakness or draw it out in its worst form.*

For example, detective stories, crime stories, and thrillers often set up a close connection between the hero's weakness—when it exists—and the "mean streets," or world of slavery in which the hero operates.

VERTIGO
(novel by Pierre Boileau and Thomas Narcejac, screenplay by Alec Coppel and Samuel Taylor, 1958)

The world of *Vertigo* highlights the hero's psychological weakness in the opening scene. While chasing a criminal over the rooftops of San Francisco, Scottie slips and hangs by his fingertips five floors above the ground. He looks down, and vertigo overwhelms him. A fellow cop falls to his death trying to help him, which creates a guilt that haunts Scottie for the rest of the story. This technique of the story world highlighting the hero's weakness is repeated later when Scottie's vertigo prevents him from climbing a tower to save the woman he loves from committing suicide. Indeed, this technique is the source of *Vertigo*'s greatest strength as a story: the killer uses the detective's own weakness—his vertigo—as the main trick in getting away with murder.

Creating a world of slavery to express or accentuate your hero's weakness is also useful in drama and melodrama.

SUNSET BOULEVARD
(by Charles Brackett & Billy Wilder & D. M. Marshman, Jr., 1950)

In *Sunset Boulevard*, the hero's weakness is a predilection for money and the finer things in life. Sure enough, he finds himself hiding out in a rundown mansion with an aging movie star who has money to burn, as long as he fulfills her wishes. Like vampires, the movie star and her mansion feed on the hero, and they are rejuvenated as the hero falls into an opulent slavery.

A Streetcar Named Desire
(by Tennessee Williams, 1947)

A Streetcar Named Desire is a perfect example of how the world of slavery at the beginning of the story expresses the hero's great weakness. Blanche is a fragile, self-deceptive woman who wants to hide in a dream world of romance and pretty things. But instead, she is thrust into a hot, cramped apartment with her sister and brutish brother-in-law. Rather than give her the illusion of romance, this hellhole, with its apelike king, Stanley, relentlessly presses in on her until she breaks.

Casablanca
(play Everybody Comes to Rick's *by Murray Burnett and Joan Alison, screenplay by Julius J. Epstein, Philip G. Epstein, and Howard Koch, 1942)*

Casablanca is a love story with an opening world of slavery that constantly jabs at Rick's weakness. His fabulous bar, the Café Américain, reminds him at every turn of the love he lost in romantic Paris. The club is also all about making money, which Rick can do only if he pays off a traitorous French police captain. Every magnificent corner of his bar shows Rick how far he has fallen into a self-centered cynicism while the world cries out for leaders.

Fantasy is another story form that places special emphasis on this technique of matching the world of slavery to the hero's weakness. A good fantasy always starts the hero in some version of a mundane world and sets up his psychological or moral weakness there. This weakness is the reason the hero cannot see the true potential of where he lives and of who he can be, and it is what propels him to visit the fantasy world.

Field of Dreams
(novel Shoeless Joe *by W. P. Kinsella, screenplay by Phil Alden Robinson, 1989)*

In *Field of Dreams*, the hero, Ray, lives on a farm in Iowa near a town that wants to ban books. He builds a baseball diamond on his property even though the other farmers think he's crazy and his brother-in-law wants the farm for its practical and monetary value. Ray's need is to do something he's passionate about and make amends with his deceased father. Building a baseball diamond—which brings back the dead baseball star Shoeless Joe Jackson—creates a utopian world where Ray lives and allows him to have one last communion with his father.

MARY POPPINS
(books by P. L. Travers, screenplay by Bill Walsh and Don Da Gradi, 1964)
In *Mary Poppins*, the household is a restrictive place, governed by a rule-bound father whose god is the clock. The apparent main character, Mary Poppins, is what I call a traveling angel, "practically perfect in every way," so she has no weaknesses. In fact, she is the agent for showing others their true potential and the negative potential of their enslaving world. The children are rebellious in a self-destructive way and have no sense of the wondrous world of enchantment that lies outside their door in London and also within their own minds.

The father, who is the main opponent, has an even greater weakness than his children. He sees the world as a business, and though he doesn't enter the fantasy worlds, he does benefit from his children's visits to them and from the magical nanny. At the end, the father's world of business has become a place where he can fly a kite with his kids.

Other traveling-angel comedies that show a similar connection between the hero and an enslaving world are *Crocodile Dundee*; *The Music Man*; *Amélie*; *Chocolat*; *Good Morning, Vietnam*; and *Meatballs*.

How the Story World and the Hero Develop Together

Notice that each of the major story elements so far—premise, designing principle, seven steps, characters, and moral argument—matches and connects with all the other elements to create a deeply textured but organic unit, with everything working together. This is the orchestration so essential to great storytelling.

In the beginning of the story, all the elements weave together and express the same thing. The hero (probably) lives in a world of slavery that highlights, amplifies, or exacerbates his great weakness. He then goes up against the opponent best able to exploit that weakness. In Chapter 8 on plot, you'll see how another element at the beginning, the "ghost," expresses the hero's weakness as well.

The connection between hero and world extends from the hero's slavery throughout his character arc. In most stories, because the hero and the world are expressions of each other, the world and the hero develop together. Or if the hero doesn't change, as in much of Chekhov, the world doesn't change either.

Let's look at some of the classic ways the hero and the world change, contrast, or don't change over the course of a story.

Hero: Slavery to Greater Slavery to Freedom
World: Slavery to Greater Slavery to Freedom

The hero begins the story in a world of slavery. He struggles to reach his goal and experiences decline as the world closes in. But then, through self-revelation, he fulfills his need and becomes free in a world that is better off because of what he has done.

This pattern is found in *Star Wars* episodes 4–6, *The Lord of the Rings*, *The Verdict*, *The Lion King*, *The Shawshank Redemption*, *It's a Wonderful Life*, and *David Copperfield*.

Hero: Slavery to Greater Slavery or Death
World: Slavery to Greater Slavery or Death

In these stories, the main character begins enslaved by his own weakness and by a world pressing in. Because of the cancer in the hero's soul, the world that depends on him is rotten as well. In seeking a goal, the hero learns a negative self-revelation that destroys both him and the world that relies on him. Or he is crushed by an enslaving world he cannot understand.

Examples are *Oedipus the King*, *Death of a Salesman*, *A Streetcar Named Desire*, *The Conversation*, *The Conformist*, *Sunset Boulevard*, *Three Sisters*, *The Cherry Orchard*, and *Heart of Darkness*.

Hero: Slavery to Greater Slavery or Death
World: Slavery to Great Slavery to Freedom

In this approach, used in some tragedies, you break the connection between hero and world at the end of the story. The hero has a self-revelation, but it comes too late to set him free. He does make a sacrifice before he dies or falls, which sets the world free after he is gone.

We see this sequence in *Hamlet*, *The Seven Samurai*, and *A Tale of Two Cities*.

Hero: Slavery to Temporary Freedom to Greater Slavery or Death
World: Slavery to Temporary Freedom to Greater Slavery or Death

This technique has the hero enter a subworld of freedom at some point during the middle of the story. This is the world in which the character *should* live if he realizes his true self. Failing to do so and moving on, or discovering the rightness of this world too late, eventually destroys the hero.

This pattern occurs in *The Wild Bunch*, *The Treasure of the Sierra Madre*, *Butch Cassidy and the Sundance Kid*, and *Dances with Wolves*.

Hero: Freedom to Slavery or Death
World: Freedom to Slavery or Death

These stories begin in a utopian world in which the hero is happy but vulnerable to attack or change. A new character, changing social forces, or a character flaw causes the hero and his world to decline and eventually fall.

This sequence is found in *King Lear*, *How Green Was My Valley*, and such King Arthur stories as *Le Morte d'Arthur* and *Excalibur*.

Hero: Freedom to Slavery to Freedom
World: Freedom to Slavery to Freedom

The hero again starts off in a world of freedom. An attack comes from outside or within the family. The hero and the world decline, but he overcomes the problem and creates a stronger utopia.

This approach is used in *Meet Me in St. Louis*, *Amarcord*, and to a lesser degree in *Cinema Paradiso*.

Hero: Apparent Freedom to Greater Slavery to Freedom
World: Apparent Freedom to Greater Slavery to Freedom

At the beginning of the story, the world appears to be a utopia but is actually a place of extreme hierarchy and corruption. The characters fight ruthlessly to win, often with many dying in the process. Eventually, the hero fights through the corruption to create a more just society, or he is simply one of the last ones standing.

Examples include *L.A. Confidential, Jurassic Park, The Magnificent Ambersons,* and *Blue Velvet.*

A brilliant variation on this sequence is found in *Goodfellas,* which combines the gangster and black comedy forms. The story moves from the apparent freedom of the mob community to greater slavery of the hero and death for all of his friends.

TIME IN THE STORY WORLD

Now that the story world is connected to the hero, we have to look at the different ways the story world itself can develop. Time is the fourth major element—along with natural settings, man-made spaces, and tools—that you use to construct your story world.

Before we look at the many ways that time is expressed through the world—or more exactly, how the story world is expressed through time—we need to get beyond two fallacies that many storytellers have about time.

Fallacies of Past and Future

What we might call the fallacy of the past is common in historical fiction. The idea is that the writer of historical fiction is depicting a different world, based on its own set of values and moral codes. Therefore, we should not judge those people by our standards.

The fallacy of the past comes from the misguided notion that a writer of historical fiction is first and foremost writing history. As a storyteller, you are always writing fiction. You use the past as a pair of glasses through which the audience can see itself more clearly today. Therefore, withholding judgment about people in the past is absurd; we show them *in order* to judge ourselves by comparison.

You make this comparison in two ways. Negatively, you show values dominant in the past that still hurt people today. We see this with the Puritan values in Nathaniel Hawthorne's *The Scarlet Letter* and Arthur Miller's *The Crucible.* Positively, you show values from the past that are still good and should be brought back. For example, *She Wore a Yellow Ribbon* glorifies such values as duty, honor, and loyalty found on a military outpost in 1870s America.

What we might call the fallacy of the future is common in science fiction stories. Many writers think science fiction is about predicting what will happen in the future, what the world will actually be like. We saw this thinking at the end of 1983 when everyone was debating whether and in what ways George Orwell had been right about 1984.

The fallacy here is that stories set in the future are about the future. They're not. You set a story in the future to give the audience another pair of glasses, to abstract the present in order to understand it better. One key difference between science fiction and historical fiction is that stories set in the future highlight not so much values as the forces and choices that face us today and the consequences if we fail to choose wisely.

True time in a story is "natural" time. It has to do with the way the world develops and in turn furthers the development of the story. Some of the top techniques of natural time are seasons, holidays, the single day, and the time endpoint.

Seasons

The first technique of natural story time is the cycle of the seasons and the rituals that come with them. In this technique, you place the story, or a moment of the story, within a particular season. Each season, like each natural setting, conveys certain meanings to the audience about the hero or the world.

If you go further and show the *change* of the seasons, you give the audience a detailed and powerful expression of the growth or decay of the hero or the world.

If you cover all four seasons in your story, you tell the audience you are shifting from a linear story, which is about some kind of development, to a circular story, which is about how things ultimately remain the same. You can present this positively or negatively. A positive circular story usually emphasizes man's connection to the land. Human beings are animals, and happy to be so. The cycle of life, death, and rebirth is natural and worthy of celebration, and we can learn much by studying the secrets nature reveals at its gentle, steady pace. Thoreau's *Walden* uses the seasons in this way.

A negative circular story usually emphasizes that humans are bound by the forces of nature, just like other animals. This approach is tricky

because it can quickly grow dull. Indeed, the great weakness of many nature documentaries is that the plot, which almost always matches the seasons, is predictable and hence boring. An animal might give birth in the
spring, hunt and be hunted in the summer, mate in the fall, and face star-
vation in the winter. But sure enough, the animal returns in the spring to
give birth again.

The classic method of connecting the seasons to the story line—done
beautifully in *Meet Me in St. Louis* and *Amarcord*—uses a one-to-one connection of season to drama and follows this course:

- Summer: The characters exist in a troubled, vulnerable state or in a
  world of freedom susceptible to attack.
- Fall: The characters begin their decline.
- Winter: The characters reach their lowest point.
- Spring: The characters overcome their problem and rise.

You may want to use this classic connection or, to avoid cliché, purposely cut against it. For example, a character might decline in the spring
and rise again in the winter. By changing the normal sequence, you not
only short-circuit the audience's expectations but also assert that humans, though of the natural world, are not enslaved by its patterns.

Holidays and Rituals

Holidays, and the rituals that mark them, give you another technique for
expressing meaning, pacing the story, and showing its development. A ritual is a philosophy that has been translated into a set of actions that are
repeated at specific intervals. So any ritual you use is already a dramatic
event, with strong visual elements, that you can insert in your drama. A
holiday expands the scope of the ritual to a national scale and so allows
you to express the political as well as the personal and social meaning of
the ritual.

If you wish to use a ritual or holiday in your story, you must first examine the philosophy inherent in that ritual and decide in what way you
agree or disagree with it. In your story, you may wish to support or attack
all or part of that philosophy.

A CHRISTMAS STORY
(screenplay by Jean Shepherd & Leigh Brown & Bob Clark, 1983)

THE GREAT AMERICAN FOURTH OF JULY AND OTHER DISASTERS
(novel In God We Trust, All Others Pay Cash *by Jean Shepherd, screenplay by Jean Shepherd, 1982)*

The humorist Jean Shepherd is a master at constructing a story around a particular holiday. He begins by combining a holiday with a storyteller reminiscing about his family. This sets up a utopia of childhood for the audience, where each viewer nestles in the recognition of living happily within a family. The particular holiday creates a time passageway, rocketing the viewer back to his childhood. Shepherd does this by having the voice-over storyteller recount the funny things that happened every year on that holiday. For example, his little brother always wore a snowsuit that was too big for him. His dad always got a gift that would infuriate his mom. He always had to deal with the neighborhood bullies. And what about the time Flick got his tongue stuck on the flagpole?

Shepherd supports the philosophy of the holiday not in a straightforward or religious way but by pretending to make fun of it, by laughing at the silly things people do at this time every year. But those silly things also make him feel good, especially because they happen every year and because the people of his memory will never grow old. This is the power of the perennial story.

If you use this technique, it is important that you understand the relationship between the ritual, the holiday, and the season in which the holiday occurs. Then orchestrate all of these elements to express change, whether in the hero or in the world.

HANNAH AND HER SISTERS
(by Woody Allen, 1986)

You can see how to connect a holiday to your story and show character change in *Hannah and Her Sisters*. In this film, the holiday is Thanksgiving. A uniquely American celebration going back to colonial times, it embodies the formation of a community to give thanks for a bountiful harvest and the beginnings of a nation. But Woody Allen doesn't use Thanksgiving to structure the story and provide the underlying theme in the normal way. Instead of focusing on the philosophy of the holiday, Allen creates a story of simultaneous action that crosscuts among three sisters and their husbands or boyfriends. At the beginning of the story, there is no community, either among the characters or in the story structure itself. Allen creates community through the structure by interweaving three different love stories and by using the holiday of Thanksgiving three different times.

The structure works like this. The story begins at a Thanksgiving dinner that all the characters attend with the wrong partners. Then the story fractures into crosscuts among the six individuals. In the middle of the story, they all come together at Thanksgiving again, and this time most are with new, but still wrong, people. The story fractures again into its many simultaneous strands, with the characters struggling and apart. The story ends with each of the characters together at Thanksgiving a third time, but this time part of a real community, because each is now coupled with the right partner. Story and holiday become one. These characters don't talk about Thanksgiving; they live it.

The Single Day

The single day is another increment of time that has very specific effects when used in a story. The first effect is to create simultaneous story movement while maintaining narrative drive. Instead of showing a single character over a long development—the linear approach of most stories—you present a number of characters acting at the same time, right now, today. But the ticking of the hours keeps the story line moving forward and gives the story a sense of compression.

If you use a twelve-hour clock, setting the entire story in one day or one night, you create a funnel effect. The audience senses not only that each of the story strands will be settled at the end of the twelve hours but also that the urgency will increase as the deadline nears. *American Graffiti*, *Ferris Bueller's Day Off*, and *Smiles of a Summer Night* use this method.

If you use a twenty-four-hour clock, you lessen the urgency and increase the sense of the circular. No matter what may have happened, we return to the beginning, with everything the same, and start all over again. Some writers use this circular sense to highlight change even more.

In this technique, you show that while most things do remain the same, the one or two things that have changed in the last twenty-four hours are that much more significant. This technique is the underlying foundation of stories as different as *Ulysses* and *Groundhog Day*. (The television show *24* reverses this technique, using the twenty-four-hour clock, stretched over an entire television season, to heighten suspense and pack the plot.)

Notice that this twenty-four-hour circular day has many of the same thematic effects as the four seasons. Not surprisingly, both techniques are often connected with comedy, which tends to be circular, emphasizes society as opposed to the individual, and ends in some kind of communion or marriage. Techniques of circular time are also associated with the myth form, which is based on circularity of space. In many classic myth stories, the hero starts at home, goes on a journey, and returns home to find what was already within him.

Eugene O'Neill uses the single-day technique in *Long Day's Journey into Night*. But unlike *Ulysses*, which covers almost twenty-four hours and evokes the positive qualities of circularity, *Long Day's Journey into Night* covers only about eighteen hours, from morning into night. This gives the story a declining line, from hope to despair, as the family becomes increasingly nasty and the mother moves toward drugged-out madness.

A second major effect of the single-day technique is to emphasize the everyday quality of the drama that is being played out. Instead of cutting out dead time and showing only the big dramatic moments, you show the little events and the boring details that make up the average person's life (as in *One Day in the Life of Ivan Denisovich*). Implied in this "day in the life" approach is that drama is just as valid, if not more so, for the little guy as for the king.

The Perfect Day

A variation on the single-day technique is the perfect day. The perfect day is a time version of the utopian moment and as such is almost always used to structure a section of the story, rather than the story itself. Implied in the technique is that everything is in harmony, which limits how long you can use it, since too much time without conflict will kill your story.

The perfect-day technique usually connects a communal activity with a twelve-hour day or night. Communal activity is the crucial element in any utopian moment. Attaching it to a natural increment of time, like dawn to dusk, intensifies the feeling of everything working well together because the harmony is grounded in a natural rhythm. The writers of *Witness* understood this very well when they connected the perfect day with the Amish community building a barn and the two leads falling in love.

Time Endpoint

A time endpoint, also known as a ticking clock, is a technique in which you tell the audience up front that the action must be completed by a specific time. It is most common in action stories (*Speed*), thrillers (*Outbreak*), caper stories (where the characters pull off some kind of heist, as in *Ocean's Eleven*), and suicide mission stories (*The Guns of Navarone*, *The Dirty Dozen*). A time endpoint gives you the benefit of intense narrative drive and great speed, although at the expense of texture and subtlety. It also creates an even faster funnel than the twelve-hour day, which is why it is often used when writers want to give an action story epic scope. The time endpoint lets you show literally hundreds of characters acting simultaneously and with great urgency, without stopping the narrative drive. In these kinds of stories—*The Hunt for Red October* is an example—the time endpoint is usually connected to a single place where all the actors and forces must converge.

A less common but very effective use of the time endpoint is in comedy journey stories. Any journey story is inherently fragmented and meandering. A comic journey makes the story even more fragmented because the forward narrative drive stops every time you do some comic business. Jokes and gags almost always take the story sideways; the story waits while a character is dropped or diminished in some way. By telling the audience up front that there is a specific time endpoint to the story, you give them a forward line they can hang on to through all the meandering. Instead of getting impatient to know what comes next, they relax and enjoy the comic moments along the way. We see this technique in comic journey stories like *The Blues Brothers* and Jacques Tati's *Traffic*.

STORY WORLD THROUGH STRUCTURE

Now that you've explored some techniques for making your story world develop over time, you have to connect the world with the hero's development *at every step of the story*. The overall arc—such as slavery to freedom—gives you the big picture of how the world of your story will change. But now you have to detail that development through story structure. Structure is what allows you to express your theme without sermonizing. It is also the way you show the audience a highly textured story world without losing narrative drive.

How do you do this? In a nutshell, you create a visual seven steps. Each of the seven key story structure steps tends to have a story world all its own. Each of these is a unique visual world within the overall story arena. Notice what a huge advantage this is: the story world has texture but also changes along with the change in the hero. To the seven structure steps you attach the other physical elements of the world, like natural settings, man-made spaces, technology, and time. This is how you create a total orchestration of story and world.

These are the structure steps that tend to have their own unique subworld ("apparent defeat or temporary freedom" and "visit to death" are not among the seven key structure steps):

- Weakness and need
- Desire
- Opponent
- Apparent defeat or temporary freedom
- Visit to death
- Battle
- Freedom or slavery

- **Weakness and Need**   At the beginning of the story, you show a subworld that is a physical manifestation of the hero's weakness or fear.
- **Desire**   This is a subworld in which the hero expresses his goal.
- **Opponent**   The opponent (or opponents) lives or works in a unique place that expresses his power and ability to attack the hero's great weakness. This world of the opponent should also be an extreme version of the hero's world of slavery.

- **Apparent Defeat or Temporary Freedom** Apparent defeat is the moment when the hero wrongly believes he has lost to the opponent (we'll discuss it in more detail in Chapter 8 on plot). The world of the hero's apparent defeat is typically the narrowest space in the story up to that point. All of the forces defeating and enslaving the hero are literally pressing in on him.

  In those rare stories where the hero ends enslaved or dead, he often experiences a moment of temporary freedom at the same point when most heroes experience apparent defeat. This usually occurs in some kind of utopia that is the perfect place for the hero if he will only realize it in time.

- **Visit to Death** In the visit to death (another step we'll discuss in Chapter 8), the hero travels to the underworld, or, in more modern stories, he has a sudden sense that he will die. He should encounter his mortality in a place that represents the elements of decline, aging, and death.

- **Battle** The battle should occur in the most confined place of the entire story. The physical compression creates a kind of pressure-cooker effect, in which the final conflict builds to its hottest point and explodes.

- **Freedom or Slavery** The world completes its detailed development by ending as a place of freedom or greater slavery and death. Again, the specific place should represent in physical terms the final maturation or decline of the character.

Here are some examples of how the visual seven steps work and how you attach the other four major elements—natural settings, man-made spaces, technology, and time—of the story world (indicated *in italics*).

Star Wars
(by George Lucas, 1977)
Outer space is the overall world and arena.

- **Weakness and Need, Desire?** *Desert wilderness.* In this barren landscape, where somehow farming is done, Luke feels stuck. "I'll never get out of here," he complains. The event that triggers Luke's desire is a hologram, a miniature, of Princess Leia asking for help.

- **Opponent** *Death Star.* Fantasy allows you to use abstract shapes as real objects. Here the opponent's subworld, the Death Star, is a giant sphere. Inside, Darth Vader interrogates Princess Leia. Later the Death Star commanders learn that the emperor has disbanded the last remnants of the republic, and Darth Vader shows them the deadly power of the Force.

- **Apparent Defeat and Visit to Death** *Collapsing garbage dump with a monster under water.* Combining "apparent defeat" and "visit to death," writer George Lucas places the characters in water, with a deadly creature underneath. And the room isn't just the narrowest space in the story up to that point; it is a collapsing room, which means it gives us a narrowing of space and time.

- **Battle** *Trench.* Realistically, a dogfight would occur in open space where the pilots have room to maneuver. But Lucas understands that the best battle occurs in the tightest space possible. So he has the hero dive his plane into a long trench, with walls on both sides, and the endpoint of the hero's desire, the weak spot where the Death Star can be destroyed, at the far end of the trench. As if that's not enough, Luke's main opponent, Darth Vader, is chasing him. Luke takes his shot, and that small spot at the end of the trench is the convergent point of the entire film. An epic that covers the universe funnels down, visually and structurally, to a single point.

- **Freedom** *Hall of Heroes.* The warriors' success is celebrated in a large hall where all the other warriors give their public approval.

THE WILD BUNCH

(story by Walon Green and Roy N. Sickner, screenplay by Walon Green and Sam Peckinpah, 1969)

This story uses a single-line journey through barren territory, and it gets progressively more barren. The story also places the characters in a society that is undergoing fundamental change, from village to city. New technology, in the form of cars and machine guns, has arrived, and the Bunch doesn't know how to adapt to this new world.

- **Problem** *Town.* The story begins when soldiers enter a town in the American Southwest. But this is a dystopian town, because the soldiers are really outlaws and the lawmen waiting to capture them are worse than the outlaws. Between them they have a gunfight that massacres a good number of the townspeople. The Wild Bunch has entered the town to rob the bank, but they have been betrayed by one of their own, and many of them do not make it out alive.

- **Weakness and Need**   *Barren cantina.*   After the massacre, the Bunch almost breaks apart in a barren cantina until their leader, Pike, gives them an ultimatum: either they stick together or they die. Their problem worsens when they discover that the silver coins they had stolen from the bank are worthless.

- **Desire**   *Campfire.*   Lying in front of a warm fire, Pike tells his second in command, Dutch, his desire: he'd like to make one last score and back off. Dutch immediately underscores the hollowness of this desire by asking, "Back off to what?" This line foreshadows the overall development of the story from slavery to greater slavery and death.

- **Temporary Freedom**   *Under the trees.*   Although its overall development goes from slavery to death, *The Wild Bunch* uses the technique of the utopian place in the middle of the story. Here the Bunch stops at a Mexican village, home of one of their comrades, Angel. This is the one communal place in the entire story, set under the trees, where children play. This is an arcadian vision, and it is where these hardscrabble men should live. But they move on, and they die.

- **Visit to Death**   *Bridge.*   Once again, this step occurs at the narrowest space in the story so far, which is on a bridge. If the Bunch gets to the other side, they are free, at least temporarily. If they don't, they die. The writers add the technique of the narrowing of time; the dynamite on the bridge is already lit when the Bunch gets stuck trying to cross.

- **Battle**   *Coliseum of Mapache.*   A big, violent battle of this sort would almost certainly occur in wide-open spaces. But these writers know that a great story battle needs walls and a small space to get maximum compression. So the four remaining members of the Bunch walk into a coliseum, which is stuffed with hundreds of opponents. When this pressure cooker explodes, it is one of the great battles in movie history.

■ **Slavery or Death** *Wind-blown ghost town.*   The story ends not just with the death of the main characters but with the destruction of the entire town. To increase the sense of devastation, the writers add wind.

MEET ME IN ST. LOUIS

(novel by Sally Benson, screenplay by Irving Brecher and Fred F. Finklehoffe, 1944)

The overall arena is small-town America, centered on a single large house. Setting their story at the turn of the twentieth century, the writers place the characters in a society changing from town to city. They structure the story based on the four seasons, using the classic one-to-one connection between the change of the seasons and the fall and rise of the family.

■ **Freedom** *Summer in the warm house.*   The opening scene shows a utopian world, a perfect balance of land, people, and technology. Horse and carriage coexists with horseless carriage on a tree-lined drive. A boy on a bicycle rides up to the large, gabled house, and inside we go, starting with the warmest, most communal room in the house, the kitchen. The writers build the sense of community—a utopia within the house—by having one of the girls in the family sing the title song ("Meet Me in St. Louis") while she walks upstairs. This establishes the musical, shows the audience the details of the main story space, and introduces most of the minor characters.

The girl then passes the song, like a baton, to her grandfather, who walks through another part of the house. This technique adds to the community, not just literally by showing us more characters but also qualitatively because this is an extended family where three generations live together happily under one roof. Having introduced the minor characters, the main song, and the nooks and crannies of the warm house, the writers take us full circle out the window, where we meet the main character, Esther, with the best voice of all, singing the title song as she climbs the front steps.

Matching the utopian world, the hero, Esther, is happy as she begins the story. She has no weakness, need, or problem yet, but she is vulnerable to attack.

- **Weakness and Need, Problem, Opponent** *Autumn in the terrifying house.* With season number two, autumn, the warm house now looks terrifying. Sure enough, the season and house are matched with Halloween, the holiday that acknowledges the dead. This is also where the family begins its decline. It is breaking apart because the two older girls may get married and move away and also because the opponent, the father, decides the family should move from small-town St. Louis to big-city New York.

  The writers use Halloween to extend their critique beyond this one family to the society itself. The two little girls are about to go trick-or-treating, and they spread rumors about one of their neighbors, claiming he poisons cats. Later, the youngest girl, Tootie, falsely claims that Esther's boyfriend molested her. This is the dark side of small-town life, where lies and rumors can destroy someone in an instant.

- **Apparent Defeat** *Winter in the bleak house.* With winter, the family reaches its lowest point. They are packed and ready to move. Esther sings Tootie a sad song about the hope for a happier Christmas next year: "Someday soon we all will be together, if the fates allow. Until then we'll have to muddle through somehow." This family community is about to fragment and die.

- **New Freedom** *Spring in the warm house.* As a comedy and a musical, this story ends with the characters passing through the crisis—father decides to keep the family in St. Louis—and emerging, in spring, with the family community reborn. There are not one but two marriages, and the now even larger family heads off to enjoy the World's Fair. The World's Fair is another subworld, a temporary utopia and miniature future of America, built to show this family, and the audience, that we can have individual opportunity without destroying community, "right here in our own back yard."

IT'S A WONDERFUL LIFE
(short story "The Greatest Gift" by Philip Van Doren Stern, screenplay by Frances Goodrich & Albert Hackett and Frank Capra, 1946)

One of the greatest examples of connecting story with world, this advanced social fantasy is designed to allow the audience to see, and compare in great detail, two distinct versions of an entire town. This small town is a miniature of America, and the two versions are based on two different sets of values, both of which are central to American life.

The arena is Bedford Falls, a bustling little town of two-story buildings where someone can wave hello from the second floor to a friend on the street below. The story uses the holiday of Christmas as one of its foundations, although it really tracks the philosophy of Easter by using the hero's "death" and rebirth for its basic structure.

- ■ **Weakness and Need**   *Night sky, Bedford Falls from above.*   The story starts with an omniscient, third-person narrator (an angel) and later is carried by an actual character, the angel Clarence. Clarence has a weakness: he doesn't have his wings. Helping George is how he will fulfill his need. George's weakness is that his despair has led him to the point of suicide. This setup is designed to allow the audience to review many years of George's life very quickly and eventually to place the two versions of the town side by side.

  The subworld of these two weaknesses, Clarence's and George's, is a God's-eye view of the arena, which is the town, and the night sky, which is a physical manifestation of the religious elements of the story.

- ■ **Desire**   *George's warm house growing up and the deserted house where he and Mary make a wish.*   After high school, George lives at home in a buzzing household with his father, mother, brother, and maid Annie. His father is a benevolent man, and there is much love between him and George. But George is bursting to leave this confining small town. George tells his father his goal: "You know what I've always talked about—build things . . . design new buildings—plan modern cities." This scene places the visual subworld and the story structure step in conflict (usually the subworld matches the step). The warm house shows what a loving family can be like. But George's intense desire to leave suggests the oppression of the small-town world, especially one controlled by a tyrant.

  George again expresses his desire when he and Mary walk home after falling into the pool at a dance. They spot an old, deserted house on the hill—the terrifying house—which for George is the symbol of negative small-town life. He throws a rock at it and tells Mary, "I'm shaking the dust of this crummy little town off my feet and I'm going to see the world . . . and then I'm going to build things." Of course, he ends up living in that house, which his wife tries to make cozy and warm. But to his mind, the house is haunted and remains his tomb.

- **Opponent** *Potter's bank and office.* Henry Potter is "the richest and meanest man in the county." When Clarence first sees him riding in his "elaborate horse-drawn carriage," he asks, "Who's that—a king?" Potter is the enemy of George and the Building and Loan because they are all that keep Potter from owning everything and everyone in town. Potter's lair is his bank, from which he controls the town.

- **Apparent Defeat** *Bridge in Bedford Falls.* George's apparent defeat occurs when he faces the shame of bankruptcy due to Uncle Billy's losing $8,000. George crosses to the middle of the bridge under a heavy snowfall and a hard wind. At this narrow place of passage, George decides to end his life.

- **Visit to Death** *Opponent's dystopian town of Pottersville.* The angel Clarence shows George what the town would be like if he had never lived and was unable to check Potter's influence. Potter values business, money, power, and keeping the common man down. So begins George's long journey through the deadly subworld of Pottersville, a perfect representation of Potter's values.

The detailing of this subworld, accomplished in the writing, is superb, and the whole sequence is done while George is on the run. Main Street is a string of bars, nightclubs, liquor stores, and pool halls, and dissonant jazz is playing over the scene (some of us actually like this vision). As described in the screenplay, "Where before it was a quiet, orderly small town, it has now become in nature like a frontier village."

Unlike Bedford Falls, Potter's version of a town has no community. Nobody recognizes George, and nobody knows one another. Even more important, all the minor characters, who have been defined in great detail up to this point, are shown as having fulfilled their worst potential. The contrast with their earlier selves is startling but believable. That really could be Ernie the cab driver living a dark version of his life. That really could be Mr. Gower, the druggist, who's now a bum. That really could be George's mother, turned nasty, running a boardinghouse. (The only miss is Donna Reed as a spinster.) This suggests that all people are a range of possibilities and that whether they are at their best or at their worst depends on the world they live in and the values they live by.

George ends his trip to Pottersville—and his long visit to death— with a visit to the graveyard on a dark snowy night. Here he sees his brother's grave and then narrowly escapes shots fired by a cop. This returns him, full circle, to the bridge, the transition point where he was about to commit suicide.

■ **Freedom**   *The hero's utopian town of Bedford Falls.*   When George discovers that he is alive, he experiences the intense liberation that comes from seeing the value of his own life and, even more, what he has been able to achieve as a human being. This is a profound self-revelation for any person. In a moment of intense but inspiring irony, he runs joyously down the main street of the town that only hours before had driven him almost to suicide. It is the same town, but the simple, tree-lined street with its family businesses has become a winter wonderland. George now experiences this once-boring town as a utopia because it is a community that cares. The big old drafty house, once haunted and confining, has become warm because the family that loves him is there, and it is soon filled with all the minor characters whose lives he improved and who are now happy to return the favor.

It's a Wonderful Life shows a very close match between story and visual world. Unlike the big sensational worlds in fantasies like *The Lord of the Rings* and the Harry Potter stories, this film uses visual techniques in the everyday setting of a suburban, middle-class, midcentury American world (*Big* is a more recent example of this). *It's a Wonderful Life* is excellent social fantasy on the level of Twain and Dickens. And it borrows from them both.

Borrowing from other storytellers is a technique that you can use if you use it playfully. Keep the references light. People who get them will enjoy them. Those who don't will still appreciate the story's added texture. In *It's a Wonderful Life*, the angel who saves George is named Clarence, which is the name of the ally in Twain's *Connecticut Yankee in King Arthur's Court*. Clarence is reading *The Adventures of Tom Sawyer* when he is called to action. And of course, the story is an American version of Dickens's *A Christmas Carol*, with a heavy dose of *David Copperfield* thrown in.

Notice that you can borrow all the way up to the designing principle of another story. But if you do, you must change it enough to make it unique. Your audience will appreciate, even on a subliminal level, the artistry of making that change. *It's a Wonderful Life* is not about a crotchety old American who visits Christmas past, present, and future in New York. It is about a middle-class American whose whole life is laid out in detail and who then sees an alternative version of what his hometown would be like had he not lived. That is a wonderful change to make to the designing principle of *A Christmas Carol*. You may be surprised to learn that audiences didn't take to this film when it first came out. Though *It's a Wonderful Life* is very sentimental, it may have been too dark a social satire for the mass audience of its day. But over time, the excellence of the film, especially in connecting character to story world, has won over the crowd.

SUNSET BOULEVARD

(by Charles Brackett & Billy Wilder & and D. M. Marshman, Jr., 1950)

Sunset Boulevard is a cutting satire about a modern kingdom whose royalty are movie stars. These kings and queens live and die by selling beauty. *Sunset Boulevard* appeals especially to people who know story—not only because its main character is the modern-day storyteller, a screenwriter, but also because its visual world is laden with all kinds of story forms and story references. These are just a few of the story world techniques in this brilliant script.

The overall world is Hollywood, which the writers set up as a kingdom, with a court of royalty and a rabble of hardworking peasants. By using a writer as a voice-over storyteller, the writers are able to make all kinds of literary connections to the world.

■ **Problem**   *Hollywood apartment.*   Screenwriter Joe Gillis is out of work and broke, and he lives in a run-down apartment. He is also a Hollywood factory writer, "cranking out two stories a week." His problem gets worse when two men come to his apartment to repossess his car.

- **Weakness and Need, Opponent** *Run-down mansion and pool.* When he first sees the run-down mansion—the terrifying house—of Norma Desmond, Joe thinks this secret subworld has just saved him. He can hide his car there, rewrite Norma's awful script, and make some good money. But he has just entered the opponent's subworld, from which he will never escape. It holds him because it feeds his great weakness, which is his hunger for money.

    Here's how Joe, the screenwriter, describes the world:

    > It was a great big white elephant of a place. The kind crazy movie people built in the crazy '20s. A neglected house gets an unhappy look. This one had it in spades. It was like that old woman in *Great Expectations*, that Miss Havisham and her rotting wedding dress, and her torn veil, taking it out on the world, because she'd been given the go-by.

    As he retreats to the guest house, Joe makes his way past the overgrown vines and thorns, just like the prince in *Sleeping Beauty*. Out his window, he sees the empty swimming pool, crawling with rats. The images of death and sleep in this world are everywhere.

- **Opponent, Apparent Defeat** *House revitalized, Joe captured at the pool.* This fairy-tale world, with its haunted house, its thorns, and its Sleeping Beauty, is also the home of a vampire. As Joe becomes more deeply ensnared in the trap of easy living, Norma and the house are revitalized. The pool is now clean and filled, and when Joe emerges from a swim, Norma, flush with new blood, dries off her bought young man with a towel, as if he were her baby.

- **Battle, Death** *Shooting at the pool.* In a short, one-sided battle, Norma shoots Joe when he tries to walk out on her. He falls into the swimming pool, and this time the vampire has left him dead.

- **Opponent's Slavery** *Norma on the staircase, descending into madness.* With such a great human opponent, *Sunset Boulevard* does not end with the death of the hero. The opponent literally descends into madness. Her ability to distinguish fantasy from reality now gone, she is both her character—"Down below, they're waiting for the Princess"—and an actress performing in another Hollywood movie. As the newsreel cameras roll, Norma walks down the grand staircase of the "palace" into a deep sleep from which no prince will awaken her.

ULYSSES
(by James Joyce, 1922)

At first we might be wary of looking at Joyce's *Ulysses* to learn techniques of great storytelling, precisely because many people consider it the greatest novel of the twentieth century. Its incredible complexity and brilliance would seem to take it far beyond the grasp of us mere writing mortals, and its intentionally obscure references and techniques would seem to make it totally unfit for those wishing to write popular stories in the form of films, novels, plays, and television scripts.

Nothing could be further from the truth. Although Joyce may have had tremendous natural talent as a writer, he was also one of the most *trained* storytellers in history. Even if he opted to use that training to write with a complexity that you might want to avoid, for all kinds of legitimate reasons, the techniques he used have universal application for great storytelling in any medium.

Ulysses is the novelist's novel. Its secondary main character, Stephen, is a man struggling to become a great writer. It uses a wider, more advanced array of storytelling techniques than any book ever written (the possible exception is Joyce's *Finnegans Wake*, but no one has actually read it from beginning to end, so it doesn't count). In myriad ways, Joyce challenges other writers, saying, in effect, Can you figure out what I'm doing, and can you do it yourself? Let's give it a try.

As a modern version of the *Odyssey*, the story form in *Ulysses* is a combination of myth, comedy, and drama. The overall arena is the city of Dublin, but the story primarily takes place not in a home but on the road. As in many myths, the main hero, Leopold Bloom, goes on a journey and returns home. But because this is a comic, or "mock heroic," myth, little or no learning is apparent upon the hero's return.

Like so many other advanced stories, *Ulysses* is set at the epoch-changing turn of the twentieth century, amid the shift between town and city. Dublin has many elements of the town but also many elements of the city—even the advanced, oppressive city. From the very beginning, we are deep inside the guilt that is so common in stories set in a town: Stephen has a housemate who makes him feel guilty for refusing to pray at his mother's deathbed.

The primary hero, Bloom, is both the everyman hero of the city and the bumbler of the advanced, oppressive city. Where Odysseus is a frustrated warrior, Bloom is a frustrated nobody. He is Charlie Chaplin's tramp, Charles Schulz's Charlie Brown, *Seinfeld*'s George Costanza. He's also a timid cuckold who knows what his wife and her lover are doing but does nothing to stop it. In many ways, Joyce's story world doesn't come from the usual combination of elements. For example, Dublin is an oppressive city not because of increasing technology, the slavery of the future, but because of the stultifying power of the past, primarily English rule and the Catholic church.

Besides using the myth of the *Odyssey* and the shifting society, Joyce builds the story structure on the technique of the twenty-four-hour day. This circular time matches the circular space of the myth and comedy forms, further defining the everyday quality of its hero and highlighting and comparing the actions of a vast web of characters in the city.

Joyce also uses the twenty-four-hour day to set up the character opposition between his primary and secondary heroes. The opening three sections of the story, which track the journey of the secondary hero, Stephen, occur from 8 a.m. to about noon. Joyce then returns to the 8 a.m. start to track his primary hero, Bloom. This time comparison constantly triggers the reader to imagine what these two men are doing at approximately the same moment, and Joyce provides a number of parallels between them to help the reader compare and contrast them.

Joyce comes up with a number of unique techniques when depicting the minor characters of his story world. Because so much of his theme concerns the slavery of this world, he gives many of his minor characters a weakness and need of their own. Usually it is some variation of being tied too strongly to the Catholic church, going along with the dominance of England, or placing too much faith in the heroes of Ireland's past and its comfortable but ultimately debilitating stereotypes.

The character web of *Ulysses* is among the most detailed in story history. Along with the key fictional characters are a number of real people who lived in Dublin at the time the story is set, 1904. Intermingled with these real people are many fictional minor characters that Joyce has used in other stories (most notably in his short story collection, *The Dubliners*). All of this gives the story world a rich texture of reality that is at the same time deeply grounded, because each of these real or imagined people has a detailed character and history that have already been defined, whether the reader is familiar with them or not.

Joyce is a master at connecting key structure steps to the visual subworlds of the story. One of the benefits of founding a modern-day journey through the city on Odysseus's travels is that it lets Joyce create identifiable subworlds within an amorphous city. It also allows him, in this incredibly complex story, to imbue each subworld with one or two main structure steps. This technique anchors the reader in the storm and flow of a huge epic and highlights the two heroes' main lines of psychological and moral development no matter how complex things get.

Here is a thumbnail sketch of the major story structure steps, the section of the *Odyssey* on which they are based (in parentheses), and the subworld of Dublin in which they take place (*in italics*).

- **Stephen's Weakness and Need, Problem, Opponent, Ghost** (Telemachus) *Martello Tower.* It is 8 a.m. in an apartment at Martello Tower, which overlooks the beach at Dublin Bay. Resident Stephen Dedalus is a troubled young man. He has returned from writing in Paris because of the death of his mother. He is aimless and doubts himself. He also feels tremendous guilt for refusing his mother's dying wish that he pray for her. Like Odysseus's son, Telemachus, he wonders who and where his true father is. His roommate, Buck Mulligan, apparently his friend but in reality his enemy, needles him for his failure to pray when his mother lay dying.

   This tower home, which Joyce connects to Hamlet's castle, is a prison for the sensitive Stephen, who shares it with the tyrant Mulligan and the haughty Englishman Haines. Though Stephen pays the rent, he lets Mulligan borrow his key to the apartment.

- **Stephen's Weakness and Need, Problem, Ghost** (Nestor) *Deasy's School.* Though he wants to be a writer, Stephen is forced to teach, for very little money, at a boys' school. The schoolroom, with its noisy, cheating students, depresses him and reminds him of the ghosts of his youth. For a would-be artist like Stephen, this school is a trap.

- **Stephen's Weakness and Need, Problem, Ghost** (Proteus) *Sandymount Strand.* Stephen strolls along the beach, where he sees images of birth and death and a three-masted ship that reminds him of the crucifixion. He is confused about what is real and what is appearance, about who he must become versus what others want to make of him. Again, he wonders who his true father is.

- **Bloom's Weakness and Need, Problem** (Calypso) *Bloom's kitchen and his butcher shop.* At 8 a.m., Leopold Bloom is making breakfast for his wife, Molly, who is still sleeping. Odysseus was enslaved by a woman, Calypso, for seven years. Bloom is enslaved by his wife. But his slavery is self-imposed. Quirky and isolated, Bloom is somewhat estranged from Molly, both sexually and emotionally. He needs deeply to be accepted and loved.

  In the kitchen and at the butcher shop, Bloom shows his attraction to bodily pleasures, including food, women, and sex. Like Stephen, Bloom leaves the house without his key.

- **Bloom's Weakness and Need, Problem, Desire** (Lotus Eaters) *A street on the way to the postal annex and the chemist's.* Bloom would prefer to avoid his troubles or, like the Lotus Eaters, forget about them entirely. Like Stephen, Bloom is reactive and aimless. Over the course of the story, he comes up with a succession of petty desires that go nowhere. At the post office, he feels guilty about his correspondence with a woman named Martha, but he is also unwilling to go beyond words to consummation. At the drug-filled world of the chemist's shop, Bloom's desire is to escape and to overcome his loneliness.

- **Opponents, Ghost** (Hades) *Carriage trip through the streets to the graveyard.* Bloom joins some men he thinks are his friends on a carriage ride to a man's funeral. But these men treat him as an outsider. They pass Blazes Boylan, a man Bloom knows will have sex with his wife later that day. Like Odysseus in the land of the dead, Bloom recalls his father's suicide and the death of his little boy, Rudy, some ten years before.

- **Desire, Opponents** (Aeolus) *Newspaper offices.* In one of Odysseus's adventures, he is blown off course within sight of his home when his men open the bag of adverse winds that Aeolus, the wind god, had sealed tight.

  The modern traveler, Bloom, sells newspaper ads. At the office, he tries very hard to make a sale but is unable to close it because of his boss. He also has to listen to a bunch of blowhards who slight him and make misguided comments about the false glories of Ireland's past.

- **Story World, Opponent, Ghost** (Lestrygonians) *Streets of Dublin, Burton Hotel restaurant, Davy Byrne's pub, National Museum.* This miniature odyssey (and there are many miniatures in *Ulysses*) shows Bloom walking through the middle of Dublin, with many details of the people and quotidian events of that world.

  At the Burton Hotel, Bloom is so disgusted by the way some piggish patrons eat that he is forced to leave. Because Bloom is on a journey and because he is a man who avoids confrontation, his main opponent, Boylan, is not present to provide ongoing conflict, but he is constantly on Bloom's mind. At Davy Byrne's pub, Bloom checks the clock and realizes that Molly's rendezvous with his enemy is little more than two hours away.

  At the end of this section, Bloom spots Boylan on the street. He slips into the museum to avoid talking to him but then must feign interest in the buttocks of statues of Greek goddesses to keep from being caught.

- **Stephen's Opponents, Revelation, Bloom's Opponent** (Scylla and Charybdis) *National Library.* At the library, the place of the mind, the theoretical and artistic Stephen propounds his theories of Shakespeare to some of Dublin's literary elite. But like Bloom, Stephen is an outsider who has not been invited to their upcoming soiree. Buck Mulligan arrives and makes fun of him again. Stephen has an important revelation that the chasm between him and Mulligan is too great, and he will no longer treat Mulligan as a friend.

  At the library, Bloom has his own run-in with Stephen's nemesis. Mulligan had seen Bloom slip into the museum and mocks his deep interest in the bottoms of goddesses.

- **Story World** (Wandering Rocks) *Streets of Dublin.* The Wandering Rocks section is the entire story world of *Ulysses* in miniature, placed at the very center of the book. Joyce gives small defining moments to many of the minor characters of this city, both comical and sad, as they make their own odyssey through their day.

- **Bloom's Weakness and Need, Opponent, Apparent Defeat** (Sirens) *Bar at the Ormond Hotel.* Like the Sirens who lure sailors to their deaths with their song, two barmaids tease Bloom at the Ormond Hotel bar. The sentimental Irish songs he hears there are painful for him because they remind him of his lost son and his problems with Molly. And Bloom knows the very moment Blazes Boylan is entering his home. This is Bloom's lowest point, and it highlights his loneliness and deep sense of alienation.

- **Opponent** (Cyclops) *Barney Kiernan's pub.* In Barney Kiernan's pub, Bloom stands up to the Irish nationalist "Citizen," who is the modern Cyclops. Ironically, Bloom also knows that at that very moment, his ongoing opponent, Boylan, is having sex with his wife. But even here, at his most heroic, Bloom cannot hide some of his own weaknesses. He comes across as "Mister Knowall," a tedious sermonizing blowhard.

  The bar where Bloom confronts one of his biggest opponents, the "Citizen," is like a cave. And over the course of the section, this place gets darker, more violent, and more filled with hate.

- **Opponent, Drive** (Nausicaa) *Sandymount Strand.* On the same strand that Stephen walked a few hours before, Bloom sees an attractive woman who so tempts him with her physical charms that he masturbates. But she is just another fake ally, and the moment is another false drive, a diversion keeping Bloom from reconnecting with his wife.

- **Bloom's Drive and Revelation, Stephen's Opponent** (Oxen of the Sun) *National Maternity Hospital, Burke's Pub, streets of Dublin.* Bloom visits the hospital to check on Mrs. Purefoy, who has been trying for three days to deliver her baby.

  Stephen has been drinking with some friends and at Burke's Pub further fritters away his money buying drinks he can't afford. He gets into a fight with Mulligan, hurts his hand, and then proceeds to a brothel.

Bloom becomes concerned for Stephen and decides to stay with him to make sure he is all right. Until this point, Bloom, the reactive, aimless man, has had a number of little desires, most of them frustrated, that have taken him through his day. But now he has a serious drive that is focused on finding a son, and Stephen, his friend's son, will be that man.

■ **Stephen's Opponent, Self-Revelation, and Moral Decision; Bloom's Drive and Moral Decision** (Circe) *Brothel.* In the Circe section (where in the *Odyssey* men are turned into pigs), a drunken Stephen goes to a brothel. His dead mother, appearing in a hallucination, tries to increase his guilt so that he will return to the church. Stephen says no to that way of life and smashes the chandelier with his walking stick (his sword), finally ridding himself of the past that has trapped him for so long.

Bloom runs to the brothel and seeks out Stephen with intense determination. Bloom defends Stephen against the madam, Bella Cohen, who tries to take Stephen's money and demands far too much as payment for damage to the chandelier. Ironically, Bloom uses blackmail for his most moral act of the day: he threatens to reveal publicly that Bella has been using prostitution to send her son to Oxford.

■ **Limited Self-Revelation and Moral Decision for Both Men** (Eumaeus) *Fitzharris coffeehouse.* The two men head over to a little coffeehouse. After his self-revelation at the brothel, Stephen knows what he must do with his future. He lends a man some money and tells him his teaching job will soon be available at the school.

At the coffeehouse, Bloom and Stephen enjoy a long conversation on many topics. But though they experience a moment of communion, they are ultimately too different to sustain a friendship beyond this night. Bloom is too practical, too much a philistine, for the extremely theoretical and artistic Stephen.

Now Bloom's drive shifts again, this time to whether he will be able to return to Molly, in the sense of marriage and home. Though he is afraid of Molly's wrath, he decides to bring Stephen with him, saying, "Lean on me." One sign that *Ulysses* is more complex psychologically and morally than most stories is that Bloom's moral decision is not strictly altruistic. He thinks Stephen could help him write an ad. He also believes the young man will provide him with material for a story he wants to write, and he can benefit from Stephen's higher sensibilities.

- **Thematic Revelation** (Ithaca) *Bloom's kitchen and bedroom.* The new "father" and "son" share another communal moment, drinking cocoa in Bloom's kitchen, the same site where the "enslaved" Bloom fixed Molly's breakfast the previous morning. Stephen heads home, and Bloom goes to bed. Using a question-and-answer catechism technique to tell the story, Joyce begins the process of lifting *Ulysses* above these few characters to a cosmic perspective, a thematic revelation, just as he did at the end of his short story "The Dead." Though the two men have had a small but real communion, when Stephen leaves, Bloom feels the "cold of interstellar space."

- **Molly's Weakness and Need, Problem, Partial Self-Revelation, Moral Decision** (Penelope) *Bloom and Molly's bed.* In bed, Molly retells the story of *Ulysses* from her point of view, but her journey is completely in her mind. She expresses her deep loneliness and her feeling of being unloved by her husband. She is also well aware of her husband's many weaknesses and needs. In her marriage bed, with Bloom now sleeping beside her (though head to feet), she recalls her affair earlier that day with Blazes Boylan.

But finally Molly is the woman of "yes." The sense that Bloom and Molly's love may be reborn is found in her thought that this morning she will fix her husband breakfast and serve him eggs, and in her memory of Bloom when, deeply in love, she agreed to be his wife and fed him "seedcake." In this grand circular journey ending back home, there is the hint that a "remarriage" between Bloom and Molly might just occur.

CREATING THE STORY WORLD—WRITING EXERCISE 5

- **Story World in One Line** Use the designing principle of your story to come up with a one-line description of the story world.
- **Overall Arena** Define the overall arena and how you will maintain a single arena throughout the story. Remember that there are four main ways to do this:
  1. Create a large umbrella and then crosscut and condense.
  2. Send the hero on a journey through generally the same area, but one that develops along a single line.
  3. Send the hero on a circular journey through generally the same area.
  4. Make the hero a fish out of water.
- **Value Oppositions and Visual Oppositions** Return to the character web of your story, and identify the value oppositions between your characters. Assign visual oppositions that complement or express these value oppositions.
- **Land, People, and Technology** Explain the unique combination of land, people, and technology that will make up the world of your story. For example, your story may take place in a lush wilderness inhabited only by small nomadic groups using the simplest of tools. Or it may play out in a modern city where nature has virtually disappeared and technology is highly advanced.
- **System** If your hero lives and works in a system (or systems), explain the rules and hierarchy of power, along with your hero's place in that hierarchy. If a larger system is enslaving your hero, explain why he is unable to see his own enslavement.
- **Natural Settings** Consider if any of the major natural settings— ocean, outer space, forest, jungle, desert, ice, island, mountain, plain, or river—are useful to your story world as a whole. Make sure you don't use any of them in a predictable or implausible way.
- **Weather** In what way might weather help you detail your story world? Focus on dramatic moments in the story—such as revelations and conflicts—when using special weather conditions. Again, avoid clichés.
- **Man-made Spaces** How do the various man-made spaces in which your characters live and work help you express the story structure?

- **Miniatures** Decide if you want to use a miniature. If you do, what is it and what precisely does it represent?
- **Becoming Big or Small** Is it appropriate for a character to become big or small over the course of the story? How does it reveal the character or theme of your story?
- **Passageways** If a character moves from one subworld to a very different subworld, come up with a unique passageway.
- **Technology** Describe the crucial technology in your story, even if it involves only the most mundane and everyday tools.
- **Hero's Change or World Change** Look again at the overall change in your hero. Decide whether the world will change along with the hero or not and how.
- **Seasons** Is one or more of the seasons important to the story? If so, try to come up with a unique way to connect the seasons to the dramatic line.
- **Holiday or Ritual** If the philosophy of a holiday or ritual is central to your story, decide in what way you agree or disagree with that philosophy. Then connect the holiday or ritual at the appropriate story points.
- **Visual Seven Steps** Detail the visual subworlds that you will attach to the main structure steps in your story. Look especially at these structure steps:
  1. weakness or need
  2. desire
  3. opponent
  4. apparent defeat or temporary freedom
  5. visit to death
  6. battle
  7. freedom or slavery

Figure out how to connect the major natural settings and man-made spaces to the subworlds you use. Concentrate on the following three subworlds:

1. *Weakness subworld*: If your hero starts the story enslaved, explain how the initial subworld is an expression or accentuation of the hero's great weakness.
2. *Opponent subworld*: Describe how the opponent's world

expresses his power and ability to attack the hero's great weakness.

3. *Battle subworld*: Try to come up with a place of battle that is the most confined space of the entire story.

As practice, let's break down the story world of one of the most popular stories ever written.

HARRY POTTER AND THE SORCERER'S STONE
(novel by J. K. Rowling, screenplay by Steven Kloves, 2001)

■ **Story World in One Line**　A school for wizards in a giant magical medieval castle.

■ **Overall Arena**　All of the Harry Potter stories combine myth, fairy tale, and the schoolboy-coming-of-age story (as in *Goodbye, Mr. Chips*; *Tom Brown's School Days*; and *Dead Poets Society*). So *Harry Potter and the Sorcerer's Stone* uses the fantasy structure of beginning in the mundane world and then moving to the main arena, which is the fantasy world. That world and arena is the Hogwarts School, set in a castle surrounded by lush nature. The story plays out over the course of the school year in a large but defined place with seemingly infinite subworlds.

■ **Value Oppositions and Visual Oppositions**　The story has a number of value oppositions on which the visual oppositions are based.

1. *Harry and the wizards of Hogwarts versus Muggles*: The first opposition is between wizards and Muggles. Muggles, who are average, nonmagical people, value possessions, money, comfort, sensual pleasure, and themselves above all. The wizards of Hogwarts School value loyalty, courage, self-sacrifice, and learning.

    Visually, Muggles live in average suburban houses on average suburban streets, where everything is homogenized to look the same, where there is no magic and no community, and nature has been so tamed that it's almost gone.

    The Hogwarts' world is a magical kingdom unto itself, a huge castle surrounded by wild nature, a school that teaches not only magic but also the values on which the school was founded.

2. *Harry versus Lord Voldemort*: The main opposition is between good wizard Harry and evil wizard Voldemort. Where Harry values friendship, courage, achievement, and fairness, Voldemort believes only in power and will do anything, including committing murder, to get it. Harry's visual world is the "shining city on the hill," the community of scholars at Hogwarts. Voldemort's world is the Dark Forest that surrounds the school and the dark underworld below the school where his power is strongest.

3. *Harry versus Draco Malfoy*: The third major opposition is student to student. Young Draco Malfoy is aristocratic and disdainful of the poor. He values status and winning at all costs. Draco is set in visual opposition to Harry, Ron, and Hermione by being placed in a competing house, Slytherin, with its own flags and colors.

■ **Land, People, and Technology**   The story is set in the present, but it is really a throwback to an earlier societal stage with a very different combination of land, people, and technology than the audience expects. This is a modern-day prep school set in a medieval world of castles, lakes, and forests. The technology is another hybrid: magic with a high-tech sheen, where the latest witch's broom is the Nimbus 2000 and the techniques of magic are taught with all the depth and rigor of a modern-day university.

■ **Systems**   The Harry Potter stories fuse two systems: the prep school and the world of magic. This fusion is the gold of the story idea (and worth billions of dollars). Writer J. K. Rowling has taken great pains to detail the rules and workings of this hybrid system. The headmaster and head wizard is Professor Dumbledore. Teachers such as Professor McGonagall and Professor Snape teach courses in potions, defense against the dark arts, and herbology. Students are divided into four houses: Gryffindor, Slytherin, Hufflepuff, and Ravenclaw. The wizard world even has its own sport, Quidditch, with as precise a set of rules as any sport in the "real" world.

As a first-year student who is only eleven, Harry is at the bottom of the hierarchy in this world. His great potential suggests he will rise to the top over the course of the seven stories and seven years. But for now he represents the audience, and they learn how this magical system works at the same time he does.

- **Natural Settings**   Hogwarts castle is built beside a mountain lake and is surrounded by the Dark Forest.
- **Weather**   Weather is used to some dramatic effect but in a fairly predictable way. It is raining heavily when Hagrid arrives at the hut where Harry's foster family has hidden. There is lightning on Halloween when the troll attacks the school. And it is snowing at Christmas.
- **Man-made Spaces**   Rowling makes full use of the techniques of man-made spaces in storytelling. She sets up the magic world by first showing the mundane. For his first eleven years, Harry lives enslaved in a bland suburban house on a bland suburban street. After learning he is a wizard, Harry in effect goes back in time when he and Hagrid go shopping on the nineteenth-century Dickensian street of Diagon Alley. The street is still recognizably English, but its quaint shops and swirl of community make it an exciting halfway house on the journey to the magical medieval kingdom of Hogwarts School. Along with Ollivander's Wand Shop is Gringott's Bank, whose goblin clerks and cavernous vaults suggest a Dickensian Hall of the Mountain King. Harry then takes a nineteenth-century locomotive, the Hogwarts Express, deep into the fairy-tale world of Hogwarts.

The castle of Hogwarts School is the ultimate warm house, with infinite nooks and crannies, filled with a community of students and teachers. The center of the warm house is the great dining hall, the cathedral-like space hung with banners that hark back to King Arthur and the days of chivalry. This is where the community comes together as a whole and where all can give praise when one of their members has done well.

Within this warm house is a labyrinth of diversity. The Escher-like stairways shift position and lead to often unpredictable locations. Students must use a secret password to get to their rooms.

This warm house also has its terrifying places. There is the forbidden area on the third floor, dusty and empty, with a room and a trapdoor guarded by a huge three-headed dog. This trapdoor is really the passageway to the cellarlike Underworld of the school. Down there is a room with giant chess pieces, and the battle of the mind played out there is a life-and-death struggle.

- **Miniatures**   The sport of Quidditch is a miniature of this magical world and Harry's place in it. Just as Hogwarts is a hybrid of the boarding school and the world of magic, Quidditch combines rugby, cricket, and soccer with flying broomsticks, witchcraft, and the jousting contests of the knights of old England. Through Quidditch, the two archrival houses in the school, Gryffindor and Slytherin, can engage in mock witch battle and show off the more spectacular action elements of their craft.

  As befits his reputation as a wizard of great potential, Harry wins the coveted role as his team's Seeker, and he is the youngest to fill the position in a century. Of course, the concept of the Seeker has larger connotations from myth and philosophy, and it describes Harry's overall quest, not just in *Sorcerer's Stone* but in the entire Harry Potter series.

- **Becoming Big or Small**   This technique is not used much in *Sorcerer's Stone*, but the three friends in effect become small when they must battle the giant troll in the bathroom; the three-headed dog is enormous, and Hagrid is a gentle giant.

- **Passageways**   Rowling uses three passageways in the story. The first is the brick wall Hagrid "opens" by spinning the bricks like a Rubik's Cube. With this gateway, Harry moves from the mundane world of his Muggle upbringing to the wizard street of Diagon Alley. The second passageway is platform 9¾ at the train station, where Harry follows the Weasley boys right through the brick archway to board the Hogwarts Express. The final passageway is the trapdoor to the Underworld of Hogwarts, guarded by the three-headed dog.

- **Technology**   The technology is among the most inventive of all the elements of *Sorcerer's Stone* and is fundamental to the huge popularity of the Harry Potter series. This is magic tech, and it has the dual appeal of the power of modern high technology allied with the charm of animals and magic. For example, owls deliver the mail by dropping it in the hands of the recipient. Wands, the ultimate tool of the wizard's power, are sold in a special wand store, and each wand chooses its owner. The favorite method of personal transportation is the broomstick, and the latest model, the Nimbus 2000, has specs as quantified as a computer's. The sorting hat reads the mind and heart of its wearer and determines what house fits him best.

Rowling even creates tools that signify false change and false value. The wish mirror takes one of the classic tools of storytelling—indeed, a symbol for storytelling itself—and shows the viewer what he most desperately dreams of becoming. The image he sees is a double of the self, but it shows a false desire on which the viewer can waste his entire life. The invisibility cloak, a tool from ancient philosophy, allows the wearer to exercise his deepest desires without paying a cost. It allows him to take greater risks, but the danger if he fails is huge. The Sorcerer's Stone can turn metal into gold and make an elixir so that the drinker never dies. But that is false growth, a change that has not been earned by hard work.

- **Hero's Change and World Change**   By the end of the story, Harry has overcome the ghost of his parents' death and learned of the power of love. But the timeless Hogwarts School, set within a lush natural world, does not change.
- **Seasons**   Rowling connects the circularity of the school year—including the seasons—with the deeply natural setting of Hogwarts School. This creates a subtle tie between the maturation of the students, especially Harry, and the wisdom and rhythms of nature.
- **Holiday or Ritual**   *Sorcerer's Stone* includes Halloween and Christmas as punctuation points in the rhythm of the school year, but the author doesn't comment on the underlying philosophy of either.

Now let's examine the visual seven steps and the story elements associated with them (indicated *in italics*).

- **Harry's Problem, Ghost**   *Suburban house, room under the stairs.*   As in many myth stories (such as the stories of Moses and Oedipus and many tales by Dickens), Harry appears first as a baby, a foundling to be raised by others. The wizards hint at his ghost (the event from Harry's past that will haunt him) and the fame that will precede him, which is why they are placing him with a Muggle family they know to be horrible. Indeed, Harry spends his first eleven years stuffed into a cagelike room under the stairs. His greedy and selfish aunt, uncle, and cousin boss him around and keep him ignorant of who he really is.

- **Weakness and Need** *Snake exhibit at the zoo, the great hall at Hogwarts School.* Harry doesn't know his origins or his great potential as a wizard. He and the audience get a sense of what he doesn't know when he visits the snake exhibit at the zoo. In this place, wild nature is completely tamed and imprisoned. Harry is shocked at his ability to talk to the snake and free him while also imprisoning his nasty cousin in the snake's cage.

   Later, in the great dining hall of Hogwarts, both Harry's potential and his need are underscored in front of the entire school when the sorting hat says he has courage, a fine mind, talent, and a thirst to prove himself. Yet in his first classes, Harry's lack of self-mastery and training as a wizard are painfully clear.

- **Desire, Ghost** *Hut, great hall, trapdoor.* Because it is the first in a seven-book series, *Sorcerer's Stone* must set up a number of desire lines.

1. *Overall desire for the series*: to go to Hogwarts School and learn to become a great wizard.

   Harry gains the first part of this desire when Hagrid comes to the hut where Harry's foster family has hidden him away. Hagrid informs Harry that he is a wizard, born to wizards who were murdered, and that he has been accepted into Hogwarts School. Learning to become a great wizard will require all seven books.

2. *Desire line that tracks this book*: to win the school cup.

   This goal is set when Harry and the other first-year students gather in the great hall, learn the rules of the school, and are placed in one of four houses by the sorting hat. Notice that this collects all the episodes of a myth, played out over the course of an amorphous school year, and places them on a single, quantifiable track. The desire line begins in the hall where all the students are gathered, and it ends in the same hall where all cheer when Harry and his friends win the victory for their house.

3. *Desire line for the second half of this story*: to solve the mystery of the Sorcerer's Stone under the trapdoor.

   The desire to win the school cup gives shape to the school year. But a lot of episodic business must be accomplished, especially in this opening story of the series. Rowling must introduce numerous characters, explain the rules of magic, and provide many details of the world, including the Quidditch match. So a second, more focused desire becomes necessary.

When Harry, Ron, and Hermione accidentally end up on the restricted third floor and find the trapdoor guarded by the three-headed dog, they gain the desire that funnels this world-heavy story to a fine point. *Sorcerer's Stone* becomes a detective story, a form that has one of the cleanest and strongest spines in all of storytelling.

■ **Opponents** *Suburban house, classes, stadium, bathroom.* Harry faces his first opponents, Uncle Vernon, Aunt Petunia, and Cousin Dudley, in his own house. Like Cinderella, he must do all the chores, and he is forced to live in a tiny room under the stairs. Harry's ongoing opponent among the students is Draco Malfoy, with whom he must contend in many of his classes. As a member of Gryffindor house, Harry battles Draco's house, Slytherin, in the Quidditch match in the stadium. Harry and his friends fight the giant troll in the girls' bathroom.

■ **Opponent, Apparent Defeat** *Dark Forest.* Lord Voldemort is Harry's long-term, behind-the-scenes, most powerful opponent. Rowling, in this first of seven Potter books, faces a difficult story problem. Since she must sustain this opposition for seven books, and because Harry is only eleven years old in the first book, she must start Voldemort in a highly weakened state. Here in *Sorcerer's Stone*, Voldemort can barely keep himself alive and must work through the mind and body of Professor Quirrell.

Still, Voldemort and his subworlds are dangerous. The Dark Forest is filled with deadly plants and animals, and Harry and the other students can easily get lost there. Harry enters the terrifying Dark Forest at night, and there he comes upon the vampirelike Lord Voldemort drinking the blood of a unicorn. Even in his weakened state, Voldemort is powerful enough to kill. Only the last-second intervention of a centaur saves Harry's life.

■ **Opponent, Battle** *Underworld of Hogwarts (trapdoor, Devil's Snare, enclosed room).* Harry, Ron, and Hermione go to the restricted third floor to find the Sorcerer's Stone. But when they get past the three-headed dog (like Cerberus guarding Hades), fall through the trapdoor, and drop below the strangling roots of the Devil's Snare, they are in the Underworld of Hogwarts, Voldemort's other subworld. There they must win the violent battle of the abstract but deadly wizard's chess match.

Harry's battle with Voldemort takes place in an enclosed room—a tight space. The room itself is at the bottom of a long flight of stairs, which gives the effect of being at the point of a vortex.

Harry faces Voldemort and Professor Quirrell alone there, and when he tries to escape, Quirrell rings the room with fire. Voldemort attacks Harry's great weakness—his desperate wish to be with the parents he never knew—by promising to bring them back if Harry gives him the stone.

■ **Self-Revelation**   *Room of fire, infirmary.*   Under extreme attack from Voldemort and Professor Quirrell, Harry takes a stand as a wizard for good. Recovering in the infirmary, he learns from Professor Dumbledore that his body is literally infused with and protected by love. Somehow his skin burned the evil Quirrell to death because of the love Harry's mother showed for him when she sacrificed her life so that he might live.

■ **New Equilibrium**   *Train station.*   With the school year over, the students are about to go through the passageway back to the mundane world. But Harry is now armed with a picture book that Hagrid gives him that shows him in the loving arms of the parents he never knew.

CHAPTER 7

Symbol Web

A LOT OF WRITERS think of symbols as those pesky little things that were only important in lit class. Big mistake. If instead you think of symbols as jewels sewn into the story tapestry that have great emotional effect, you'll have some idea of the power of this set of story techniques.

Symbol is a technique of the small. It is the word or object that stands for something else—person, place, action, or thing—and is repeated many times over the course of the story. Just as character, theme, and plot are big puzzles to fool and please the audience, symbol is the small puzzle that works its magic deep below the surface. Symbols are crucial to your success as a storyteller because they give you a hidden language that emotionally sways the audience.

HOW SYMBOLS WORK

A symbol is an image with special power that has value to the audience. Just as matter is highly concentrated energy, a symbol is highly concentrated meaning. In fact, it is the most focused condenser-expander of any storytelling technique. A simple guide to using symbol might be "Refer and repeat." Here's how it works: you start with a feeling and create a symbol that will cause that feeling in the audience. You then repeat the symbol, changing it slightly.

Feeling → symbol → feeling in the audience
Changed symbol → stronger feeling in the audience

Symbols work on the audience in a very sneaky but powerful way. A symbol creates a resonance, like ripples in a pond, every time it appears. As you repeat the symbol, the ripples expand and reverberate in the minds of the audience often without their being consciously aware of it.

SYMBOL WEB

You may recall that I said that the single biggest mistake in creating character is to see a character as a single, unique individual. That's the quickest way to make sure that none of your characters is a unique individual. Similarly, the single biggest mistake in creating a symbol is to see it as a single object.

KEY POINT: *Always create a* web *of symbols in which each symbol helps define the others.*

Let's step back for a moment and look once more at how the various subsystems of the story body fit together. The character web shows a deeper truth about how the world works by comparing and contrasting people. Plot shows a deeper truth about how the world works through a sequence of actions with a surprising but powerful logic. The symbol web shows a deeper reality about how the world works by referring objects, people, and actions to other objects, people, and actions. When the audience makes that comparison, even if partially or fleetingly, they see the deepest nature of the two things being compared.

For example, to compare Tracy Lord to a goddess in *The Philadelphia Story* emphasizes her beauty and grace, but also her coldness and fierce sense of superiority to others. To compare the serene forest world of

Lothlorien to the terrifying mountain world of Mordor in *The Lord of the Rings* highlights the contrast between a sweet, life-giving community of equals and a fiery, death-dealing world of tyranny. To compare airplanes to horses in *For Whom the Bell Tolls* encapsulates how an entire culture valuing mechanized, impersonal force is replacing a horse culture valuing personal chivalry, loyalty, and honor.

You create the symbol web by attaching symbols to any or all of these elements: the entire story, the structure, characters, theme, story world, actions, objects, and dialogue.

STORY SYMBOLS

At the level of the story idea or premise, a symbol expresses the fundamental story twists, the central theme, or the overall story structure and unifies them under one image. Let's look at some examples of story symbols.

THE ODYSSEY

The central story symbol in the *Odyssey* is in the title itself. This is the long journey that must be endured.

ADVENTURES OF HUCKLEBERRY FINN

The central symbol here, by contrast, is not Huck's journey down the Mississippi; it is the raft. On this fragile, floating island, a white boy and a black slave can live as friends and equals.

HEART OF DARKNESS

The symbolic heart of darkness of the title is the deepest part of the jungle, and it represents the physical, psychological, and moral endpoint of Marlow's trip up the river.

SPIDER-MAN, BATMAN, SUPERMAN

These titles describe hybrid men with special powers. But the titles also imply characters who are divided within themselves and separated from the human community.

THE CHERRY ORCHARD

The cherry orchard suggests a place of timeless beauty but also one that is impractical and thus expendable in a real world that develops.

THE SCARLET LETTER

The scarlet letter starts literally as the symbol by which a woman is forced to advertise her immoral act of love. But it becomes the symbol of a different morality based on real love.

A PORTRAIT OF THE ARTIST AS A YOUNG MAN

The portrait of this artist begins with his symbolic name, Dedalus. Daedalus was the architect and inventor who built the labyrinth in Greek mythology. Connected with this name is the symbol of wings, which Daedalus built so that he and his son, Icarus, could escape the labyrinth. Many critics have commented that Joyce created the story structure of *Portrait* as a series of trial flights for his artistic hero to make his escape from his past and his country.

HOW GREEN WAS MY VALLEY

This story of a man recounting his childhood in a Welsh mining village has two main symbols: the green valley and the black mine. The green valley is the literal home of the hero. It is also the beginning of the overall story process and emotional journey by which the hero will move from green nature, youth, innocence, family, and home to a blackened, mechanized factory world, a shattered family, and exile.

ONE FLEW OVER THE CUCKOO'S NEST

The two symbols of the title, the crazy place and the free spirit who flies, again suggest the overall process of the story of a fun-loving prisoner stirring up the patients in a mental institution.

NETWORK

The network is literally a television broadcasting company and symbolically a web that traps all who are entangled within it.

Alien

An alien is the symbolic outsider, and as a story structure, it is the terrifying other who comes within.

Remembrance of Things Past

The key symbol is the madeleine cookie, which, when eaten, causes the storyteller to remember the entire novel.

A Farewell to Arms

The farewell to arms for the hero is desertion, the central action of the story.

The Catcher in the Rye

The catcher in the rye is a symbolic fantasy character the hero wants to be, and it is emblematic of both his compassion and his unrealistic desire to stop change.

Symbol Line

In coming up with a web of symbols that you can weave through your story, you must first come up with a single line that can connect all the main symbols of the web. This symbol line must come out of the work you have done on the designing principle of the story, along with the theme line and the story world you have already created.

For practice, let's return one more time to the designing principles of the stories we discussed in Chapter 2, "Premise," this time to find the symbol line.

Moses, in the Book of Exodus

- **Designing Principle**   A man who does not know who he is struggles to lead his people to freedom and receives the new moral laws that will define him and his people.
- **Theme Line**   A man who takes responsibility for his people is rewarded by a vision of how to live by the word of God.
- **Story World**   A journey from an enslaving city through a wilderness to a mountaintop.

- **Symbol Line** God's word made physical—via such symbols as the burning bush, plague, and the tablet of the Ten Commandments.

ULYSSES
- **Designing Principle** In a modern odyssey through the city, over the course of a single day, one man finds a father and the other man finds a son.
- **Theme Line** The true hero is the man who endures the slings and arrows of everyday life and shows compassion to another person in need.
- **Story World** A city over the course of twenty-four hours, with each of its parts being a modern version of a mythical obstacle.
- **Symbol Line** The modern Ulysses, Telemachus, and Penelope.

FOUR WEDDINGS AND A FUNERAL
- **Designing Principle** A group of friends experiences four utopias (weddings) and a moment in hell (funeral) as they all look for their right partner in marriage.
- **Theme Line** When you find your one true love, you must commit to that person with your whole heart.
- **Story World** The utopian world and rituals of weddings.
- **Symbol Line** The wedding versus the funeral.

HARRY POTTER BOOKS
- **Designing Principle** A magician prince learns to be a man and a king by attending a boarding school for sorcerers over the course of seven school years.
- **Theme Line** When you are blessed with great talent and power, you must become a leader and sacrifice for the good of others.
- **Story World** A school for wizards in a giant magical medieval castle.
- **Symbol Line** A magical kingdom in the form of a school.

THE STING
- **Designing Principle** Tell the story of a sting in the form of a sting, and con both the opponent and the audience.

- **Theme Line** A little lying and cheating are OK if you bring down an evil man.
- **Story World** A fake place of business in a run-down Depression-era city.
- **Symbol Line** The trickery by which a person gets stung.

Long Day's Journey into Night

- **Designing Principle** As a family moves from day into night, its members are confronted with the sins and ghosts of their past.
- **Theme Line** You must face the truth about yourself and others and forgive.
- **Story World** The dark house, full of crannies where family secrets can be hidden away.
- **Symbol Line** From increasing darkness to a light in the night.

Meet Me in St. Louis

- **Designing Principle** The growth of a family over the course of a year is shown by events in each of the four seasons.
- **Theme Line** Sacrificing for the family is more important than striving for personal glory.
- **Story World** The grand house that changes its nature with each season and with each change of the family that lives in it.
- **Symbol Line** The house changing with the seasons.

Copenhagen

- **Designing Principle** Use the Heisenberg uncertainty principle to explore the ambiguous morality of the man who discovered it.
- **Theme Line** Understanding why we act, and whether it is right, is always uncertain.
- **Story World** The house in the form of a courtroom.
- **Symbol Line** The uncertainty principle.

A Christmas Carol

- **Designing Principle** Trace the rebirth of a man by forcing him to view his past, his present, and his future over the course of one Christmas Eve.

- **Theme Line**   A person lives a much happier life when he gives to others.
- **Story World**   A nineteenth-century London countinghouse and three different homes—rich, middle-class, and poor—glimpsed in the past, present, and future.
- **Symbol Line**   Ghosts from the past, present, and future result in a man's rebirth at Christmas.

IT'S A WONDERFUL LIFE

- **Designing Principle**   Express the power of the individual by showing what a town, and a nation, would be like if one man had never lived.
- **Theme Line**   A man's riches come not from the money he makes but from the friends and family he serves.
- **Story World**   Two different versions of the same small town in America.
- **Symbol Line**   Small-town America through history.

CITIZEN KANE

- **Designing Principle**   Use a number of storytellers to show that a man's life can never be known.
- **Theme Line**   A man who tries to force everyone to love him ends up alone.
- **Story World**   The mansion and separate "kingdom" of a titan of America.
- **Symbol Line**   One man's life made physical—through such symbols as the paperweight, Xanadu, the news documentary, and the sled.

SYMBOLIC CHARACTERS

After defining the symbol line, the next step to detailing the symbol web is to focus on character. Character and symbol are two subsystems in the story body. But they are not separate. Symbols are excellent tools for defining character and furthering your story's overall purpose.

When connecting a symbol to a character, choose a symbol that represents a defining principle of that character or its reverse (for example,

Steerforth, in *David Copperfield*, is anything but a straightforward, up-standing guy). By connecting a specific, discrete symbol with an essential quality of the character, the audience gets an immediate understanding of one aspect of the character in a single blow.

They also experience an emotion they associate from then on with that character. As this symbol is repeated with slight variations, the char-acter is defined more subtly, but the fundamental aspect and emotion of the character becomes solidified in their minds. This technique is best used sparingly, since the more symbols you attach to a character, the less striking each symbol becomes.

You might ask, "How do I choose the right symbol to apply to a char-acter?" Return to the character web. No character is an island. He is de-fined in relation to the other characters. In considering a symbol for one character, consider symbols for many, beginning with the hero and the main opponent. These symbols, like the characters they represent, stand in opposition to one another.

Also think about applying two symbols to the same character. To put it another way, create a symbol opposition *within* the character. This gives you a more complex character while still giving you the benefit of symbol.

To sum up the process of applying symbol to character:

1. Look at the entire character web before creating a symbol for a single character.
2. Begin with the opposition between hero and main opponent.
3. Come up with a single aspect of the character or a single emotion you want the character to evoke in the audience.
4. Consider applying a symbol opposition within the character.
5. Repeat the symbol, in association with the character, many times over the course of the story.
6. Each time you repeat the symbol, vary the detail in some way.

A great shorthand technique for connecting symbol to character is to use certain *categories* of character, especially gods, animals, and machines. Each of these categories represents a fundamental *way of being* as well as a *level of being*. Thus when you connect your individual character to one of these types, you give that character a basic trait and level that the audience immediately recognizes. You can use this technique at any time, but it is found most often in certain genres, or storytelling forms, that are highly metaphorical, such as myth, horror, fantasy, and science fiction.

Let's look at some stories that use the technique of symbolic characters.

God Symbolism

A PORTRAIT OF THE ARTIST AS A YOUNG MAN
(by James Joyce, 1914)

Joyce connects his hero, Stephen Dedalus, to the inventor Daedalus, who built wings to escape slavery in the labyrinth. This gives Stephen an ethereal quality and suggests his essential nature as an artistic man trying to break free. But then Joyce adds texture to that primary quality by using the technique of symbolic opposition within the character: he attaches to Stephen the opposing symbols of Daedalus's son, Icarus, who flies too close to the sun (too ambitious) and dies, and the labyrinth, which Daedalus also made, in which Stephen finds himself lost.

THE GODFATHER
(novel by Mario Puzo, screenplay by Mario Puzo and Francis Ford Coppola, 1972)

Mario Puzo also connects his character to a god but highlights a very different aspect of God than Joyce does. Puzo's is the God the Father who controls his world and metes out justice. But he is a vengeful God. This is a man-God with a dictatorial power no mortal should have. Puzo also adds symbolic opposition within the character when he connects this God to the devil. Equating the normal opposites of sacred and profane is fundamental to this character and the entire story.

THE PHILADELPHIA STORY
(play by Philip Barry, screenplay by Donald Ogden Stewart, 1940)

Writer Philip Barry connects the hero, Tracy Lord, not just to aristocracy but to the concept of the goddess. Besides the "lordly" quality of her last name, both her father and her ex-husband refer to her as a "bronze goddess." She is both reduced and elevated by this symbolic attachment. The story turns on whether she will succumb to the worst aspects of "goddessness"—her cold, haughty, inhuman, unforgiving side—or the best—a greatness of soul that will allow her, ironically, to find and be her most human and forgiving self.

Other uses of the godlike hero include *The Matrix* (Neo = Jesus), *Cool Hand Luke* (Luke = Jesus), and *A Tale of Two Cities* (Sydney Carton = Jesus).

Animal Symbolism

A STREETCAR NAMED DESIRE
(by Tennessee Williams, 1947)

In *A Streetcar Named Desire*, Tennessee Williams equates his characters to animals in a way that diminishes them but also grounds them in biologically driven behavior. Stanley is referred to as a pig, a bull, an ape, a hound, and a wolf to underscore his essentially greedy, brutal, and masculine nature. Blanche is connected to a moth and a bird, fragile and frightened. Williams repeats these symbols in various forms as the story plays out. Eventually, the wolf eats the bird.

BATMAN, SPIDER-MAN, TARZAN, CROCODILE DUNDEE

Comic book stories are modern myth forms. So not surprisingly, they literally equate their characters with animals from the very start. This is the most metaphorical, over-the-top symbol making you can do. Batman, Spider-Man, even Tarzan the Ape Man all call attention to their characters' connection to animals by their names, their physiques, and their dress. These characters don't just have certain animal-like traits, like Stanley Kowalski, that affect them in subtle but powerful ways. They are animal men. They are fundamentally divided characters, half man and half beast. The nasty state of nature of human life forces them to turn to some animal to benefit from its unique powers and to fight for justice. But the cost is that they must suffer from an uncontrollable division within and an insurmountable alienation from without.

Equating a character with an animal can be very popular with an audience because it is a form of getting big (but not so big as to make the story dull). To be able to swing through the trees (*Tarzan*) or swing through the city (*Spider-Man*) or to have power over the animal kingdom (*Crocodile Dundee*) are dreams that lie deep in the human mind.

Other stories that use animal symbols for characters are *Dances with Wolves*, *Dracula*, *The Wolf Man*, and *The Silence of the Lambs*.

Machine Symbolism

Connecting a character to a machine is another broad way of creating a symbolic character. A machine character, or robot man, is usually someone with mechanical and thus superhuman strength, but it is also a human being without feeling or compassion. This technique is used most often in horror and science fiction stories where over-the-top symbols are part of the form and thus accepted. When good writers repeat this symbol over the course of the story, they do not add detail to it, as with most symbolic characters. They *reverse* it. By the end of the story, the machine man has proved himself the most human of all the characters, while the human character has acted like an animal or a machine.

FRANKENSTEIN, OR THE MODERN PROMETHEUS
(novel by Mary Shelley, 1818; play by Peggy Webling, screenplay by John L. Balderston and Francis Edward Faragoh & Garrett Fort, 1931)
Connecting character to machine was an approach first developed by Mary Shelley in *Frankenstein*. Her human character at the beginning of the story is Dr. Frankenstein. But he is soon elevated to god status as a man who can create life. He creates the machine man, the monster who, because he is manufactured from parts, lacks the fluid motion of a human being. A third character, the hunchback, is the in-between symbolic character, the subhuman man who is shunned as a freak by the human community but works for Dr. Frankenstein. Notice how these symbolic characters are defined and contrasted by simple but clear types. Over the course of the story, it is precisely because he is treated as a lower type, a machine to be chained, burned, and then discarded, that the monster rebels and seeks revenge against his cold, inhuman, godlike father.

Other stories that use the character-as-machine technique are *Blade Runner* (the replicants), *The Terminator* (Terminator), *2001: A Space Odyssey* (HAL), and *The Wizard of Oz* (the Tin Woodman).

Other Symbolism

THE SUN ALSO RISES
(by Ernest Hemingway, 1926)

The Sun Also Rises is a textbook example of creating a symbolic character without using metaphorical character types like god, animal, or machine. Hemingway sets up a symbolic opposition within hero Jake Barnes by showing a strong, confident man of integrity who is also impotent from a war wound. The combination of strength and impotence creates a character whose essential quality is that of being lost. As a result, he is a deeply ironic man, going from one sensuous moment to the next but unable to function on that basic level. As a man who is not a man, he is a totally realistic character who also comes to stand for a whole generation of men who are simply drifting.

SYMBOL TECHNIQUE: THE SYMBOLIC NAME

Another technique you can use to connect symbol to character is to translate the character's essential principle into a name. A genius at this technique, Charles Dickens created names whose images and sounds immediately identify his characters' fundamental natures. For example, Ebenezer Scrooge is clearly a man who loves money and will do anything to anyone to get it. Uriah Heep may try to hide behind the formal facade of "Uriah," but his essential slimy nature seeps out in "Heep." We know Tiny Tim is the ultimate good boy long before he utters the phrase "God bless us, every one."

Vladimir Nabokov has pointed out that this technique is much less common in post-nineteenth-century fiction. That's probably because the technique can call attention to itself and be too obviously thematic.

Done properly, however, the symbolic name can be a marvelous tool. But it's a tool that usually works best when you are writing a comedy, since comedy tends toward character type.

For example, here are some of the guests at one of Gatsby's parties in *The Great Gatsby*. Notice how Fitzgerald often lists names that suggest a failed attempt to appear as American aristocracy: the O.R.P. Schraeders and the Stonewall Jackson Abrams of Georgia; Mrs. Ulysses Swett. He then follows with the harsh reality of who these people really are or what became of them:

> From East Egg, then, came the Chester Beckers and the Leeches, and a man named Bunsen, whom I knew at Yale, and Doctor Webster Civet, who was drowned last summer up in Maine. And the Hornbeams and the Willie Voltaires. . . . From farther out on the Island came the Cheadles and the O.R.P. Schraeders, and the Stonewall Jackson Abrams of Georgia, and the Fishguards and the Ripley Snells. Snell was there three days before he went to the penitentiary, so drunk on the gravel drive that Mrs. Ulysses Swett's automobile ran over his right hand.

Another technique that uses symbolic character names is mixing "real" with fictional characters, such as in *Ragtime*, *The Wind and the Lion*, *Underworld*, *Carter Beats the Devil*, and *The Plot Against America*. These historical characters are not "real" at all. Their famous legacy has given them an iconic and in some cases godlike quality in the mind of the reader. They become, in effect, the mythical gods and heroes of a nation. Their names have a prefabricated power, like the flag, that the writer can support or cut against.

SYMBOL TECHNIQUE: SYMBOL CONNECTED TO CHARACTER CHANGE

One of the more advanced techniques in the area of character is using a symbol to help track the character change. In this technique, you choose a symbol you want the character to become when he undergoes his change.

To use this technique, focus on the structural framing scenes at the beginning and end of the story. Attach the symbol to the character when you are creating the character's weakness or need. Bring the symbol back at the moment of character change, but with some variation from when you first introduced it.

THE GODFATHER
(novel by Mario Puzo, screenplay by Mario Puzo and Francis Ford Coppola, 1972)

The Godfather film executes this technique to perfection. The opening scene is a prototypical Godfather experience: a man has come to the Godfather, Vito Corleone, to ask for justice. The scene is essentially a negotiation, and by the end, the man and the Godfather have come to an agreement. In the final line of the scene, the Godfather says, "Someday, and that day may never come, I will ask you for a favor in return." This line, which sums up the negotiation, subtly suggests that a Faustian bargain has just been concluded and that the Godfather is the devil.

The writers apply the devil symbol again near the end of the story when Michael, the new Godfather, attends the christening of his nephew while his minions gun down the heads of the five New York crime families. As part of the baby's christening, the priest asks Michael, "Do you renounce Satan?" Michael responds, "I do renounce him," even as he is becoming Satan by his actions at this very moment. Michael then promises to protect this child for whom he is literally becoming a godfather, even though, as the Godfather, he will have the child's father murdered as soon as the christening is over.

This battle scene is followed by what would normally be a self-revelation scene. But Michael has become the devil, so the writers purposely deprive him of a self-revelation and give it instead to his wife, Kay. She watches from another room as Michael's minions gather around to congratulate him on his new "exalted" position, and the door to the new king of the underworld is closed in her face.

Notice the subtlety by which the symbol is applied to the opening framing scene. No one uses the word "devil" in the first scene. The writers attach the symbol to the character by an ingenious construction of the scene where the word "Godfather" comes at the end, just before the final line of dialogue that vaguely hints at a Faustian bargain. It's because of the subtlety with which the symbol is applied, not in spite of it, that this technique has such a dramatic impact on the audience.

SYMBOLIC THEMES

After story symbol and character symbol, the next step in creating a symbol web is to encapsulate entire moral arguments in symbol. This produces the most intense concentration of meaning of all the symbol techniques. For this reason, symbolic theme is a highly risky technique. If done in an obvious, clumsy way, the story feels preachy.

To make a theme symbolic, come up with an image or object that expresses a *series* of actions that hurt others in some way. Even more powerful is an image or object that expresses two series of actions—two moral sequences—that are in conflict with each other.

THE SCARLET LETTER

(by Nathaniel Hawthorne, 1850)

Hawthorne is a master of symbolic theme. The scarlet letter *A* appears at first glance to represent the simple moral argument against adultery. It is only over the course of the story that this very obvious symbol comes to represent two opposing moral arguments: the absolute, inflexible, and hypocritical argument that chastises Hester in public and the much more fluid and true morality that Hester and her lover have actually lived in private.

BEAU GESTE

(novel by Christopher Wren, screenplay by Robert Carson Percival, 1939)

This story of three brothers who join the French Foreign Legion shows a crucial feature of the technique of symbolic theme: it works best when you do it *through the plot*. In the beginning of the story, the three brothers are children playing a game of King Arthur. While the oldest brother is hiding in a suit of armor, he overhears some information about a family sapphire known as the Blue Water. Years later, as an adult, he steals the jewel and joins the Foreign Legion, all to save his aunt's name and the family's reputation. That knight's armor comes to symbolize an act of chivalry and self-sacrifice, the *beau geste* that is the central theme of the story. By embedding this symbol in the plot, the writers allow the connection between symbol and theme to evolve and grow over the course of the story.

THE GREAT GATSBY

(by F. Scott Fitzgerald, 1925)

The Great Gatsby showcases a writer with tremendous ability at attaching symbol to theme. Fitzgerald uses a web of three major symbols to crystallize a *thematic sequence*. These three symbols are the green light, the spectacles billboard in front of the dump, and the "fresh, green breast of the new world." The thematic sequence works like this:

1. The green light represents modern America. But the original American dream has been perverted to seeking material wealth and the golden girl who is desirable only because she is beautifully wrapped.
2. The spectacles billboard in front of the dump stands for America behind the material surface, totally used up, the mechanical refuse created by America the material. The machine has eaten the garden.
3. The "fresh, green breast of the new world" symbolizes the natural world of America, newly discovered and full of potential for a new way of living, a second chance at a Garden of Eden.

Notice that the symbol sequence is out of chronological order. But it is in the right *structural* order. Fitzgerald introduces the "fresh, green breast of the new world" on the very last page. This is a brilliant choice, because the lush nature and huge potential of the new world are made shockingly real by their stark contrast to what has actually been done to that new world. And this contrast comes at the very end of the story, after Nick's self-revelation. So structurally, this symbol, and what it stands for, explodes in the minds of the audience as a stunning thematic revelation. This is masterful technique and a part of creating a work of art.

SYMBOL FOR STORY WORLD

In Chapter 6, I talked about many of the techniques used to create the world of the story. Some of these techniques, like miniature, are also symbol techniques. Indeed, one of the most important functions of symbol is to encapsulate an entire world, or set of forces, in a single, understandable image.

Natural worlds like the island, mountain, forest, and ocean have an inherent symbolic power. But you can attach additional symbols to them to heighten or change the meaning audiences normally associate with them. One way to do that is to infuse these places with magical powers. This technique is found in Prospero's island (*The Tempest*), Circe's island (the *Odyssey*), the forest in *A Midsummer Night's Dream*, the Forest of Arden in *As You Like*

It, the Dark Forest in the Harry Potter stories, and the Forest of Lothlorien in *The Lord of the Rings*. Strictly speaking, magic is not a specific symbol but a different set of forces by which the world works. But making a place magical has the same effect as applying a symbol. It concentrates meaning and charges the world with a force field that grabs an audience's imagination.

You can create symbols that convey this supernatural set of forces. An excellent example is in *Moonstruck*.

MOONSTRUCK

(by John Patrick Shanley, 1987)

John Patrick Shanley uses the moon to give a physical manifestation to the notion of fate. This is especially useful in a love story where what is really at stake is not the individual characters as much as the love between them. The audience must feel that this is a great love and that it would be a tragedy if it doesn't grow and last. One way of getting this across to an audience is to show that the love is necessary, that it is fated by powers far greater than these two mere humans. Shanley connects the two main characters, Loretta and Ronny, to the moon by establishing Loretta from the beginning as unlucky in love. This creates a sense of the larger forces at work. Loretta's grandfather tells a group of old men that the moon brings the woman to the man. At dinner, Loretta's uncle, Raymond, tells the story of how Loretta's father, Cosmo, courted her mother, Rose. One night, Raymond woke up to see a huge moon, and when he looked out the window, he saw Cosmo in the street below gazing up at Rose's bedroom.

Shanley then uses the crosscut technique to place the entire family under the power of the moon and connect it with love. In quick succession, Rose gazes out at the huge full moon; Loretta and Ronny, after their first lovemaking, stand together at the window and watch it; and Raymond awakes and tells his wife it's Cosmo's moon, back again. These two old people, long married, are inspired to make love. The sequence ends with the grandfather and his pack of dogs howling at the big moon over the city. The moon becomes the great generator of love, bathing the entire city in moonlight and fairy dust.

You may also want to create a symbol when you write a story in which the world evolves from one stage of society to another, like village to city.

Social forces are highly complex, so a single symbol can be valuable in making these forces real, cohesive, and understandable.

SHE WORE A YELLOW RIBBON
(stories by James Warner Bellah, screenplay by Frank Nugent and Laurence Stallings, 1949)

This story tracks a captain's last days before retiring from the U.S. Cavalry on a remote western outpost around 1876. Paralleling the end of the captain's professional life is the end of the frontier (the village world) and the warrior values that it embodies. To highlight and focus this change for the audience, writers Frank Nugent and Laurence Stallings use the buffalo as a symbol. A big, blustery sergeant, retiring just days before the captain, celebrates with a drink at the post saloon. He says to the bartender, "The old days are gone forever. . . . Did you hear about the buffalo coming back? Herds of them." But the audience knows they won't be back for long, and men like the captain and the sergeant will be gone forever too.

ONCE UPON A TIME IN THE WEST
(story by Dario Argento & Bernardo Bertolucci & Sergio Leone; screenplay by Sergio Leone & Sergio Donati, 1968)

This huge, operatic Western begins with the murder of a man and his children at their home in the wilderness. His mail-order bride arrives at the house to find that she is already a widow and the owner of an apparently worthless property in the middle of the American desert. While rummaging through her late husband's possessions, she finds a toy town. This toy town is both a miniature and a symbol of the future, a model of the town the dead man envisioned when the new railroad finally arrives at his doorstep.

CINEMA PARADISO
(story by Giuseppe Tornatore, screenplay by Giuseppe Tornatore and Vanna Paoli, 1989)

The movie house of the title is both the symbol of the entire story and the symbol of the world. It is a cocoon where people come together to experience the magic of movies and in the process create their community. But as the town evolves into a city, the movie house devolves, decaying until it is replaced by a parking lot. The utopia dies, and the community fragments and dies as well. This movie house shows the ability of a symbol to concentrate meaning and move an audience to tears.

THE MATRIX
(by Andy Wachowski and Larry Wachowski, 1999)

NETWORK
(by Paddy Chayevsky, 1976)

If you place your story in something as large and complex as a society or an institution, a symbol is almost required if you want to reach an audience. Both *The Matrix* and *Network* owe much of their success to the symbol that represents the story and the social world in which they occur. The terms "matrix" and "network" suggest a single unit that is also a web of enslaving threads. These symbols tell the audience up front that they are entering a complex world of many forces, some of which are hidden from view. This not only warns them to stop trying to figure everything out immediately but also assures them that fun revelations are on the way.

SYMBOLIC ACTIONS

A single action is normally part of a larger sequence of actions that comprise the plot. Each action is a kind of car in the long train of the hero and opponent competing for the goal. When you make an action symbolic, you connect it to another action or object and so give it charged meaning. Notice that making an action symbolic makes it stand out from the plot sequence. It calls attention to itself, in effect saying, "This action is especially important, and it expresses the theme or character of the story in miniature." So be careful how you use it.

WUTHERING HEIGHTS
(novel by Emily Brontë, 1847; screenplay by Charles MacArthur and Ben Hecht, 1939)

When Heathcliff pretends to fight the black knight for Cathy at their "castle" on the moors, he is expressing their make-believe world of romance and Cathy's determination to live in a world of riches and nobility. Heathcliff is also playing out, in miniature, the overall story in which he fights the well-born Linton for Cathy's hand.

WITNESS
(by Earl W. Wallace & William Kelley, story by William Kelley, 1985)
By helping build a barn with the other men while trading glances with Rachel, John is signaling his willingness to leave the violent world of the cop and build a loving bond in a community of peace.

A TALE OF TWO CITIES
(by Charles Dickens, 1859)
Like Christ on the cross, Sydney Carton willingly sacrifices his life to the guillotine so that others may live. "It is a far, far better thing that I do than I have ever done; it is a far, far better rest that I go to than I have ever known."

GUNGA DIN
(poem by Rudyard Kipling, story by Ben Hecht & Charles MacArthur, screenplay by Joel Sayre & Fred Guiol, 1939)
Indian "coolie" Gunga Din wants more than anything to be a soldier in the regiment like the three British soldiers he reveres. In the final battle, with his soldier friends badly wounded and captured, Din blows his bugle, thereby exposing himself to certain death and saving his regiment from walking into a trap.

SYMBOLIC OBJECTS

Symbolic objects almost never exist alone in a story because alone they have almost no ability to refer to something else. A web of objects, related by some kind of guiding principle, can form a deep, complex pattern of meaning, usually in support of the theme.

When creating a web of symbolic objects, begin by going back to the designing principle of the story. This is the glue that turns a collection of individual objects into a cluster. Each object then not only refers to another object but also refers to and connects with the other symbolic objects in the story.

You can create a web of symbolic objects in any story, but they are easiest to see in certain story forms, especially myth, horror, and Western. These genres have been written so many times that they have been honed to perfection. That includes objects that have been used so often that they have become recognizable metaphors. They are prefabricated symbols whose meaning the audience understands immediately at some level of conscious thought.

Let's look at the web of symbolic objects in some stories that best represent these highly metaphorical genres.

Myth Symbol Web

Myth is the oldest and to this day the most popular of all story forms. The ancient Greek myths, which are one of the foundation pillars of Western thought, are allegorical and metaphorical, and you should know how they work if you want to use them as the basis for your own story.

These stories always present at least two levels of beings: gods and humans. Don't make the common mistake of thinking that this was necessarily the ancient Greeks' view of how the world really works. The two levels in these stories don't express the belief that gods rule man. Rather, the gods are that aspect of man by which he can achieve excellence or enlightenment. The "gods" are an ingenious psychological model in which a web of characters represents character traits and ways of acting you wish to attain or avoid.

Along with this highly symbolic set of characters, myths use a clearly prescribed set of symbolic objects. When these stories were originally told, audiences knew that these symbols always represented something else, and they knew exactly what the symbols meant. Storytellers achieved their effects by juxtaposing these key symbols over the course of the story.

The most important thing to understand about these metaphorical symbols is that they also represent something *within the hero*. Here are some of the key symbols in myth and what they probably meant to ancient audiences. Of course, even with these highly metaphorical symbols, there is no fixed meaning; symbols are always ambiguous to some degree.

- Journey: The life path
- Labyrinth: Confusion on finding the path to enlightenment
- Garden: Being at one with the natural law, harmony within oneself and with others
- Tree: Tree of life
- Animals (horse, bird, snake): Models on the path to enlightenment or hell
- Ladder: Stages to enlightenment
- Underground: Unexplored region of the self, land of the dead
- Talisman (sword, bow, shield, cloak): Right action

THE ODYSSEY
(by Homer)

I believe that the *Odyssey* is the most artistic and most influential Greek myth in storytelling history. Its use of symbolic objects is one reason. To see the symbol techniques, you must begin, as always, with the characters.

The first thing you notice about the characters is that Homer has moved from the powerful warrior who fights to the death (the *Iliad*) to the wily warrior who searches for home and lives. Odysseus is a very good fighter. But he is much more a searcher, a thinker (schemer), and a lover.

This character shift dictates a change in symbolic theme as well, from matriarchy to patriarchy. Instead of a story where the king must die and the mother remains, Odysseus returns to retake the throne. As in most great stories, Odysseus undergoes character change. He returns home the same man but a greater person. This we see by his biggest moral decision: by returning home, Odysseus chooses mortality over immortality.

One of the central oppositions of symbolic character in storytelling is man versus woman. Unlike Odysseus, who learns by journeying, Penelope stays in one place and learns through dreams. She also makes decisions based on her dreams.

Homer builds the web of symbolic objects in the *Odyssey* based on the characters and the theme. This is why the web is based on male objects: ax, mast, staff, oars, and bow. For the characters, these objects all represent some version of directionality and right action. In contrast to these symbols is the tree that supports Odysseus and Penelope's marriage bed. This is the tree of life, and it represents the idea that marriage is organic. It grows or it decays. When the man wanders too far or too long in his quest for glory (the ultimate warrior value), the marriage and life itself die.

Horror Symbol Web

The horror genre is about the fear of the inhuman entering the human community. It is about crossing the boundaries of a civilized life—between living and dead, rational and irrational, moral and immoral—with destruction the inevitable result. Because horror asks the most fundamental question—what is human and what is inhuman?—the form has taken on a religious mind-set. In American and European horror stories, that religious mind-set is Christian. As a result, the character web and symbol web in these stories are almost completely determined by Christian cosmology.

In most horror stories, the hero is reactive, and the main opponent, who pushes the action, is the devil or some version of the devil's minion. The devil is the incarnation of evil, the bad father, who will lead humans to eternal damnation if not stopped. The moral argument in these stories is always couched in simple binary terms: the battle between good and evil.

The symbol web also starts with a binary opposition, and the symbolic, visual expression of good versus evil is light versus dark. The primary symbol on the light side is of course the cross, which has the power to turn back even Satan himself. The dark symbols are often different animals. In pre-Christian myth stories, animals like the horse, stag, bull, ram, and snake were symbols of ideals that would lead a person to right action and a higher self. In Christian symbolism, those animals represent evil action. That's why the devil is horned. Animals like the wolf, ape, bat, and snake represent the lifting of sanctions, the success of passion and the body, and the path to hell. And these symbols exert their greatest power in darkness.

DRACULA
(novel by Bram Stoker, play by Hamilton Deane & John L. Balderston, script by Garrett Fort, 1931)

The vampire Dracula, one of the "undead," is the ultimate creature of the night. He lives off the blood of humans whom he kills or infects to make them his slaves. He sleeps in a coffin, and he will burn to death if he is exposed to sunlight.

Vampires are extremely sensual. They gaze longingly at the bare neck of a victim, and they are overwhelmed by their lust to bite the neck and suck the blood. In vampire stories like *Dracula*, sex equals death, and the blurring of the line between life and death leads to a sentence far worse than death, which is to live in an unending purgatory, roaming the world in the dark of night.

Dracula has the power to turn into a bat or a wolf, and he usually lives in ruins that are crawling with rats. He is a uniquely European character in that he is a count, a member of the aristocracy. Count Dracula is part of an aging, corrupt aristocracy that parasitically feeds on the common people.

Dracula is extremely powerful at night. But he can be stopped if someone knows his secret. He shrinks at the sight of the crucifix and burns when sprayed with holy water.

Other classic horror stories that play with this symbol set are *The Exorcist* and *The Omen*. *Carrie* uses the same set but reverses its meaning. Here the Christian symbols are associated with bigotry and closed-mindedness, and Carrie kills her evangelical mother by teleporting a crucifix into her heart.

Western Symbol Web

The Western is the last of the great creation myths, because the American West was the last livable frontier on earth. This story form is the national myth of America and has been written and rewritten thousands of times. So it has a highly metaphorical symbol web. The Western is the story of millions of individuals journeying west, taming the wilderness, and building a home. They are led by a lone-warrior hero who can defeat the barbarians and make it safe for the pioneers to form a village. Like Moses, this warrior can lead his people to the Promised Land but not enter it himself. He is doomed to remain unmarried and alone, forever traveling the wilderness until he and it are gone.

The heyday of the Western genre was from about 1880 to 1960. So this story form has always been about a time and place that was already past, even when it first became popular. But it is important to remember that as a creation myth, the Western was always a vision of the *future*, a national stage of development that Americans had collectively decided they wanted, even though it was set in the past and could not be created in fact.

The vision of the Western is to conquer the land, kill or transform the "lower" "barbarian" races, spread Christianity and civilization, turn nature into wealth, and create the American nation. The designing principle of the Western story form is that the entire process of world history is being repeated on the clean slate of the pristine American wilderness, so America is the world's last chance to regain paradise.

Any national story becomes a religious story, depending on its definition of certain rituals and values and the intensity with which it is believed. Not surprisingly, such a national religious story produces a highly metaphorical symbol web.

The symbol web of the Western begins with the horseman. He is both hunter and warrior, and he is the ultimate expression of the warrior culture. He also takes on certain features of the English national myth of King Arthur. He is the natural knight, a common man of pure and noble character who lives by a moral code of chivalry and right action (known as the Code of the West).

The Western hero does not wear armor, but he wears the second great symbol of this symbol web, the six-gun. The six-gun represents mechanized force, a "sword" of justice that is highly magnified in power. Because of his code and the values of the warrior culture, the cowboy will never draw his gun first. And he must always enforce justice in a showdown in the street, where all can see.

Like the horror story, the Western always expresses binary values of good and evil, and these are signaled by the third major symbol of the web, the hat. The Western hero wears a white hat; the bad man wears black.

The fourth symbol of the form is the badge, which is in the shape of another symbol, the star. The Western hero is always the enforcer of right, often to his own detriment, since his violence usually ostracizes him. He may temporarily join the community in an official way if he becomes a lawman. He imposes the law not just upon the wilderness but also upon the wildness and passion within each person.

The final major symbol of the Western web is the fence. It is always a wooden fence, slight and fragile, and it represents the skin-deep control the new civilization has over the wilderness of nature and the wildness of human nature.

The Western symbol web is used to great effect in stories like *The Vir-*

ginian, Stagecoach, My Darling Clementine, and the most schematic and metaphorical of all Westerns, *Shane.*

SHANE

(novel by Jack Schaefer, screenplay by A. B. Guthrie, Jr., and Jack Sher, 1953)
Shane's schematic quality makes it easy to see the Western symbols, but it
calls so much attention to those symbols that the audience always has the
sense that "I'm watching a classic Western." This is the great risk in using
highly metaphorical symbols.

That being said, *Shane* takes the mythical Western form to its logical
extreme. The story tracks a mysterious stranger who, when first seen, is already on a journey. He rides down from the mountain, makes one stop,
and then returns to the mountain. The film is a subgenre I call the "traveling angel story," which is found not only in Westerns but also in detective stories (the Hercule Poirot stories), comedies (*Crocodile Dundee; Amélie;
Chocolat; Good Morning, Vietnam*), and musicals (*Mary Poppins, The Music
Man*). In the traveling angel story, the hero enters a community in trouble,
helps the inhabitants fix things, and then moves on to help the next community. Here in its Western version, Shane is the traveling warrior angel
who fights other warriors (cattlemen) to make it safe for the farmers and
the villagers to build a home and a village.

Shane also has a highly symbolic character web. There is the angel-like
hero versus the satanic gunslinger; the family-man farmer (named Joseph)
versus the grizzled, ruthless, unmarried cattleman; the ideal wife and
mother (named Marian); and the child, a boy who worships the man who
is good with a gun. These abstract characters are presented with almost
no individual detail. For example, Shane has some ghost in his past involving the use of guns, but it's never explained. As a result, the characters
are just very appealing metaphors.

All the standard Western symbols are here in their purest form. The
gun is crucial to any Western. But in *Shane*, it's placed at the center of the
theme. The film asks the question by which every man in the story is
judged: Do you have the courage to use the gun? The cattlemen hate the
farmers because they put up fences. The farmers fight the cattlemen so
they can build a real town with laws and a church. Shane wears light buck-
skin; the evil gunslinger wears black. The farmers buy supplies with which

they can build their homes at the general store. But the store has a door that opens into the saloon where the cattlemen drink and fight and kill. Shane tries to build a new life of home and family when he's in the general store, but he can't help being sucked into the saloon and back to his old life as a lone warrior who is great with a gun.

This isn't to say that *Shane* is a bad piece of storytelling. It has a certain power precisely because its symbol web is so clean, so well drawn. There is no padding here. But for that same reason, it feels like a schematic story, with a moral argument that is just this side of moral philosophy, as almost all religious stories are.

SYMBOL TECHNIQUE: REVERSING THE SYMBOL WEB

The great flaw of using a prefabricated metaphorical symbol web is that it is so self-conscious and predictable that the story becomes a blueprint for the audience, not a lived experience. But in this flaw lies a tremendous opportunity. You can use the audience's knowledge of the form and the symbol web to reverse it. In this technique, you use all the symbols in the web but twist them so that their meaning is very different from what the audience expects. This forces them to rethink all their expectations. You can do this with any story that has well-known symbols. When you are working in a specific genre like myth, horror, or Western, this technique is known as undercutting the genre.

McCabe and Mrs. Miller
(novel by Edmund Naughton, screenplay by Robert Altman &
Brian McKay, 1971)

McCabe and Mrs. Miller is a great film with a brilliant script. A big part of its brilliance lies in its strategy for reversing the classic Western symbols. This reversal of symbols is an outgrowth of the traditional Western theme. Instead of characters bringing civilization to the wilderness, *McCabe and Mrs. Miller* shows an entrepreneur who builds a town from out of the wilderness and who is destroyed by big business.

The reverse symbolism begins with the main character. McCabe is a gambler and dandy who makes a fortune by opening a whorehouse. He creates a community out of the western wilderness through the capitalism of sex. The second main character, the love of McCabe's life, is a madam who smokes opium.

The visual subworlds also reverse the classic symbols. The town is not the rational grid of clapboard buildings on the flat, dry plain of the Southwest. It's a makeshift wood and tent town carved out of the lush, rainy forest of the Northwest. Instead of a bustling community under the benevolent gaze of the marshal, this town is fragmented and half-built, with listless, isolated individuals who stare suspiciously at any stranger.

The key symbolic action of the Western is the showdown, and this too is reversed. The classic showdown happens in the middle of the main street where the whole town can see. The cowboy hero waits for the bad man to draw first, still beats him, and reaffirms right action and law and order for the growing community. In *McCabe and Mrs. Miller*, the hero, who is anything but a lawman, is chased all over town by three killers during a blinding snowstorm. None of the townspeople see or care about McCabe's right action or whether the town's leader lives or dies. They are off dousing the flames of a church that no one attends.

McCabe and Mrs. Miller flips the symbolic objects of classic Westerns as well. The law does not exist. The church sits empty. In the showdown, one of the killers hides behind a building and picks off McCabe with a shotgun. McCabe, who only appears to be dead, shoots the killer between the eyes using a hidden derringer (in classic Westerns, the weapon of women!). Instead of the chaps and white, wide-brimmed hat of the cowboy, McCabe wears an eastern suit and a bowler.

McCabe and Mrs. Miller, with its strategy of undercutting a genre, gives us some of the best techniques for making old metaphorical symbols new. It is an education in great storytelling and a landmark of American film.

Examples of Symbol Web

The best way to learn the techniques of symbol web is to see them in use. As we look at different stories, you will notice these techniques apply equally well in a wide array of story forms.

EXCALIBUR

(novel Le Morte d'Arthur *by Thomas Malory, screenplay by Rospo Pallenberg and John Boorman, 1981)*

If the Western is the national myth of the United States, you could argue that the King Arthur story is the national myth of England. Its power and appeal are so vast that this one tale informs thousands of stories throughout Western storytelling. For that reason alone, we as modern-day storytellers should know how its crucial symbols work. As always, we begin with the character symbols.

King Arthur is not just a man and not just a king. He is the modern centaur, the metal horseman. As such, he is the first superman, the Man of Steel, the male taken to the extreme. He is the ultimate embodiment of warrior culture. He represents courage, strength, right action, and establishing justice through combat in front of others. Ironically, as masculinity taken to the extreme, he lives by a code of chivalry that places woman high on a pedestal of absolute purity. This turns the entire female gender into a symbol, divided into the Christian binary opposites of Madonna and whore.

King Arthur also symbolizes the modern leader in conflict. He creates a perfect community in Camelot, based on purity of character, only to lose it when his wife falls in love with his finest and purest knight. The conflict between duty and love is one of the great moral oppositions in storytelling, and King Arthur embodies it as well as any character ever has.

Arthur's ally is Merlin, the mentor-magician *par excellence*. He is a throwback character to the pre-Christian worldview of magic, so he represents knowledge of the deeper forces of nature. He is the ultimate craftsman-artist of nature and human nature, and of human nature as an outgrowth of nature. His spells and advice always begin with a deep understanding of the needs and cravings of the unique person before him.

Arthur's opponents possess a symbolic quality that hundreds of writers have borrowed over the years. His son is Mordred, the evil child whose very name represents death. Mordred's ally is his mother, Morgana (also known as Morgan le Fay), an evil sorceress.

The knights are supermen like Arthur. They stand above the common man not just in their abilities as warriors but also in their purity and greatness of character. They must live by the chivalric code, and they seek the Holy Grail, by which they can enter the Kingdom of Heaven. In their journeys, the knights act as Good Samaritans, helping all in need and by their right action proving their purity of heart.

Excalibur and other versions of the King Arthur story are filled with symbolic worlds and objects. The premier symbolic place is Camelot, the utopian community where members suppress their human craving for individual glory in exchange for the tranquillity and happiness of the whole. This symbolic place is further symbolized by the Round Table. The Round Table is the republic of the great, where all the knights have an equal place at the table, alongside their king.

Excalibur is named after the other major symbolic object of the King Arthur story, the sword. Excalibur is the male symbol of right action, and only the rightful king, whose heart is pure, can draw it from the stone and wield it to form the ideal community.

The symbols of King Arthur infuse our culture and are found in stories such as *Star Wars, The Lord of the Rings, Hope and Glory, A Connecticut Yankee in King Arthur's Court, The Fisher King,* and thousands of American Westerns. If you want to use King Arthur symbols, be sure to twist their meaning so they become original to your story.

THE USUAL SUSPECTS
(by Christopher McQuarrie, 1995)

The Usual Suspects tells a unique story in which the main character creates his own symbolic character using the techniques that we've been talking about, while the story is happening. Appropriately named Verbal, he is apparently a small-time crook and ally but is actually the hero, a master criminal (the main opponent), and a storyteller. In telling the customs interrogator what happened, he constructs a terrifying, ruthless character named Keyser Soze. He attaches to this character the symbol of the devil, in such a way that Keyser Soze gains mythical power to the point that just the mention of his name strikes terror in the heart. At the end of the story, the audience learns that Verbal *is* Keyser Soze, and he is a master criminal in part *because* he is a master storyteller. *The Usual Suspects* is great storytelling and symbol making at the highest level.

STAR WARS

(by George Lucas, 1977)

One of the main reasons *Star Wars* has been so popular is that it is founded on the technique of symbolic theme. This apparently simple fantasy adventure story has a strong theme that is concentrated in the symbol of the light saber. In this technologically advanced world where people travel at light speed, both heroes and opponents fight with a saber. Obviously, this is not realistic. But it is realistic enough in *this* world to be an object that can take on thematic power. The light saber symbolizes the samurai code of training and conduct that can be used for good or evil. It is impossible to overestimate the importance of this symbolic object and the theme it represents to the worldwide success of *Star Wars*.

FORREST GUMP

(novel by Winston Groom, screenplay by Eric Roth, 1994)

Forrest Gump uses two objects to stand for themes: the feather and the box of chocolates. You could criticize the writers' technique of attaching symbol to theme as heavy-handed. In this everyday world, a feather just floats down from the sky and lands at Forrest's feet. Obviously, the feather represents Forrest's free spirit and open, easygoing way of life. The box of chocolates is even more obvious. Forrest states, "My momma always said, 'Life is like a box of chocolates. You never know what you're gonna get.'" This is a direct thematic statement of the right way to live connected to a metaphor.

But these two symbols attached to themes work much better than they at first appear, and the reasons are instructive. First, *Forrest Gump* is a myth form connected to a drama, and the story covers about forty years. So like the feather, the story meanders over space and time with no apparent direction except the general line of history. Second, its hero is a simpleton who thinks in easy-to-remember platitudes. A "normal" character declaring outright that life is like a box of chocolates is preachy. But simple Forrest is pleased by this charming insight, learned from his beloved mother, and so is most of the audience.

ULYSSES

(by James Joyce, 1922)

Joyce takes the idea of storyteller as magician, symbol maker, and puzzle maker further than any other writer. This has benefits, but it also has costs, most notably moving the audience from an emotional response to one that is intensely intellectual. When you present literally thousands of subtle and even obscure symbols in thousands of tricky ways, you force your reader to become a story scientist or literary sleuth, determined to step as far back as possible to see how this elaborate puzzle is constructed. Like *Citizen Kane* (though for different reasons), *Ulysses* is a story that you can admire greatly for its techniques but that is very hard to love. So let's look at its symbol techniques.

Story Symbol and Symbolic Characters

Joyce sets up a web of symbolic characters primarily by overlaying onto his story the characters of the *Odyssey*, the Christ story, and *Hamlet*. He supplements his references to these major character webs with references to real people and iconic characters from Ireland's past. This strategy has a number of advantages. First, it connects character to theme: Joyce is trying to create a natural, or humanistic, religion out of his characters' actions. His everyday characters, Bloom, Stephen, and Molly, take on heroic and even godlike qualities, not just by what they do but also by their constant references to other characters like Odysseus, Jesus, and Hamlet.

This technique also places the characters of *Ulysses* within a great cultural tradition while showing them rebelling from that tradition and emerging as unique individuals. This is exactly the line of character development Stephen is struggling through over the course of the story. Oppressed by his Catholic upbringing and England's domination of Ireland but not wanting to destroy all spirituality, Stephen searches for a way to be his own person and a real artist.

Another advantage to matching characters with characters from other stories is that it gives Joyce a web of character signposts that extend throughout the book. This is immensely helpful when you are writing a story as long and complex as this. Besides being a designing principle, the character signposts allow Joyce to gauge how his leads change over the course of the story by referring to these same symbolic characters—Odysseus, Jesus, Hamlet—in different ways.

Symbolic Actions and Objects

Joyce applies these same techniques of symbolic character to the actions and objects of the story. He constantly compares the actions of Bloom, Stephen, and Molly to Odysseus, Telemachus, and Penelope, and the effect on the reader is both heroic and ironic. Bloom defeats his Cyclops and makes his escape from the dark cave of a bar. Stephen is haunted by his dead mother, just as Odysseus meets his mother in Hades and Hamlet is visited by his murdered father's ghost. Molly stays at home just like Penelope, but unlike the faithful Penelope, she becomes famous there for her infidelity.

The symbolic objects in *Ulysses* form a vast web of "sacred" things in Joyce's naturalistic, everyday religion. Both Stephen and Bloom leave their homes without their keys. Stephen has broken his glasses just the day before. But while his real sight is diminished, he has the chance to be a visionary, to gain his artistic sight over the course of the day's journey. An ad for "Plum's Potted Meat"—"A home isn't really a home without it"—refers to the lack of the sacred act of sex between Bloom and his wife and the harm it has done to their home. Stephen wields his walking stick like a sword at the chandelier in the brothel and breaks free of the past that holds him like a prison. Bloom believes that Catholic communion is a lollipop for believers, but he and Stephen have a real communion when they share coffee and then cocoa at Bloom's home.

CREATING SYMBOLS—WRITING EXERCISE 6

- **Story Symbol**   Is there a single symbol that expresses the premise, key story twists, central theme, or overall structure of your story? Look again at your premise, your theme, and your one-line description of the story world. Then write a one-line description of the main symbols in your story.
- **Symbolic Characters**   Determine the symbols for your hero and other characters. Work through the following steps:
  1. Look at the entire character web before creating a symbol for a single character.
  2. Begin with the opposition between hero and main opponent.
  3. Come up with a single aspect of the character or a single emotion you want the character to evoke in the audience.
  4. Consider applying a symbol opposition within the character.
  5. Repeat the symbol, in association with the character, many times over the course of the story.
  6. Each time you repeat the symbol, vary the detail in some way.
- **Character Type**   Consider connecting one or more of your characters to a character type, especially to gods, animals, and machines.
- **Symbolic Character Change**   Is there a symbol you can connect to the character change of your hero? If so, look at the scenes where you express the hero's weakness and need at the beginning of the story and his self-revelation at the end.
- **Symbolic Theme**   Look for a symbol that can encapsulate the main theme of your story. For a symbol to express the theme, it must stand for a series of actions with moral effects. A more advanced thematic symbol is one that stands for two series of moral actions that are in conflict.
- **Symbolic World**   Determine what symbols you wish to attach to the various elements of the story world, including the natural settings, man-made spaces, technology, and time.
- **Symbolic Actions**   Are there one or more specific actions that merit symbolic treatment? Figure out a symbol you can attach to each such action to make it stand out.

- **Symbolic Objects**   Create a web of symbolic objects by first reviewing the designing principle of your story. Make sure that each symbolic object you create fits with this designing principle. Then choose the objects you want to give extra meaning.
- **Symbol Development**   Chart how each symbol you use changes over the course of the story.

To see some of these techniques of symbol in practice, let's look at *The Lord of the Rings*.

THE LORD OF THE RINGS
(by J.R.R. Tolkien, 1954–1955)

The Lord of the Rings is nothing less than a modern cosmology and mythology of England. It brings together the story forms of myth, legend, and high romance, along with story and symbol references to Greek and Norse mythology, Christianity, fairy tale, the King Arthur story, and other tales of the knight errant. *The Lord of the Rings* is allegorical in the sense, as Tolkien said, that it is very applicable to our modern world and time. Allegorical means, among many other things, that the characters, worlds, actions, and objects are, of necessity, highly metaphorical. That doesn't mean they aren't unique or created by the writer. It means the symbols have references that echo against previous symbols, often deep in the audience's mind.

- **Story Symbol**   The story symbol, of course, is right in the title. The ring is the object of unlimited power that everyone craves. He who possesses it becomes a lord, with godlike powers. But that lord will inevitably be destructive. The ring is the great temptation that will pull someone from a moral, happy life. And its lure never ends.
- **Symbolic Characters**   The strength of this incredibly textured story is the rich web of symbolic characters. This is not simply man versus man, man versus animal, or man versus machine. These characters are defined and distinguished by good versus evil, by levels of power (god, wizard, man, Hobbit), and by species (man, elf, dwarf, Orc, goblin, Ent, and ghost). Myth works by character type, which is one reason it has epic scope but little subtlety in how it depicts people. By setting up such a complex and textured web of character types,

Tolkien and his audience get to have their character cake and eat it too. This is an important lesson for any writer using symbolic characters, especially if you are writing a myth-based story.

In Tolkien's character oppositions, good is symbolized by characters who sacrifice, Gandalf and Sam; by the warrior-king Aragorn, who can heal as well as kill; and by those who are one with nature and who have gained mastery of self rather than mastery over others, Galadriel and Tom Bombadil. Tolkien's hero is not the great warrior but the little "man," Hobbit Frodo Baggins, whose greatness of heart allows him to be the most heroic of all. Like Leopold Bloom in *Ulysses*, Frodo is a new kind of myth hero, defined not by the strength of his arms but by the depth of his humanity.

The opponents also possess great symbolic power. Morgoth is the original evil character who predates this story and is part of the history Tolkien created for *The Lord of the Rings*. Like Mordred of King Arthur, Maugrim of *The Chronicles of Narnia*, and Voldemort of the Harry Potter stories (English writers just love giving the bad guy a name with "mor" in it, perhaps because "mor" sounds like the French word for "death"), Morgoth conjures up in the minds of the audience the first antigod, Satan, and he is associated in name and action with death. Sauron is the main opponent in *The Lord of the Rings*; he is evil both because he seeks absolute power and because he will use it to wreak total destruction on Middle Earth. Saruman is a kind of switch character of evil who began as a wizard sent to fight Sauron but was poisoned by the taste of absolute power. Other opponents—Gollum, the Nazgul, the Orcs, the spider Shelob, and the Balrog—are various symbolic expressions of envy, hatred, brutality, and destruction.

■ **Symbolic Theme**   As always in a good story (and especially in an allegory), all the elements are founded on the thematic line and oppositions. For Tolkien, that means a Christian thematic structure emphasizing good versus evil. Evil is defined here by the love for and use of power. Good comes from caring for living things, and the highest good is to sacrifice, especially one's own life, for another.

■ **Symbolic Worlds**   The visual subworlds of *The Lord of the Rings* are as richly textured and symbolic as the character web. These worlds are also both natural and supernatural. Even the man-made spaces are infused with and extend out of the natural environment. Like the characters, these symbolic subworlds are set in opposition. In the forest world, there is the beautiful, harmonic Lothlorien and the forest of the treelike beings, the Ents, versus the evil Milkwood. The good forest worlds are also set in opposition to the mountain world, which is where the evil forces live. Sauron rules from the mountain lair of Mordor, behind the massive Morannon gate (more "mor"). The Misty Mountains are the site of the underground caverns of Moria, where the heroes visit the "underworld." Frodo passes through the Dead Marshes, a graveyard for those who have died in battle.

The "human" communities express this same natural symbolism. Like Lothlorien, which is a utopia built around trees, Rivendell is a utopia built around water and plants. The Shire, home of the Hobbits, is a village embedded in a tamed, agricultural world. These communities stand in contrast to mountain fortresses such as Mordor, Isengard, and Helm's Deep, which are founded on raw power.

■ **Symbolic Objects**   *The Lord of the Rings* is based on the quest for and possession of symbolic objects, and these are largely dug from the ground or forged in fire. Most important, of course, is the One Ring that Sauron forged in the fires of the volcano of Mount Doom. It symbolizes the desire for false values and absolute power, and whoever owns it will inevitably become totally evil and corrupt. Another circular symbol of evil is the Eye of Sauron that sees all from the top of the Dark Tower and helps Sauron in his quest for the ring.

Like King Arthur's Excalibur, Anduril, which means "flame of the west," is the sword of right action and must only be wielded by the rightful heir to the throne. Where Excalibur was stuck in stone, Anduril was broken and must be reforged so that Aragorn can defeat the forces of evil and regain his throne. Aragorn is a unique warrior-king in his use of the plant Athelas, which has the power to heal. Like Achilles, he is a fighter of great skill, but he is also in communion with nature and is an agent of life.

Of course, these are just a few of the symbols that Tolkien uses in the epic *The Lord of the Rings*. Study it carefully to master many of the techniques of symbol-making.

CHAPTER 8

Plot

P LOT IS the most underestimated of all the major story-telling skills. Most writers know the importance of character and dialogue, though they may not know how to write them well. But when it comes to plot, they think they'll just figure it out when the time comes—which of course never happens.

Because plot involves the intricate weaving of characters and actions over the course of the entire story, it is inherently complex. It must be extremely detailed yet also hang together as a whole. Often the failure of a single plot event can bring the entire story down.

Not surprisingly, plot techniques such as "three-act structure" that do not account for both the whole story and the detailed plot threads fail miserably. Writers who use the old three-act structure techniques are always complaining about second-act problems. That's because the techniques they use to create plot are fundamentally flawed. The mechanical and simplistic techniques of three-act structure don't give you a precise map showing how to weave a great plot throughout the difficult middle section of the story.

One reason writers underestimate plot is that they have many misconceptions about what it is. They often think that plot is the same as story. Or that plot simply tracks the actions of a hero going after his goal. Or that plot is the way the story is told.

Story is much larger than plot. Story is all of the subsystems of the story body working together: premise, character, moral argument, world, symbol, plot, scene, and dialogue. Story is a "many-faceted complex of form and meaning in which the line of narrative [plot] is only one amongst many aspects."[1]

Plot is the under-the-surface weaving of various lines of action or sets of events so that the story builds steadily from the beginning through the middle to the end. More particularly, plot tracks the intricate dance between the hero and *all of his opponents* as they fight for the same goal. It is a combination of what happens and how those events are revealed to the audience.

KEY POINT: *Your plot depends on how you withhold and reveal information. Plotting involves "the masterful management of suspense and mystery, artfully leading the reader through an elaborate . . . space that is always full of signs to be read, but always menaced with misreading until the very end."[2]*

ORGANIC PLOT

Plot is any description of a sequence of events: this happened, then this happened, and then this happened. But a simple sequence of events is not a good plot. It has no purpose, no designing principle that tells you which events to tell and in which order. A good plot is always organic, and this means many things:

- An organic plot shows the actions that lead to the hero's character change or explain why that change is impossible.
- Each of the events is causally connected.
- Each event is essential.
- Each action is proportionate in its length and pacing.
- The amount of plotting seems to come naturally from the main character rather than being imposed by the author on the characters. Imposed plot feels mechanical, with the wheels and gears of the story machine clearly evident. This drains the characters of their fullness

and humanity, making them feel like puppets or pawns. Plot that comes naturally from the hero is not simply one the hero concocts. It is plot that is appropriate to the character's desire and ability to plan and act.

- The sequence of events has a unity and totality of effect. As Edgar Allan Poe said, in a good plot, "no part can be displaced without ruin to the whole."[3]

PLOT TYPES

Organic plot is very difficult to grasp, much less create. That's partly because plotting always involves a contradiction. Plot is something you design, pulling actions and events out of thin air and then connecting them in some order. And yet the plot events must seem like necessary stages that develop of their own accord.

Generally, the history of plot evolves from an emphasis on taking action to learning information, which are the two "legs" by means of which every story moves. Early plot, using the myth form, shows a main character taking a series of heroic actions, which the audience is inspired to mimic. Later plot, using a broad version of the detective form, shows a hero and an audience ignorant or confused about what is happening, and their task is to determine the truth about these events and characters.

Let's look at some of the major plot types to see the different ways storytellers design the sequence of events and create an organic plot.

The Journey Plot

The first major strategy of plot came from the myth storytellers, and its main technique was the journey. In this plot form, the hero goes on a journey where he encounters a number of opponents in succession. He defeats each one and returns home. The journey is supposed to be organic (1) because one person is creating the single line and (2) because the journey provides a physical manifestation of the hero's character change. Every time the hero defeats an opponent, he *may* experience a small character change. He experiences his biggest change (his self-revelation) when he returns home to discover what was already deep within him; he discovers his deepest capabilities.

The problem with the journey plot is that it usually fails to achieve its organic potential. First, the hero almost never undergoes even slight character change when defeating each of his opponents. He simply beats the character and moves on. So each fight with a strange opponent becomes a repeat of the same plot beat and feels episodic, not organic, to the audience.

A second reason the journey plot rarely becomes organic is that the hero covers so much space and time on the trip. In such a sprawling, meandering story, the storyteller has great difficulty bringing back characters the hero encounters in the early part of the story and doing so in a natural, believable way.

Over the years, writers have been painfully aware of the problems inherent in the journey plot, and they have tried various techniques to solve them. For example, in *Tom Jones*, which uses a comic journey, the author, Henry Fielding, relies on two major structural fixes. First, he hides the true identity of the hero and that of some of the other characters at the beginning of the story. This allows him to return to some familiar characters and see them in a deeper way. Fielding is applying the revelation technique, also known as the "reveal," to the journey plot.

Second, he brings back many of the early characters over the course of Tom's journey by sending these characters on journeys of their own, all with the same destination as Tom. This creates a funnel effect and lets Tom bounce off one character and then another again and again over the course of the story.

The difficulty of creating an organic plot using the journey is clearly seen in Mark Twain's *Adventures of Huckleberry Finn*. Twain comes up with the brilliant idea of the raft, a miniature floating island, on which he can place Huck and a second character, Jim. But the vehicle is too small, so Huck and Jim have no ongoing opponents and encounter a succession of strangers "on the road." Also, with his main character stranded down the Mississippi, Twain has no idea how to bring the plot to a natural end. So he arbitrarily stops the journey and uses *deus ex machina* to save the day. There is no reason for Tom Sawyer to reappear, other than to return the plot to its comical roots, put on a spiffy polish, and say, "The End." Even Mark Twain can't get away with that.

The Three Unities Plot

The second major strategy for creating an organic plot was provided by ancient Greek dramatists like Aeschylus, Sophocles, and Euripides. Their central technique was what Aristotle referred to as the unities of time, place, and action. In this technique, the story must take place in twenty-four hours, in one location, and must follow one action or story line. The plot is organic because all actions come from the hero in a very short time of development. Notice that this technique solves the big problem of the journey plot by having opponents the hero knows and who are present throughout the story.

The problem with the three unities plot is that although the plot is organic, there isn't enough of it. Having such a short time period greatly limits the number and power of the revelations. Revelations are the learning part of plot (as opposed to taking action), and they are the keys to how complex the plot is. The short time period in these stories means that the hero knows the opponents too well. They may have hatched a plot before the start of the story, but once the story begins, they are limited in how much of themselves they can hide.

As a result, with the three unities plot, you typically have the time, opponents, and complexity of action for one big reveal. For example, Oedipus (in the world's first detective story) learns that he has killed his father and slept with his mother. That's a very big reveal, no doubt. But if you want a lot of plot, you have to have reveals peppered throughout the story.

The Reveals Plot

The third major plot type is what we might call the reveals plot. In this technique, the hero generally stays in one place, though it is not nearly so narrow an area as unity of place requires. For example, the story may take place in a town or a city. Also, the reveals plot almost always covers a longer time period than unity of time allows, even up to a few years. (When the story covers decades, you are probably writing a saga, which tends more toward the journey plot.)

The key technique of the reveals plot is that the hero is familiar with his opponents, but a great deal about them is hidden from the hero and the audience. In addition, these opponents are very skilled at scheming to get what they want. This combination produces a plot that is filled with revelations, or surprises, for the hero and the audience.

Notice the basic difference between the journey plot and reveals plot: in the journey plot, surprise is limited because the hero dispatches a large number of opponents quickly. The reveals plot takes few opponents and hides as much about them as possible. Revelations magnify the plot by going under the surface.

When done properly, the reveals plot is organic because the opponent is the character best able to attack the weakness of the hero, and the surprises come at the moments when the hero and the audience learn how those attacks have occurred. The hero must then overcome his weakness and change or be destroyed.

The reveals plot is very popular with audiences because it maximizes surprise, which is a source of delight in any story. Another name for this is the big plot, not just because there are so many surprises but also because they tend to be shocking. Although still immensely popular today—especially in detective stories and thrillers—the heyday of the reveals plot was the nineteenth century, with writers like Dumas (*The Count of Monte Cristo*, *The Three Musketeers*) and Dickens. Not surprisingly, this was also the height of stories like *The Portrait of a Lady* in which extremely powerful villains use negative plots to win.

Dickens was the master of the reveals plot, perhaps unequaled in storytelling history. But Dickens's reputation as one of the great storytellers of all time comes partly from the fact that he often expanded the reveals plot by combining it with the journey plot. Needless to say, this required tremendous plotting ability, since these two plot approaches are in many ways opposites. In the journey plot, the hero meets a vast cross section of society but quickly leaves each character behind. In the reveals plot, the hero meets a handful of people but gets to know them very well.

Antiplot

If nineteenth-century storytelling was about superplot, twentieth-century storytelling, at least in serious fiction, was about antiplot. In stories as wildly different as *Ulysses*, *Last Year at Marienbad*, *L'Avventura*, *Waiting for Godot*, *The Cherry Orchard*, and *The Catcher in the Rye*, you see almost a disdain for plot, as if it were the magic act you have to perform for the audience so you can do the more important work of character. As Northrop Frye says, "We may keep reading a novel or attending a play 'to see how it turns out.' But once we know how it turns out, and the spell ceases to bind us, we tend to forget the continuity, the very element in the play or novel that enabled us to participate in it."[4]

If you were to sum up the plot of some of these stories, it might go something like this: *The Catcher in the Rye* involves a teenage boy walking around New York City for a couple of days. In *The Cherry Orchard*, a family arrives at the old homestead, waits around for it to be sold at auction, and leaves. *L'Avventura* is a detective story in which no crime may have occurred and none is solved.

I suspect that many twentieth-century writers were not rebelling against plot per se but big plot, those sensational revelations that so shock the reader, they knock over everything else in their path. What I am calling antiplot, then, is really a range of techniques that these storytellers devised that would make the plot organic by making it express the *subtleties* of character. Point of view, shifting narrators, branching story structure, and nonchronological time are all techniques that play with plot by changing how the story is told, with the deeper aim of presenting a more complex view of human character.

These techniques might make stories feel fragmented, but they're not necessarily inorganic. Multiple points of view can express collage, montage, and character dislocation but also a sense of vitality and a flood of sensations. If these experiences contribute to the development of the character and the audience's sense of who that character is, they are organic and ultimately satisfying.

Plot digressions—which are common in antiplot—are a form of simultaneous action and sometimes backward action. They are organic if and only if they come out of who the character is. For example, *Tristram Shandy*, the ultimate antiplot novel, has often been criticized for its neverending digressions. But what these readers fail to realize is that *Tristram Shandy* isn't a story with a main plotline interrupted by digressions. It is a story of digressions interrupted by what appears to be a main plotline.

The main character, Tristram, is essentially a man who digresses, so the way the story is told is a perfectly organic expression of who the hero is.

A version of antiplot is backward storytelling, like Harold Pinter's *Betrayal*, in which the scenes are laid out in reverse chronological order. Backward storytelling actually highlights the organic unfolding of the story by highlighting the causal thread between scenes. This thread is normally buried under the surface; one scene seems to naturally follow another. But by going backward, the audience is forced to become conscious of the connecting thread between scenes. They can see that what just happened *had* to evolve from the event that came before it and the event that came before that.

Genre Plot

While serious storytellers were making plot smaller, their popular counterparts, especially in movies and novels, were making it even bigger through genre. Genres are types of stories, with predetermined characters, themes, worlds, symbols, and plots. Genre plots are usually big, emphasizing revelations that are so stunning they sometimes flip the story upside down. Of course, these big plots lose some of their power by the fact that they are predetermined. The audience knows generally what is going to happen in any genre story, so only the particulars surprise them.

These various genre plots seem organically connected to their main characters simply because they have been written so many times. All padding is gone. But these genre plots lack a huge requirement of an organic plot: they are not unique to their particular main character. They are literally generic, which means they are mechanical. In certain genres like farce and caper (heist stories), this mechanical quality is taken to such an extreme that the plots have the complexity and timing of a Swiss watch—and no character at all.

Multistrand Plot

The newest plot strategy is the multistrand plot, which was originally devised by novelists and screenwriters but has really flowered in dramatic television, beginning with the seminal show *Hill Street Blues*. In this strategy, each story, or weekly episode, is comprised of three to five major plot strands. Each strand is driven by a separate character within a single group, usually within an organization like a police precinct, hospital, or law firm. The storyteller crosscuts between these strands. When this plot strategy is executed poorly, the strands have nothing to do with each other, and the crosscut is simply used to goose the audience's attention and increase the speed. When the plot strategy is executed well, each strand is a variation on a theme, and the crosscut from one strand to another creates a shock of recognition at the moment two scenes are juxtaposed.

The multistrand plot is clearly a much more simultaneous form of storytelling, emphasizing the group, or the minisociety, and how the characters compare. But that doesn't mean this plot strategy can never be organic. The multistrand approach simply changes the developing unit from the single hero to the group. When the many strands are variations on one theme, the audience more readily experiences who we are as humans, and that can be just as insightful and moving as seeing the growth of a single person.

CREATING AN ORGANIC PLOT

Now that you are well armed with knowledge of some of the major plot strategies, the big question arises, How do you create an organic plot for your particular characters? Here is the sequence for writing an organic plot:

1. Look again at your designing principle. This is the organic germ of your story. The plot must ultimately be the detailed fruition of this principle.
2. Reacquaint yourself with the theme line. This is the moral argument you want to make, reduced to a single line. The plot must also be a detailed manifestation of this line.
3. If you have created a symbol line for the entire story, your plot should generally play out that line as well. Here you're looking for some way to sequence the symbols through the actions of hero and opponent (the plot).

4. Decide whether you wish to use a storyteller. This can have a big effect on how you tell the audience what happens and thus how you design the plot.

5. Figure out the structure in detail, using the twenty-two structure steps of every great story (which we'll discuss in a moment). This will give you most of your plot beats (major actions or events), and it will guarantee, as much as any technique can, that your plot is organic.

6. Decide if you want your story to use one or more genres. If so, you must add the plot beats unique to those genres at the appropriate places and twist them in some way so that your plot is not predictable.

Although you should decide if you want a storyteller before using the twenty-two building blocks to figure out your plot, I am going to explain these powerful and advanced tools in reverse chronology, since this is the easiest way to understand them.

TWENTY-TWO-STEP STORY STRUCTURE

The twenty-two building blocks of every great story are the crucial structure events, or stages, in the unfolding of an organic plot. We've already talked about the seven key structure steps in Chapter 3. But the seven steps come near the beginning and at the end of the story. The additional fifteen steps are found primarily in the middle of the story, where most stories fail.

The twenty-two steps are the most useful of all storytelling techniques because of their breadth and detail. They show you how to create an organic plot, regardless of the length or genre of your story. They are also the key set of tools for rewriting. One reason the twenty-two steps are so powerful is that they never tell you *what* to write, the way formulas or genres do. They show you the *most dramatic way* to tell your story to an audience. They give you an extremely precise map of your entire plot, allowing you to build the story steadily from beginning to end, and avoid the fragmented, dead middle that gives so many writers trouble. Here are the twenty-two steps:

1. Self-revelation, need, and desire
2. Ghost and story world
3. Weakness and need
4. Inciting event
5. Desire
6. Ally or allies
7. Opponent and/or mystery
8. Fake-ally opponent
9. First revelation and decision: Changed desire and motive
10. Plan
11. Opponent's plan and main counterattack
12. Drive
13. Attack by ally
14. Apparent defeat
15. Second revelation and decision: Obsessive drive, changed desire and motive
16. Audience revelation
17. Third revelation and decision
18. Gate, gauntlet, visit to death
19. Battle
20. Self-revelation
21. Moral decision
22. New equilibrium

At first glance, using the twenty-two steps may appear to stunt your creativity, to give you a mechanical story rather than an organic one. This is part of a deeper fear that many writers have of too much planning. But the result is that they try to make the story up as they go and end up with a mess. Using the twenty-two steps avoids either of these extremes and actually increases your creativity. The twenty-two steps are not a formula for writing. Instead they provide the scaffolding you need to do something really creative and know that it will work as your story unfolds organically.

Similarly, don't get hung up on the number twenty-two. A story may have more or fewer than twenty-two steps, depending on its type and length. Think of a story as an accordion. It is limited only in how much it can contract. It must have no fewer than the seven steps, because that is the least number of steps in an organic story. Even a thirty-second commercial, if it's good, will follow the seven steps.

But the longer a story gets, the more structure steps it will need. For example, a short story or a situation comedy can only hit the seven major steps in the limited time the story has to unfold. A movie, a short novel, or a one-hour drama for television will usually have at least twenty-two steps (unless the drama is multistrand, in which case each strand hits the seven steps). A longer novel, with its added twists and surprises, has far more than twenty-two structure steps. For example, *David Copperfield* has more than sixty revelations.

If you were to study the twenty-two steps in depth, you would see that they are really a combination of many systems of the story body woven into a single plotline. They combine the character web, the moral argument, the story world, and the series of actual events that comprise the plot. The twenty-two steps represent a detailed choreography of hero versus opponents as the hero tries to reach a goal and solve a much deeper life problem. In effect, the twenty-two steps guarantee that your main character drives your plot.

The table on page 270 shows the twenty-two steps broken down into four major threads, or story subsystems. Keep in mind that each step can be an expression of more than one subsystem. For example, drive, which is the set of actions the hero takes to reach the goal, is primarily a plot step. But it is also a step where the hero may take immoral action to win, which is part of the moral argument.

The following description of the twenty-two steps will show you how to use them to figure out your plot. After I explain a step, I will show you an example of that step from two films, *Casablanca* and *Tootsie*. These films represent two different genres—love story and comedy—and were written forty years apart. Yet both hit the twenty-two steps as they build their organic plots steadily from beginning to end.

Always remember that these steps are a powerful tool for writing but are not carved in stone. So be flexible when applying them. Every good story works through the steps in a slightly different order. You must find the order that works best for your unique plot and characters.

STEP	CHARACTER	PLOT	STORY WORLD	MORAL ARGUMENT
1.	Self-revelation, need, and desire			
2.	Ghost		Story world	
3.	Weakness and need			
4.		Inciting event		
5.	Desire			
6.	Ally or allies			
7.	Opponent	Mystery		
8.	Fake-ally opponent			
9.	Changed desire and motive	First revelation and decision		
10.		Plan		
11.		Opponent's plan and main counterattack		
12.		Drive		
13.				Attack by ally
14.		Apparent defeat		
15.	Obsessive drive, changed desire and motive	Second revelation and decision		
16.		Audience revelation		
17.		Third revelation and decision		
18.		Gate, gauntlet, visit to death		
19.		Battle		
20.	Self-revelation			
21.				Moral decision
22.	New equilibrium			

1. Self-Revelation, Need, and Desire

Self-revelation, need, and desire represent the overall range of change of your hero in the story. A combination of Steps 20, 3, and 5, this frame gives you the structural "journey" your hero will take. You'll recall that in Chapter 4, on character, we started at the endpoint of your hero's development by figuring out his self-revelation. Then we returned to the beginning to get his weakness and need and his desire. We must use the same process when determining the plot.

By starting with the frame of the story—self-revelation to weakness, need, and desire—we establish the endpoint of the plot first. Then every step we take will lead us directly where we want to go.

When looking at the framing step of the plot, ask yourself these questions, and be very specific in your answers:

- What will my hero learn at the end?
- What does he know at the beginning? No character is a completely blank slate at the start of the story. He believes certain things.
- What is he *wrong* about at the beginning? Your hero cannot learn something at the end of the story unless he is wrong about something at the beginning.

CASABLANCA

- **Self-Revelation**   Rick realizes he cannot withdraw from the fight for freedom simply because he was hurt by love.
- **Psychological Need**   To overcome his bitterness toward Ilsa, regain a reason for living, and renew his faith in his ideals.
- **Moral Need**   To stop looking out for himself at the expense of others.
- **Desire**   To get Ilsa back.
- **Initial Error**   Rick thinks of himself as a dead man, just marking time. The affairs of the world are not his concern.

TOOTSIE

- **Self-Revelation**   Michael realizes he has treated women as sex objects and, because of that, he has been less of a man.

- **Psychological Need**   To overcome his arrogance toward women and learn to honestly give and receive love.
- **Moral Need**   To stop lying and using women to get what he wants.
- **Desire**   He wants Julie, an actress on the show.
- **Initial Error**   Michael thinks he is a decent person in dealing with women and that it is OK to lie to them.

2. Ghost and Story World

Step 1 sets the frame of your story. From Step 2 on, we will work through the structure steps in the order that they occur in a typical story. Keep in mind, however, that the number and sequence of steps may differ, depending on the unique story you wish to tell.

Ghost

You are probably familiar with the term "backstory." Backstory is everything that has happened to the hero before the story you are telling begins. I rarely use the term "backstory" because it is too broad to be useful. The audience is not interested in everything that has happened to the hero. They are interested in the essentials. That's why the term "ghost" is much better.

There are two kinds of ghosts in a story. The first and most common is an event from the past that still haunts the hero in the present. The ghost is an open wound that is often the source of the hero's psychological and moral weakness. The ghost is also a device that lets you extend the hero's organic development backward, before the start of your story. So the ghost is a major part of the story's foundation.

You can also think of this first kind of ghost as the hero's *internal opponent*. It is the great fear that is holding him back from action. Structurally, the ghost acts as a counterdesire. The hero's desire drives him forward; his ghost holds him back. Henrik Ibsen, whose plays put great emphasis on the ghost, described this structure step as "sailing with a corpse in the cargo."[5]

HAMLET
(by William Shakespeare, circa 1601)

Shakespeare was a writer who knew the value of a ghost. Before page 1, Hamlet's uncle has murdered his father, the king, and then married

Hamlet's mother. As if that wasn't enough ghost, Shakespeare introduces in the first few pages the actual ghost of the dead king, who demands that Hamlet take his revenge. Hamlet says, "The time is out of joint: O cursed spite, / That ever I was born to set it right!"

IT'S A WONDERFUL LIFE

(short story "The Greatest Gift" by Philip Van Doren Stern, screenplay by Frances Goodrich & Albert Hackett and Frank Capra, 1946)

George Bailey's desire is to see the world and build things. But his ghost—his fear of what the tyrant Potter will do to his friends and family if he leaves—holds him back.

A second kind of ghost, though uncommon, is a story in which a ghost is not possible because the hero lives in a paradise world. Instead of starting the story in slavery—in part because of his ghost—the hero begins free. But an attack will soon change all that. *Meet Me in St. Louis* and *The Deer Hunter* are examples.

A word of caution is warranted here. Don't overwrite exposition at the start of your story. Many writers try to tell the audience everything about their hero from the first page, including the how and why of the ghost. This mass of information actually pushes your audience away from your story. Instead, try *withholding* a lot of information about your hero, including the details of his ghost. The audience will guess that you are hiding something and will literally come toward your story. They think, "There's something going on here, and I'm going to figure out what it is."

Occasionally, the ghost event occurs in the first few scenes. But it's much more common for another character to explain the hero's ghost somewhere in the first third of the story. (In rare instances, the ghost is exposed in the self-revelation near the end of the story. But this is usually a bad idea, because then the ghost—the power of the past—dominates the story and keeps pulling everything backward.)

Story World

Like the ghost, the story world is present from the very beginning of the story. It is where your hero lives. Comprised of the arena, natural settings, weather, man-made spaces, technology, and time, the world is one of the main ways you define your hero and the other characters. These characters and their values in turn define the world (see Chapter 6, "Story World," for details).

KEY POINT: *The story world should be an expression of your hero. It shows your hero's weaknesses, needs, desires, and obstacles.*

KEY POINT: *If your hero begins the story enslaved in some way, the story world will also be enslaving and should highlight or exacerbate your hero's great weakness.*

You place your hero within a story world from page 1. But many of the twenty-two steps will have a unique subworld of their own.

Note that conventional wisdom in screenwriting holds that unless you are writing fantasy or science fiction, you should sketch the world of your story quickly so that you can get to the hero's desire line. Nothing could be further from the truth. No matter what kind of story you are writing, you must create a unique and detailed world. Audiences love to find themselves in a special story world. If you provide a story world, viewers won't want to leave, and they will return to it again and again.

CASABLANCA

- **Ghost**   Rick fought against the Fascists in Spain and ran guns to the Ethiopians fighting the Italians. His reason for leaving America is a mystery. Rick is haunted by the memory of Ilsa deserting him in Paris.
- **Story World**   *Casablanca* spends a great deal of time at the beginning detailing a very complex story world. Using voice-over and a map (a miniature), a narrator shows masses of refugees streaming out of Nazi-occupied Europe to the distant desert outpost of Casablanca in North Africa. Instead of getting quickly to what the main character wants, the film shows a number of refugees all seeking visas to leave Casablanca for the freedom of Portugal and America. This is a community of world citizens, all trapped like animals in a pen.

   The writers continue to detail the story world with a scene of the Nazi Major Strasser being met at the airport by the French chief of police, Captain Renault. Casablanca is a confusing mix of political power, a limbo world: Vichy French are allegedly in charge, but real power rests with the Nazi occupiers.

Within the story arena of Casablanca, Rick has carved out a little island of power in his grand bar and casino, Rick's Café Américain. He is depicted as the king in his court. All the minor characters play clearly defined roles in this world. Indeed, part of the pleasure the audience takes from the film is seeing how comfortable all the characters are in the hierarchy. Ironically, this film about freedom fighters is, in that sense, very antidemocratic.

The bar is also a venal place, a perfect representation of Rick's cynicism and selfishness.

TOOTSIE

- **Ghost** There is no specific event in Michael's past that is haunting him now. But he has a history of being impossible to deal with, which is why he can no longer get work as an actor.
- **Story World** From the opening credits, Michael is immersed in the world of acting and the entertainment business in New York. This is a world that values looks, fame, and money. The system is extremely hierarchical, with a few star actors at the top who get all the jobs and a mass of struggling unknowns at the bottom who can't find roles and must wait on tables to pay the rent. Michael's life consists of teaching the craft of acting, going on endless auditions, and fighting with directors over how to play a part.

Once Michael disguised as Dorothy wins a part on a soap opera, the story shifts to the world of daytime television. This is theater totally dominated by commerce, so actors perform silly, melodramatic scenes at top speed and move quickly to the next setup. This is also a very chauvinistic world, dominated by an arrogant male director who patronizes every woman on the set.

The man-made spaces of Michael's world are the tiny apartments of the struggling actors and the television studio in which the show is shot. The studio is a place of make-believe and role-playing, perfect for a man who is trying to pass as a woman. The tools of this world are the tools of the acting trade: voice, body, hair, makeup, and costume. The writers create a nice parallel between the makeup

Michael uses to play a part in the theater and the makeup Michael uses to play a woman in front of and behind the camera.

The make-believe, chauvinistic soap opera world expresses and exacerbates Michael's great weaknesses: he is a chauvinist who will lie and betray the trust of others in order to get a part.

3. Weakness and Need

- **Weakness**   The hero has one or more character flaws that are so serious they are ruining his life. Weaknesses come in two forms, psychological and moral. They are not mutually exclusive; a character can have both.

  All weaknesses are psychological. The inner person is damaged in some way. A weakness is also moral if it causes someone else to get hurt. A character with a moral weakness always has a direct negative effect on someone else.

KEY POINT: *Many writers think they've given their hero a moral weakness when it is only psychological. The key test for a moral weakness is if the hero is clearly hurting at least one other person at the beginning of the story.*

- **Need**   Need is what the hero must fulfill in order to have a better life. It almost always requires that he overcome his weaknesses by the end of the story.
- **Problem**   The problem is the trouble or crisis your hero faces at the very beginning of the story. He is aware of the crisis but does not know how to solve it. The problem is usually an outgrowth of the hero's weakness and is designed to quickly show that weakness to the audience. While it should be present at the beginning of the story, it is far less important than weakness and need.

CASABLANCA

Rick seems not to want or need anything. But he is only hiding his need. He seems stronger than others, self-contained. While his cynicism does reveal a man who is deeply troubled, he is the master of his world. He runs his club as a kind of benevolent dictator. He is also a man who controls women. And he is a man of extreme contradictions: though he is now cynical, bitter, and often immoral, he was a freedom fighter for various good causes in the not-too-distant past.

What is unique in this story is that the main character, though very much in control, begins as an observer and a reactor. Rick is a man of great power and history, but he has chosen to withdraw from his rightful domain in the world, back to his club in one of the world's lost corners, Casablanca—and back into himself. Rick is a lion caged in a cell of his own making.

- **Weaknesses** Rick is cynical, disillusioned, reactive, and selfish.
- **Psychological Need** To overcome his bitterness toward Ilsa, regain a reason for living, and renew his faith in his ideals.
- **Moral Need** To stop looking out for himself at the expense of others.
- **Problem** Rick is trapped in Casablanca and trapped in his own bitter world.

Tootsie

- **Weaknesses** Michael is selfish, arrogant, and a liar.
- **Psychological Need** To overcome his arrogance toward women and learn to honestly give and receive love.
- **Moral Need** To stop lying and using women to get what he wants.
- **Problem** Michael is desperate to find work as an actor.

Openings

Ghost, story world, weakness, need, and problem constitute the all-important opening of your story. There are three kinds of structural openings in storytelling in which these elements are established.

Community Start

The main character lives in a paradise world where the land, people, and technology are in perfect harmony. As a result, the hero has no ghost. He is happy, with only the most minor problem, if any, but is also vulnerable to attack. This attack will come soon, either from without or within. *Meet Me in St. Louis* and *The Deer Hunter* have this warm, communal opening.

Running Start

This classic opening, designed to catch the reader in the first few pages, is actually made up of a number of structural elements. The hero has a strong ghost. He lives in a world of slavery, has a number of serious weaknesses, has both a psychological and a moral need, and faces one or more problems. Most good stories use this opening.

Slow Start

The slow start is not one in which the writer simply fails to include all the structure steps of the running start. Rather, the slow start involves stories with a purposeless hero.

Purposeless people do of course exist. But stories about them are extremely sluggish. Because the hero's self-revelation is to learn his true desire (and thereby gain a purpose), the first three-quarters of the story have no goal, and the story has no narrative drive. Very few stories are able to overcome this huge structural flaw, but *On the Waterfront* and *Rebel Without a Cause* are two that do.

4. Inciting Event

This is an event from the outside that causes the hero to come up with a goal and take action.

The inciting event is a small step, except for one thing: it connects need and desire. At the beginning of the story, when weakness and need are being established, the hero is typically paralyzed in some way. You need some kind of event to jump-start the hero out of his paralysis and force him to act.

KEY POINT: To find the best inciting event for your story, keep in mind the catchphrase "from the frying pan into the fire."

The best inciting event is one that makes your hero think he has just overcome the crisis he has faced since the beginning of the story. In fact, due to the inciting event, the hero has just gotten into the worst trouble of his life.

For example, in *Sunset Boulevard*, Joe is an unemployed screenwriter.

Two men come to repossess his car, so he takes off. Suddenly, his tire blows (inciting event). Joe turns into Norma Desmond's driveway and thinks he has gotten away. In fact, he has just fallen into a trap from which he will never escape.

CASABLANCA

Ilsa and Laszlo enter Rick's. They are the outsiders who will shake Rick out of his steady and masterful but unhappy position.

TOOTSIE

Michael's agent, George, tells him that no one will hire him because of his horrible personality. This prompts Michael to put on women's clothes and try out for a soap opera.

5. Desire

The desire is your hero's particular goal. It provides the spine for the entire plot. In our discussion of the seven steps in Chapter 3, I mentioned that a good story usually has one goal that is specific and extends through most of the story. To these elements we must add one more: start the goal at a low level.

One of the ways you build a story is by increasing the importance of the desire as the story progresses. If you start the desire at too high a level, it can't build, and the plot will feel flat and repetitious. Start the desire low so you have somewhere to go.

As you build the desire over the course of the story, be sure you don't create an entirely new desire. Rather, you should increase the intensity and the stakes of the desire you start with.

CASABLANCA

Rick wants Ilsa. But as a love story, this desire is blunted because Ilsa is also Rick's first opponent. Bitter at her for abandoning him in Paris, he first wants to hurt her.

With Rick's desire for Ilsa frustrated, the story shifts focus to someone else's desire: Laszlo's wish to get exit visas for himself and his wife. But the writers make Rick's desire clear early on, which placates the impatient audience during Laszlo's actions because they know Rick's desire will take over soon enough. The waiting makes the desire percolate and boil.

Near the end of the story, Rick comes up with a second, conflicting desire, which is to help Ilsa and Laszlo escape. Having such a conflicting desire early on would give the story two spines. But when the conflicting desire comes near the end and remains hidden until the last moment, it becomes both a revelation and part of Rick's self-revelation.

Tootsie

At first, Michael wants to get an acting job. But he accomplishes this quite early in the story. The goal that actually serves as the spine of the film is Michael's desire for Julie, one of the actresses on the show.

PLOT TECHNIQUE: LEVELS OF DESIRE

Part of the success of your story is based on the level of the desire you give the hero. A desire that remains low throughout the story reduces your hero and makes any complexity of plot virtually impossible. For example, the lowest desire line is simple survival. The hero is under attack and wants to escape. This reduces the hero to the level of an animal. The plot in escape stories simply repeats the same beat of running away.

Here are the levels of some classic desire lines, from lowest to highest:

1. Survive (escape)
2. Take revenge
3. Win the battle
4. Achieve something
5. Explore a world
6. Catch a criminal
7. Find the truth
8. Gain love
9. Bring justice and freedom
10. Save the Republic
11. Save the world

6. Ally or Allies

Once the hero has a desire line, he will usually gain one or more allies to help him overcome the opponent and reach the goal. An ally is not simply a sounding board for the hero's views (although that is valuable, especially in theater, film, and television). An ally is a key figure in the character web and one of the main ways by which you define your hero.

KEY POINT: Consider giving the ally a desire line of his own. You have relatively little time to define this character. The quickest way to make the audience think they are seeing a complete person is to give that character a goal. For example, the Scarecrow in The Wizard of Oz *wants a brain.*

KEY POINT: Never make the ally a more interesting character than the hero. Remember the rule from our discussion of premise: always write a story about your most interesting character. If your ally is more interesting than your hero, redesign the story so that the ally is the hero.

CASABLANCA

Rick's allies are the various role players in the bar: Carl, the professor turned waiter; Sacha, the Russian bartender; Emil, the croupier; Abdul, the bouncer; and Rick's sidekick, Sam, the piano player.

TOOTSIE

Michael's roommate, Jeff, is writing a play, *Return to the Love Canal*, that Michael wants to put on so he can play the lead.

PLOT TECHNIQUE: SUBPLOT

In Chapter 4, on character, we talked about the subplot having a very precise definition and function in a story: a subplot is used to compare how the hero and another character approach generally the same situation.

Remember two key rules about subplot:

must affect the hero's main plot, or it shouldn't be
all. If the subplot doesn't serve the main plot, you have
ltaneous stories that may be clinically interesting to the
e, but they make the main plot seem too long. To connect the
t to the main plot, make sure the two dovetail neatly, usually
near the end. For example, in *Hamlet*, the subplot character, Laertes,
allies with Hamlet's main opponent, Claudius, and he and Hamlet
duel in the battle scene.

2. The subplot character is usually *not* the ally. The subplot character
   and the ally have two separate functions in the story. The ally helps
   the hero in the main plot. The subplot character drives a different
   but related plot that you compare to the main plot.

Most Hollywood movies today have multiple genres, but they rarely
have true subplots. A subplot extends the story, and most Hollywood
films are too interested in speed to put up with that. Where we see true
subplots most often is in love stories, which is a form that tends to have a
thin main plot. An example is *Moonstruck*, which has two subplots, one involving the heroine's father, the second involving her mother. The main
plot and the subplots all deal with the problem of fidelity in marriage.

Subplot is not one of the twenty-two steps because it's not usually
present and because it is really a plot of its own with its own structure. But
it's a great technique. It improves the character, theme, and texture of
your story. On the other hand, it slows the desire line—the narrative drive.
So you have to decide what is most important to you.

If you are going to use a subplot, you only have enough time to work
through the seven key steps. But be aware that if you can't cover all seven,
it won't be a complete story and will seem forced. Because of the limited
time, you want to introduce your subplot as early in the story as is naturally appropriate.

7. Opponent and/or Mystery

The opponent is the character who wants to prevent the hero from reaching his goal. The relationship between this character and your hero is the
most important in your story. If you set up the opposition properly, your

plot will unwind just as it should. If you don't, no amount of rewriting will make any difference.

The best opponent is the *necessary* one: the character best able to attack the great weakness of your hero. Your hero will be forced either to overcome that weakness and grow or else be destroyed. Look again at Chapter 4 on character for all the elements needed for a great opponent.

There are two main reasons opponent and mystery are closely related:

1. A mysterious opponent is more difficult to defeat. In average stories, the hero's only task is to defeat the opponent. In good stories, the hero has a two-part task: uncover the opponent and then defeat him. This makes the hero's job doubly difficult and his success a far greater accomplishment.

   For example, Hamlet doesn't know that the king really killed his father, because he heard it from a ghost. Othello doesn't know that Iago wants to bring him down. Lear doesn't know which daughter really loves him.

2. In certain kinds of stories, like detective and thriller, there must be a mystery to compensate for a missing opponent. Since detective stories purposely hide the opponent until the end, the audience needs something to replace an ongoing conflict between hero and opponent. In this kind of story, you introduce a mystery at about the time you would normally introduce the main opponent.

Before introducing your main opponent, ask yourself these key questions:

- Who wants to stop the hero from getting what he wants and why?
- What does the opponent want? He should be competing for the same goal as the hero.
- What are the opponent's values, and how do they differ from the hero's? Most writers never ask this question, and it's a big mistake. A story without a conflict of values, as well as characters, cannot build.

CASABLANCA

Because *Casablanca* is essentially a love story, Rick's first opponent is his lover, Ilsa Lund. A woman of mystery, she has not told Rick that she was, and still is, married to Victor Laszlo. Rick's second opponent is Ilsa's competing suitor, Laszlo, the great man who has impressed half the world. Though both men hate the Nazis, Rick and Laszlo represent two very different versions of a great man. Laszlo is great on the political and societal level, whereas Rick is great on the personal level.

Major Strasser and the Nazis provide the outside opposition and the danger that move the stakes of the love story to a much higher level. Strasser is not mysterious in any way, because he doesn't need to be; in Casablanca, he is all-powerful.

TOOTSIE

Because *Tootsie* uses the farce form (along with romantic comedy) for its structure, it does not use the mysterious opponent technique. Farce has more opponents than any other form and works by having a lot of opponents attack the hero at a progressively faster rate of speed. These are the main opponents who attack Michael's weaknesses:

1. Julie forces Michael to confront how he has mistreated and abused women.
2. Ron, the arrogant director, doesn't want Dorothy (Michael) for the role and remains hostile toward her.
3. Les, Julie's father, unknowingly shows Michael the effects of his dishonesty when he becomes attracted to Dorothy.
4. John, another actor on the show, makes unwanted advances toward Dorothy.

PLOT TECHNIQUE: THE ICEBERG OPPONENT

Making the opponent mysterious is extremely important, no matter what kind of story you are writing. Think of the opponent as an iceberg. Some of the iceberg is visible above the water. But most of it is hidden below the surface, and that is by far the more dangerous part. There are four techniques that can help you make the opposition in your story as dangerous as possible:

1. Create a *hierarchy* of opponents with a number of alliances. All of the opponents are related to one another; they are all working together

to defeat the hero. The main opponent sits at the top of this pyramid, with the other opponents below him in power. (See our discussion of four-corner opposition in Chapter 4. An example of this technique as used in *The Godfather* can be found at the end of this chapter.)

2. Hide the hierarchy from the hero and the audience, and hide each opponent's true agenda (true desire).

3. Reveal all this information in pieces and at an increasing pace over the course of the story. This means you'll have more reveals near the end of the story. As we shall see, how you reveal information to hero and audience is what makes or breaks your plot.

4. Consider having your hero go up against an obvious opponent early in the story. As the conflict intensifies, have the hero discover attacks from a stronger hidden opposition or attacks from that part of the opponent that has been hidden away.

8. Fake-Ally Opponent

The fake-ally opponent is a character who appears to be an ally of the hero but is actually an opponent or working for the main opponent.

Plot is driven by reveals, which come from the steps the hero takes to uncover the true power of the opposition. Every time a hero discovers something new about an opponent—a revelation—the plot "turns," and the audience is delighted. The fake-ally opponent increases the opponent's power because the fact of his opposition is hidden. The fake-ally opponent forces the hero and the audience to dig below the tip of the iceberg and find what the hero is truly up against.

The fake-ally opponent is also valuable because he's inherently complex. This character often undergoes a fascinating change in the course of the story. By pretending to be an ally of the hero, the fake-ally opponent starts to feel like an ally. So he becomes torn by a dilemma: he works for the opponent but wants the hero to win.

You usually introduce the fake-ally opponent after the main opponent, but not always. If the opponent has come up with a plan to defeat the hero before the story even begins, you may introduce the fake-ally opponent first.

CASABLANCA

Although he is always charming and friendly to Rick, Captain Renault protects himself by working for the Nazis. Renault is much more open in his opposition than most fake-ally opponents, who work undercover. At the very end, Renault flips to become Rick's true ally. This is one of the biggest kicks of the story and is a good example of the storytelling power that comes from switching a character from ally to opponent or from opponent to ally.

TOOTSIE

Sandy is not the usual fake-ally opponent either, fooling the hero and the audience from the beginning. She starts off as an actress friend of Michael's. She becomes a fake-ally opponent when Michael dresses up as a woman to try out for a part in a soap opera that Sandy wants for herself. When she catches him trying on her clothes, he must extend the deception even further by pretending he has fallen in love with her.

9. First Revelation and Decision: Changed Desire and Motive

At this point in the story, the hero gets a revelation—or reveal—which is a surprising piece of new information. This information forces him to make a decision and move in a new direction. It also causes him to adjust his desire and his motive. Motive is why the hero wants the goal. All four of these events—revelation, decision, changed desire, and changed motive—should occur at the same time.

The reveals are the keys to the plot, and they are usually missing in average stories. In many ways, the quality of your plot comes down to the quality of your revelations. Keep these techniques in mind:

1. The best reveals are those where the hero gets information about an *opponent*. This kind of information intensifies the conflict and has the most effect on the outcome of the plot.
2. The changed desire must be a *bend* of the original desire, not a break in it. Think of the changed desire as a river that changes course. You don't want to give your hero an entirely new desire at this point, or

you have started a new story. You want to adjust, intensify, and build the original desire line.

3. Each revelation must be explosive and *progressively stronger than the one that preceded it*. The information should be important, or it won't pop the story. And each reveal should build on the one before it. When we talk about the plot "thickening," this is what is actually happening. Think of the revelations as the gears in a car. With each reveal the car (story) picks up speed until at the final one the vehicle is zooming. The audience has no idea how they ended up moving so fast, but they sure are having a good time.

If your revelations don't build in intensity, the plot will stall or even decline. This is deadly. Avoid it at all costs.

Note that Hollywood has become more plot-conscious in recent years, and that makes many screenwriters' reliance on three-act structure even more dangerous. Three-act structure, you will recall, requires that your story have two or three plot points (reveals). Aside from the fact that this advice is just plain wrong, it will give you a lousy plot with no chance of competing in the real world of professional screenwriting. The average hit film in Hollywood today has seven to ten major reveals. Some kinds of stories, including detective stories and thrillers, have even more. The sooner you abandon three-act structure and learn the techniques of advanced plotting, the better off you will be.

CASABLANCA
- **Revelation**   Ilsa shows up at Rick's bar later that night.
- **Decision**   Rick decides to hurt her as deeply as he can.
- **Changed Desire**   Until Ilsa arrived, Rick simply wanted to run his bar, make money, and be left alone. Now he wants her to feel as much pain as he feels.
- **Changed Motive**   She deserves it for breaking his heart in Paris.

TOOTSIE
- **Revelation**   Michael realizes he has real power when "Dorothy" acts like a bitch at the soap opera audition and gives Ron, the director, a piece of her mind.

- **Decision**   Michael, as Dorothy, decides to behave like a no-nonsense, powerful woman.
- **Changed Desire**   No change. Michael still wants the job.
- **Changed Motive**   Now he sees how to have the job on *his* terms.

TWENTY-TWO STEPS TECHNIQUE: ADDED REVELATIONS

The more revelations you have, the richer and more complex the plot. Every time your hero or audience gains new information, that's a revelation.

KEY POINT: The revelation should be important enough to cause your hero to make a decision and change his course of action.

TOOTSIE

- **Revelation**   Michael realizes he is attracted to Julie, one of the actresses on the show.
- **Decision**   Michael decides to become friends with Julie.
- **Changed Desire**   Michael wants Julie.
- **Changed Motive**   He is falling in love with her.

10. Plan

The plan is the set of guidelines and strategies the hero will use to overcome his opponent and reach the goal.

KEY POINT: Beware of having your hero simply play out the plan. This gives you a predictable plot and a superficial hero. In good stories, the hero's initial plan almost always fails. The opponent is too strong at this point in the story. The hero needs to dig deep and come up with a better strategy, one that takes into account the power and weapons at the opponent's disposal.

CASABLANCA

Rick's initial plan to win Ilsa back is both arrogant and passive: he knows she will come to him, and he tells her so. His main plan, which he figures out relatively late in the story, is to use Ugarte's exit visas to help Ilsa and Laszlo escape the Nazis. The advantage of having such a late plan is that the plot twists (reveals) near the end are rapid and breathtaking.

TOOTSIE

Michael's plan is to maintain his disguise as a woman while convincing Julie she should free herself from her boyfriend, Ron. He also has to fend off the advances of Les and John without their finding out that Dorothy is a man. And he must deceive Sandy about his interest in her and his role on the soap opera.

PLOT TECHNIQUE: TRAINING

Most heroes are already trained to do what they must do to succeed in the story. Their failure in the early part of the plot comes because they have not looked within and confronted their weaknesses.

But training is an important part of certain genres, and in these stories, it is often the most popular part of the plot. Training is most common in sports stories, war stories (including the suicide mission, as in *The Dirty Dozen*), and caper stories (usually involving a heist, as in *Ocean's Eleven*). If you include training in your story, it will probably come right after the plan and before the main action and conflict lines kick in.

11. Opponent's Plan and Main Counterattack

Just as the hero has a plan and takes steps to win, so does the opponent. The opponent comes up with a strategy to get the goal and begins to execute a line of attack against the hero. I cannot emphasize enough how important this step is, and yet most writers are largely unaware of it.

As I've already mentioned, plot comes largely from reveals. To get reveals, you have to hide the ways the opponent attacks the hero. So you want to devise a detailed plan for the opponent with as many hidden attacks as possible. Each of these hidden attacks, when sprung on the hero, is another reveal.

KEY POINT: *The more intricate the opponent's plan, and the better you hide it, the better your plot will be.*

CASABLANCA

- **Opponent's Plan**   Ilsa tries to convince Rick that she left him at the station for good reasons and that Laszlo must escape Casablanca. Major Strasser's plan is to pressure Captain Renault to hold Laszlo in Casablanca and intimidate anyone, including Rick, who might help Laszlo escape.
- **Main Counterattack**   After Rick turns down Laszlo's offer to buy the letters, Ilsa comes to Rick's and threatens him with a gun. Strasser's main attack occurs after Laszlo inspires the Frenchmen in the bar by having the band play "La Marseillaise." Strasser orders the bar closed and warns Ilsa that she and Laszlo must return to Occupied France or Laszlo will be either imprisoned or killed. Later that night, he has Captain Renault arrest Laszlo.

TOOTSIE

As a romantic comedy and farce, each of Michael-Dorothy's opponents has a plan, based on who they think the character is. The plot is ingeniously constructed, using an escalating series of attacks by these opponents: Dorothy has to share a room and bed with Julie, Dorothy has to take care of Julie's screaming baby, Julie mistakenly thinks Dorothy is gay, Les proposes, John forces himself on Dorothy, and Sandy is enraged at Michael for lying to her.

This cyclone effect is one of the pleasures of the farce form, and *Tootsie* gives it a strong emotional impact that is missing from most farces. Michael's gender switches are playing with people's feelings of love and screwing them up at a faster and more complicated rate. This is great writing.

12. Drive

The drive is the series of actions the hero performs to defeat the opponent and win. Comprising what is usually the biggest section of the plot, these actions begin with the hero's plan (Step 10) and continue all the way to his apparent defeat (Step 14).

During the drive, the opponent is usually too strong, so the hero is losing. As a result, he becomes desperate and often starts taking immoral steps to win. (These immoral actions are part of the moral argument of the story; see Chapter 5.)

KEY POINT: *During the drive, you want plot* development, *not repetition. In other words, change the hero's action in a fundamental way. Don't keep hitting the same plot beat (action or event).*

For example, in a love story, two characters falling in love may go to the beach, then to the movies, then to the park, and then out to dinner. These may be four different actions, but they are the same plot beat. That's repetition, not development.

For the plot to develop, you must make your hero react to new information about the opponent (revelations again) and adjust his strategy and course of action accordingly.

CASABLANCA

The unique feature of Rick's drive is that it is *postponed*. This is not a sign of bad writing. It comes from Rick's character, his weakness and desire. Rick is paralyzed by bitterness and the belief that nothing in the world has value anymore. He wants Ilsa, but she is his opponent and is with another man. So in the early and middle parts of the story, Rick speaks with Ilsa but doesn't actively try to get her. Indeed, he begins by driving her away.

This postponement of the desire, though required by Rick's character, has a cost. It results in lulls where audience interest flags. Laszlo seeking exit visas from Ferrari, Laszlo at the police station, Laszlo seeking exit visas from Rick, Laszlo with Ilsa, Laszlo escaping from the underground meeting—all are deflections from the hero's driving line.

But postponing the drive also has two big benefits. First, the writers use Laszlo's actions to build the epic, political side of the story. Even though these actions have nothing to do with the hero's drive, they are necessary in this particular story because they give Rick's final reveal and decision worldwide importance.

Second, by waiting so long to show Rick beginning his quest, the film gains the advantage of having the climaxes and revelations fall quickly one after the other.

When Ilsa comes to Rick's room and declares her love, Rick finally acts,

THE ANATOMY OF STORY

and the story catches fire. Of course, the great irony of Rick's sudden burst of action is that he is really taking steps to make sure that he *doesn't* get Ilsa. The change in the main character's motive and goal—from wanting Ilsa to helping her and Laszlo fly away together—happens just after Rick begins his quest for Ilsa. Indeed, much of the excitement of this final quarter of the film is the result of uncertainty as to which of the two goals Rick is really seeking.

KEY POINT: This uncertainty between the two goals works only because it exists for a short time and is part of the big reveal in the final battle.

■ **Drive Steps**
1. Rick recalls his time in Paris with Ilsa.
2. Rick accuses Ilsa of being a whore when she returns to the café.
3. Rick attempts to make up with Ilsa in the marketplace, but she rejects him.
4. Rick refuses to turn the letters of transit over to Renault.
5. After seeing Ilsa, Rick helps the Bulgarian couple win enough money to pay off Renault.
6. Rick turns down Laszlo's offers for the letters. He tells him to ask Ilsa why.
7. Rick turns down Ilsa's request for the letters, and she confesses she still loves him.
8. Rick tells Ilsa he will help Laszlo escape—alone.
9. Rick has Carl sneak Ilsa out of the club while he talks to Laszlo, who is then arrested.

Tootsie
■ **Drive Steps**
1. Michael buys women's clothes and tells Jeff how tough it is to be a woman.
2. He lies to Sandy about his newfound source of money.
3. He arranges to do his own makeup and hair.
4. He improvises to avoid kissing a man.
5. He is friendly to Julie.
6. He lies to Sandy about being sick.

7. He makes another date with Sandy.

8. He helps April rehearse.

9. He helps Julie with her lines and asks her why she puts up with Ron.

10. He lies to Sandy when he's late for their date.

11. He improvises new lines to make Dorothy a tougher woman.

12. He improvises lines with Julie.

13. He asks George to help him get deeper roles, now that he's learned so much as a woman.

14. Michael, as a man, comes on to Julie, but she rejects him.

15. As Dorothy, he tells Ron not to call him "Tootsie."

16. He lies to avoid Sandy so he can go to the country with Julie.

17. He falls in love with Julie out on the farm.

18. The producer tells Michael they want to renew Dorothy's contract.

13. Attack by Ally

During the drive, the hero is losing to the opponent and becoming desperate. When he starts taking immoral steps to succeed, the ally confronts him.

At this moment, the ally becomes the conscience of the hero, saying, in effect, "I'm trying to help you reach your goal, but the way you're doing it is wrong." Typically, the hero tries to defend his actions and does not accept the ally's criticism. (See Chapter 10, "Scene Construction and Symphonic Dialogue," for details on writing moral dialogue.)

The attack by the ally provides the story with the second level of conflict (hero versus opposition is the first). The ally's attack increases the pressure on the hero and forces him to begin questioning his values and way of acting.

CASABLANCA

■ **Ally's Criticism**   Rick is criticized not by one of his allies but by his first opponent, Ilsa. In the marketplace, she accuses him of not being the man she knew in Paris. When Rick bluntly propositions her, she tells him she was married to Laszlo before she met him.

■ **Hero's Justification**   Rick offers no justification except to say he was drunk the night before.

Tootsie

- **Ally's Criticism**   When Michael pretends to be sick so he can ditch Sandy and go to the country with Julie, Jeff asks him how long he intends to keep lying to people.
- **Hero's Justification**   Michael says lying to a woman is better than hurting her with the truth.

14. Apparent Defeat

During the drive, the hero is losing to the opponent. About two-thirds to three-quarters of the way into the story, the hero suffers an apparent defeat. He believes he has lost the goal and his opponent has won. This is the hero's lowest point.

The apparent defeat provides an important punctuation to the overall structure of any story because it is the moment when the hero hits bottom. It also increases the drama by forcing him to come back from defeat to win at the end. Just as any sporting event is more exciting when the losing home team comes back to win, so is a story when a hero the audience loves battles back from what seems like certain defeat.

KEY POINT: The apparent defeat is not a small or temporary setback. It should be an explosive, devastating moment for the hero. The audience must really feel that the hero is finished.

KEY POINT: You want only one apparent defeat. Although the hero can and should have many setbacks, he should have only one moment that clearly seems to be the end. Otherwise, the story will lack shape and dramatic power. To see the difference, think of a car barreling down a hill and either going over two or three nasty bumps or smashing into a brick wall.

Casablanca

Rick's apparent defeat occurs fairly early in the drive when Ilsa visits him after the bar closes for the night. Drunk, he remembers their romance in Paris and the terrible ending when she failed to show up for the train. When she tries to explain what happened, he bitterly attacks her and drives her away.

TOOTSIE

George tells Michael there is no way Michael can break his contract with the soap opera. He must continue to live this nightmare as a woman.

Apparent Victory

In stories where the hero ends in greater slavery or death, this step is an apparent victory. The hero reaches the height of success or power, but everything goes downhill from here. This is also the moment when the hero often enters a subworld of temporary freedom (see Chapter 6, "Story World"). An example of a story with an apparent victory is *Goodfellas*, when the characters pull off the Lufthansa heist. They think they have made the score of a lifetime. In fact, this success begins a process that will end in the death and destruction of them all.

15. Second Revelation and Decision: Obsessive Drive, Changed Desire and Motive

Just after the apparent defeat, the hero almost always has another major revelation. If he doesn't, the apparent defeat is real, and the story is over. So at this point, the hero gets a new piece of information that shows him that victory is still possible. Now he decides to get back into the game and resume his quest for the goal.

This major revelation has a galvanizing effect on the hero. Where before he wanted the goal (desire and drive), now he is obsessed with it. The hero will do virtually anything to win.

In short, at this point in the plot, the hero becomes tyrannical in his quest to win. Notice that while he is strengthened by this information, he is also continuing the moral decline he began during the drive. (This is another step in the moral argument of your story.)

This second revelation also causes the hero to change his desire and motive. Again the story turns in a new direction. Make sure that all five of these elements—revelation, decision, obsessive drive, changed desire, and changed motive—occur, or this moment will deflate and the plot will flag.

CASABLANCA

■ **Revelation** Ilsa tells Rick that she was married to Laszlo before she met him, which is why she deserted Rick in Paris.

- **Decision** Rick seems to make no clear decision, but he does tell Renault that if anyone uses the letters, he will.
- **Changed Desire** Rick no longer wants to hurt Ilsa.
- **Obsessive Drive** Rick's first obsessive drive occurs when Ilsa shows up at the club and he desperately wants to hurt her because of the pain she caused him. This is another unique element in *Casablanca*. Rick begins at a much higher level of passion and obsession than the heroes in most stories. At the same time, this high level of desire has somewhere to go because Rick ends the story by going off to help save the world.

  Notice also that Rick only *appears* to become more immoral as the story progresses. In fact, he has decided to help Ilsa and Laszlo escape together and is determined to make that happen.
- **Changed Motive** Rick has forgiven Ilsa for what she did.

TOOTSIE
- **Revelation** The soap opera producer tells Dorothy that they want to sign her to another year's contract.
- **Decision** Michael decides to get George to break his contract.
- **Changed Desire** Michael wants to escape the hassle of his masquerade and get close to Julie.
- **Obsessive Drive** Michael is determined to escape Dorothy.
- **Changed Motive** Michael feels increasing guilt because of the decent way Julie and Les have treated him.

Additional Revelation
- **Revelation** Les proposes to Dorothy.
- **Decision** Dorothy leaves Les at the bar.
- **Changed Desire** Michael wants to stop misleading Les.
- **Changed Motive** No change. Michael continues to feel guilty about his actions.

Notice that Michael's moral decline increases here, even though he is feeling guilty and trying to escape his predicament. The longer he keeps up this charade, the more pain he inflicts on those around him.

16. Audience Revelation

The audience revelation is the moment when the audience—*but not the hero*—learns an important piece of new information. Often this is when the audience learns the true identity of the fake-ally opponent and the fact that the character they thought was the hero's friend is really an enemy.

No matter what the audience learns here, this revelation is a valuable moment for a number of reasons.

1. It provides an exciting pop in what is often a slow section of the plot.
2. It shows the audience the true power of the opposition.
3. It allows the audience to see certain hidden plot elements played out dramatically and visually.

Notice that the audience revelation marks a major shift in the relationship of hero to audience. In most stories up to this point (farce being a notable exception), the audience learns information at the same time as the hero. This creates a one-to-one connection—an identity—between hero and audience.

But with an audience revelation, for the first time the audience learns something *before* the hero. This creates distance and places the audience in a *superior* position to the hero. There are a number of reasons why this is valuable, the most important being that it allows the audience to step back and see the hero's overall process of change (culminating at the self-revelation).

CASABLANCA

Rick forces Renault at gunpoint to call the airport tower. But the audience sees that the Captain has actually called Major Strasser.

TOOTSIE

This step does not occur in *Tootsie*, primarily because Michael is scamming the other characters. Because he is fooling them, he is in control. So the audience learns things at the same time as Michael.

17. Third Revelation and Decision

This revelation is another step in the hero's learning what he needs to know to beat the opponent. If the story has a fake-ally opponent, this is often the moment the hero discovers that character's true identity (what the audience learned in Step 16).

As the hero finds out more and more about the true power of the opposition, you might think he would want to back out of the conflict. On the contrary, this information makes the hero feel stronger and more determined to win because he can now see all that he's up against.

CASABLANCA
- **Revelation**   Ilsa comes to Rick for the letters and confesses that she still loves him.
- **Decision**   Rick decides to give Ilsa and Laszlo the letters of transit, but he keeps this decision hidden from Ilsa and the audience.
- **Changed Desire**   Rick wants to save Laszlo and Ilsa from the Nazis.
- **Changed Motive**   Rick knows that Ilsa must go with Laszlo and help him with his cause.

TOOTSIE
- **Revelation**   When Michael gives Sandy chocolates that Les gave Dorothy, Sandy calls him a liar and a fake.
- **Decision**   Michael decides to go to George and find some way out of his contract.
- **Changed Desire**   Unchanged; Michael wants to leave the soap opera.
- **Changed Motive**   Unchanged; he cannot go on lying to all these people.

Additional Revelation
- **Revelation**   When Dorothy gives Julie a present, Julie tells Dorothy she cannot see her anymore because it would be leading her on.
- **Decision**   Michael decides to tell the truth about his masquerade.
- **Changed Desire**   Unchanged; Michael wants Julie.
- **Changed Motive**   Michael loves Julie and realizes he can't have her as long as he plays the role of Dorothy.

18. Gate, Gauntlet, Visit to Death

Near the end of the story, the conflict between hero and opponent intensifies to such a degree that the pressure on the hero becomes almost unbearable. He has fewer and fewer options, and often the space through which he passes literally becomes narrower. Finally, he must pass through a narrow gate or travel down a long gauntlet (while being assaulted from every direction).

This is also the moment when the hero visits "death." In myth stories, the hero goes down to the underworld and foresees his own future in the land of the dead.

In more modern stories, the visit to death is psychological. The hero has a sudden realization of his own mortality; life is finite, and it could end very soon. You might think that this realization would cause him to flee the conflict, since it could cause his death. Instead, it spurs him to fight. The hero reasons, "If my life is to have meaning, I must take a stand for what I believe in. I will take that stand here and now." Thus the visit to death is a testing point that often triggers the battle.

The gate, gauntlet, and visit to death is the most movable of the twenty-two steps and is often found in other parts of the plot. For example, the hero may visit death during the apparent defeat. He may pass through the gauntlet during the final battle, as in the trench fight in *Star Wars* or the tower in *Vertigo*. Or he may pass through it after the battle, as Terry Malloy does at the end of *On the Waterfront*.

CASABLANCA

This step occurs during Rick's efforts to reach the airport with Ilsa, Laszlo, and Renault and Major Strasser's attempt to catch up with them.

TOOTSIE

Michael experiences a gauntlet of escalating nightmares when he must baby-sit Julie's screaming infant, Amy; deal with Julie's rejection when he tries to kiss her; dance with Les, who has fallen in love with Dorothy; get rid of John, the soap opera actor who also wants Dorothy; and refute Sandy's accusations when he gives her the candy Les gave him.

19. Battle

The battle is the final conflict. It determines who, if anyone, wins the goal. A big, violent conflict, though common, is the least interesting form of battle. A violent battle has lots of fireworks but not much meaning. The battle should give the audience the clearest expression of what the two sides are fighting for. The emphasis should not be on which is the superior force but which ideas or values win out.

The battle is the funnel point of the story. Everything converges here. It brings together all the characters and the various lines of action. It occurs in the smallest space possible, which heightens the sense of conflict and unbearable pressure.

The battle is where the hero usually (but not always) fulfills his need and gains his desire. This is also where he is most like his main opponent. But in that similarity the crucial differences between them become even clearer.

Finally, the battle is where the theme first explodes in the minds of the audience. In the conflict of values, the audience sees clearly for the first time which way of acting and living is best.

CASABLANCA

At the airport, Rick holds a gun on Renault and tells Ilsa she must leave with Laszlo. Rick tells Laszlo that Ilsa has been faithful. Laszlo and Ilsa get on the plane. Major Strasser arrives and tries to stop the plane, but Rick shoots him.

TOOTSIE

During a live broadcast of the soap opera, Michael improvises a complicated plot to explain that his character is actually a man and then pulls off his disguise. This simultaneously shocks the audience and the other people on the show. When he's finished, Julie slugs him and leaves.

The final conflict between Michael and Julie is fairly mild (Julie's punch). The big conflict has been replaced with a big reveal whereby Michael strips off his disguise in front of cast, crew, and a national viewing audience.

One of the brilliant touches of this script is that the complex plot that Michael improvises for his character tracks the same process of female liberation that he has undergone by playing a woman.

20. Self-Revelation

By going through the crucible of battle, the hero usually undergoes change. For the first time, he learns who he really is. He tears aside the facade he has lived behind and sees, in a shocking way, his true self. Facing the truth about himself either destroys him—as in *Oedipus the King*, *Vertigo*, and *The Conversation*—or makes him stronger.

If the self-revelation is moral as well as psychological, the hero also learns the proper way to act toward others. A great self-revelation should be *sudden*, for better dramatic effect; *shattering* for the hero, whether the self-revelation is positive or negative; and *new*—it must be something the hero did not know about himself until that moment.

Much of the quality of your story is based on the quality of the self-revelation. Everything leads to this point. You must make it work. There are two pitfalls to making it work that you should be aware of:

1. Make sure that what the hero learns about himself is truly meaningful, not just fine-sounding words or platitudes about life.
2. Don't have the hero state directly to the audience what he has learned. That is a mark of bad writing. (Chapter 10, "Scene Construction and Symphonic Dialogue," explains how to use dialogue to express the self-revelation without preaching.)

PLOT TECHNIQUE: DOUBLE REVERSAL

You may want to use the technique of the double reversal at the self-revelation step. In this technique, you give a self-revelation to the opponent as well as to the hero. Each learns from the other, and the audience sees two insights about how to act and live in the world instead of one.

Here's how you create a double reversal:

1. Give both the hero and the main opponent a weakness and a need.
2. Make the opponent human. That means, among other things, that he must be capable of learning and changing.

3. During or just after the battle, give the opponent as well as the hero a self-revelation.

4. Connect the two self-revelations. The hero should learn something from the opponent, and the opponent should learn something from the hero.

5. Your moral vision as the author is the best of what both characters learn.

CASABLANCA

■ **Psychological Self-Revelation**   Rick regains his idealism and a clear sense of who he really is.

■ **Moral Self-Revelation**   Rick realizes that he must sacrifice to save Ilsa and Laszlo and that he must rejoin the fight for freedom.

■ **Revelation and Double Reversal**   Renault announces he's become a patriot too and will join Rick on the new path.

TOOTSIE

■ **Psychological Self-Revelation**   Michael realizes he's never really loved because he doesn't look beyond a woman's physical attributes.

■ **Moral Self-Revelation**   He sees how his own arrogance and disdain for women has hurt himself and the women he has known. He tells Julie he learned more about being a man by living as a woman than he ever learned by living as a man.

21. Moral Decision

Once the hero learns the proper way to act in the self-revelation, he must make a decision. The moral decision is the moment when he chooses between two courses of action, each of which stands for a set of values and a way of living that affects others.

The moral decision is the proof of what the hero has learned in the self-revelation. By taking this action, the hero shows the audience what he has become.

CASABLANCA

Rick gives Laszlo the letters, makes Ilsa leave with him, and tells Laszlo that Ilsa loves him. He then heads off to risk his life as a freedom fighter.

Tootsie
Michael sacrifices his job and apologizes to Julie and Les for lying.

PLOT TECHNIQUE: THEMATIC REVELATION

In Chapter 5, "Moral Argument," I talked about the thematic revelation as a revelation gained not by the hero but by the audience. The audience sees how people in general should act and live in the world. This allows the story to grow beyond the bounds of these particular characters to affect the audience in their own lives.

Many writers shy away from this advanced technique because they don't want to sound preachy in their final moment with the audience. But done properly, the thematic revelation can be stunning.

KEY POINT: *The trick is in how you draw the abstract and the general from the real and the specific of your characters. Try to find a particular gesture or action that can have symbolic impact on the audience.*

Places in the Heart
(by Robert Benton, 1984)

An example of a brilliant thematic revelation is found at the end of *Places in the Heart*, the story of a woman, played by Sally Field, in the American Midwest of the 1930s whose sheriff husband is accidentally killed by a drunken black boy. Klansmen lynch the boy and later drive out a black man who's been helping the widow farm her land. In a subplot, a man has an affair with his wife's best friend.

The movie's final scene takes place in a church. As the preacher speaks of the power of love, the adulterer's wife takes his hand for the first time since his affair almost destroyed their marriage, and he feels the overwhelming power of forgiveness. The communion plate is passed down one row after another. As each person drinks the wine, he says, "Peace of God." Every character we've seen in the story drinks the wine of communion. And slowly, an amazing thematic revelation comes to the audience. The banker, who was one of the hero's opponents, drinks. The black man who was driven off—and has long since left the story—also drinks. The

Sally Field character drinks. Sitting beside her is her dead husband, and he drinks. And beside him, the black boy who killed him and died because of it drinks too. "Peace of God."

From a realistic depiction of the characters in this story, the scene gradually evolves into a moment of universal forgiveness that the audience shares. The impact is profound. Don't avoid this magnificent technique for fear that you may sound pretentious. Take a chance. Do it right. Tell a great story.

22. New Equilibrium

Once the desire and need have been fulfilled (or tragically left unfulfilled), everything goes back to normal. But there is one big difference. Because of his self-revelation, the hero is now at either a higher or a lower level.

CASABLANCA
Rick has regained his idealism and sacrificed his own love for the sake of someone else's freedom and a higher cause.

TOOTSIE
Michael has learned to be honest and less selfish about himself and his career. By telling the truth, he is able to reconcile with Julie and begin a real romance.

The twenty-two steps comprise a powerful tool that gives you an almost limitless ability to create a detailed, organic plot. Use it. But realize that it is a tool that requires much practice to master. So apply it to everything you write and everything you read. As you apply it, keep two points in mind:

1. Be flexible. The twenty-two steps are not fixed in their order. They are not a formula by which you whip your story into conformity. This is the *general* order by which humans try to solve life problems. But every problem and every story is different. Use the twenty-two steps as a framework for the organic unfolding of your unique characters solving their specific problems.

2. Beware of breaking the order. This second caution is the opposite of the first, and again, it's based on the fact that these steps are how

humans solve life problems. The twenty-two steps represent an organic order, the development of a single unit. So if you try to change the order too drastically in an effort to be original or surprising, you risk a story that seems fake or contrived.

REVELATIONS SEQUENCE

Good writers know that revelations are the key to plot. That's why it's so important that you take some time to separate the reveals from the rest of the plot and look at them as one unit. Tracking the revelations sequence is one of the most valuable of all storytelling techniques.

The key to the revelations sequence is to see if the sequence builds properly.

1. The sequence of revelations must be logical. They must occur in the order in which the hero would most likely learn of them.
2. They must build in intensity. Ideally, each reveal should be stronger than the one that came before it. This is not always possible, especially in longer stories (for one thing, it defies logic). But you want a general buildup so that the drama increases.
3. The reveals must come at an increasing pace. This also heightens the drama because the audience gets hit with a greater *density* of surprise.

The most powerful of all reveals is known as a *reversal*. This is a reveal in which the audience's understanding of everything in the story is turned on its head. They suddenly see every element of the plot in a new light. All reality changes in an instant.

A reversal reveal is most common, not surprisingly, in detective stories and thrillers. In *The Sixth Sense*, the reversal reveal comes when the audience discovers that the Bruce Willis character has been dead for most of the movie. In *The Usual Suspects*, the reversal reveal comes when the audience discovers that the meek Verbal has been making up the entire story and that he is the terrifying opponent, Keyser Soze.

Notice that in both of these movies, the big reversal reveal comes right at the end of the story. This has the advantage of sending the audience out of the theater with a knockout punch. It's the biggest reason these movies were huge hits.

But you must be careful with this technique. It can reduce the story to a mere vehicle for plot, and very few stories can support such domination by the plot. O. Henry gained great fame using the reversal technique in his short stories (such as "The Gift of the Magi"), but they were also criticized for being forced, gimmicky, and mechanical.

Let's look at the revelations sequences in some stories besides *Casablanca* and *Tootsie*.

ALIEN

(story by Dan O'Bannon and Ronald Shusett, screenplay by Dan O'Bannon, 1979)

- **Revelation 1**   The crew realizes that the Alien is using the air vents to move through the ship.
- **Decision**   They decide to flush the Alien toward the airlock and vent it into space.
- **Changed Desire**   Ripley and the others want to kill the Alien.
- **Changed Motive**   They must kill the Alien or die.

- **Revelation 2**   Ripley learns from the computer, MOTHER, that the crew is expendable in the name of science.
- **Decision**   Ripley decides to challenge Ash's actions.
- **Changed Desire**   She wants to know why this was hidden from the crew.
- **Changed Motive**   She suspects that Ash is not on the crew's side.

- **Revelation 3**   Ripley discovers that Ash is a robot that will kill her if necessary to protect the Alien.
- **Decision**   Ripley, with Parker's aid, attacks and destroys Ash.
- **Changed Desire**   She wants to stop the traitor among them and get off the spaceship.
- **Obsessive Drive**   She will oppose and destroy anything and anyone who aids the Alien.
- **Changed Motive**   Her motive remains self-preservation.

- **Revelation 4** After his robot head is revived, Ash tells Ripley that the Alien is a perfect organism, an amoral killing machine.
- **Decision** Ripley orders Parker and Lambert to prepare for immediate evacuation and the destruction of the spaceship.
- **Changed Desire** Ripley still wants to kill the Alien, but it now means destroying the ship.
- **Changed Motive** Unchanged.

- **Audience Revelation** The Alien remains an unknown, terrifying force throughout. So the audience learns things at generally the same time as Ripley and the crew, depriving them of a sense of superiority over the characters and increasing their fear.

- **Revelation 5** Ripley discovers that the Alien has cut her off from the shuttle pod.
- **Decision** She races back to abort the self-destruct sequence.
- **Changed Desire** Ripley doesn't want to blow up with the ship.
- **Changed Motive** Unchanged.

- **Revelation 6** Ripley discovers that the Alien is hiding on the shuttle.
- **Decision** She gets into a spacesuit and opens the shuttle to the vacuum of space.
- **Changed Desire** Ripley still wants to kill the Alien.
- **Changed Motive** Unchanged.

Notice that the final revelation is the classic horror one: the place you escape to is actually the deadliest place of all.

BASIC INSTINCT
(by Joe Eszterhas, 1992)
- **Revelation 1** Nick discovers that a professor was killed while Catherine was attending school at Berkeley.
- **Decision** Nick decides to follow Catherine.
- **Changed Desire** Nick wants to solve the murder and bring Catherine down off her throne.
- **Changed Motive** Nick and the police thought Catherine had been cleared but now think otherwise.

- **Revelation 2** Nick finds out that Catherine's friend Hazel is a murderer and that Catherine knew the professor who was killed.
- **Decision** He decides to continue following Catherine.
- **Changed Desire** Unchanged.
- **Changed Motive** Unchanged.

- **Revelation 3** Nick finds out that Catherine's parents died in an explosion.
- **Decision** He decides that Catherine is the killer and goes after her.
- **Changed Desire** Unchanged.
- **Obsessive Drive** He will beat this brilliant killer if it's the last thing he does (and it may well be).
- **Changed Motive** Unchanged.

- **Revelation 4** Nick's fellow cop, Gus, tells him that an internal affairs cop named Nilsen died with a large sum of money in the bank, as if someone had paid him off.
- **Decision** Nick makes no clear decision based on this information, but he does decide to uncover the source of this money.
- **Changed Desire** Nick wants to find out why Nilsen had all this money.
- **Changed Motive** Unchanged.

- **Revelation 5** Nick discovers that his ex-girlfriend, Beth, changed her name, that Nilsen had her file, and that Beth's husband was killed in a drive-by shooting.
- **Decision** Nick decides to try to prove that Beth is the real killer.
- **Changed Desire** He wants to know if Beth is committing these murders and pinning the blame on Catherine.
- **Changed Motive** He still wants to solve the murder.

- **Revelation 6** Gus tells Nick that Beth was Catherine's college roommate and lover.
- **Decision** Nick decides to go with Gus to confront Beth.
- **Changed Desire** Nick still wants to solve the murders, but now he's certain Beth is the killer.
- **Changed Motive** Unchanged.

Notice with the detective thriller, the revelations get bigger and *closer to home.*

"THEME OF THE TRAITOR AND THE HERO"
(by Jorge Luis Borges, 1956)

Borges is a rare example of a writer who has great reveals, even in very short stories, but they don't dominate the story at the expense of character, symbol, story world, or theme. Inherent to Borges's philosophy as a writer is an emphasis on learning or exploring as a way out of a labyrinth that is both personal and cosmic. As a result, his revelations have tremendous thematic power.

"Theme of the Traitor and the Hero" is a short story made up almost totally of revelations. In it, the unnamed storyteller explains that he is formulating a story whose details are not yet revealed to him. His narrator, Ryan, is the great-grandson of Kilpatrick, one of Ireland's greatest heroes, who was murdered in a theater on the eve of a victorious revolt.

- **Revelation 1**   While writing a biography of Kilpatrick, Ryan discovers a number of troubling details of the police investigation, such as a letter Kilpatrick received, warning him not to attend the theater, much like the letter Julius Caesar received warning him of his murder.
- **Revelation 2**   Ryan senses that there is a secret form of time in which events and lines of dialogue are repeated throughout history.
- **Revelation 3**   Ryan learns that words a beggar spoke to Kilpatrick were the same as those found in Shakespeare's *Macbeth*.
- **Revelation 4**   Ryan discovers that Kilpatrick's best friend, Nolan, had translated Shakespeare's plays into Gaelic.
- **Revelation 5**   Ryan finds out that Kilpatrick ordered the execution of a traitor—identity unknown—just days before his own death, but that order doesn't square with Kilpatrick's merciful nature.
- **Revelation 6**   Kilpatrick had previously given his friend Nolan the job of uncovering the traitor in their midst, and Nolan had discovered that the traitor was Kilpatrick himself.
- **Revelation 7**   Nolan devised a scheme whereby Kilpatrick would be assassinated in a dramatic way so that he would die a hero and trigger the revolt. Kilpatrick agreed to play his part.

- **Revelation 8**   With so little time for the plan, Nolan had to steal elements from Shakespeare's plays to complete the scheme and make it dramatically convincing to the people.
- **Revelation 9**   Because the Shakespearean elements are the least dramatic in the scheme, Ryan realizes that Nolan used them so that the truth of the scheme, and Kilpatrick's identity, would one day be uncovered. Ryan, the narrator, is part of Nolan's plot.
- **Audience Revelation**   Ryan keeps his final discovery a secret and instead publishes a book glorifying Kilpatrick.

THE STORYTELLER

To use a storyteller or not, that is the question. And it's one of the most important decisions you must make in the writing process. I am talking about it here in connection with plot because the storyteller can radically change the way you sequence the plot. But if you are writing an organic story, a storyteller has just as much effect on your depiction of character.

Here's the rub (to carry the *Hamlet* metaphor a bit further). The storyteller is one of the most misused of all techniques, because most writers don't know the implications of the storyteller or its true value.

The vast majority of popular stories in movies, novels, and plays don't use a recognizable storyteller. They are linear stories told by an omniscient storyteller. Someone is telling the story, but the audience doesn't know who and doesn't care. These stories are almost always fast, with a strong, single desire line and a big plot.

A storyteller is someone who recounts a character's actions, either in the first person—talking about himself—or in the third person—talking about someone else. Using a recognizable storyteller allows you greater complexity and subtlety. Stated simply, a storyteller lets you present the actions of the hero along with commentary on those actions.

As soon as you identify the person who is telling the story, the audience immediately asks, Why is that person telling this story? And why does this particular story need a teller, need to be recounted right now before my eyes? Notice that a storyteller calls attention to himself and, at least initially, can distance the audience from the story. This gives you, the writer, the benefit of detachment.

A storyteller also lets the audience hear the voice of the character who is doing the telling. People bandy about the term "voice" all the time, as if it were some golden key to great storytelling. When we talk about letting the audience hear the character's voice, we are really putting the audience in the character's *mind*, right now as he speaks. It is a mind expressed in the most precise and unique way possible, which is what the character talks about and how he says it. Being in the character's mind implies that this is a real person, with prejudices, blind spots, and lies, even when he isn't aware of them himself. This character may or may not be trying to tell the truth to the audience, but whatever truth comes out will be highly subjective. This is not the word of God or an omniscient narrator. Taken to its logical extreme, the storyteller blurs, or even destroys, the line between reality and illusion.

Another important implication of a storyteller is that he is recounting what happened in the past, and that immediately brings memory into play. As soon as an audience hears that this story is being *remembered*, they get a feeling of loss, sadness, and "might-have-been-ness." They also feel that the story is complete and that the storyteller, with only the perspective that comes after the end, is about to speak with perhaps a touch more wisdom.

Some writers use this combination—someone speaking personally to the audience and telling the story from memory—to fool them into thinking that what they are about to hear is more, not less, truthful. The storyteller says in effect, "I was there. I'm going to tell you what really happened. Trust me." This is a tacit invitation to the audience *not* to trust and to explore the issue of truth as the story unfolds.

Besides heightening the issue of truth, the storyteller gives the writer some unique and powerful advantages. It helps you establish an intimate connection between character and audience. It can make your characterization subtler and help you distinguish one person from another. Furthermore, the use of a storyteller often signals a shift from a hero who acts—usually a fighter—to a hero who creates—an artist. The act of telling the story now becomes the main focus, so the path to "immortality" shifts from a hero taking glorious action to a storyteller who tells about it.

A storyteller is tremendously liberating when it comes to constructing the plot. Because the actions of the plot are framed by someone's memories, you can leave chronology behind and sequence the actions in whatever way makes the most structural sense. A storyteller also helps you string together actions and events that cover great stretches of time and place or when the hero goes on a journey. As we've discussed, these plots often feel fragmented. But when framed by a remembering storyteller, the actions and events suddenly have a greater unity, and the huge gaps between the story events seem to disappear.

Before we discuss the best techniques when using a storyteller, here's what to avoid. Don't use the storyteller as a simple frame. The story begins with the storyteller saying in effect, "I'd like to tell you a story." He then recounts the events of the plot in chronological order and ends by saying, "That's what happened. It was some amazing story."

This kind of framing device is quite common and is worse than useless. Not only does it call attention to the storyteller for no reason, but it also fails to take advantage of any of the implications and strengths of the storyteller technique. It seems to exist only to let the audience know that they should appreciate this story because it is being told in an "artistic" way.

However, there are a number of techniques that will let you take full advantage of the storyteller. The reason these techniques are so powerful is that they are inherent in the structure of *a person who needs to tell a story* and of *a story that needs to be told*. But don't think you must use all of them at once. Every story is unique. Pick the techniques that are right for you.

1. Realize that your storyteller is probably your true main character.

Whether you use first- or third-person narration, nine out of ten times, the storyteller is your true hero. The reason is structural. The act of telling the story is the equivalent of taking the self-revelation step and splitting it in half. At the beginning, the storyteller is looking back to try to understand the impact his actions or someone else's actions have had on him. In recounting those actions—of another or of himself at some earlier time—the storyteller sees an external model of action and gains a profound personal insight that changes his life in the present.

2. Introduce the storyteller in a dramatic situation.

For example, a fight has just occurred, or an important decision must be made. This places the storyteller *within* the story, creating suspense about the storyteller himself and giving the storyteller's tale a running start.

- *Sunset Boulevard*: The storyteller, dead man Joe Gillis, has just been shot by his lover, Norma Desmond.
- *Body and Soul*: The storyteller is about to enter the boxing ring, where he will throw the championship fight.
- *The Usual Suspects*: The storyteller may be the only survivor of a mass killing and is being interrogated by the cops.

3. Find a good trigger to cause him to tell the story.

Instead of "I'm going to tell you a story," the storyteller is personally motivated by a story problem in the present. And this story problem, this personal motivation, is directly linked to why he has to tell *this* story right now.

- *Body and Soul*: The storyteller hero is a corrupt boxer. He is about to throw the title fight, so he needs to understand how he got to this point before the fight begins.
- *The Usual Suspects*: The interrogator threatens to put a contract out on Verbal's life unless he talks.
- *How Green Was My Valley*: The hero is devastated that he is being driven out of his beloved valley. He needs to know why this happened before he goes.

4. The storyteller should not be all-knowing at the beginning.

An all-knowing storyteller has no dramatic interest in the present. He already knows everything that happened, so he becomes a dead frame. Instead, the storyteller should have *a great weakness that will be solved by telling the story*, and thinking back and telling the story should be a struggle for him. This way, the storyteller is dramatic and personally interesting in the present, and the act of telling the story is itself heroic.

- *Cinema Paradiso*: The hero, Salvatore, is wealthy and famous but also sad and in despair. He has known many women but never really loved any of them. And he hasn't visited his hometown in Sicily for thirty years. When he learns that his old friend Alfredo has died, it causes him to remember growing up in the place to which he vowed he would never return.
- *The Shawshank Redemption*: "Red" Redding, serving a life sentence for murder, has just been turned down again for parole. He is a man

without hope and believes he needs the walls of the prison to survive. One day, Andy arrives and walks the gauntlet between the lines of jeering prisoners that all new prisoners must walk. Red bets that Andy will be the first new prisoner to cry that night. Andy doesn't make a sound.

- *Heart of Darkness*: This is ultimately a detective story where the "crime"—the "horror" of what Kurtz might have done and said—is never known or solved. Part of the mystery is Marlow's true motive for telling and retelling his tale. One clue may be his final words to Kurtz's "Intended," when she asks him the last thing Kurtz said before he died. Instead of his actual words—"The horror! The horror!"—Marlow lies and says, "The last word he pronounced was—your name." Marlow is guilty of telling her a lie, telling a story that promises a simple answer and a false emotion, and this is reprehensible to him. And so he is doomed, driven, to tell his tale again and again until he gets it right, even though Kurtz's experience, and the heart of darkness itself, is unknowable.

5. Try to find a unique structure for telling the tale instead of simple chronology.

The way you tell the story (through the storyteller) should be exceptional. Otherwise it's just a frame and we don't need it. A unique way of telling the story justifies a storyteller and says: this story is so unique that only a special storyteller could do it justice.

- *It's a Wonderful Life*: Two angels tell a third angel the events of a man's life that have led him to the point of committing suicide. The third angel then shows the man an alternative present: what the world would look like had he never lived.
- *The Usual Suspects*: A number of men are murdered on a docked ship. Customs agent Kujan interrogates a crippled man named Verbal who tells how it all started six weeks ago when the cops questioned five guys for a heist. The story goes back and forth between Kujan questioning Verbal and the events that Verbal describes. After he lets Verbal go, Kujan looks at the bulletin board in the interrogation room and sees all the names Verbal used in his confession. Verbal has made up all the "past" events in the present. He is both the killer and the storyteller.

6. The storyteller should try different versions of how he tells the story as he struggles to find and express the truth.

Again, the story is not some fixed thing, known from the beginning. It is a dramatic argument the writer is having with the audience. The act of telling the story and the act of an audience listening to it, and silently questioning it, should partly determine how it turns out.

The storyteller creates this give-and-take by leaving openings where he struggles with how best to tell it and lets the audience fill in the gaps. Through his struggle, he comes to understand the deeper meaning of the events, and by pulling the audience in and making them participate, he triggers the deeper meaning of their life narrative as well.

- *Heart of Darkness*: This is the antistoryteller's tale: it uses three narrators to show structurally that the "true" story is hopelessly ambiguous and can never be told. A seaman talks about a storyteller (Marlow) who is telling his shipmates a tale told to him by a man (Kurtz) whose dying words, "The horror! The horror!" are never explained. So we literally get a mystery wrapped in an enigma, an infinite regression of meaning, as obscure as "The horror" itself.

   Also, Marlow has told this tale many times, as though trying to get closer to the truth by each telling, always ending in failure. He explains that he went up the river to find the truth about Kurtz, but the closer he got to him, the murkier things became.

- *Tristram Shandy*: Three hundred years ahead of its time, *Tristram Shandy* uses this same storytelling technique in comedy. For example, the first-person narrator tells a story that goes backward as well as forward. He talks to the reader directly and admonishes the reader for not reading properly. And he complains to the reader when he has to explain something that he says should come out later.

7. Do not end the storytelling frame at the end of the story, but rather about three-quarters of the way in.

If you put the final storytelling frame at the very end of the story, the act of remembering and telling the story can have no dramatic or structural impact on the present. You need to leave some room in the story for the act of recounting the change to the storyteller himself.

- *It's a Wonderful Life*: Clarence, the angel, listens to the story of George's life until the moment when George is about to commit suicide. This recounting of past events concludes with about a third of the story to go. In the final third of the story, Clarence shows George an alternative and helps him change.
- *Cinema Paradiso*: The hero, Salvatore, finds out that his friend Alfredo has died. He thinks back to his childhood, which he spent mostly at the Cinema Paradiso, where Alfredo was the projectionist. The memory ends when Salvatore leaves his hometown as a young man to make his name in Rome. Back in the present, he returns to his hometown for the funeral and sees that the Cinema Paradiso has become a boarded-up ruin. But Alfredo has left him a gift, a reel of all the great kissing scenes the priest ordered cut when Salvatore was just a boy.

8. The act of telling the story should lead the storyteller to a self-revelation.

By thinking back, the storyteller gains a great insight about himself in the present. Again, the entire storytelling process is structurally one big self-revelation step for the storyteller. So telling the story is the way the storyteller-hero fulfills his need.

- *The Great Gatsby*: Nick says at the end, "That's my middle West. . . . I am part of that, a little solemn with the feel of those long winters. ⁄ . . After Gatsby's death the East was haunted for me like that. . . . So when the blue smoke of brittle leaves was in the air and the wind blew the wet laundry stiff on the line I decided to come back home."
- *The Shawshank Redemption*: Red learns to have hope and live in freedom after being inspired by his friend Andy.
- *Goodfellas*: As a black comedy, *Goodfellas* uses the first-person storyteller to highlight the ironic fact that the hero *doesn't* get a self-revelation at the end, even though it is clear that he should.

9. Consider having the storyteller explore how the act of telling the story can be immoral or destructive, to himself or to others.

This makes storytelling itself a moral issue, dramatically interesting in the present.

■ *Copenhagen*: Copenhagen is really a competition of storytellers: three characters give different versions of what happened when they met during World War II to discuss building a nuclear bomb. Each story represents a different view of morality, and each character uses his own story to attack the morality of another.

10. The act of telling the story should cause a final dramatic event.

This event is often the hero's moral decision.

Telling the story should have an effect, and the most dramatic effect is to force the storytelling hero to make a new moral decision based on his self-revelation.

■ *The Great Gatsby*: Nick decides to leave the moral decadence of New York and return to the Midwest.
■ *It's a Wonderful Life*: George decides not to commit suicide but rather to join his family and face the music.
■ *Body and Soul*: The storyteller hero, after looking back, decides not to throw the fight.
■ *The Shawshank Redemption*: Red decides not to give up outside of prison as his friend Brooks did. Instead he decides to live and join Andy, who is starting a new life in Mexico.

11. Don't promote the fallacy that a character's death allows the full and true story to be told.

In this common trigger for telling a story, the storyteller states that the character's death finally makes it possible to tell the truth about him. His deathbed scene and last words provide the final key for the truth to "fall into place."

This is a false technique. It is not your actual death that allows you to understand your life because you can finally see it whole. It is acting *as if* you will die that creates meaning by motivating you to make choices now. Finding meaning is an ongoing process of living.

Similarly, the storyteller may use the character's death (someone else's or his own) to give the *appearance* that now the full story can be told and understood. But meaning comes in the act of storytelling, in looking back again and again, and each time, the "true" story is different. Like Heisenberg's uncertainty principle, the storyteller may know *a* meaning at any one time but never *the* meaning.

- *Citizen Kane*: The meaning of Kane's dying word, "Rosebud," is not that it sums up all of Kane's life but that it can't.
- *Heart of Darkness*: Kurtz's dying words—"The horror! The horror!"—don't make the enigma of his life any clearer. They are the final mystery in a larger mystery about the heart of darkness that exists in all humans, including the storyteller Marlow, who tells the tale again and again in a vain attempt to finally get to the truth.

12. The deeper theme should be concerned with the truth and beauty of creativity, not heroic action.

By placing all actions within the storytelling frame and highlighting the importance and struggles of the storyteller recounting those actions, you make storytelling the primary action and the great accomplishment.

- *The Usual Suspects*: Verbal is a master criminal, having defeated or killed everyone who has tried to stop him. But his greatest accomplishment—indeed, the main reason he is a successful criminal—is the story he improvises that makes everyone think he is a weak, pathetic man.
- *Gilgamesh*: Gilgamesh is a great warrior. But when his friend and fellow warrior dies, he looks in vain for immortality. He is left with the immortality that comes from having his story told.
- *The Shawshank Redemption*: Andy's great gift to his friend Red (the storyteller) and the other prisoners is to show them how to live life with hope, style, and freedom, even in prison.

13. Be wary of too many storytellers.

For all its power, the storyteller has costs. The biggest one is that it places a frame between the story and the audience, and that usually drains some emotion from the story. The more storytellers you have, the more you risk distancing the audience so much that they look at the story from a cold and clinical position.

Stories that excel in their use of a storyteller are *Sunset Boulevard*, *The Conformist*, *American Beauty*, *The Usual Suspects*, *Goodfellas*, *The Shawshank Redemption*, *Forrest Gump*, *Presumed Innocent*, *The Magnificent Ambersons*, *Heart of Darkness*, *Tristram Shandy*, *Copenhagen*, *Madame Bovary*, *Citizen Kane*, *How Green Was My Valley*, *Cinema Paradiso*, *Gilgamesh*, *The Great Gatsby*, *It's a Wonderful Life*, and *Body and Soul*.

GENRES

The next major structural element that affects your plot is genre. A genre is a story form, a particular kind of story. Most stories in movies, novels, and plays are founded on at least one genre, and are usually a combination of two or three. So it is important that you know what story form, if any, you are using. Each genre has predetermined plot beats that you must include, or your audience will be disappointed.

Genres are really story subsystems. Each genre takes the universal steps of story structure, the seven and twenty-two steps, and executes them in a different way. You can tell a great story without using any genre at all. But if you do use one, you must master how your form executes these structure steps, as well as learn how each handles character, theme, story world, and symbol. Then you must use these elements in an original way so that your story is not like any other story in that form, even though in many ways it is like every other story in that genre. Audiences of genre stories like to see the familiar bones of the form, but with a new skin that makes this story fresh.

The details of the various genres lie beyond the scope of this book, and I have written extensively about them elsewhere. They are very complex, and you must commit to one or two of them if you are to have any chance of mastery. The good news is that, with practice, as all successful writers know, they can be learned.

CREATING YOUR PLOT—WRITING EXERCISE 7

- **Designing Principle and Plot**   Review the designing principle and the theme of your story. Be certain that your plot tracks these lines.
- **Symbol for Plot**   If you are using a story symbol, make sure that your plot is an expression of it.
- **Storyteller**   Figure out if you want to use a storyteller, and if so, what kind. Keep in mind the structural techniques that allow you to get the most out of the storyteller.
- **Twenty-two Steps**   Describe the twenty-two steps of your story in detail. Be sure to start with Step 1, the plot frame, so that all the other steps fall naturally into place.
- **Reveals Sequence**   Focus on the reveals sequence. List the reveals separately from the other steps. Look for the following elements to make the reveals as dramatic as possible:
  1. Make sure the sequence is logical.
  2. Try to make each reveal more intense than the one before.
  3. Check that each reveal causes your hero to change his original desire in some way.
  4. Make the reveals come at a faster pace as you move toward the end of the story.

Let's look at a twenty-two-step breakdown for *The Godfather* so that you can see how the twenty-two steps add the crucial plot details to the seven key structure steps you've already determined.

THE GODFATHER
(novel by Mario Puzo, screenplay by Mario Puzo and Francis Ford Coppola, 1972)
- **Hero**   Michael Corleone.

1. SELF-REVELATION, NEED, AND DESIRE

- **Self-Revelation**   Michael has no self-revelation. He has become a ruthless killer, but only his wife, Kay, has seen his moral decline.
- **Need**   To avoid becoming a ruthless killer.

- **Desire**   To take revenge on the men who shot his father.
- **Initial Error**   Michael believes he is different from his family and above their criminal activity.

2. GHOST AND STORY WORLD

- **Ghost**   Michael's ghost is not a single event from his past but a family legacy of crime and killing that he despises.
- **Story World**   The story world is the Mafia system of Michael's family. It is extremely hierarchical, run like the military, with strict rules. The Godfather is the absolute ruler, meting out justice as he sees fit, and the family uses murder to get what it wants. The workings of this world are laid out at the wedding of Michael's sister, to which all the characters in the story have been invited, including the hidden opponent, Barzini.

  The national reach of the family's power is then shown when a Hollywood producer fails to do what the Godfather has asked. The man wakes up with the severed head of his favorite horse beside him.

3. WEAKNESS AND NEED

- **Weaknesses**   Michael is young, inexperienced, untested, and overconfident.
- **Psychological Need**   To overcome his sense of superiority and self-righteousness.
- **Moral Need**   To avoid becoming ruthless like the other Mafia bosses while still protecting his family.
- **Problem**   Rival gang members shoot Michael's father, the head of the family.

4. INCITING EVENT

Michael's distance from his family is shattered when he reads that his father has been shot.

5. DESIRE

To take revenge on the men who shot his father and thereby protect his family.

6. ALLY OR ALLIES

Michael has a vast array of allies from his family. They include his father, Don Corleone; his brothers, Sonny and Fredo; Tom; Clemenza; and his wife, Kay.

7. OPPONENT AND/OR MYSTERY

Michael's first opponent is Sollozzo. However, his true opponent is the more powerful Barzini, who is the hidden power behind Sollozzo and wants to bring the entire Corleone family down. Michael and Barzini compete over the survival of the Corleone family and control over crime in New York.

8. FAKE-ALLY OPPONENT

Michael has an unusually large number of fake-ally opponents, which greatly increases the plot. They include the driver of the car when his father was shot; his Sicilian bodyguard, Fabrizio, who tries to kill him but blows up his wife instead; his brother-in-law, Carlo, who lures Sonny to his death; and Tessio, who goes over to Barzini's side.

9. FIRST REVELATION AND DECISION: CHANGED DESIRE AND MOTIVE

- **Revelation** The hospital in which his father is recuperating has no guards and is virtually empty. Michael realizes that men are coming to kill his father.
- **Decision** He decides to protect his father by wheeling his bed into another room and standing guard outside.
- **Changed Desire** Instead of standing apart from the family, Michael now wishes to protect his father and save his family.
- **Changed Motive** He loves his family deeply, and his drive to compete and succeed will not let him lose.

10. PLAN

Michael's first plan is to kill Sollozzo and his protector, the police captain. His second plan is to kill the heads of the other families in a single strike.

11. OPPONENT'S PLAN AND MAIN COUNTERATTACK

Michael's main opponent is Barzini. Barzini's plan is to use Sollozzo as a front man in the effort to kill Don Corleone. Once Don Corleone is incapacitated, he pays off Carlo to lure Sonny into a trap and pays Michael's bodyguard in Sicily to kill him.

12. DRIVE

- **Drive Sequence**
    1. Clemenza shows Michael how to kill Sollozzo and McCluskey.
    2. At the restaurant, Michael shoots Sollozzo and McCluskey.
    3. There is a quick montage of newspaper articles.
    4. Sonny and Tom argue because Sonny wants to kill old Tattaglia.
    5. In Sicily, Michael sees a pretty girl on the road and tells her father he wants to meet her.
    6. Michael meets Apollonia.
    7. Sonny finds Connie with a black eye. He beats up Connie's husband, Carlo, in the street.
    8. Michael and Apollonia are wed.
    9. Tom won't accept Kay's letter to Michael.
    10. Michael shows Apollonia how to drive; he learns Sonny is dead.
- **Added Revelation**   Michael sees a beautiful Italian girl on the road in Sicily.
- **Decision**   He decides to meet her.
- **Changed Desire**   He wants her.
- **Changed Motive**   He is falling in love.

13. ATTACK BY ALLY

- **Ally's Criticism**   When Michael returns from Sicily, Kay criticizes him for working for his father. She tells him he is not like that.
- **Hero's Justification**   He promises her the family will be legitimate in five years.

14. APPARENT DEFEAT

Michael's apparent defeat is a one-two punch. He finds out that his brother Sonny has been murdered and soon afterward sees his wife blown up by a bomb that was meant for him.

15. SECOND REVELATION AND DECISION: OBSESSIVE DRIVE, CHANGED DESIRE AND MOTIVE

- **Revelation**   Michael realizes that a bomb has been planted in his car and that his wife is about to start the engine.
- **Decision**   He tries to stop his wife, but he is too late.
- **Changed Desire**   Michael wants to return home to his family.
- **Obsessive Drive**   He is determined to take revenge on the men who killed his wife and brother.
- **Changed Motive**   They must pay for killing the people he loves.

16. AUDIENCE REVELATION

The audience sees Luca Brasi, Don Corleone's most dangerous ally, murdered when he meets with Tattaglia and Sollozzo.

17. THIRD REVELATION AND DECISION

- **Revelation**   Michael realizes that Tessio has gone over to the other side and that Barzini plans to kill him.
- **Decision**   He decides to strike first.
- **Changed Desire**   He wants to kill all of his enemies in one blow.
- **Changed Motive**   He wants to win the war once and for all.

18. GATE, GAUNTLET, VISIT TO DEATH

Because Michael is such a superior fighter, even fooling the audience, he doesn't pass through a gate or gauntlet before the final battle. His visit to death occurs when he sees his wife blown up by a bomb meant for him.

19. BATTLE

The final battle is a crosscut between Michael's appearance at his nephew's baptism and the killing of the heads of the five Mafia families. At the baptism, Michael says that he believes in God. Clemenza fires a shotgun into some men getting off an elevator. Moe Green is shot in the eye. Michael, following the liturgy of the baptism, renounces Satan. Another gunman shoots one of the heads of the families in a revolving door. Barzini is shot. Tom sends Tessio off to be murdered. Michael has Carlo strangled.

20. SELF-REVELATION

- **Psychological Self-Revelation**   None. Michael still believes that his sense of superiority and self-righteousness is justified.
- **Moral Self-Revelation**   None. Michael has become a ruthless killer. The writers use an advanced story structure technique by giving the moral self-revelation to the hero's wife, Kay, who sees what he has become as the door slams in her face.

21. MORAL DECISION

Michael's great moral decision happens just before the battle when he decides to kill all of his rivals as well as his brother-in-law after becoming godfather to the man's baby.

22. NEW EQUILIBRIUM

Michael has killed his enemies and risen to the position of Godfather. But morally he has fallen and become the devil. This man who once wanted nothing to do with the violence and crime of his family is now its leader and will kill anyone who betrays him or gets in his way.

CHAPTER 9

Scene Weave

WHY ARE JANE AUSTEN and Charles Dickens such great storytellers, still delighting audiences even in this high-tech, high-speed world? For one thing, they are two of the greatest scene weavers of all time.

A scene is generally one action in one time and place. It is the basic unit of what actually happens in the story, right now, as the audience experiences it. The scene weave is the sequence of these units. To be a great storyteller, you must create a weave that is like a fine tapestry, picking up one thread for a moment before letting that thread dip back under the surface before appearing again a bit later on.

The scene weave, also known as the scene list, scene outline, or scene breakdown, is the final step before writing your full story or script. It is a list of every scene you believe will be in the final story, along with a tag for any scene in which a structure step occurs.

The scene weave is an extremely valuable step in the writing process. Like the seven steps, character web, and revelations sequence, it is a way of seeing how the story fits together beneath the surface.

The scene weave is really an extension of the plot. It is your plot in minute detail. The point of the scene weave is to get one last look at the overall architecture of the story before writing it. Therefore, don't go into too much detail, because this will hide the structure. Try to describe each scene in one line. For example, a description of four scenes in *The Godfather* might look like this:

- Michael saves the Don from assassination at the hospital.
- Michael accuses police captain McCluskey of working for Sollozzo. The Captain slugs him.
- Michael suggests that he kill the Captain and Sollozzo.
- Clemenza shows Michael how to execute Sollozzo and the Captain.

Notice that only the single essential action of each scene is listed. If you keep your description to one or two lines, you will be able to list your scene weave in a few pages. Next to the scene description, list any structure step (such as desire, plan, or apparent defeat) that is accomplished during that scene. Some scenes will have these structure tags, but many will not.

KEY POINT: Be prepared to change your scene weave when you start writing individual scenes.

When it comes to actually writing a scene, you may find that the basic action occurring in that scene is not what you thought. You will only know that for sure when you get "inside" the scene and write it. So be flexible. What's important at this point in the process is to get an overview of what you think the single main action of each scene will be.

Be aware that the average Hollywood movie has forty to seventy scenes. A novel ordinarily has twice that number and, depending on length and genre, possibly a great many more.

Your story may have subplots, or subsections, that when woven together create the plot. If you have more than one subplot or subsection, label each scene with a plotline and subsection number. This will allow you to look at the scenes of each subplot as a separate unit and make sure each subplot builds properly.

Once you have the complete scene weave before you, see if you need to make the following changes:

- *Reorder scenes.* First, focus on getting the overall sequence of the story right. Then look at the juxtapositions between individual scenes.
- *Combine scenes.* Writers often create a new scene for no other reason than to get in a good line of dialogue. Whenever possible, combine scenes so that each one is packed, but make sure each scene accomplishes essentially one action.
- *Cut or add scenes.* Always trim fat. Remember, story pacing has to do not only with the length of a scene but also with the choice of scenes. Once you have trimmed all the fat, you may find gaps in the scene weave that require a whole new scene. If so, add it to the list in the right spot.

KEY POINT: *Order the scenes by structure, not chronology.*

Most writers choose the next scene according to which action (scene) comes next in time. The result is a padded story with many useless scenes. Instead, you want to choose a scene by how it furthers the development of the hero. If it doesn't further that development or set it up in a crucial way, cut the scene.

This technique guarantees that every scene in the story is essential and in the right order. Typically, you end up with a chronological scene sequence, but not always.

KEY POINT: *Pay special attention to the* juxtaposition *of scenes.*

Especially in film and television, where the change of scene or story line is instantaneous, the juxtaposition of two scenes can be more important than what happens in any individual scene. In these juxtapositions, you want to look first at the contrast of content. In what way, if at all, does the next scene comment on the previous scene?

Then look at the contrast of proportion and pacing. Does the next scene or section have the right importance and length compared to the previous scene or section?

A good rule of thumb is this: find the line and keep the line.

There are some scenes—such as subplot scenes—that only set up the narrative drive. Go ahead and put them in. But you can never get away from the narrative line for too long without your story collapsing.

You can create powerful juxtapositions in all kinds of ways. One of the best, especially in film and television, is the juxtaposition between sight and sound. In this technique, you split these two communication tracks to create a third meaning.

M

(by Thea von Harbou and Fritz Lang, 1931)

A classic example of this technique occurs in the great German film *M*. In *M*, a child murderer buys a little girl a balloon. In the next scene, a woman prepares dinner and then calls for her child, Elsie. As she continues to call the little girl's name, the visual track splits from the sound track, and the audience sees an empty stairwell, a block of apartments, Elsie's empty chair, and her plate and spoon at the kitchen table, while the ever more desperate cries of the mother calling "Elsie!" are heard. The visual line ends with the shot of a balloon that catches in some electrical wires and then floats away. This contrast between the sound line and the visual line produces one of the most heartbreaking moments in the history of film.

Perhaps the most common technique of juxtaposition in scene weave is the crosscut. In the crosscut, you jump back and forth between two or more lines of action. This technique has two main effects:

1. It creates suspense, especially when you cut back and forth at an increasing pace, as when someone is rushing to save a victim in danger.
2. It compares two lines of action, two pieces of content, and makes them equal. This expands your thematic pattern. Anytime you jump back and forth between two lines of action, you go from a simple linear development of your story (usually of a single character) to show a deeper pattern present in the entire society.

An example of the content crosscut is a sequence in *M* in which the story goes back and forth between a group of cops and a group of criminals. Each is trying to figure out how to find the child murderer, so the crosscut shows the audience how two types of people they normally consider opposites are in many ways identical.

THE GODFATHER

(novel by Mario Puzo, screenplay by Mario Puzo and Francis Ford Coppola, 1972)

An even better example of a content crosscut occurs in the battle scene of *The Godfather*. The challenge is to create a battle scene that expresses Michael's character, what he has become as the new Godfather. By crosscutting between a number of Michael's men as they assassinate the heads of the five crime families, the writers not only provide a dense series of plot punches but also express Michael's position as a kind of corporate boss of crime. He doesn't kill these men by himself in a crime of passion. He hires men in his company who are experts at killing.

To this the writers add another crosscut, between the mass murders and Michael's renouncing of Satan as he stands as godfather to a child whose father he is about to kill. Through this crosscut, the audience sees Michael become Satan at the same moment he gains the height of his power as the Godfather.

I'd like to compare the scene weave from an early draft of *The Godfather* with the final draft. You will see how proper juxtaposition of scenes—and in this case, whole sections—can make a huge difference in the quality of the story. The key difference between these two scene weaves comes just after Michael has shot Sollozzo and Captain McCluskey in the restaurant. In the early draft, notice that the writers list all the scenes pertaining to Sonny's death and the ending of the war between the families (underlined). Then they list all the scenes of Michael in Sicily, ending with the murder of his wife (in italics).

THE GODFATHER: EARLY DRAFT

1. At a restaurant, Michael, Sollozzo, and McCluskey talk; Michael gets a gun and shoots them.
2. Montage of newspaper articles.
3. <u>Sonny finishes sex with a girl and goes to his sister Connie's house.</u>
4. <u>Sonny finds Connie with a black eye.</u>

5. <u>Sonny beats up Connie's husband, Carlo, in the street.</u>
6. Tom won't accept Kay's letter to Michael.
7. Don Corleone is brought home from the hospital.
8. Tom tells Don Corleone what happened; the Don is sad.
9. <u>Sonny and Tom argue because Sonny wants to kill old Tattaglia.</u>
10. <u>A nasty fight breaks out between Connie and Carlo; Connie calls home; Sonny is mad.</u>
11. <u>Sonny is blasted in the tollbooth.</u>
12. <u>Tom tells Don Corleone that Sonny is dead—Don Corleone says to settle the war.</u>
13. <u>Don Corleone and Tom bring Sonny's body to undertaker Bonasera.</u>
14. <u>Don Corleone makes peace with the heads of the families.</u>
15. <u>Don Corleone knows it was Barzini who was the leader.</u>
16. *In Sicily, Michael sees a pretty girl on the road and tells her father he wants to meet her.*
17. *Michael meets Apollonia.*
18. *Michael and Apollonia are wed.*
19. *Wedding night.*
20. *Michael shows Apollonia how to drive; he learns Sonny is dead.*
21. *Michael's car blows up with Apollonia driving.*

This scene sequence has a number of problems. It places the plot-heavy and more dramatic scenes of Sonny's killing and the revelation about Barzini first. So there is a big letdown when the plot moves to Sicily. Moreover, Michael in Sicily is a long and relatively slow sequence, so the overall story comes to a screeching halt, and the writers have tremendous difficulty getting the "train" started again after that section concludes. Putting all the scenes with Apollonia together also highlights the sudden and somewhat unbelievable nature of Michael's marrying a Sicilian peasant girl. The dialogue tries to gloss over this fact by saying Michael has been hit by a thunderbolt. But when the audience sees all these scenes at one time, the explanation is not convincing.

THE GODFATHER: FINAL DRAFT

In the final script, the writers overcome this potentially fatal flaw in their scene weave by crosscutting between the Sonny line and the Michael line.

1. At a restaurant, Michael, Sollozzo, and McCluskey talk; Michael gets a gun and shoots them.
2. Montage of newspaper articles.
3. Don Corleone is brought home from the hospital.
4. Tom tells Don Corleone what happened; the Don is sad.
5. <u>Sonny and Tom argue because Sonny wants to kill old Tattaglia.</u>
6. *In Sicily, Michael sees a pretty girl on the road and tells her father he wants to meet her.*
7. *Michael meets Apollonia.*
8. <u>Sonny finishes sex with a girl and goes to his sister Connie's house.</u>
9. <u>Sonny finds Connie with a black eye.</u>
10. <u>Sonny beats up Connie's husband, Carlo, in the street.</u>
11. *Michael and Apollonia are wed.*
12. *Wedding night.*
13. Tom won't accept Kay's letter to Michael.
14. <u>A nasty fight breaks out between Connie and Carlo; Connie calls home; Sonny is mad.</u>
15. <u>Sonny is blasted in the tollbooth.</u>
16. <u>Tom tells Don Corleone that Sonny is dead—Don Corleone says to settle the war.</u>
17. <u>Don Corleone and Tom bring Sonny's body to undertaker Bonasera.</u>
18. *Michael shows Apollonia how to drive; he learns Sonny is dead.*
19. *Michael's car blows up with Apollonia driving.*
20. <u>Don Corleone makes peace with the heads of the families.</u>
21. <u>Don Corleone knows it was Barzini who was the leader.</u>

By crosscutting between these two story lines, the slower Sicilian line is never onscreen long enough to kill the narrative drive of the story. Also, both lines funnel to a single point, which is the hero's apparent defeat, his lowest point in the story (see Chapter 8, "Plot"), where Sonny's murder is followed almost immediately by Apollonia's. This one-two punch is then trumped by the great reveal that Barzini was behind it all along. This revelation of Barzini as the true opponent hurtles the rest of the plot to its stunning conclusion.

Of all the techniques we've covered, scene weave is the one best understood by using a case study approach. Let's start with an easy example, from TV's *ER*, because television drama is all about weaving a rich tapestry where multiple story lines are juxtaposed.

MULTISTRAND PLOT SCENE WEAVE

The television multistrand plot crosscuts between three to five major story lines, each with its own hero. Telling this many stories in about forty-five minutes (sixty minutes minus commercials) means that no plotline can have much depth in any one episode. The writers hope to make up for that over the course of the entire season and the many seasons the show remains on the air.

KEY POINT: *In a multistrand weave, the quality of the overall story comes primarily from the juxtaposition of the plotlines. You compare what a number of people in a minisociety are facing at the same time. The audience gets to see in compressed form how lead characters use different solutions when trying to solve generally the same problem.*

KEY POINT: *With three to five plots, you can't cover the twenty-two steps for any one line, but each must cover the seven major structure steps. Anything less than the seven steps means that that line isn't a complete story, and the audience will find it unnecessary and annoying.*

KEY POINT: *With multiple main characters and so many lines, you give shape to the overall story and maintain narrative drive by* making the hero of one line the opponent of another. *This keeps the story from exploding ever outward with, for example, five heroes, five opponents, myriad minor characters, and so on.*

One of the reasons *ER* and other TV dramas use this multistrand crosscut is that it gives the episode dramatic density. There is no lull in these stories. The audience sees only the dramatic punch scenes of each plotline. In the case of *ER*, creator Michael Crichton, the greatest premise writer in Hollywood, figured out how to combine the benefits of the medical drama and the action genre in one show. To this mix, Crichton added a character web that covers a broad range of classes, races, ethnic back-grounds, nationalities, and genders. That's a very potent and popular combination.

ER: "THE DANCE WE DO"

(by Jack Orman, 2000)

The episode we want to study has five plotlines, each of which extends back and builds on a number of previous episodes:

- **Plot 1**   Abby's mother, Maggie, is visiting. She is bipolar and has a history of going off her medication, erupting, and then disappearing for long stretches.
- **Plot 2**   Dr. Elizabeth Corday is being sued and must undergo a deposition. Opposing counsel contends she botched an operation that resulted in his client's paralysis.
- **Plot 3**   Gangbangers killed Dr. Peter Benton's nephew in a previous episode. The boy's girlfriend, Kynesha, shows up at the hospital with her face badly beaten.
- **Plot 4**   Dr. Mark Greene has been keeping a secret from his girlfriend, Elizabeth (Dr. Corday), and from the other doctors. Today he finds out if his brain tumor is fatal.
- **Plot 5**   Because of a previous drug problem, Dr. Carter is required to undergo regular testing if he wants to continue working at the hospital.

The first thing you notice about this episode is that the plotlines have an underlying unity. They are all variations of the same problem. That makes the juxtapositions pay off. On the superficial level, many of these plots concern characters with a drug problem. More important, all five show different effects of lying and telling the truth.

The power of the weave of "The Dance We Do" comes from two prin-ciples of storytelling: how each plot is a variation on truth and lying and how all five stories *funnel down* to the most powerful revelation or self-revelation that the lead character and the plot are capable of.

Teaser

1. Abby's mother, Maggie, who is bipolar, finds Abby counting her pills. Abby wants to give her mother a blood test to make sure she is taking her medication. *Plot 1: weakness and need, opponent*

(Commercial)

Act 1

2. Dr. Greene assures his girlfriend, Dr. Elizabeth Corday, that she wasn't negligent and that her deposition will go fine. She tells him not to jog into any more street signs. *Plot 2: weakness and need; Plot 4: problem and need*

3. At the hospital, Maggie begs Abby not to go through with the blood test because it will just make them both feel bad. Abby reluctantly agrees. *Plot 1: desire, opponent*

4. A woman named Stephanie is looking for Dr. Malucci. Maggie rushes in saying a girl was thrown from a car. *Plot 3: weakness and need*

5. Dr. Cleo Finch, Abby, and Maggie help the injured girl, Kynesha. Abby sends her mother away. *Plot 3: weakness and need*

If you look at this scene weave in detail, you see that each plotline hits the seven steps. So each story is strong on its own. With that foundation, the writer can then play with the juxtaposition of individual scenes in different plotlines.

6. Opposing attorney Bruce Resnick is overly friendly when he meets Elizabeth at the deposition. *Plot 2: opponent*

7. Cleo tells Dr. Peter Benton he shouldn't take this patient because she is his deceased nephew's girlfriend. He takes the case. *Plot 3: ghost, desire*

8. Greene learns from his doctor he has an inoperable tumor. *Plot 4: revelation*

(Commercial)

Act 2

9. Carter corrects Greene's incorrect diagnosis. Greene reminds Carter they must do a blood and urine test on him because of Carter's drug problem. *Plot 5: weakness and need, opponent; Plot 4: desire*

10. Peter, Cleo, and Abby check to see if Kynesha was raped. She insists she was just beaten by a bunch of girls. *Plot 3: opponent*

11. In the deposition, Elizabeth says she first had to operate on the nephew of her former lover, Peter (Dr. Benton). She was upset about the boy's death when she operated on the opposing lawyer's client. *Plot 2: drive, opponent*

12. Carter jokes while Abby takes his blood. Greene isn't amused. Abby learns her mother has

In scene 10 (Plot 3), Kynesha arrives at the hospital beat up and possibly raped. She is the girlfriend of the nephew who died some time ago. In the very next scene (11, Plot 2), the attorney asks Dr. Corday if she was upset about that boy's death when she performed the operation on his client. So scene 10 (Plot 3) is a later moment of the same plotline referred to in scene 11 (Plot 2).

had a problem outside a clothing store. *Plot 5: opponent; Plot 1: revelation*

13. Kynesha won't tell Peter who beat her up. He tells her the reason his nephew was shot and killed was because he was visiting her. She says the gang killed him because he tried to get her out of the gang. *Plot 3: revelation*

14. Abby has to help her mother avoid a shoplifting charge. *Plot 1: opponent*

15. Greene says Carter hasn't been taking his medicine and it's in his contract. Carter says enough is enough. Greene collapses and convulses. *Plots 4 and 5: combining personal stories through opposition between doctors*

(Commercial)

Act 3

16. Greene wakes up and refuses Carter's request that he get a head CT. *Plot 4: drive*

17. Opposing attorney Resnick points out that Elizabeth performed the operation on his client very quickly and that she was rushing to get to a personal appointment. *Plot 2: opponent*

18. Maggie insists she was in the right. Abby tells her mother she needs stitches. *Plot 1: opponent*

Scenes 16 (Plot 4), 17 (Plot 2), and 18 (Plot 1) each show a character— Greene, Elizabeth, and Maggie—lying to others and denying the extent of a problem even to himself or herself.

19. The cops say they must hear Kynesha tell them who shot Peter's nephew or they can't arrest anyone. Kynesha won't talk to the cops. *Plot 3: opponent*

20. Greene tells Carter he has a brain tumor and he probably won't be able to work after today. *Plot 5: revelation*

In scene 20 (Plot 5), Greene finally tells someone the truth about himself. It is immediately followed by scene 21 (Plot 2), where his girlfriend, Elizabeth, is told by her lawyer that she has to hide the truth.

21. Elizabeth's lawyer tells her to keep her answers to yes or no to limit information. She says that's hiding the truth. *Plot 2: opponent*

22. Maggie flirts with Abby's boyfriend, Dr. Kovac, while he puts in the stitches. She's high. Abby apologizes. Her mother attacks her and then runs. Kovac carries her screaming to the table while Maggie begs Abby not to do this. *Plot 1: opponent*

The final scene and the dramatic funnel of Act 3, scene 22 (Plot 1), shows the terrible result of lying, of "doing the dance." At her workplace, Abby experiences the most intense public humiliation when her mother debases herself.

(Commercial)

Act 4

23. Elizabeth walks in for the final session of her deposition to find her paralyzed ex-patient sitting there in a wheelchair. Her lawyer says not to let him rattle her. *Plot 2: revelation, drive*

In Scene 23 (Plot 2), the beginning of the final act, Elizabeth has to confront the effects of her sloppy work when the patient who is suing her shows up at the deposition in his wheelchair.

24. The hospital psychologist tells Abby she will admit her mother if she wants, but Abby doesn't care. She walks away. *Plot 1: drive*

25. Peter puts Kynesha in a cab with some final advice on taking care of her injuries. She gives him the finger. *Plot 3: opponent*

26. The opposing lawyer says the anesthesiologist told Elizabeth there could be spinal fluid leaking. She lies when she insists she did a full inspection. *Plot 2: battle, audience revelation*

27. Carter tells Abby her mother took off. Abby says she disappears for four months and then returns; it's the "dance we do." *Plots 5 and 1: combining personal stories as one drug addict learns about another; Plot 1: self-revelation*

28. Kynesha tells Peter the cops came to her house and now the gang is going to kill her. Peter puts her in his car. *Plot 3: Opponent*

29. Elizabeth tells Greene it went badly. She says she lied. She rushed the operation. Greene says God owes us one. He tells her that his headaches weren't from hockey. They hug. *Plot 2: self-revelation and revelation*

At this late point in the story, the battles and the self-revelations come fast and furious, which is one of the great storytelling benefits of the multistrand technique. In the battle scene of Plot 2 (scene 26), at her deposition, Elizabeth makes her big moral decision and lies. Then Abby from Plot 1 explains to Carter, who's been lying about his own drug taking in Plot 5, how she and her mother do a never-ending dance of drugs and lying and hurting each other.

In the next-to-last scene of the episode, both Greene and Elizabeth help each other confront the negative truth.

30. Abby gets out of the bed she shares with Kovac, turns on the water in the bathroom tub and cries. *Plot 1: old equilibrium*

The final scene is a brilliant dramatic twist given to the first plotline. By beginning and ending with a Plot 1 scene, the writer frames the entire episode and helps unify all the plotlines of the story. Abby gets up in the middle of the night and turns on the bathwater so she can cry in the bathroom and not awaken her boyfriend. For these people, doing the dance they do, things will always stay the same. It's an old equilibrium, not a new one. For Abby, this realization about herself and her mother is tragic. The audience suddenly understands that real life isn't a story where people always change and grow in the end. And that hurts. This is beautiful scene weave.

SCENE WEAVE—WRITING EXERCISE 8

- **Scene List**   List every scene in your story. Try to describe the scene in one sentence.
- **Twenty-two-Step Tags**   Tag any scene that includes one of the twenty-two structure steps. If your story has more than one plotline or subsection, label each scene with the appropriate plotline.
- **Ordering Scenes**   Study the order of scenes. Make sure the scene sequence builds by structure, not chronology.
  1. See if you can cut scenes.
  2. Look for opportunities to combine two scenes into one.
  3. Add a scene wherever there are gaps in the story's development.

Because scene weave can best be understood by practicing it, I'd like to change our usual pattern of ending the chapter with a single example and look at the scene weaves of a number of stories. Of course, each scene weave is unique to that story and its requirements. But as you look at each example, notice how the different genres present various scene weave challenges that the writers must solve.

DETECTIVE OR CRIME SCENE WEAVE

L.A. CONFIDENTIAL
(novel by James Ellroy, screenplay by Brian Helgeland & Curtis Hanson, 1997)

L.A. Confidential has one of the best and most advanced scene weaves in recent years. It is shaped like a huge funnel, starting with three cop heroes in the corrupt world of the Los Angeles Police Department. Over the course of the story, the writers weave these three distinct lines into one. They keep the narrative drive moving forward by making the heroes opponents to each other as they all seek the killer at the end of the funnel.

This setup lets the writers compare, through crosscutting, the three heroes and their different approaches to crime solving and justice. It also allows them to create a dense set of reveals as the funnel tightens down to a single point.

In the following scene weave, Bud White is Hero 1, Jack Vincennes is Hero 2, Ed Exley is Hero 3, and Captain Smith is the main opponent, though he appears to be an ally.

1. As the writer of *Hush Hush* gossip magazine, Sid Hudgens does a voice-over montage about Los Angeles as a paradise but says it's only an image. Under the surface, mobster Mickey Cohen runs organized crime. Cohen has been arrested, and now the crime vacuum must be filled. *Story world*

In the opening scene, a voice-over sets up the world of the story—Los Angeles in the 1950s—and the basic thematic opposition on which the world is based—an apparent utopia that is corrupt underneath.

2. Officer Bud White arrests a parole violator for beating his wife. *Hero 1*

3. Sid agrees to pay Sgt. Jack Vincennes, technical adviser on the television show *Badge of Honor*, to arrest an actor for marijuana possession so Sid can get pictures. *Hero 2: need, fake-ally opponent*

4. Sgt. Ed Exley answers a reporter's questions about being an up-and-coming cop. Cap. Dudley Smith suggests that Ed doesn't have the stomach for detective work because Ed refuses to break the law to catch a criminal. Ed insists on being a lieutenant of detectives. *Hero 3: desire, main opponent, fake-ally opponent*

The next few scenes introduce the three heroes and the Captain, who is a fake-ally opponent:

- *Bud is a tough-guy cop who protects women (scenes 2, 5, 6). During one of his early scenes (scene 6), the writers quietly introduce the second major opponent, Patchett. But he is not acting as an opponent yet.*

- *Jack is the slick, corrupt cop who is technical adviser on a cop show and makes arrests for extra money (scenes 3, 7, 8).*

- *Ed is the young, up-and-coming star cop who insists on being legally and morally clean (scene 4).*

5. Bud is buying liquor for the office Christmas party when he meets Lynn Bracken, a Veronica Lake look-alike. *Hero 1: desire*

6. Outside, Bud roughs up Leland Meeks, an ex-cop who's the driver for Pierce Patchett. A bandaged woman who looks like Rita Hayworth tells Bud she's OK. Bud's partner Dick Stensland says he recognizes Meeks but doesn't know him. *Hero 1: opponent, story world, ally*

7. Jack arrests actor Matt Reynolds and a girl while Sid photographs them for *Hush Hush* magazine.

8. While collecting marijuana evidence in Matt's apartment, Jack finds a card for "Fleur de Lis." Sid narrates the write-up and pays him. *Hero 2: revelation*

9. Stensland tells some of the other cops at the station that they're late because Bud had to help a damsel in distress.

10. When Jack brings in Matt and the girl, he hands Ed his $10 for being watch commander. Ed refuses it. *Hero 2 vs. Hero 3: opponent*

11. Cops bring in some Mexicans for beating up two cops earlier that evening. Drunk, the cops, led by Stensland, push past Ed and beat up the Mexicans.

These early scenes lead to a watershed event that defines all three heroes and the corrupt police world. All the cops but Ed beat up some Mexican prisoners (scene 11). In this and the next few scenes, Ed becomes an opponent to both Bud and Jack (scenes 10–15).

Bud and Jack join in. *Heroes 1 and 2: opponent*

12. Bud refuses to testify about the other cops in the brawl and is suspended from duty.

13. Ed agrees to testify and suggests that the Chief nail Stensland and Bud. The Chief promotes Ed to lieutenant. Ed tells them how they can force Jack to give corroborating testimony. *Hero 3: drive, story world*

14. The Chief threatens to take Jack off the show unless he testifies. He agrees.

15. Before giving testimony, Jack asks Ed how he was paid off. He warns Ed to watch out for his fellow cops, especially Bud. *Hero 2 vs. Hero 3: opponent*

16. The Captain returns Bud's badge and gun and asks Bud to join him on a special assignment, a "muscle job," working out of homicide. *Hero 1: desire*

17. Two of Cohen's mobsters are assassinated in their car. *Opponent's plan*

18. Cohen's narcotics man is gunned down in his home. *Opponent's plan*

19. At the isolated Victory Motel, Bud beats a mobster, and the Captain tells the man it's time to get out of town. *Hero 1: drive*

From scenes 16 through 23, the story fragments into three lines that are crosscut: Bud gets a new position working as muscle for the Captain, the hidden opponent kills a number of gangsters, and Jack finds a clue that will eventually lead to one of the two main opponents.

20. In his new assignment in vice, Jack notices the "Fleur de Lis" sign on some pornography that's going around town. *Hero 2: revelation*

21. Jack tries to find out about an organization called Fleur de Lis but gets nowhere. Sid knows nothing about it. *Hero 2: drive*

22. Stensland hands in his badge and gun, says goodbye to his fellow cops, and knocks a box out of Ed's hands as he walks out.

23. Stensland tells Bud he has a confidential date that night but will have a drink with him later in the week. *Hero 3: opponent*

24. Alone at the station, Ed takes a homicide call for the Night Owl coffee shop. *Hero 3: inciting event*

25. Ed investigates the crime scene and finds a pile of bodies in the men's room. *Hero 3: desire*

26. The Captain takes over the case and makes Ed his second in command. One of the murder victims is Stensland. *Hero 3: revelation*

27. Bud finds Stensland's body in the morgue. Ed tells him what appears to have happened.

28. A woman has trouble identifying the body of her daughter because so much

Now comes the inciting event, the case in which a number of people are murdered at the Night Owl coffee shop, including Bud's ex-partner (scenes 24–26). This is the beginning of the funneling effect where the three lines are eventually woven into one. Each hero now goes after the suspects, who, again, are minorities.

about the girl has been changed. Bud recognizes her as Susan Lefferts, the woman who looked like Rita Hayworth in the car. *Hero 1: revelation*

29. The Captain tells his men that three young black men were seen shooting shotguns and driving a maroon car in the vicinity of the murders. The Chief tells the men to use whatever means necessary. *Fake-ally opponent plan; Heroes 1, 2, and 3: drive*

30. Bud goes off to investigate something on his own. Ed agrees to help Jack check a hunch. *Heroes 1, 2, and 3: drive*

31. Bud asks the liquor store owner for Susan's address. *Hero 1: drive*

32. Patchett tells Bud that the dead girl looked injured that night because she had just had plastic surgery to make her look like Rita Hayworth. Susan was part of his stable of movie star look-alikes for hire. *Hero 1: revelation*

33. Bud tells a councilman client of Lynn's to take off. She explains her deal with Patchett. Bud asks to see her again, then takes it back. *Hero 1: desire*

34. A black boxer with a brother in jail tells Jack and Ed where they can find a guy driving a maroon car. *Heroes 2 and 3: revelation*

The next few scenes represent a false drive in which all three heroes, guided by the fake-ally opponent (the Captain), go after the wrong guys (scenes 29, 30, 34–38). Again, the law enforcers are corrupt. Jack and Ed nab the suspects, and Ed shines when he does the interrogation. But his cop opponent, Bud, charges in, takes the law into his own hands, and murders the main suspect in the name of justice (scenes 37 and 38).

35. Jack and Ed find two detectives already at the maroon car. As they move in to make the arrest, Ed prevents the other two cops from shooting the three blacks.

36. The Captain tells Ed that the shells from the shotguns in the back of the maroon car are identical to those found at the murder scene. While conducting the interrogation, Ed uses the sound system to pipe information back and forth to the three suspects to get them to talk. *Hero 3: revelation*

37. Ed gets one of the men to admit to hurting a girl, and Bud barges in and threatens to kill the guy to get the address. *Heroes 1 and 3: revelation*

38. Bud enters the house first and finds a girl tied to the bed. He shoots a black man in the chest and then plants a gun to make it look like the man fired at him first. *Hero 1: drive*

39. Ed tells Bud he doesn't believe the naked guy had a gun. Bud replies that the man got justice and then tries to punch Ed. They get word that the Night Owl suspects have escaped. *Hero 1 vs. Hero 3: opposition*

40. Ed checks the transcript to see where the three black guys got their drugs and asks one of

In this section of the script, the writers avoid a fragmented story line by focusing on the opposition between heroes Bud and Ed (scene 39). Ed tracks down the escaped suspects. In the shootout, everyone is killed but him (scenes 40 and 41). A major section of the story ends with the drive apparently accomplished (scenes 42–44).

the Captain's men to help him out. *Hero 3: revelation*

41. In the shootout, everyone is killed but Ed. *Hero 3: drive*

42. The Captain and the other cops congratulate Ed on a good job and call him "Shotgun Ed."

43. Ed gets a medal for valor in the line of duty.

44. Jack receives a warm welcome on his return to the set of *Badge of Honor.*

45. Lynn sees Bud watching her from his car.

46. The councilman tells a man he won't vote for Patchett's project. The man shows the councilman photos of himself in bed with Lynn. *Opponent's plan*

The writers now bring the opponent Patchett from background to foreground with a number of scenes showing his reach in the city (scenes 46–49).

47. The councilman announces that he will vote for the project.

48. Patchett is at the opening of construction for the new Santa Monica freeway.

49. Patchett smiles as Lynn flirts with a client at one of his parties.

50. Bud is disgusted as the Captain has another mobster beaten at the Victory Motel. The Captain watches Bud drive away.

51. Bud knocks on Lynn's door, and she takes him in. They kiss on the bed. *Hero 1: drive (second)*

52. Sid pays Jack $50 to catch the DA in a rendezvous with the young actor, Matt Reynolds,

The story returns to simultaneous action lines, again crosscutting between the three heroes. The unifying element in all three lines is that each character is becoming disillusioned by his normal desire:

■ *Bud is disgusted being the Captain's muscle and falls in love with the prostitute, Lynn, who is also connected to opponent Patchett (scenes 50, 51, 53, 57).*

later that night. Matt asks Jack if they met at a "Fleur de Lis" party. Sid and Jack promise Matt a part on the show if he will go through with having sex with the DA. *Hero 2: drive*

53. Bud and Lynn take in a movie together.

54. Jack is disgusted with himself and leaves the $50 bill Sid paid him on the bar. *Hero 2: self-revelation, moral decision*

55. Jack finds Matt already dead at the motel. *Hero 2: revelation*

56. The rape victim tells Ed she lied about when the three black men left her that night. *Hero 3: revelation*

57. In bed, Lynn tells Bud she is going back to her hometown to open a dress shop in a couple of years. He tells her he got his scar by trying to save his mother, but his father beat her to death. Bud wants to leave strong-arm stuff and work homicide. He suspects something is wrong with the Night Owl case. Lynn says he's smart enough. *Hero 1: ghost, desire (new)*

58. Bud checks the photos of the Night Owl evidence. He recalls that both Stensland and Susan were killed there. *Hero 1: revelation*

59. Susan's mother identifies Stensland as her daughter's

- Jack gets a young actor killed by helping Sid set up a sexual rendezvous between the actor and the DA (scenes 52, 54, 55).
- Ed realizes he killed the wrong guys in the Night Owl case (scenes 56, 60).

From this point on, the story gains focus and narrative drive as the heroes pursue the real killer in the case. At first, each hero searches separately, using his own techniques and for his own reasons of redemption (scenes 58–62).

boyfriend. Bud checks a bad smell and finds Meeks's corpse under the house. *Hero 1: revelation*

60. Ed is troubled about the Night Owl case and finds out Bud was asking about it that morning. *Hero 3: revelation*

61. Ed learns from Susan's mother that Bud already checked under the house. *Hero 3: revelation*

62. Ed delivers the body to the morgue and tells them to speak only to him.

63. Ed asks Jack to tail Bud because he can't trust any other cop in homicide. He explains that "Rolo Tomasi" was the name he gave to the man who killed his cop father and got away with it. It's why Ed became a cop, but he's lost sight of justice. Jack says he can't remember why he became a cop. He agrees to help Ed with the Night Owl case if Ed will help him solve Matt's murder. *Heroes 2 and 3: ghost, desire, self-revelation, moral decision*

64. Mobster Johnny Stompanato tells Bud that Meeks supposedly had a large supply of heroin but skipped out. Jack watches them. *Hero 1: revelation*

65. Jack and Ed see Bud kissing Lynn in her apartment. *Hero 2 and 3: revelation*

The funneling picks up speed when Ed and Jack team up (scene 63). This section includes the moment when Ed has sex with Bud's girlfriend, Lynn (scene 72). The fire of opposition between these two men intensifies.

66. Jack tells Ed all the strands are connected to "Fleur de Lis."

67. Ed tries to question Stompanato. He mistakes the real Lana Turner for a look-alike whore. *Hero 2 and 3: drive*

68. Jack and Ed question Patchett about Matt and why Bud is seeing Lynn, but he says nothing.

69. When Ed and Jack leave, Patchett calls Sid. *Opponent's plan*

70. The coroner tells Jack that the dead man was Meeks. *Hero 2: revelation*

71. Jack asks to see Meeks's arrest records when he worked vice.

72. Lynn tells Ed she likes Bud for all the reasons he isn't like Ed, a political animal who will screw himself to get ahead. Ed starts kissing her. She moves so Sid can get good photographs of them having sex. *Hero 3: desire (second)*

73. Jack goes to the Captain's home. He noticed that some years ago the Captain supervised a case where Stensland and Meeks investigated Patchett. The Captain shoots Jack. Jack's last words are "Rolo Tomasi." *Fake-ally opponent attack; Hero 2: revelation*

74. The Captain tells the squad to hunt mercilessly for Jack's killer. The Captain asks Ed

By meticulously setting up the story world and creating three apparently distinct story lines at the beginning, the writers are now able to hit the audience with a series of revelations. The teamwork between Ed and Jack ends with the biggest revelation of all, an audience stunner: the Captain murders Jack (scene 73).

about an associate of Jack's, Rolo Tomasi. *Fake-ally opponent plan; Hero 3: revelation*

75. The Captain wants Bud to join him at the Victory Motel to help break the man who may have killed Jack.

76. The coroner tells Ed that he told Jack the body was that of ex-cop Meeks. *Hero 3: revelation*

77. The Captain questions Sid about Jack and Patchett while Bud punches him. When Sid says he photographed Lynn screwing a cop, Bud goes nuts, grabs the photos, and takes off. *Fake-ally opponent attack; Hero 1: revelation*

78. The Captain moves in for the kill as Sid pleads that he, Patchett, and the Captain are a team. *Audience revelation*

79. Ed asks a clerk to find the daily report books that will list who Meeks arrested when he was a vice cop.

80. Lynn tells Bud she thought she was helping him when she slept with Ed. Bud punches her. *Hero 1: opponent*

81. Ed sees on the daily log that Meeks and Stensland reported to the Captain. Bud beats Ed. Ed pulls a gun and tells him the Captain killed Jack and wants Bud to kill him. Bud thinks Stensland killed Meeks

Bud and Ed search separately for a little longer until they have a minibattle, after which they agree to work together (scene 81). This team drives the rest of the story.

over heroin. Ed explains that Dudley's cops must have framed the three blacks, and somehow it's all connected to Patchett. *Hero 3: revelation; Hero 1 vs. Hero 3: opposition*

82. Ed tells the DA he wants the Captain and Patchett investigated. When the DA refuses, Bud shoves his head in the toilet and hangs him out the window. The DA confesses that the Captain and Patchett are taking over Cohen's rackets, but the DA was unable to prosecute because they had incriminating pictures of him. *Opponent; Heroes 1 and 3: revelation*

83. Ed and Bud find Patchett dead next to a fake suicide note. *Heroes 1 and 3: revelation*

84. Ed has local cops take Lynn to the station under an assumed name to protect her from the Captain.

85. Lynn tells Ed she doesn't know anything about the Captain.

86. Bud finds Sid dead in his office. He gets word from Ed to meet him at the Victory Motel. *Hero 1: revelation*

87. When Bud arrives, he and Ed realize they've been set up. In a shootout, Bud and Ed kill a number of the Captain's men. Bud drops under the floorboards of the house. Ed is

More revelations funnel the two leads into a battle with the Captain and his men that ends with Ed shooting the Captain in the back (scene 87).

hit. Two men come in to finish him off when Bud rises from the floor and kills them. The Captain shoots Bud twice. Ed calls the Captain Rolo Tomasi, the guy who gets away with it. Bud stabs the Captain's leg. The Captain shoots Bud again, but Ed draws a shotgun on him. The Captain promises Ed he'll be chief of detectives if Ed arrests him and doesn't kill him. Sirens approach. Ed shoots the Captain in the back. *Heroes 1 and 3: revelation, battle; Hero 3: self-revelation, moral decision*

88. In interrogation, Ed explains that the Captain was behind the murders of Susan, Patchett, Sid, and Jack and was taking over crime in Los Angeles. Outside the room, the DA tells the Chief that they may save the department's reputation by turning the Captain into a hero. Ed tells them they'll need more than one hero to make it work. *Story world*

89. The Chief presents Ed with another medal. Lynn watches from the back.

90. Ed thanks Bud, who's bandaged heavily in the back seat of Lynn's car, and says goodbye to Lynn. She drives away, back to her hometown. *New equilibrium, Heroes 1 and 3*

Ever the politician, Ed turns this murder into another medal for himself (scene 89). He says goodbye to his polar opposite, Bud, the simple guy who goes off to live in a small town with Lynn (scene 90).

CROSSCUT SCENE WEAVE

THE EMPIRE STRIKES BACK

(story by George Lucas, screenplay by Leigh Brackett and Lawrence Kasdan, 1980)

The Empire Strikes Back is a textbook example of the crosscut weave. To see why the writers might want to use this approach for such a large part of the plot (scenes 25–58), you have to look at the structural requirements of the story. First, *The Empire Strikes Back* is the middle episode of a trilogy that begins with *Star Wars* and ends with *The Return of the Jedi*, so it lacks the opening focus of the first episode, when the main character is introduced, and the closing focus of the third episode, when everything converges in the final battle. The crosscut strategy allows the writers to use the middle story to expand the trilogy to the widest possible scope, in this case, the universe. But they still have to keep narrative drive. And that's made even trickier by the fact that this is a middle episode of a trilogy that must somehow stand on its own.

The crosscut's deepest capability is to compare content, by juxtaposing characters or lines of action. That doesn't happen here. But the film does take advantage of the *plot* capabilities of the crosscut, which are to increase suspense, set up cliffhangers, and jam more action into the limited time a movie has.

The most important reason the writers use the crosscut scene weave here has to do with the hero's development, as it should. In *The Empire Strikes Back*, Luke must undergo extensive training in the ways of "the Force" if he is to become a Jedi Knight and defeat the evil Empire. But that poses a big problem for the writers. Training is only one structure step, and it isn't even one of the crucial twenty-two steps. So making the long training sequence part of a linear scene weave—tracking only Luke—would have stopped the plot in its tracks. By crosscutting Luke's training scenes (listed here in italics) with the big action scenes of Han Solo, Princess Leia, and Chewbacca escaping Darth Vader's men (listed here underlined), the writers are able to give Luke's training and his character development the time they need without the plot grinding to a halt.

1. Luke and Han patrol the ice planet of Hoth. An ice beast knocks Luke off his tauntaun and drags him away. *Problem*
2. Han returns to the rebel base. Chewbacca repairs the *Falcon*. *Allies*
3. Han requests a dismissal to pay off a huge debt to Jabba the Hutt. Han says goodbye to Leia. *Allies*
4. Leia and Han argue about their imagined and true feelings for each other.
5. C-3PO and R2-D2 report that Luke is still missing. Han requests a report from the deck officer. *Allies*
6. Despite the deck officer's warnings of fatal freezing levels, Han vows to search for Luke.
7. Luke escapes from the ice beast's lair.
8. C-3PO and R2-D2 worry about Luke at the rebel base.
9. Luke struggles to stay alive in the freezing cold. Han searches for him. *Visit to death*
10. Leia reluctantly agrees to close the time-locked doors of the base. Chewbacca and the droids fear for Han and Luke.
11. Obi-Wan Kenobi instructs Luke to seek training from Yoda. Han arrives to save Luke. *Inciting event*
12. Small rebel fighter planes search for Luke and Han and find them.
13. Luke thanks Han for saving his life. Han and Leia continue their romantic sparring.
14. The general reports a strange signal coming from a new probe on the planet. Han decides to check it out.
15. Han and Chewbacca destroy the imperial probe droid. The general decides to evacuate the planet. *Revelation*
16. Darth Vader learns about the report from Hoth. He orders an invasion. *Opponent*
17. Han and Chewbacca repair the *Falcon*. Luke says goodbye to them.
18. The rebel general learns of approaching imperial forces. The general deploys an energy shield for protection.
19. Vader kills the hesitant admiral and orders a ground attack of Hoth. *Opponent's plan and attack*
20. Imperial forces attack the rebel base. Luke and his team of flyers fight back. *Battle*

21. Han and Chewbacca argue as they repair the *Falcon*. C-3PO says goodbye to R2-D2, who will accompany Luke.

22. Luke's fighter plane crashes. He escapes the walker just before it destroys his plane. *Battle*

23. Han orders Leia to board the last transport ship before it leaves. Imperial forces enter the base.

24. Luke blows up an imperial walker while another walker destroys the main power generator.

25. Han, Leia, and C-3PO are cut off from the transport ship. They now run to the *Falcon*.

26. Vader and the imperial forces enter the rebel base. The *Falcon* escapes.

27. *Luke and R2-D2 escape from Hoth. Luke informs R2-D2 that they will be traveling to Dagobah. Desire*

28. With TIE fighters chasing them, Han tries in vain to implement hyperdrive. Han steers the *Falcon* into an asteroid field.

29. *Luke lands in a barren, desolate Dagobah swamp. Plan*

30. Vader orders the imperial fleet to follow the *Falcon* into the asteroid field.

31. C-3PO works on the hyperdrive function. Han and Leia continue their romantic sparring.

32. *Yoda finds Luke but hides his own identity. Yoda promises to bring Luke to Yoda. Ally*

33. C-3PO discovers the hyperdrive malfunction. Han and Leia finally kiss.

34. The emperor announces that Luke Skywalker is their new enemy. Vader vows to turn Luke over to the Dark Side. *Opponent's plan*

35. *Yoda reveals himself to Luke as the Jedi master. Yoda worries about Luke's impatience and his commitment. Revelation*

36. TIE fighters search for the *Falcon* in the asteroid field.

37. Han, Leia, and Chewbacca search for life outside the *Falcon*. Han flies the *Falcon* out of a giant serpent. *Revelation, opponent*

38. *Luke trains with Yoda in the swamp. Luke leaves him to face a strange challenge from the Force. Need, drive*

39. *Luke enters a cave and fights with the specter of Darth Vader. Luke cuts off the specter's head and sees his own face. Need, revelation*

40. Vader instructs bounty hunters to search for the *Falcon*. The admiral announces that they have found the *Falcon*.

41. TIE fighters chase the *Falcon* out of the asteroid field. Han flies the *Falcon* directly toward the star cruiser.

42. The admiral watches the *Falcon* fly directly toward the cruiser. The radar man loses the *Falcon* on the radar screen.

43. *Luke continues his training. He fails to raise his X-wing fighter from the swamp. Yoda raises it with little trouble. Apparent defeat*

44. Vader kills another admiral for his blunder and promotes another officer.

45. The *Falcon* hides in the star cruiser's garbage chute. Han decides to make repairs at Lando Calrissian's mining colony.

46. *Luke foresees Han and Leia in pain in a city in the clouds. Luke wants to save them. Revelation*

47. Han has trouble landing in Lando's colony. Leia worries about Han's troubled past with Lando.

48. Lando greets Han and the others. They discuss their stormy history. A hidden stormtrooper blows C-3PO apart. *Fake-ally opponent*

49. *Yoda and Kenobi plead with Luke not to stop his training. Luke promises to return after he saves his friends. Attack by ally*

50. The *Falcon* is almost repaired. Leia worries about missing C-3PO.

51. Chewbacca finds C-3PO in the junk pile. Lando flirts with Leia.

52. Lando explains his operations to Han and Leia. Lando leads the unwitting pair to Darth Vader.

53. *Luke nears the mining colony. Drive*

54. In a jail cell, Chewbacca repairs C-3PO.

55. Vader promises to give Han's body to the bounty hunter. Lando complains about the changes to their deal. *Opponent's plan and attack*

56. Lando explains the arrangement to Han and Leia. Han hits Lando. Lando claims that he did what he could.

57. Vader inspects a carbon-freezing cell meant for Luke. Vader promises to test it on Han first. *Opponent's plan*

58. *Luke approaches the colony.*

59. Vader prepares to freeze Han. Leia tells Han that she loves him. Han survives the freezing process. *Opponent's attack*

60. Luke battles stormtroopers. Leia warns Luke about the trap. Luke explores a passageway.

61. Luke finds Vader in the carbon-freezing chamber. They battle with their light sabers. *Battle*

62. Lando's men free Leia, Chewbacca, and C-3PO. Lando tries to explain his predicament. They rush to save Han.

63. The bounty hunter loads Han's body into his spaceship and leaves. The rebels fight the imperial soldiers.

64. Luke and Vader continue their battle. Luke escapes the freezing chamber. Pressurized air sucks Luke into an airshaft. *Battle*

65. Lando and the others head for the *Falcon*. He orders an evacuation of the city. They escape in the *Falcon*.

66. Luke fights Vader on the airshaft walkway. Vader reveals that he is Luke's father. Luke rejects the Dark Side and falls. *Battle and self-revelation*

67. Leia feels Luke's cry for help. Chewbacca flies the *Falcon* back to the colony to rescue Luke. TIE fighters approach.

68. The admiral confirms that he deactivated the hyperdrive in the *Falcon*. Vader prepares to intercept the *Falcon*.

69. Luke wonders why Kenobi never told him about his father. R2-D2 repairs the hyperdrive. The *Falcon* escapes.

70. Vader watches the *Falcon* disappear.

71. Lando and Chewbacca promise to save Han from Jabba the Hutt. Luke, Leia, and the droids watch them leave. *New equilibrium*

LOVE STORY SCENE WEAVE

PRIDE AND PREJUDICE

(novel by Jane Austen, 1813; screenplay by Aldous Huxley and Jane Murphin, 1940)

1. Writing on screen: "It happened in old England in the village of Meryton." *Story world*
2. While shopping, Mother and two of her daughters, Lizzy and Jane, find out that the new arrivals in town are the rich Mr. Bingley and his sister, along with the even richer Mr. Darcy. *Inciting event, desire, main opponent*
3. Mother tells the girls they must hurry home to send Father over to meet the Bingleys before the other fathers get there.
4. Mother rounds up her other daughters: the bookish Mary, and Lydia and Kitty, who are with two officers, one of whom is Mr. Wickham. *Allies, subplots 2, 3, and 4*
5. The carriage with Mother and all the girls passes Mrs. Lucas's carriage as the two matrons rush to make their daughters' availability known. *Minor opponent*
6. Mother insists that Father, Mr. Bennet, call on Mr. Bingley right away so he can meet their

In the first scene after the title, the writers get right to the desire: to find a husband. This gives the story a line on which the writers can then describe the story world (scenes 3–6).

daughters. Father reminds her that his estate must pass to a male heir, their cousin Mr. Collins. He also says he met Mr. Bingley last week and has already invited him to the upcoming ball. *Story world*

7. At the ball, Wickham flirts with Lizzy. *Fake-ally opponent*

8. When Darcy, Bingley, and Miss Bingley arrive, Lizzy calls Darcy supercilious. While dancing, Bingley is impressed with Jane's kindness. *Subplot 1: desire*

9. While Lydia and Kitty drink with Wickham and the other officer, Miss Bingley tells Jane her fear of being marooned out here in the wilderness. *Second opponent*

10. Lizzy and her best friend, Charlotte Lucas, overhear Darcy talk about how low-class the local girls are and how Bingley has latched on to the only pretty one. Darcy doesn't want to deal with Lizzy's provincial wit or her insufferable mother. *Revelation, Subplot 5*

11. Lizzy refuses Darcy's offer to dance and instead dances with Wickham, with whom Darcy does not get along. *Opponent*

12. Everyone is excited that Jane is going to Netherfield Park to have lunch with Bingley. Mother gives her advice on how to act.

At the ball (scenes 7–11), it's back to setting up the main spine of the love story between the heroine, Lizzy, and Darcy. But by giving the family five daughters, the writers also interweave five subplots (four sisters and Charlotte) to compare women and how they find a husband. A similar technique is used in The Philadelphia Story *when one woman must choose from three different suitors. The five subplots give the story tremendous density and texture while still being entertaining. In fact, the subplots are a big part of what delights the audience in this film. They like having little story moments for each of the minor characters that play off the same problem facing the main characters.*

There's another big advantage to this scene weave: setting up the story world, the hero's line, and the five subplots will provide the writers a dense succession of reveals later on. Having this many reveals is rare, and welcome, in a love story form that often lacks plot. Best of all (for the audience), the use of the five daughters, and the subplot for each, enables the writers to end this comedic love story

13. Mother makes Jane change clothes and take a horse so that if it rains, she'll have to stay the night. *Subplot 1: drive*

14. Jane rides in the heavy rain.

15. Jane and Bingley are delighted when the doctor says her cold will require her to stay at Bingley's home for a week. Miss Bingley is shocked that Lizzy has walked to the house and come alone, but Darcy disagrees.

16. Lydia and Kitty want to go to the village while Mother practices singing, and Father jokes about sending all the girls over to the Bingley house.

17. Darcy and Miss Bingley don't feel that most women are accomplished, but Lizzy disagrees. Miss Bingley suggests that she and Lizzy walk about the room, and Darcy makes a witty comment about not joining them. *Opponent*

18. Dull Mr. Collins tells Mother his patron, Lady Catherine de Bourgh, has advised him to marry. When he suggests Jane, Mother says she is practically engaged, so Mr. Collins turns his attentions to Lizzy. *Third opponent, second suitor*

19. There is an invitation from Bingley to a garden party at his home at Netherfield Park.

20. At the party, Collins chases

with not just one marriage but several, including a bad one.

In the early setup of the story world, the writers explain the logic on which this system is based: property goes to the male heir, so women must marry and marry well. This logic shapes every plotline in the story. So the writers come up with a number of different characters to compare. With Miss Bingley and Charlotte, the hero's opponent and ally, the writers compare the women. With Mr. Wickham and Mr. Collins, they compare the suitors. Notice that the comparisons begin at the first party (scenes 7–11).

The party is also where the writers introduce a strong initial opposition between the eventual lovers, Lizzy and Darcy (scenes 8, 10, 11). But instead of playing it out, they put that line on hold and play out Subplot 1, between sister Jane and Mr. Bingley (scenes 12–15). By going to the subplot, the writers allow Lizzy to spend more time getting to know Darcy yet still maintain the opposition she has with him (scene 17).

Enter the line of the second competing suitor, Mr. Collins, who is also an opponent to the whole family, since he will inherit their estate (scene 18). He is a stuffy fool, which highlights the central conflict within Lizzy and the other women in this world, which is the need to marry well (even if he's dull) versus the desire to marry for love.

after Lizzy. At Lizzy's urging, Darcy sends him off in the wrong direction. *Third opponent*

21. Darcy gives Lizzy an archery lesson only to find that she is much better than he is. Referring to Wickham, Lizzy asks Darcy what he would think of a wealthy, good-looking man who would refuse to accept an introduction from a man who was poor. Darcy says a gentleman would not have to explain his actions. *Opponent*

22. Back at the main house, Lizzy finds Mary singing badly in front of everyone. Miss Bingley sarcastically compliments Lizzy on her family. *Revelation, second opponent*

23. Darcy finds Lizzy crying on the veranda and admires her loyalty to Wickham. But when she and Darcy overhear Mother say that Jane is sure to marry Bingley, Darcy leaves and Lizzy calls him condescending for failing her at the first test of loyalty. *Opponent, revelation*

24. Mr. Collins proposes to Lizzy. She says no, but he thinks she means yes. *Revelation*

25. Mother wants Father to convince Lizzy, but he doesn't want her to marry Mr. Collins.

26. Mother opens Bingley's letter to Jane and is devastated to

The second party (scenes 20–23) allows the writers to bring together in one tight knot a number of lines: Darcy along with the competing suitors of Wickham and Mr. Collins; a moral argument between Lizzy and Darcy; Subplot 1 with Jane and Bingley; the female opponent, Miss Bingley; and the subplots with Lizzy's sisters that become an opposition as they embarrass her in front of Darcy. These are all-important combining scenes where the community and all the characters are together.

The Subplot 1 breakup between Bingley and Jane (scenes 26, 28) is

learn that Bingley and Darcy have gone to London. Jane cries. *Revelation*

27. Wickham tells Lizzy that he was intended for the church, but that Darcy disregarded his own father's will and kept Wickham from his annuity. *False revelation*

28. Lizzy finds Jane crying because a letter from Miss Bingley says that Bingley will be seeing another woman. *Revelation*

29. When Mrs. Lucas and Charlotte arrive with news that Charlotte will marry Mr. Collins, Mother is angry that Charlotte will become the lady of this house. *Subplot 5: revelation*

30. Lizzy begs Charlotte to hold off the marriage for a time, but Charlotte refuses.

31. After Charlotte and Mr. Collins are married, Lizzy visits. Lady Catherine arrives. *Fake-opponent ally*

32. Lady Catherine gives Collins orders. She is very harsh, and Charlotte is afraid of her.

33. Darcy joins them for dinner. Lady Catherine is shocked at how Lizzy and her sisters have been raised.

34. As Lizzy plays piano, Lady Catherine suggests to Darcy that it is fated that he and her daughter, Anne, will be together.

followed by another apparent defeat for Lizzy (scene 29): the marriage between her best friend and ally, Charlotte, and the second suitor, the foolish Mr. Collins (Subplot 5).

35. Lizzy angrily tells Charlotte that Bingley left Jane because Darcy wanted to save him from an impossible marriage.

36. Darcy asks Lizzy to marry him, even though her family is unsuitable. Lizzy refuses him due to his haughty manner, his treatment of Wickham, and the fact that he has destroyed the happiness of her sister. *Revelation, breakup*

37. Lizzy returns to find out from Jane that Lydia has run off with Wickham and that they are not married. Father has gone to London to look for them. Darcy arrives. *Revelation, subplot 2*

38. Darcy tells Lizzy that Wickham did this to his own sister. He offers to help, but she says all is being done, so he leaves. Lizzy tells Jane she now realizes she loves Darcy. *Revelation, partial self-revelation*

39. Miss Bingley happily reads a letter saying that Lydia has not been found and that Mr. Bennet has given up the search. Bingley is upset by the news.

40. The family is getting ready to move. Father gets word that their uncle has found Lydia and that Wickham has asked for surprisingly little money. *Revelation*

41. Lydia and Wickham arrive and

Next is the surprising revelation: Darcy expresses his love for Lizzy and proposes (scene 36). This is followed by a breakup (although the relationship never connected in the first place) because both characters still suffer from their psychological and moral weaknesses of pride and prejudice. The weave concludes with a dense series of reveals beginning with the audience revelation that Wickham is really an opponent (scene 37), the revelation that Darcy is good (scene 38), the hero's revelation that she loves Darcy (scene 38), the Subplot 2 marriage between Wickham and sister Lydia (scene 41), the Subplot 1 "marriage" between Jane and Bingley (scene 45), the hero's "marriage" to Darcy (scene 45), and the promise of marriage for the daughters of Subplots 3 and 4 (scene 47). This is the cyclonic series of revelations I mentioned when I talked about the plot in Tootsie. *This kind of plot density is rare in love stories and is a big plus for the audience.*

announce they are married.
Wickham says his new wealth
is due to the death of his
uncle. *Revelation*

42. Lizzy refuses to promise Lady
Catherine that she won't marry
Darcy and doesn't care if Lady
Catherine were to strip Darcy of
his inheritance. Lady Catherine
informs Lizzy of what Darcy
did for her sister. *Revelation*

43. Outside, Lady Catherine tells
Darcy of Lizzy's comments. She
agrees that Lizzy is right for
him because he needs someone
to stand up to him. Darcy is
overjoyed. *Audience revelation*

44. Darcy enters the house with
news of Bingley.

45. In the garden, Darcy and Lizzy
spot Bingley kissing Jane's
hand. Lizzy realizes how she
has misjudged Darcy, but he
says he is the one who should
be ashamed for his arrogance.
He asks her again to marry,
and they kiss. *Subplot 1: self-
revelations, double reversal*

46. At the window, Mother shows
Father that Lizzy and Darcy
are kissing and imagines the
10,000 pounds a year Lizzy
will have while poor Jane will
have to make do with only
5,000. *New equilibrium*

47. In the next room, Kitty flirts
with one man while Mary

sings, accompanied by a man
playing the flute. Mother is excited
that three daughters are married
and two are tottering on the brink.
*Subplots 3 and 4: marriages, new
equilibrium*

SOCIAL FANTASY SCENE WEAVE

IT'S A WONDERFUL LIFE

*(short story "The Greatest Gift" by Philip Van Doren Stern, screenplay by
Frances Goodrich & Albert Hackett and Frank Capra, 1946)*

1. The whole town is praying.
   Two angels call in a low-level
   angel, Clarence, to help George.
   If he succeeds, Clarence can get
   his own wings. *Ghost, story
   world, weakness and need*
2. As a boy in 1919, George saves
   his younger brother, Harry,
   from falling through the ice.
   Story world
3. Young George works at
   Gower's drugstore. Violet and
   Mary are there. George reads
   that Gower's son died. Gower
   tells George to bring pills, but
   George sees they're poison.
   Story world
4. George tries to ask advice
   from his dad, but he's busy
   asking Potter for more time
   for people to pay their
   mortgages. George argues
   with Potter. *Main opponent*

The writers start with a narrator (an
angel) in the sky talking about a crisis
moment for the hero (scene 1). This
allows them to present the entire arena
of the story, the town, and begin with
some dramatic intensity. This also gives
the writers permission to go back and
explain the hero's past because they have
promised that the audience will be
rewarded with high drama later on (the
suicide). Most important of all, it sets up
the fantasy payoff at the end of the story
when George gets to see what the town
would be like if he had never lived.

This umbrella opening—
encapsulating the entire town—is
followed by a series of scenes of the hero
as a boy (scenes 2–5). They define not
only the hero's essential character but
also the character of the key
inhabitants of the town. The childhood
scenes also set up the intricate web of
connections of both character and

5. Gower slaps George, but George explains Gower's mistake.

6. It is 1928. The adult George gets a free suitcase from Gower for his trip. *Desire*

7. On the street, George says hi to cop Bert, cab driver Ernie, and to Violet. *Allies*

8. George and Harry have fun before dinner. George tells his father he doesn't want to work at the Building and Loan. *Ghost, story world*

9. At Harry's graduation dance, George sees Sam and meets a grown-up and very pretty Mary. They dance, and fall into the pool. *Desire (second)*

10. George and Mary walk home together, sing, and throw rocks at an old house on Sycamore. George is about to kiss Mary when she loses her robe and has to hide naked in the bushes. George finds out his father has had a stroke. *Desire 1 and 2, plan*

11. At a board meeting, Potter wants to close the Building and Loan. George stands up for it. George learns that the Building and Loan can stay if he runs it. *Opponent, revelation, desire and plan 1 derailed*

12. George and Uncle Billy pick up Harry at the train station. Harry shows up with a wife and a job offer. *Revelation*

action that the writers will pay off in the last part of the story.

The scene weave then jumps to the hero as an adult, clearly stating his desire line to leave town and see the world (scene 6). Many of the minor characters now appear as adults (scenes 7–9), and the audience sees how these people are essentially the same as they were when they were kids.

Next is a sequence in which each scene plays out the same pattern: (1) the hero states his desire to go, (2) frustration keeps him in town, and (3) a second conflicting desire ties him even more tightly to the town. For example:

- George wants to leave town, but his father dies and he has to run the Building and Loan (scenes 10 and 11).

- He is about to leave, but brother Harry comes home married with a great job offer in another town (scenes 12 and 13).

- George falls in love with Mary, helps the town get through the Depression, fights off Potter, builds Bailey Park, and has children (scenes 15–25).

13. On the porch, George sits with Uncle Billy. His mother suggests he see Mary.

14. On the street, George runs into Violet, but she doesn't want to walk in the woods.

15. George reluctantly enters Mary's house. They argue. Sam calls. George suggests he build his factory in Bedford Falls. George kisses Mary. *Revelation*

16. George and Mary wed.

17. In a cab on the way to their honeymoon, they see a run on the bank. At the Building and Loan, Uncle Billy says the bank called their loan. Potter offers George's customers 50 cents on the dollar. George pleads with people not to take Potter's offer. Each takes a little of George's personal money instead. *Revelation, drive*

18. George and the others celebrate the $2 they have left at end of the day. He gets a call from Mary to meet her at Sycamore.

19. Bert and Ernie are putting posters on the old house. Mary has fixed up the place. *Revelation*

20. George helps the Martini family move out of the Potter's Field slum and into a new house in Bailey Park. *Plan 2*

21. The tax collector tells Potter he's losing business to George.

22. George and Mary say hi to rich Sam and his wife.

23. Potter offers George a job at $20,000 a year. George, at first delighted, says no. *Revelation*

24. George thinks of Potter's offer and his dreams. Mary says she's pregnant. *Revelation*

25. Montage of more babies, fixing the house, George discouraged, war, men fighting. Harry is a hero and saves a ship. George is an air raid warden. *Drive (losing)*

26. This morning, George hands out newspapers of Harry winning the Medal of Honor. He talks on the phone to Harry in Washington, D.C. The bank examiner arrives to check the books.

27. Over at the bank, Uncle Billy is depositing $8,000 when he goads Potter. Uncle Billy accidentally hands the money to Potter. *Audience revelation*

28. At the Building and Loan, George helps Violet with money. Uncle Billy says he's lost the $8,000. *Revelation, fake-ally opponent*

29. George and Uncle Billy look for the money on the street.

30. At Uncle Billy's, George is desperate. He says one of them will go to prison, and it won't be him.

31. At home, George snaps at the kids, learns that daughter

Now the weave does something unique: after a sequence of scenes covering almost three decades, the writers go through a series of scenes that cover one day (scenes 26–34). These are the events that lead up to the crisis referred to in the opening scene, George's suicide. The scenes conclude at the moment the angel's voice-over began, where the writers deliver on the promised excitement of the opening (scene 34).

Zuzu is sick, visits her, tells off her teacher on the phone, and then tells off the teacher's husband. George smashes things and leaves. Mary calls Uncle Billy. *Attack by ally*

32. George begs Potter for help. Potter suggests he ask his friends. George has no collateral but his life insurance policy. *Drive*

33. At Martini's, the teacher's husband slugs George after George prays for help.

34. George smashes his car into a tree. He walks onto a bridge. He's about to commit suicide when a man jumps in. George dives in and saves him. *Apparent defeat, revelation*

35. In the toll keeper's house, Clarence says he's an angel who saved George. Clarence can win his wings by helping George. He realizes he can show George what it would have been like if George hadn't been born. George notices his lip is not bleeding, his bad ear is good, and his clothes are dry. *Revelation*

36. George can't find his car by the tree. *Gauntlet, revelation*

37. Martini's is now Nick's bar. Nick is about to toss George and Clarence out. George sees a bum. It's Mr. Gower, who was in jail for twenty years for poisoning a kid. Nick tosses

Next comes the key scene sequence of the story: Clarence will show George an alternative present and an alternative town as they would be had George never lived (scenes 35–42). This is where investing time to set up the story world—George's connection to the townspeople—pays off.

The writers present a series of reveals in which George sees all the minor characters in their most negative form (scenes 37, 39, 40, 42). He and the audience also see the web of connections that George has made, and it's quite a web.

them out in the snow.
Gauntlet, revelation

38. Outside, George calls Clarence screwy. He goes off to see Mary.

39. George runs through ugly Pottersville. Violet is a tramp, Ernie is a bitter cab driver. George's place on Sycamore is a ghost house. George fights Bert the cop and runs. *Gauntlet, revelation*

40. George's mother is old and suspicious of him. She says Uncle Billy is crazy. *Gauntlet, revelation*

41. George visits Bailey Park, now a cemetery. He sees Harry's grave. *Visit to death*

42. At the library, George tries to talk to Mary, who's a spinster, but she flees, terrified. George runs as Bert shoots. *Battle*

43. Back at the bridge, George begs to live again. Bert arrives and recognizes him as George. George is ecstatic. He still has Zuzu's flower. *Self-revelation*

44. George happily runs through Bedford Falls. *Revelation*

45. At home, the sheriff is waiting. George embraces Mary and the kids. Friends come in with a basket of money. Harry arrives. A bell rings, and George congratulates Clarence on winning his wings. *New equilibrium, new community*

The story ends with George back in the actual present, but now happy in spite of the fact that he has still lost all that money. George's web of connections pays off again when the town comes to his rescue (scenes 43–45).

This is a scene weave that makes the most of the big social contrasts on which social fantasy is based. The overall sequence is dense, and the juxtaposition of scenes is excellent.

CHAPTER 10

Scene Construction and Symphonic Dialogue

S CENES ARE WHERE the action is—literally. Using description and dialogue, you translate all the elements of premise, structure, character, moral argument, story world, symbol, plot, and scene weave into the story the audience actually experiences. This is where you make the story come alive.

A scene is defined as one action in one time and place. But what is a scene made of? How does it work?

A scene is a ministory. This means that a good scene has six of the seven structure steps: the exception is self-revelation, which is reserved for the hero near the end of the story. The self-revelation step within a scene is usually replaced by some twist, surprise, or reveal.

CONSTRUCTING THE SCENE

To construct any scene, you must always achieve two objectives:

- Determine how it fits into and furthers the overall development of the hero.
- Make it a good ministory.

These two requirements determine everything, and the arc of the hero's overall development always comes first.

KEY POINT: Think of a scene as an upside-down triangle.

The beginning of the scene should frame what the whole scene is about. The scene should then funnel down to a single point, with the most important word or line of dialogue stated last:

Beginning broad frame of the scene

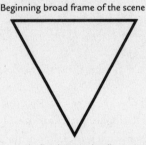

Ending key word or line

Let's look at the ideal sequence you should work through to construct a great scene. Ask yourself the following questions:

1. *Position on the character arc*: Where does this scene fit within the hero's development (also known as the character arc), and how does it further that development?
2. *Problems*: What problems must be solved in the scene, or what must be accomplished?
3. *Strategy*: What strategy can be used to solve the problems?
4. *Desire*: Which character's desire will drive the scene? (This character may be the hero or some other character.) What does he want? This desire provides the spine of the scene.
5. *Endpoint*: How does that character's desire resolve? By knowing your endpoint in advance, you can focus the entire scene toward that point.

The endpoint of the desire also coincides with the point of the inverted triangle, where the most important word or line of the scene is positioned. This combination of the endpoint of the desire with the key word or line creates a knockout punch that also kicks the audience to the next scene.

6. *Opponent*: Figure out who opposes the desire and what the two (or more) characters fight about.

7. *Plan*: The character with the desire comes up with a plan to reach the goal. There are two kinds of plans that a character can use within a scene: direct and indirect.

   In a direct plan, the character with the goal states directly what he wants. In an indirect plan, he pretends to want one thing while actually wanting something else. The opposing character will have one of two responses: he will recognize the deception and play along, or he will be fooled and end up giving the first character exactly what he really wants.

   A simple rule of thumb can help you decide which sort of plan the character should use. A direct plan increases conflict and drives characters apart. An indirect plan decreases conflict initially and brings characters together, but it can cause greater conflict later on when the deception becomes clear.

   Remember, the plan refers to how the character tries to reach a goal within the scene, not in the overall story.

8. *Conflict*: Make the conflict build to a breaking point or a solution.

9. *Twist or reveal*: Occasionally, the characters or the audience (or both) are surprised by what happens in the scene. Or one character tells another off. This is a kind of self-revelation moment in a scene, but it is not final and may even be wrong.

Note that many writers, in an attempt to be "realistic," start the scene early and build slowly toward the main conflict. This doesn't make the scene realistic; it makes it dull.

KEY POINT: Start the scene as late as possible without losing any of the key structure elements you need.

COMPLEX OR SUBTEXT SCENES

The classic definition of subtext is a scene where the characters don't say what they really want. This may be true, but it doesn't tell you how to write it.

The first thing to understand about subtext is that conventional wisdom is wrong: it's not always the best way to write the scene. Subtext characters are usually afraid, in pain, or simply embarrassed to say what they really think or want. If you want a scene with maximum conflict, don't use subtext. On the other hand, if it's right for your particular characters and the scene they are in, by all means use it.

A subtext scene is based on two structural elements: desire and plan. For maximum subtext, try these techniques:

- Give *many* characters in the scene a hidden desire. These desires should be in direct conflict with one another. For example, A is secretly in love with B, but B is secretly in love with C.
- Have all the characters with hidden desires use an indirect plan to get what they want. They say one thing while really wanting something else. They may be trying to fool the others, or they may use subterfuge they know is obvious but hope the artifice is charming enough to get them what they really want.

DIALOGUE

Once you've constructed the scene, you use description and dialogue to write it. The fine art of description is not within the scope of a book on story. But dialogue is.

Dialogue is among the most misunderstood of writing tools. One misconception has to do with dialogue's function in the story: most writers ask their dialogue to do the heavy lifting, the work that the story structure should do. The result is dialogue that sounds stilted, forced, and phony.

But the most dangerous misconception about dialogue is the reverse of asking it to do too much; it is the mistaken belief that good dialogue is real talk.

KEY POINT: *Dialogue is not real talk; it is highly selective language that sounds like it* could *be real.*

KEY POINT: *Good dialogue is always more intelligent, wittier, more metaphorical, and better argued than in real life.*

Even the least intelligent or uneducated character speaks at the highest level at which that person is capable. Even when a character is wrong, he is wrong more eloquently than in real life.

Like symbol, dialogue is a technique of the small. When layered on top of structure, character, theme, story world, symbol, plot, and scene weave, it is the subtlest of the storyteller's tools. But it also packs tremendous punch.

Dialogue is best understood as a form of music. Like music, dialogue is communication with rhythm and tone. Also like music, dialogue is best when it blends a number of "tracks" at once. The problem most writers have is that they write their dialogue on only one track, the "melody." This is dialogue that explains what is happening in the story. One-track dialogue is a mark of mediocre writing.

Great dialogue is not a melody but a symphony, happening on three major tracks simultaneously. The three tracks are story dialogue, moral dialogue, and key words or phrases.

Track 1: Story Dialogue—Melody

Story dialogue, like melody in music, is the story expressed through talk. It is talk about what the characters are doing. We tend to think of dialogue as being opposed to action: "Actions speak louder than words," we say. But talk is a form of action. We use story dialogue when characters talk about the main action line. And dialogue can even carry the story, at least for short periods of time.

You write story dialogue the same way you construct a scene:

- Character 1, who is the lead character of the scene (and not necessarily the hero of the story), states his desire. As the writer, you should know the endpoint of that desire, because this gives you the line on which the dialogue of the scene (the spine) will hang.
- Character 2 speaks against the desire.
- Character 1 responds with dialogue that uses a direct or indirect plan to get what he wants.
- Conversation between the two becomes more heated as the scene progresses, ending with some final words of anger or resolution.

An advanced dialogue technique is to have the scene progress from dialogue about action to dialogue about being. Or to put it another way, it goes from dialogue about what the characters are doing to dialogue about who the characters really are. When the scene reaches the hottest point, one of the characters says some form of the words "You are . . ." He then gives details of what he thinks about the other person, such as "You are a liar" or "You are a no-good, sleazy . . ." or "You are a winner."

Notice that this shift immediately deepens the scene because the characters are suddenly talking about how their actions define who they essentially are as human beings. The character making the claim "You are . . ." is not necessarily right. But just the simple statement makes the audience sum up what they think of these characters so far in the story. This technique is a kind of self-revelation within the scene, and it often includes talk about values (see Track 2, moral dialogue). This shift from action to being is not present in most scenes, but it is usually present in key scenes. Let's look at an example of this shift in a scene from *The Verdict*.

THE VERDICT
(novel by Barry C. Reed, 1980; screenplay by David Mamet, 1982)
In this scene, Mr. Doneghy, brother-in-law of the victim, accosts attorney Frank Galvin for turning down a settlement offer without consulting him first. We come in about halfway through the scene:

INT. COURTHOUSE CORRIDOR—DAY

> DONEGHY
>
> . . . Four years . . . my wife's been crying to sleep what they, what, what they did to her sister.

> GALVIN
>
> I *swear* to you I wouldn't have turned the offer down unless I thought I could win the case . . .

> DONEGHY
>
> What you *thought*!? What you *thought* . . . I'm a working *man*, I'm trying to get my wife out of *town*, we *hired* you, we're *paying* you, I got to find out from the other *side* they offered two hundred . . .

> GALVIN
>
> I'm going to win this *case* . . . Mist . . . Mr. Doneghy . . . I'm going to the jury with a solid case, a *famous* doctor as an *expert* witness, and I'm going to win eight hundred thousand dollars.

> DONEGHY
>
> You guys, you guys, you're all the same. The doctors at the *hospital*, *you* . . . it's "What I'm going to do for you"; but you screw up it's "We did the best that we could. I'm dreadfully sorry . . ." And people like me live with your mistakes the rest of our lives.

Track 2: Moral Dialogue—Harmony

Moral dialogue is talk about right and wrong action, and about values, or what makes a valuable life. Its equivalent in music is harmony, in that it provides depth, texture, and scope to the melody line. In other words, moral dialogue is not about story events. It's about the characters' attitudes toward those events.

Here's the sequence in moral dialogue:

- Character 1 proposes or takes a course of action.
- Character 2 opposes that action on the grounds that it is hurting someone.

■ The scene continues as each attacks and defends, with each giving reasons to support his position.

During moral dialogue, characters invariably express their values, their likes or dislikes. Remember, a character's values are actually expressions of a deeper vision of the right way to live. Moral dialogue allows you, at the most advanced level, to compare in argument not just two or more actions but two or more ways of life.

Track 3: Key Words, Phrases, Taglines, and Sounds—Repetition, Variation, and Leitmotif

Key words, phrases, taglines, and sounds are the third track of dialogue. These are words with the potential to carry special meaning, symbolically or thematically, the way a symphony uses certain instruments, such as the triangle, here and there for emphasis. The trick to building this meaning is to have your characters say the word many more times than normal. The repetition, especially in multiple contexts, has a cumulative effect on the audience.

A tagline is a single line of dialogue that you repeat many times over the course of the story. Every time you use it, it gains new meaning until it becomes a kind of signature line of the story. The tagline is primarily a technique for expressing theme. Some classic taglines are "Round up the usual suspects," "I stick my neck out for nobody," and "Here's looking at you, kid," from *Casablanca*. From *Cool Hand Luke*: "What we've got here is failure to communicate." From *Star Wars*: "May the Force be with you." From *Field of Dreams*: "If you build it, he will come." *The Godfather* uses two taglines: "I'll make him an offer he can't refuse" and "It's not personal; it's business."

Butch Cassidy and the Sundance Kid shows us a textbook example of how to use the tagline. When the line is first uttered, it has no special meaning. After robbing a train, Butch and Sundance can't shake a posse. Butch looks back at the men way off in the distance and says, "Who are those guys?" A while later, the posse is even closer, and Sundance repeats the line, this time with a hint of desperation. As the story progresses, it becomes clear that Butch and Sundance's main task is to figure out the identity of "those guys." Those guys aren't just another posse our heroes can easily lose. They are the future stage of society. They are all-star lawmen, from all over the American West, hired by a corporate boss back East that Butch, Sundance, and the audience never even meet. But if Butch and Sundance don't figure out who those guys are in time, they will die.

SCENES

Let's look at how particular kinds of scenes both execute and modify the basic principles of scene construction and symphonic dialogue.

The Opening

The opening scene is the foundation of every character and every action in the story, which is why it is probably the most difficult to write well. As the first scene in the upside-down triangle that is the full story, it must set a frame around the broadest scope of the story. The first scene tells the audience generally what the story is about. But it must also be a ministory of its own, with characters and actions that are dramatically compelling and provide an opening punch.

That's why it's helpful to think of the first scene as an inverted triangle inside the larger inverted triangle of the story:

First scene of the story

End of the story

In providing the big frame around the story, the opening scene also suggests the thematic patterns—of identity and opposition—that the author wants to weave throughout. But always these big patterns must be grounded in particular characters so that the scene doesn't come across as theoretical or preachy.

The best way to master the principles of the opening scene is to see them in action. Let's break down the first two scenes of *Butch Cassidy and the Sundance Kid*.

BUTCH CASSIDY AND THE SUNDANCE KID
(by William Goldman, 1969)

The first two scenes of *Butch Cassidy and the Sundance Kid* constitute one of the greatest openings in movie history. Author William Goldman's scene construction and dialogue not only please and catch the audience immediately but also lay out the patterns and oppositions that determine the whole story.[1]

Scene 1: Butch at the Bank

In the first scene, a man (the audience doesn't yet know his identity) cases a bank while the bank closes down for the night.

- **Position on the Character Arc**   This is the story's opening scene and the first look at the main character, Butch. It is also Step 1 in the hero's process: a robber in the Old West who ends up dead.
- **Problems**
  1. Introduce the world of the story, particularly outlaws in an American West that has almost disappeared.
  2. Introduce the main character, who is the first of two buddies.
  3. Suggest that the heroes, like the West itself, are getting old and are almost gone.
- **Strategy**
  1. Create a prototypical Butch and Sundance experience that introduces the key thematic patterns.
  2. Indicate the basic *process* of the entire story in one scene, which is everything closing down.
  3. Make it lighthearted and funny while suggesting a darker underbelly and future.
  4. Show a guy looking to rob a bank but finding it much harder than in the old days.

5. Trick the audience by not revealing up front who this man is. By forcing them to figure out that this is really a bank robber casing the bank, the author makes the final joke funnier but also defines the hero as a confident trickster and a man of words.

- **Desire**   Butch wants to scope out a bank to rob.
- **Endpoint**   He finds that the bank is much more secure, and it is closing for the night.
- **Opponent**   The guard and the bank itself.
- **Plan**   Butch uses deception, pretending to be interested in the bank for its looks.
- **Conflict**   The bank, like a living thing, is closing down around Butch.
- **Twist or Reveal**   The man looking at the bank is casing it in order to rob it.
- **Moral Argument and Values**   Aesthetics versus practicality. Of course, the joke comes when aesthetics are applied to a bank, especially by someone who would like to rob it. But this opposition isn't just good for a laugh at the end. It is the fundamental value difference in the story. This story world is becoming more practical, but Butch and Sundance are, above all, men of style, in love with a way of life that is rapidly disappearing.
- **Key Words and Images**   Bars going down, time ending, light going out, space closing in.

The dialogue in the scene points toward a punch line, with the key word and line of the scene last: "It's a small price to pay for beauty." But the trick to the scene is that the punch line comes at the same moment as the reveal about the main character: this man is a trickster (bank robber) who has a way with words. The line has two opposing meanings. On the one hand, this man doesn't care about the bank's beauty; he wants to rob it. On the other hand, the line really does define the man; he is a man of style, and that will eventually kill him.

Scene 2: Sundance and the Poker Game

In this scene, a man named Macon calls another man a cheat at cards. Macon tells the man to leave the money and get out. The man turns out to be the notorious Sundance Kid, and Macon barely escapes with his life.

- **Position on the Character Arc**   This scene marks Sundance's opening position on the arc of a robber who will end up dead and adds details to Butch's opening character as well.
- **Problems**
  1. Introduce the second lead of the two buddies, and show how he is different from Butch.
  2. Show the two men as friends in action; above all, show that they are a *team*.
- **Strategy**   Goldman creates a second prototypical scene that has no effect on the plot. Its only purpose is to clearly define these two men in a snapshot.
  1. In contrast to the first scene, this scene defines the characters through conflict and crisis because crisis clarifies essence right away.
  2. This second scene primarily defines Sundance, but it also defines Butch by showing him acting in contrast to Sundance.
  3. It shows both men working together as a team, like great musicians. Sundance creates the conflict; Butch tries to relieve it. Sundance is a man of few words; Butch is a talker, a classic trickster con man.
  4. To create a crisis scene, Goldman starts with a classic Western story beat, the poker game, with its built-in audience expectations, and then flips it. Instead of a normal showdown, this is the goofy way a guy defends his honor when he's called a cheat. And then Goldman flips the classic scene again and creates an even greater Western hero: it turns out this goofy guy really is that good.
  5. Goldman's key strategy for the scene is to trick the audience about who Sundance is at the same time Sundance tricks his opponent. More on this in a moment.

- **Desire** Macon wants to take all of Sundance's money and toss him out of the saloon with his tail between his legs.
- **Endpoint** Macon is humiliated but gets to see that he made the smart choice when Sundance shows his ability with a gun.
- **Opponent** Sundance and then Butch.
- **Plan** Macon uses no deception. He directly tells Sundance to leave or die.
- **Conflict** As Macon and Sundance square off over the card game, the conflict escalates to the point of a gun battle, with one man sure to end up dead. Butch then tries to defuse the conflict by negotiating a deal but fails.
- **Twist or Reveal** The key to the whole scene is the way Goldman constructs it around the revelations. Notice that he withholds information so that he can flip the audience at the same time he flips Macon. The author starts Sundance in an apparently weaker position and exacerbates it when, like a little kid, Sundance insists he wasn't cheating. Sundance weakens even further in the audience's eyes when Butch reminds him that he's getting older and may be over the hill.

  So when the tables suddenly turn, Sundance's effect on the audience is huge. Sure, they see he's an action hero by the way he uses his gun at the end of the scene. But what really shows his greatness is his ability to fool the audience and his willingness to look like he could lose. He's that good.
- **Moral Argument and Values** This situation is an extreme example of warrior culture: the showdown in public, the contest of physical ability and courage, the power of a man's name and reputation. Butch would never get into this bind; he is from a later social stage than Sundance. He just wants everyone to stay alive and get along.
- **Key Words and Images** Getting old, time closing down on them— but not quite yet.

The dialogue in the showdown is very lean, often with a single line for each character, which heightens the sense of these combatants trading verbal blows. More important, the language is highly stylized and witty, with the precise rhythm and timing of a stand-up comic's routine. Even Sundance, the man of action, is the master of verbal brevity. When Macon asks him, "What's the secret of your success?" he responds simply, "Prayer." Sundance's first line in the film is one word, and its stylish and confident insolence defines him perfectly.

Notice that the second section of the scene shifts to a conflict between Sundance and Butch. These buddies are so close they will argue even when one of them is facing a life-and-death situation. Butch's dialogue is also lean and stylish, but it shows Butch's unique values as a conciliator along with the story's major theme of getting older and being over the hill.

The heart of the scene plays out the absurdity of the solution that both Butch and Sundance concoct for this apparently deadly fix. Even though he appears to be in a weak position, Sundance says, "If he invites us to stay, then we'll go." Incredibly, Butch takes this proposition to Macon, but he tries to soften the humiliation by saying, "What would you think about maybe asking us to stick around?" and "You don't have to mean it or anything." Besides showing the audience their strengths by stylishly flipping this familiar Western situation on its head, Butch and Sundance show their greatness as a *team*, and they do it by being a *comedy* team.

After this long setup, Butch then snaps the punch line when he says, "Can't help you, Sundance." And again, notice that Goldman puts the key word of the line, "Sundance," last. Suddenly, the power positions flip, the terrifying Macon is now terrified, and the comedy teamwork between Butch and Sundance moves quickly to the final point. Macon says, "Stick around, why don't you?" and Butch, always affable and considerate, replies, "Thanks, but we got to be going."

The scene ends with an obvious setup when Macon asks Sundance how good he is and Sundance responds with a remarkable display of physical ability, confirming in action what the audience has already guessed by Sundance's words. But again notice that the key thematic line of the story comes last, forming the final point of the triangle of this opening scene and suggesting the final point of the entire movie. Butch says, "Like I been telling you—over the hill." This obviously sarcastic comment is clearly wrong in light of Sundance's recent physical display and the verbal display earlier when Butch and Sundance conned Macon and the audience. It's only later, in hindsight, that the audience sees that these two *are* over the hill, but they don't know it, and so they die. This is brilliant scene writing.

SCENE-WRITING TECHNIQUE: THE FIRST SENTENCE

The opening sentence of the story takes the principles of the opening scene and compresses them into one line. The first line is the broadest statement of the story and frames what the story will be about. At the same time, it must have dramatic power, some kind of punch. Let's look at three classic opening sentences. I have included a number of lines that follow the opening sentence so you can see how the sentence fits the author's overall strategy for the scene and the story.

PRIDE AND PREJUDICE
(by Jane Austen, 1813)

- **Position on the Character Arc** Before the hero is even introduced, there is the world of the story—specifically, the world of women looking for a husband.
- **Problems**
  1. Jane Austen needs to let the reader know this is a comedy.
  2. She has to give some suggestion of the world of this story and its rules of operation.
  3. She has to let the reader know this story will be told from a woman's point of view.
- **Strategy** Begin with a mock-serious first sentence that seems to state a universal fact and act of altruism but is really an opinion about an act full of self-interest. The content of the first sentence tells the reader the story is about marriage, about women and their families chasing men, and the essential connection in this world of marriage to money.

  Having presented the general arena of the story comically in the first sentence, the author proceeds to a particular family who will play out the opening principle over the course of the story. Notice there is not an ounce of fat in these opening lines.

It is a truth universally acknowledged, that a single man in possession of a good fortune, must be in want of a wife.

However little known the feelings or views of such a man may be on his first entering a neighborhood, this truth is so well fixed in the minds of the surrounding families, that he is considered as the rightful property of some one or other of their daughters.

"My dear Mr. Bennet," said his lady to him one day, "have you heard that Netherfield Park is let at last?"

Mr. Bennet replied that he had not.

"But it is," returned she; "for Mrs. Long has just been here, and she told me all about it."

Mr. Bennet made no answer.

"Do not you want to know who has taken it?" cried his wife impatiently.

"*You* want to tell me, and I have no objection to hearing it."

That was invitation enough.

DAVID COPPERFIELD
(by Charles Dickens, 1849–1850)

- **Position on the Character Arc**   By using a storyteller, the writer creates a hero who is at the end of the arc but is talking about the very beginning. So the hero at the opening will be very young, but with a certain wisdom.
- **Problems**
  1. In telling the story of a man's life, where do you start and where do you end?
  2. How do you tell the audience the *kind* of story you are going to tell them?
- **Strategy**   Use a first-person storyteller. Have him say, in the chapter title, "I am born." Three little words. But they have tremendous punch. That chapter title in effect is the opening sentence of the book. The storyteller is planting the flag of his own life. "I am important, and this will be a great story," he says. He is also indicating that he's telling a coming-of-age story in myth form, starting with the birth of the hero. This story has big ambitions.

  Dickens follows this short but punchy line with "Whether I shall turn out to be the hero of my own life . . ." Immediately he is telling the audience that his hero thinks in terms of stories (and is in fact a writer) and is concerned with fulfilling the potential of his life. He then goes back to the exact moment of his birth, which is extremely presumptuous. But he does so because it has a dramatic element to it: as a baby, he awoke to life at the midnight tolling of the bell.

Notice another result of this opening strategy: the audience gets nestled in the story. The author is saying, "I'm going to take you on a long but fascinating journey. So sit back and relax and let me lead you into this world. You won't be sorry."

I AM BORN.

Whether I shall turn out to be the hero of my own life, or whether that station will be held by anybody else, these pages must show. To begin my life with the beginning of my life, I record that I was born (as I have been informed and believe) on a Friday, at twelve o'clock at night. It was re-marked that the clock began to strike, and I began to cry, simultane-ously.

In consideration of the day and hour of my birth, it was declared by the nurse, and by some sage women in the neighborhood who had taken a lively interest in me for several months before there was any pos-sibility of our becoming personally acquainted, first, that I was destined to be unlucky in life; and secondly, that I was privileged to see ghosts and spirits; both these gifts inevitably attaching, as they believed, to all unlucky infants of either gender, born toward the small hours on a Fri-day night.

THE CATCHER IN THE RYE
(by J. D. Salinger, 1951)

- **Position on the Character Arc**   Holden Caulfield is in a sanitarium remembering what happened to him the previous year. So he is close to the end of his development, but without the final insights that will come to him by reviewing and telling his own story.
- **Problems**
  1. He has to figure out where to begin his story about himself and what to include.
  2. He wants to tell the reader who he really is by the *way* he tells his own story, not just by what he says about himself.

3. He must express the basic theme and value that will guide the story and the character.

■ **Strategy**

1. Write in the first person, which puts the reader in the mind of the hero and tells the reader that this is a coming-of-age story. But since the hero is speaking from a sanitarium and talks with a "bad boy" vernacular, the audience will know that this is the opposite of the usual coming-of-age story.

2. Surprise the reader by making the storyteller antagonistic to him. Put the reader on warning, right up front, that this isn't going to be the usual fluffy, phony kid's story and he (Holden) is not going to "suck up" to the reader to get his sympathy. The implication is that this narrator will be brutally honest. In other words, telling the truth as he sees it is a moral imperative for him.

3. Make it a long and rambling sentence so that the form of the sentence expresses who the hero is and what the plot will be like.

4. Refer immediately and with disdain to *David Copperfield*, the ultimate nineteenth-century version of the coming-of-age story. This will let the reader know that everything the narrator says will be opposite *David Copperfield*. Instead of big plot and big journey, this will be small plot, perhaps even antiplot, and small journey. It also hints at ambition: the author implies that he's going to write a coming-of-age story for the twentieth century that's just as good as the best of the nineteenth.

   Most important, the reader will know that the guiding value for the hero and how he tells his story is "nothing phony." Get ready for real characters, real emotions, and real change, if it happens at all.

If you really want to hear about it, the first thing you'll probably want to know is where I was born, and what my lousy childhood was like, and how my parents were occupied and all before they had me, and all that David Copperfield kind of crap, but I don't feel like going into it, if you want to know the truth. . . . I'll just tell you about this madman stuff that happened to me around last Christmas just before I got pretty run-down and had to come out here and take it easy.

Values in Conflict

Great drama is not the product of two individuals butting heads; it is the product of the values and ideas of the individuals going into battle. Conflict of values and moral argument are both forms of moral dialogue (Track 2). Conflict of values involves a fight over what people believe in. Moral argument in dialogue involves a fight over right and wrong action.

Most of the time, values come into conflict on the back of story dialogue (Track 1), because this keeps the conversation from being too obviously thematic. But if the story rises to the level of a contest between two ways of life, a head-to-head battle of values in dialogue becomes necessary.

In a head-to-head battle of values, the key is to ground the conflict on a particular course of action that the characters can fight about. But instead of focusing on the right or wrong of a particular action (moral argument), the characters fight primarily about the larger issue of what is a good or valuable way to live.

IT'S A WONDERFUL LIFE

(short story "The Greatest Gift" by Philip Van Doren Stern; screenplay by Frances Goodrich & Albert Hackett and Frank Capra, 1946)

It's a Wonderful Life is superb not only in its ability to show the texture of a town in magnificent detail but also in its ability to show the values of two ways of life. The scene where George and Potter argue about the future of the Building and Loan is the most important argument in the film. The writers make Potter an even greater opponent by allowing him to express in detail the values and indeed the logic system by which he lives. And these values are in direct opposition to George's values.

As a social fantasy, this isn't just an argument between two people on the personal level. This is about how an entire society should live. So this dialogue is also political. It's not political in any specific way, which quickly becomes dated. This is human politics, how people live under leaders. What's really brilliant here is the way the writers make this big picture talk extremely emotional and personal. They focus on a single action—closing the Building and Loan—and personalize it with the death of the hero's father.

Notice that with the exception of a short interchange in the middle, this scene is really two monologues. Both monologues are quite long and break the conventional Hollywood wisdom requiring short snippets of back-and-forth talk. That's because each character needs time to build his case for an entire way of life. If the writers didn't ground this in a personal fight between two people who despise each other, it would come across as dry political philosophy.

- **Position on the Character Arc**   With the death of his father, George has experienced the first frustration of his life's desire (to see the world and build things) and made his first act of self-sacrifice for his family and his friends. Now he is about to go off to college to pursue his dreams.
- **Problem**   The writers must mount a fight about the values on which the town and America itself should be built without sermonizing.
- **Strategy**
  1. Have the hero and the main opponent argue over the future of an institution that funds everything else in the town, the Building and Loan, as well as about the man who built the institution but has now died.
  2. Focus the entire philosophical argument down to one word, "richer," in the last line of the hero's monologue.
- **Desire**   Potter wants to close the Building and Loan.
- **Endpoint**   He fails because George stops him.
- **Opponent**   George.
- **Plan**   Potter directly calls for the closing of the Building and Loan, and George directly opposes him.
- **Conflict**   The conflict intensifies when Potter moves from talking about the institution to talking about George's father.
- **Twist or Reveal**   Young George is able to go head to head with this man who bullies everyone else.
- **Moral Argument and Values**   The exchange between these men is worth close inspection because it is a classic example of values in conflict. Notice how well both these monologues are sequenced. These men are making very specific arguments, representing two opposing political and philosophical systems.

Potter's argument and values

1. There is an important distinction between being a businessman and being a man of high ideals.

2. High ideals without common sense can ruin the entire town. From this, the audience knows that the town itself is the battleground and that the central question of the film will be, What way of life will make that battleground, that world, a better place in which to live?

3. Potter goes to a particular example, Ernie Bishop, the friendly taxi driver, someone the audience knows and likes. Ernie has already shown the audience that he is not a risky man, but Potter claims that Ernie got money to build a house only because of a personal relationship he had with George.

4. The consequence of this kind of business, says Potter, is a discontented lazy rabble instead of a thrifty working class. Here is the sinister implication of Potter's system of values: America is a class society in which Potter feels justified ruling those in the lower class. At this point, the dialogue may go too far: Potter is not only the classic patriarch but also the evil capitalist.

5. Potter ends by attacking the very thing that George represents: the starry-eyed dreamer and the sort of personal, communal contact that makes a town a worthwhile place in which to live.

George's argument and values

KEY POINT: *The writers set up George's argument by having his father make the same case to him a few scenes before, at which time George gave the opposing view. This makes George's eloquence both more believable and more poignant.*

---

1. George makes a brilliant opening move by conceding a point to Potter: his father was no businessman, and he himself has no taste for the penny-ante Building and Loan.

2. He then shifts the argument so that it is primarily about his father. His father was selfless, although that selflessness resulted in neither George nor Harry being able to go to college.

3. He attacks Potter on Potter's ground, which is business. He says that his father helped others get out of Potter's slums, and that made them better citizens and better customers, able to increase the wealth and welfare of the entire community.

4. He kicks the argument up a level by making the case for the heroism of the little man. The people that Potter called "lazy rabble" are the ones who do most of the working and paying and living and dying in the community. They are, in short, the strength of the community, its heart and soul. And if the community is to be a place where all people can have fulfilling lives, then no one can be treated as a member of a lower class.

5. George concludes with the most essential argument of all, that of the inalienable rights of a human being. His father treated people as human beings, as ends in themselves, whereas Potter treats people as cattle, as mindless animals to be herded wherever he chooses. In other words, Potter treats them as means to his own end, the end of making money.

KEY POINT: *At the same time the writers make their most encompassing argument—the rights of the common man—they are also focusing on the most personal level, with the key line and key word coming last.*

Potter is doing all of this, says George, because he is "a warped, frustrated old man." This line is crucially important in the film, not simply because it describes Potter but even more because frustration is George's most obvious characteristic.

Now comes the final line, the endpoint of the scene: "Well, in my book [my father] died a much richer man than you'll ever be!" One word, "richer," has two different values. The more obvious one—how much money a person makes—defines Potter. But the deeper one, meaning a personal contribution to others and from others in return, defines George.

■ **Key Word**   Richer.

INT. BAILEY BUILDING AND LOAN OFFICE—DAY

> POTTER
>
> Peter Bailey was not a business man. That's what killed him. He was a man of high ideals, so called, but ideals without common sense can ruin this town.
>
> *(picking up papers from table)*
>
> Now you take this loan here to Ernie Bishop . . . You know, that fellow that sits around all day on his brains in his taxi. You know . . . I happen to know the bank turned down this loan, but he comes here and we're building him a house worth five thousand dollars. Why?

George is at the door of the office, holding his coat and papers, ready to leave.

> GEORGE
>
> Well, I handled that, Mr. Potter. You have all the papers there. His salary, insurance. I can personally vouch for his character.

> POTTER
>
> *(sarcastically)*
>
> A friend of yours?

> GEORGE
>
> Yes, sir.

> POTTER
>
> You see, if you shoot pool with some employee here, you can come and borrow money. What does that get us? A discontented, lazy rabble instead of a thrifty working class. And all because a few starry-eyed dreamers like Peter Bailey stir them up and fill their heads with a lot of impossible ideas. Now I say . . .

George puts down his coat and comes around to the table, incensed by what Potter is saying about his father.

> GEORGE
>
> Just a minute—just a minute. Now, hold on, Mr. Potter. You're *right*

when you say that my father was no *business* man. I know that. Why
he ever started this cheap, penny-ante Building and Loan, I'll *never*
know. But neither you nor anyone else can say anything against his
character, because his whole life was . . . Why, in the twenty-five
years since he and Uncle Billy started this thing, he never once
thought of himself. Isn't that right, Uncle Billy? He didn't save
enough money to send *Harry* to school, let alone me. But he *did* help
a few people get out of your slums, Mr. Potter. And what's wrong
with that . . . Here, you're all businessmen here. Doesn't it make
them better citizens? Doesn't it make them better customers?
You . . . you said . . . What'd you just say a minute ago? . . . They
had to wait and save their money before they even ought to think of
a decent home? Wait! Wait for what? Until their children grow up
and leave them? Until they're so old and broken down that they . . .
Do you know how long it takes a working man to save five thousand
dollars? Just remember this, Mr. Potter, that this rabble you're
talking about . . . they do most of the working and paying and living
and dying in this community. Well, is it too much to have them
work and pay and live and die in a couple of decent rooms and a
bath? Anyway, my *father* didn't think so. People were human beings
to him, but to you, a warped, frustrated old man, they're cattle.
Well, in my book he died a much richer man than you'll ever be!

SHADOW OF A DOUBT

(story by Gordon McDonell, screenplay by Thornton Wilder, Sally Benson, and Alma Reville)

Shadow of a Doubt is probably the best thriller script ever written. It is the
story of dapper Uncle Charlie who comes to stay with his sister's family in
a small American town. His niece, Young Charlie, worships him but
comes to believe that he may be the serial killer known as the Merry
Widow Murderer.

Thornton Wilder's script is a model for combining drama techniques
with the thriller genre to transcend the form. This approach can be seen in
the famous scene in which Uncle Charlie hints at his moral justification
for the murders. A lesser writer would have made the killer opaque, an evil

monster who needs no justification because he is inherently monstrous. But that would reduce the story to the chronicle of a killing machine.

Instead, Wilder gives the killer a detailed and *understandable* moral argument, which makes this man far more terrifying. Uncle Charlie attacks the dark underbelly of American life—the grasping for money and the vast majority who never realize the American dream—which the rest of us try to sweep under the rug.

- **Position on the Character Arc**   The opponent does not have a character arc of his own in the story. But this scene occurs at a crucial point in the hero's development. Young Charlie is already deeply suspicious of the uncle she once worshiped. But she is at this moment teetering between her old attraction and her new revulsion. And she is desperate to understand how and why this could happen.
- **Problem**   How do you have the opponent suggest his motive for killing without coming right out and admitting it?
- **Strategy**   Put the entire family around the dinner table so that the justification will be within the family and part of everyday, normal American life. Have Uncle Charlie's sister, Mrs. Newton, tell him he will be giving a talk to her women's club so that Uncle Charlie can have a natural reason to muse about older women. Then have the horrifying come out of the mundane.
- **Desire**   Uncle Charlie wants to justify his loathing for women, especially older women, to his niece and scare her off as well.
- **Endpoint**   He finds he has gone too far.
- **Opponent**   His niece, Young Charlie.
- **Plan**   Uncle Charlie uses an indirect plan of philosophizing about city women in general, which both preserves his cover and also makes the point to the one person at the table he knows will understand.
- **Conflict**   Even though Young Charlie counterattacks only once, the conflict builds steadily through Uncle Charlie's increasingly hateful view of women.
- **Twist or Reveal**   The dapper Uncle Charlie thinks most older women are no better than animals that should be put to death.

■ **Moral Argument and Values**   Uncle Charlie's moral argument is terrifyingly precise. He begins by calling older women useless. Then he reduces them to sensual beasts devouring money. He ends with the argument that it is actually morally right to put such fat old animals out of their misery. The values in opposition are usefulness and human versus money, sensuality, uselessness, and animals.

■ **Key Words**   Money, wives, useless, greedy, animals.

This dialogue is chilling because it is simultaneously mundane and murderous. It begins with everyday husbands and wives but moves toward the point of view of women as animals. Notice that the key last line is in the form of a question. Uncle Charlie doesn't come right out and say that these women should be slaughtered. He asks his niece what should be done, and the force of his terrible logic can allow her no other conclusion.

The brilliance of the scene construction and dialogue can be found even in the comical bit that Wilder tags onto the end. Uncle Charlie's older sister, Mrs. Newton, is blissfully unaware of what her younger brother is really saying. So she brings the scene back to its origin, Uncle Charlie's talk to her women's club, which the audience knows is like letting the wolf guard the henhouse. And Uncle Charlie's mothering older sister has a nice widow already picked out for him.

INT. DINING ROOM—NIGHT

Uncle Charlie is now pouring out the wine. He does this meticulously, talking casually:

UNCLE CHARLIE
What kind of audience will it be?

MRS. NEWTON
Oh, women like myself. Pretty busy with our homes, most of us.

MR. NEWTON
Women's clubs!

ROGER
For a while it was astrology.

ANN

When I get up my next club, I'm going to have it a reading club. I'm going to be the treasurer and buy all the books.

Uncle Charlie passes the glasses around.

CLOSE UP—YOUNG CHARLIE

Receives her glass of wine. She abruptly drains half of it. Her eyes return to Uncle Charlie.

Uncle Charlie seems to be in a brooding mood for a moment; then says from some deep, inner resentment:

UNCLE CHARLIE

Women keep busy in towns like this. In the cities it's different. The cities are full of women . . . middle aged . . . widows . . . their husbands are dead . . . the husbands who've spent their lives making thousands . . . working . . . working . . . working . . . and then they die and leave their money to their wives . . . their silly wives. And what do the wives do? These useless women? You see them in . . . hotels, the best hotels, every day by the thousands . . . eating the money, drinking the money, losing the money at bridge . . . playing all afternoon and all night . . . smelling of money . . . proud of their jewelry . . . proud of nothing else . . . horrible, faded, fat and greedy women . . .

Suddenly Young Charlie's voice cuts in from the f.g. [foreground]

YOUNG CHARLIE'S VOICE
(a cry wrung from her)
But they're alive! They're human beings!

He looks up across at her, as though awakened.

UNCLE CHARLIE

Are they? Are they, Charlie? Are they human or are they fat, wheezing animals? And what happens to animals when they get too fat and too old?
(he suddenly calms down)

> (laughing)
>
> I seem to be making a speech here.

YOUNG CHARLIE

Hastily picks up her fork. Her eyes lowered. We hear Mrs. Newton say:

MRS. NEWTON

Well, for heaven's sake, Charles, don't talk about women like that in front of my club. You'll be tarred and feathered! The idea!

> (teasing him)

And that nice Mrs. Potter is going to be there, too. She was asking about you.

Monologue

Monologue is an especially valuable technique in the storyteller's craft. Dialogue lets the writer get at truth and emotion through the crucible of conflict between two or more characters. Monologue gets at truth and emotion through the crucible of conflict a person has with himself.

A monologue is a ministory within the mind of the character. It is another form of miniature, a summation of who the character is, his central struggle, and the process he is going through over the course of the story. You can use it to show the audience a character's mind in depth and detail. Or you can use it to show the intensity of the pain the character is suffering.

To write a good monologue, you must first and foremost tell a complete story, which means, as always, hitting the seven structure steps and ending with the key word or key line last.

THE VERDICT

David Mamet uses a monologue to conclude the battle scene in *The Verdict*. Because it is part of the hero's closing argument to the jury, Mamet doesn't have to justify using a monologue in a "realistic" medium like mainstream American film. This monologue is a beautiful piece of writing, and not just because it tells a complete story. It actually tells *two* stories: the path of the woman he is defending and the path of his own life.

- **Position on the Character Arc**   Frank has already had his self-revelation. But this is the final step of his arc: he proves the self-revelation by winning the case in trial.
- **Problem**   How do you sum up the case so that it has the maximum dramatic power?
- **Strategy**   Make the case and the call to moral action for the jury by secretly describing Frank's own personal development.
- **Desire**   Frank wants to convince the jury to stand up for justice.
- **Endpoint**   He recognizes that each juror is a human being who wants to do what is right.
- **Opponent**   The rich and powerful out there who pound on us every day and make us weak.
- **Plan**   His plan is to speak from his heart and so make justice real.
- **Conflict**   The monologue shows a man struggling to know and do what is right even as he is asking the jury to do the same.
- **Twist or Reveal**   The audience realizes that Frank isn't just talking about this case. He is talking about himself.
- **Moral Argument and Values**   Frank's moral argument for acting with justice is a complete seven-step story. He begins with people being lost, feeling like powerless victims (weakness). People want to be just (desire), in spite of the rich and powerful who beat them down (opposition). If we can realize we have power (plan), if we believe in ourselves (self-revelation), we can act with justice (moral decision, battle, and new equilibrium).
- **Key Words**   Justice, believe.

Take a look at this film to see what a great actor can do with a beautifully written monologue.

Closings

Chekhov said that the last ninety seconds are the most important of any play. That's because the final scene is the ultimate convergent point of the story. Occasionally, the last scene includes one more plot kick, in the form of a revelation. But usually, plot business has already been taken care of. The final scene then becomes, like the opening scene, a miniature of the entire story. The author highlights the thematic patterns one more time, and the audience realizes that this representation of characters is also the way of the larger world. In short, the audience has a thematic revelation.

To write a great closing scene, you must realize that it is the point of the upside-down triangle of the full story and that the scene itself is an upside-down triangle, with the key word or line—of the scene and the entire story—coming last:

Story

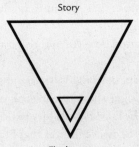

Final scene

Done well, the final scene gives you the ultimate funnel effect: that key word or line at the end sets off a huge explosion in the hearts and minds of the audience and resonates long after the story is over.

Let's look at some great final scenes to see how scene construction and dialogue work at this crucial moment in the story.

THE SUN ALSO RISES
(by Ernest Hemingway, 1926)

This story tracks the meandering of a group of friends as they travel around Europe and of a particular man who can't be with the woman he loves because of a war wound. This is a great love that cannot be, so these characters spiral down to a point where life is nothing but a succession of grabs at sensation. They are purposeless people, aware of their trap but unable to find a way out.

The final scene is prototypical of the characters' actions in the book. After eating dinner, Jake and Lady Brett Ashley are again on the move. Someone is driving them somewhere in a taxi. As the scene funnels toward the endpoint, Brett says the ultimate Brett line: "Oh, Jake, we could have had such a damned good time together." This mundane, even throwaway line, also symbolizes the entire story. The might-have-been of grand romantic tragedy has been reduced to having a good time.

The line is topped by the ultimate Jake line: "Yes. Isn't it pretty to think so?" Cursed not just by his injury but also by a sensibility that lets him have an illusion and see through it too, Jake is doomed for eternity.

THE SEVEN SAMURAI
(by Akira Kurosawa & Shinobu Hashimoto & Hideo Oguni, 1954)

In *The Seven Samurai*, the storyteller's craft is taken to the rarified level of highest art. This is one of the great scripts, masterfully executing virtually every technique described in this book. Its final scene leaves the audience devastated and yet strangely inspired that so much insight into human beings is possible.

In this story, the seven samurai have come together out of altruism and a love of their warrior craft to protect a village from marauding bandits. Katsushiro, a young samurai apprentice, has fallen in love with Shino, a peasant girl. Now the fight is over; the samurai and the villagers have won. But four of the great warriors lie in graves on the hill. And Shino has turned her back on the young warrior and joined the other farmers to plant the next season's crop.

With Shichiroji, the other surviving samurai, the lead samurai, Kanbei, witnesses Katsushiro's heartbreak, the farmers planting new life, and the four graves of his comrades on the hill. And he has a final insight. Though victorious, he knows the samurai have lost, and their entire way of life is over. The deep differences between people, erased for a moment, have returned, and the heroism of the four dead warriors is as lasting as a gust of wind.

Seen in such a shortened form, this moment may appear to be a baldly stated self-revelation. But for many reasons, it doesn't come across that way. First, it comes after an epic struggle in which seven samurai defeat forty bandits just to save a few farmers who are strangers to them. So it's a tremendous emotional twist. Second, this is a huge revelation, and it comes in the very last moment of the story, much like the shocking reversals at the end of *The Sixth Sense* and *The Usual Suspects*. Finally, it is also a thematic revelation in which the hero sees the death of an entire, and in many ways beautiful, social world.

EXT. VILLAGE—DAY

Kanbei lowers his head and looks at the ground. He takes a few steps toward camera and then stops, looking back toward the paddy fields. Then he turns and walks back to stand beside Shichiroji again.

KANBEI

We've lost again.

Shichiroji is surprised. He looks questioningly at Kanbei.

KANBEI

No, the farmers are the winners, not us.

Kanbei turns away from camera and looks up; Shichiroji does likewise; the camera tilts up the side of the burial hill, losing the two samurai and holding on the four samurai burial mounds silhouetted against the sky. The samurai music comes in over the planting music as the wind blows up the dust among the mounds.

THE GREAT GATSBY

(by F. Scott Fitzgerald, 1925)

The Great Gatsby is justly famous for its closing. Gatsby is dead. Nick has realized the falseness of his quest for success in the big city and has decided to return to the Midwest. The final page finds Nick looking one last time at this rich enclave of the East Coast.

Fitzgerald's final sequence bears careful study. Through Nick, he says the big mansions have closed for the season. This is a specific fact in the story that also symbolizes the end of the phony utopia of rich parties that died along with Gatsby. He then jumps back in time and up in scope when Nick imagines the island at America's beginnings, when it was a natural Eden, all potential, "a fresh, green breast of the new world" and "the last and greatest of all human dreams." This creates a stark comparison to the same island today, where real desires by real people like Gatsby, Daisy, and Tom have turned the lush forests into the false idols of big houses and fancy, meaningless parties.

From this big-picture comparison, Fitzgerald focuses back down to one person, Gatsby again, whose own desire pointed laserlike to the green light at the end of Daisy's dock. Gatsby is the false dreamer who, like the classic myth hero, does not know that he already had it all back in the "dark fields" of the Midwest where he started.

As Fitzgerald closes in on the point of the triangle at the end of the scene and the story, he speaks of the symbol of that fake desire, the green light. Unlike so many stories that end falsely with the hero's desire accomplished and everything settled for good, Fitzgerald ends on the desire that never stops, the effort that redoubles as our human goal recedes into the distance. His last line is a thematic revelation that stands for the entire story: "So we beat on, boats against the current, borne back ceaselessly into the past."

BUTCH CASSIDY AND THE SUNDANCE KID
(by William Goldman, 1969)

Just as *Butch Cassidy and the Sundance Kid* has one of the great openings in movie history, it also has one of the great endings. And in many ways, the final scene is a mirror image of the first two scenes.

- **Position on the Character Arc**   The tragedy of these immensely likable guys is that they can't change. They can't learn. The new world that's coming on fast is too much for them. They can only die.
- **Problem**   How do you create an ending that expresses the heroes' essential qualities and shows the result of their not being able to learn?
- **Strategy**   As in the first scene, the characters find themselves in a tight room with everything closing in fast around them. As in the second scene, the characters face a crisis that defines them. First, they are defined by the way both men face death with extreme confidence—they have no doubt that they can get out of this. And Butch is already planning their next stop. Second, the crisis shows their differences: Butch is still coming up with ideas, while Sundance is the one who has to get them out of the trouble that always ensues.

Again, Goldman showcases the beauty of their teamwork when Butch runs out to get ammunition and Sundance covers him. If Sundance was impressive when he shot Macon's gun across the floor, he is downright dazzling when he whirls and shoots every policeman in sight. But what makes the audience *love* this team is how they work together comically. Their never-ending comic bickering, present from the beginning, with Butch the excited one and Sundance the cool skeptic, shows the audience once more that this really is a marriage made in heaven.

But Goldman sets up one more contrast in the scene that expresses the main theme and the lack of character change: these two guys can't see the world that's coming. Goldman crosscuts their comic bickering over Butch's latest idea for dodging the future—Australia—with the arrival of what appears to be the entire Bolivian army. The increasingly extreme contrast between what the heroes know and what the audience knows underlines what has always been there from the beginning: Butch and Sundance can't see beyond their little personal world. Lovable as they are, they aren't that smart.

With this contrast, a final audience revelation hits home: even supermen must die. And isn't it painful when they do?

Once again, the last line is the key line of the scene and the story. When Butch asks Sundance if he saw their nemesis Lafors out there and Sundance says no, Butch replies, "Good. For a minute I thought we were in trouble."

MASTERPIECES OF SCENE CONSTRUCTION

I'd like to take one last look at the techniques of scene construction and dialogue by studying two great films, *Casablanca* and *The Godfather*. These films are masterpieces in the art of storytelling, and their scene construction and dialogue are brilliant. Because so much of your success in scene writing depends on your ability to place a scene on the arc of your hero's development, I want to explore scenes that come from the beginning and the end of these two films. To fully appreciate the excellence of scene construction and dialogue, give yourself the pleasure of seeing these films again.

CASABLANCA
(play Everybody Comes to Rick's *by Murray Burnett and Joan Alison, screenplay by Julius J. Epstein, Philip G. Epstein, and Howard Koch, 1942)*

First Scene Between Rick and Louis

In this scene, still fairly early in the story, Rick and Police Captain Louis Renault have a pleasant chat before Major Strasser arrives and Ugarte is captured.

- **Position on the Character Arc**   This is the first moment in the development of the relationship between Rick and Louis that will end in their mutual redemption and "marriage" in the final scene of the story.

    This scene is a perfect example of why you should always start constructing a scene by determining its place on the overall character arc. This is not the first scene in the movie and so it appears to be just another step in the flow of the story. Only by starting with the endpoint of Rick's arc—becoming a freedom fighter and entering a "marriage" of friendship with Louis—do you see that this is the crucial opening step in that arc.

- **Problems**
    1. Show the audience that Louis is as witty as Rick and that he is the appropriate buddy for Rick to end up with.
    2. Show that Louis has just as much moral need as Rick.
    3. Bring in more information about Rick's ghost, particularly information that shows that this cynical, hard man was once not only good but also heroic.

- **Strategy**
    1. Have Louis question Rick and introduce information about his past under the guise that it is all part of Louis's job of stopping Laszlo. This is an excellent way of introducing exposition about the main character without being dull or heavy-handed. At the same time, Rick's insistence that he was well paid for his work keeps him from seeming too sentimental and idealistic.
    2. Have Rick and Louis bet on whether Laszlo will escape. This gives the two men a desire line just between them and shows their mutual cynicism and selfishness; both will turn a freedom fighter's quest to defeat the Nazis into a contest for money.

3. Introduce information about Laszlo and Ilsa so that both arrive on the scene already having great reputations.

4. Provide more explanations between the complex and confusing power relationships between Louis, the French police captain, and the Nazi, Major Strasser.

■ **Desire**   Louis wants to learn more about Rick's past. Then he wants to warn Rick not to help Laszlo escape.

■ **Endpoint**   Rick won't tell him anything and claims he doesn't care whether Laszlo escapes, except as a sporting proposition.

■ **Opponent**   Rick is Louis's opponent.

■ **Plan**   Louis asks Rick directly about his past and warns him in no uncertain terms to leave Laszlo alone.

■ **Conflict**   Rick and Louis disagree over whether Laszlo will escape, but Rick defuses any real conflict by turning their disagreement into a bet.

■ **Twist or Reveal**   The great freedom fighter Laszlo, whom we haven't met, is traveling with a remarkable woman, and hard-boiled, cynical Rick was a freedom fighter himself some years before.

■ **Moral Argument and Values**   This exchange is about *not* acting morally. The two men bet on whether Laszlo will escape, not on whether he should. Indeed, Rick insists he will not help Laszlo and wasn't acting for moral reasons when he fought for the "right" side in Ethiopia and Spain. Rick also says Laszlo will take one exit visa and leave his companion in Casablanca.

   The clear value opposition in the scene is money and self-interest versus romance and selfless fighting for right.

■ **Key Words**   Romantic, sentimentalist.

The dialogue of both characters in this scene is very stylized and witty. Louis doesn't just ask Rick about the ghost of his past. He asks, "Did you abscond with the church funds? Did you run off with the Senator's wife? I'd like to think you killed a man. It's the romantic in me." Rick doesn't just tell him to mind his own business. He says he "came to Casablanca for the waters." When Louis reminds him Casablanca is in the desert, Rick responds, "I was misinformed."

Closing Scene Between Rick and Louis

The final scene in *Casablanca* is one of the most famous in movie history. Rick has sacrificed his love for Ilsa and sent her off to help her husband, Victor Laszlo. Now he faces his former opponent but stylistic equal, Louis.

- **Position on the Character Arc**
  1. This is the endpoint of Rick's becoming a committed freedom fighter and patriot.
  2. Structurally, the scene has a double reversal, a change of two characters, Louis as well as Rick.
  3. This is the endpoint of Rick's relationship with Louis in which the two enter into a buddy "marriage."
- **Problems**
  1. How do you give the final scene the most dramatic impact possible?
  2. How do you show big changes, in *two* characters, in a believable but not boring way?
- **Strategy**
  1. Hold off the reveal of Louis's change and the creation of a new buddy team until the very end.
  2. Use a double reversal so that Rick and his equal both see the light *but maintain their hard-nosed opportunism*. What makes the scene is the return to the bet. This allows both men to make huge moral flips but still preserve their tough-guy quality and so avoid over-the-top sentimentality.
- **Desire**   Louis wants to join Rick in the fight and begin what looks like a great friendship.
- **Endpoint**   Rick welcomes him on the journey.
- **Opponent**   It appears that Rick and Louis might still be opponents over Rick's escape and the bet. But Louis finesses that.
- **Plan**   Louis hides his real intention, making it look like he could still give Rick trouble over the exit visa or the bet.

- **Conflict**   The two men negotiate over Rick's escape and the money Louis owes Rick. But Louis comes up with a stylish resolution that ends in friendship.
- **Twist or Reveal**   Louis isn't going to nail Rick; he's going to join him. But it will cost Rick the 10,000 francs he won.
- **Moral Argument and Values**   Both men accept the idea that it is time to become a patriot. But they don't entirely forget about money, either.
- **Key Words**   Patriot, friendship.

The last scene funnels down to a single point of the scene and the story: friendship. Rick may miss out on true love, but he ends up with a great and equal friend. The scene is constructed to lead to the big reveal, Louis's stylish way of joining Rick in his new moral action. The dialogue between the two men is just as snappy and sophisticated as ever. What makes it even better is that they're not even trying.

There's one last thing to notice about the dialogue. Though extremely witty, it is quite dense. The writers pack huge story flips into a few short lines, and this has tremendous impact on the audience. Rick does his noble deed. There's a line of dialogue from each, and Louis does his noble deed, dumping the Vichy water. Louis proposes the deal concerning Rick's escape. Three short lines. Rick flips it back to the bet. Three short lines. Louis combines the escape with the bet. One line. Rick realizes what's happened. And the last line is eternal friendship. That series of combinations produces a big knockout at the very end of the final scene of the film. Clearly, these writers understood how to execute Chekhov's rule about the last ninety seconds of their story.

THE GODFATHER
(novel by Mario Puzo, 1969; screenplay by Mario Puzo and Francis Ford Coppola, 1972)

To see how the writers of *The Godfather* might have constructed the scenes and written the dialogue of this great film, we have to start with the big picture, the overall story. These are some of the ways we could describe the story strategy or process they want to play out over the course of the film:

1. The passing of power from one king to the next
2. Three sons, each with different attributes, trying to be king
3. A family under attack fighting back to survive and win

Now let's look at some of the big thematic patterns the writers want to track over the course of the story. First are the patterns of identity. These are story elements we normally think of as different but that these writers want to show, on a deeper level, are the same. The three most important are these:

- Mafia family as business
- Mafia family as military
- Profane as sacred and sacred as profane: "god" as the devil

Next, we need to focus on the patterns of opposition, the key elements that the writers will contrast and place in conflict. These are the main patterns of opposition:

- Family versus the law
- Family and personal justice versus American legal justice
- Immigrant America versus mainstream and elite America
- Men versus women

Working through the scene-writing process, the *last* step we would need to take if we were writing these scenes is to clarify the values and symbols, or key words, that will come into conflict throughout the story. Only by looking at the full story can we see which objects or images are central and organic to it. Then we can tease them out and highlight them through repetition (Track 3 dialogue). In *The Godfather*, these values and symbols fall into two major clusters: honor, family, business, appearance, and crime versus freedom, country, and moral and legal action.

Opening Scene

The average writer would start *The Godfather* with a plot scene to give this big, violent story a running start. He would write the scene strictly with story dialogue (Track 1) to help kick off the plot. But writers Mario Puzo and Francis Coppola are not average writers. Guided by the principle of the inverted triangle for both story and scene, they created a prototypical experience for the opening that frames the entire story and focuses down to a single point at the end of the scene:

First scene of the story

End of the story

- **Position on the Character Arc**   Since this story tracks the end of one king and the rise of the next, the opening scene doesn't mark the beginning point of the new king (Michael). It starts with the current king (Don Corleone) and shows what he and his successor actually do.
- **Problems**   In a story about a "king" in a democracy, much needs to be accomplished in the opening scene:
  1. Introduce the Godfather, and see what a Godfather does.
  2. Start showing how this unique system of the Mafia works, including the hierarchy of characters and the rules by which they are organized and operate.
  3. Announce the epic scope of the story so that the audience knows right away one of the main thematic points: the world of this family is not some ghetto they can disdain, but one that stands for the nation.
  4. Introduce some of the thematic patterns of identity and opposition that the writers want to weave through the story.
- **Strategy**
  1. Start with the prototypical Godfather experience, in which the Godfather acts as a judge and exerts power over his unique dominion.

2. Place this essential Godfather scene within a larger, more complex story world, a wedding, where all the characters who are part of this system are gathered and where the central element of family is emphasized.

- **Desire**   Bonasera wants the Don to kill the boys who beat his daughter. Bonasera is a very minor character in this world. But he has no knowledge of the Mafia system. So he is the audience. The writers use him to drive the scene so that the audience can learn the system as he does and can *feel* what it is like to enter and connect with this world. By the way, his full name, Amerigo Bonasera, can be translated as "Good evening, America."

- **Endpoint**   Bonasera is trapped by the Don.

- **Opponent**   Don Corleone.

- **Plan**   Bonasera uses a direct plan, asking the Don to murder the two boys and asking how much he wants to be paid. This direct approach elicits a "no."

  In his efforts to reel another person into his web, the Don uses an indirect plan, making Bonasera feel guilty for the way he has treated the Don in the past.

- **Conflict**   The Don, angry at the various slights he feels Bonasera has made and continues to make toward him, refuses Bonasera's request. But there is a limit to how much the conflict can build in this scene because the Don is all-powerful and Bonasera is no fool.

- **Twist or Reveal**   The Don and Bonasera come to an agreement, but the audience realizes that Bonasera has just made a pact with the devil.

- **Moral Argument and Values**   Bonasera asks the Don to kill two boys for beating his daughter. The Don says that is not justice. He then cleverly turns the moral argument back onto Bonasera, arguing that Bonasera has slighted him and treated him with disrespect.

- **Key Words**   Respect, friend, justice, Godfather.

The opening scene of *The Godfather* clearly shows why great dialogue is not just melodic but also symphonic. If this scene were composed only of story dialogue, it would be half the length and one-tenth the quality. Instead, the writers wove the dialogue using three tracks simultaneously, and the scene is a masterpiece.

The endpoint of the scene is Bonasera saying the word "Godfather" at the same moment he is trapped in a Faustian bargain. The beginning of the scene, and the framing line of the entire story, is "I believe in America." This is a value, and it tells the audience two things: they are about to experience an epic, and the story will be about ways of success.

The scene opens with a monologue delivered in a place with almost no detail. Bonasera's monologue doesn't just tell his daughter's sad story; it is filled with values and key words such as "freedom," "honor," and "justice." Don Corleone responds with a slight moral attack, which puts Bonasera on the defensive. And then Don Corleone, acting as the Godfather-judge, gives his ruling.

There's a quick back-and-forth as they disagree over moral argument, in particular about what constitutes justice. And then Bonasera, in the role of the audience, makes a mistake, because he doesn't know the rules of the system. He doesn't know how payment is made here.

At this point, the scene flips, and the Don drives the scene. He makes a moral argument, packed with values like respect, friendship, and loyalty, designed to make Bonasera his slave. Though the Don says he simply wants Bonasera's friendship, Bonasera sees the true goal of the Don's indirect plan. He bows his head and says the key word of the scene, "Godfather." It is followed by the last and most important line of the scene when the Godfather says, "Some day, and that day may never come, I would like to call upon you to do me a service in return."

This line has the same form as the pact the devil makes with Faust. Godfather and devil merge. The "sacred" equals the profane. End of scene. Pow!

Closing Scene

This scene, which is the final point in the upside-down triangle of the full story, is simultaneously a "trial," where Connie accuses Michael of murder, and a coronation. The last scene matches the opening. The prototypical Godfather experience that ended in a pact with the devil is now the new devil crowned king.

Beginning of the story

Final scene

- ■ **Position on the Character Arc** Michael is accused of being a murderer by his sister at the same time he gains his final ascension as the new Godfather. Michael also reaches a kind of endpoint in his marriage to Kay when he poisons it beyond repair.
- ■ **Problems** How to make the moral argument against Michael without having him accept it.
- ■ **Strategy**
  1. Give Connie the argument, but have her discounted because she's hysterical and a woman.
  2. Deny Michael the self-revelation and give it to Kay instead. But make it based not on what Connie says but on what Kay sees in her husband.
- ■ **Desire** Connie wants to accuse Michael of Carlo's murder.
- ■ **Endpoint** The door closes in Kay's face.
- ■ **Opponent** Michael, Kay.
- ■ **Plan** Connie uses a direct plan, accusing Michael of her husband's murder in front of everyone.
- ■ **Conflict** The conflict starts at an intense level and then dissipates at the end.
- ■ **Twist or Revelation** Michael lies to Kay, but Kay sees what Michael has become.
- ■ **Moral Argument and Values** Connie claims that Michael is a cold-hearted murderer who doesn't care about her. Michael says nothing to Connie and instead refutes her accusations by suggesting she is sick or hysterical and needs a doctor. He then denies Connie's accusations to Kay.
- ■ **Key Words** Godfather, emperor, murderer.

WRITING SCENES—WRITING EXERCISE 9

- **Character Change**   Before writing any scene, state your hero's character change in one line.
- **Scene Construction**   Construct each scene by asking yourself these questions:
  1. Where is the scene positioned on your hero's character arc, and how does the scene take him to the next step on his line of development?
  2. What problems must you solve, and what must you accomplish in this scene?
  3. What strategy will you use to do so?
  4. Whose desire will drive the scene? Remember, this is not necessarily the hero of the story.
  5. What is the endpoint of the character's goal in this scene?
  6. Who will oppose this character's goal?
  7. What plan—direct or indirect—will the character use to accomplish his goal in the scene?
  8. Will the scene end at the height of conflict, or will there be some sort of solution?
  9. Will there be a twist, surprise, or reveal in the scene?
  10. Will one character end the scene by commenting about who another character is, deep down?
- **Scenes Without Dialogue**   First, try writing the scenes without dialogue. Let the characters' actions tell the story. This gives you the "clay" you can shape and refine in each successive draft.
- **Writing Dialogue**
  1. *Story Dialogue*: Rewrite each scene using only story dialogue (Track 1). Remember, this is dialogue about what the characters are doing in the plot.
  2. *Moral Dialogue*: Rewrite each scene, this time adding moral dialogue (Track 2). This is argument about whether those actions are right or wrong or comments about what the characters believe in (their values).

3. *Key Words:* Rewrite each scene again, highlighting key words, phrases, tagline, and sounds (Track 3). These are objects, images, values, or ideas that are central to the theme of your story.

Think of this process for writing the three tracks of dialogue in the same way that you might draw someone's portrait. First you would sketch the overall shape of the face (story dialogue). Then you would add the major shadings that give depth to the face (moral dialogue). Then you would add the most minute lines and details that make that face a unique individual (key words).

■ **Unique Voices**   Make sure that each character speaks in a unique way.

CHAPTER 11

The Never-Ending Story

A GREAT STORY lives forever. This is not a platitude or a tautology. A great story keeps on affecting the audience long after the first telling is over. It literally keeps on telling itself. How is it possible for a great story to be a living thing that never dies?

You don't create a never-ending story just by making it so good it's unforgettable. The never-ending story happens only if you use special techniques embedded in the story structure. Before we consider some of those techniques, let's look at the reverse of the never-ending story: a story whose life and power are cut short by a false ending. There are three major kinds of false endings: premature, arbitrary, and closed.

The premature ending can have many causes. One is an early self-revelation. Once your hero has his big insight, his development stops, and everything else is anticlimactic. A second is a desire the hero achieves too quickly. If you then give him a new desire, you have started a new story. A third cause of a premature ending is any action your hero takes that is not believable because it's not organic to that unique person. When you force your characters, especially your hero, to act in an unbelievable way, you immediately kick the audience out of the story because the plot "mechanics" come to the surface. The audience realizes the character is acting a certain way because *you* need him to act that way (mechanical) and not because *he* needs to (organic).

An arbitrary end is one in which the story just stops. This is almost always the result of an inorganic plot. The plot is not tracking the development of one entity, whether it is a single main character or a unit of society. If nothing is developing, the audience has no sense of something coming to fruition or playing itself out. A classic example of this is the end of *Adventures of Huckleberry Finn*. Twain tracks Huck's development, but the journey plot he uses literally paints Huck into a corner. He is forced to rely on coincidence and *deus ex machina* to end the story, disappointing those who find the rest of the story so brilliant.

The most common false ending is the closed ending. The hero accomplishes his goal, gains a simple self-revelation, and exists in a new equilibrium where everything is calm. All three of these structural elements give the audience the sense that the story is complete and the system has come to rest. But that's not true. Desire never stops. Equilibrium is temporary. The self-revelation is never simple, and it cannot guarantee the hero a satisfying life from that day forward. Since a great story is always a living thing, its ending is no more final and certain than any other part of the story.

How do you create this sense of a breathing, pulsing, ever-changing story, even when the last word has been read or the last image seen? You have to go back to where we started, to the essential characteristic of a story as a *structure in time*. It is an organic unit that develops over time, and it must keep on developing even after the audience stops watching it.

Since a story is always a whole, and the organic end is found in the beginning, a great story always ends by *signaling to the audience to go back to the beginning and experience it again*. The story is an endless cycle—a Möbius strip—that is always different because the audience is always rethinking it in light of what just happened.

The simplest way to create the never-ending story is through plot, by ending the story with a reveal. In this technique, you create an *apparent* equilibrium and then immediately shatter it with one more surprise. This reversal causes the audience to rethink all the characters and actions that have led them to this point. Like a detective who reads the same signs but sees a very different reality, the audience mentally races back to the beginning of the story and reshuffles the same cards in a new combination.

We see this technique executed beautifully in *The Sixth Sense* when the audience discovers that the Bruce Willis character has been dead since the beginning. The technique is even more astounding in *The Usual Suspects* when the wimpy narrator walks out of the police headquarters and before our eyes turns into the fearsome opponent of his own invention, Keyser Soze.

The reversal reveal, while shocking, is the most limited way of creating the never-ending story. It gives you only one more cycle with the audience. The plot was not what they first thought. But now they know. There will be no more surprises. Using this technique, you don't get a never-ending story so much as a twice-told tale.

Some writers would argue that it is impossible to create the never-ending story if your plot is too powerful, too dominant over the other story elements. Even a plot that ends with a great reversal gives the audience the sense that all the doors of the house have now shut. The key turns; the puzzle is solved; the case is closed.

To tell a story that feels different over and over again, you don't have to kill your plot. But you do have to use every system of the story body. If you weave a complex tapestry of character, plot, theme, symbol, scene, and dialogue, you will not limit how many times the audience retells the story. They will have to rethink so many story elements that the permutations become infinite and the story never dies. Here are just a few of the elements you can include to create an infinite story tapestry:

- The hero fails to achieve his desire, and the other characters come up with a new desire at the end of the story. This prevents the story from closing down and shows the audience that desire, even when it's foolish or hopeless, never dies ("I want; therefore, I am").
- Give a surprising character change to an opponent or a minor character. This technique can lead the audience to see the story again with that person as the true hero.
- Place a tremendous number of details in the background of the story world that on later viewings move to the foreground.
- Add elements of texture—in character, moral argument, symbol, plot, and story world—that become much more interesting once the audience has seen the plot surprises and the hero's character change.
- Create a relationship between the storyteller and the other characters

that is fundamentally different once the viewer has seen the plot for the first time. Using an unreliable storyteller is one, but only one, way of doing this.

■ Make the moral argument ambiguous, or don't show what the hero decides to do when he is confronted with his final moral choice. As soon as you move beyond the simple good versus evil moral argument, you force the audience to reevaluate the hero, the opponents, and all the minor characters to figure out what makes right action. By withholding the final choice, you force the audience to question the hero's actions again and explore that choice in their own lives.

The central problem I faced in this book was how to lay out a practical poetics—the craft of storytelling that exists in all story forms. It involves showing you how to create a complex living story that grows in the mind of the audience and never dies. It also means overcoming what appears to be an impossible contradiction: telling a universally appealing story that is also totally original.

My solution has been to show you the secret workings of the story world. I wanted you to discover the dramatic code—the ways human beings grow and change in a lifetime—in all its splendor and complexity. Many of the techniques for expressing the dramatic code in a powerful and original story are in this book. If you are wise, you will never stop studying and practicing them.

But mastering technique is not enough. Let me end with one final reveal: *you* are the never-ending story. If you want to tell the great story, the never-ending story, you must, like your hero, face your own seven steps. And you must do it every time you write a new story. I have tried to provide you with the plan: the strategies, tactics, and techniques that will help you reach your goal, fulfill your needs, and gain an endless supply of self-revelations. Becoming a master storyteller is a tall order. But if you can learn the craft and make your own life a great story, you will be amazed at the fabulous tales you will tell.

If you are a good reader—and I have no question that you are—you are not the same person you were when you began this book. Now that you've read it once, let me suggest . . . well, you know what to do.

CHAPTER 1   Story Space, Story Time

1. Peter S. Stevens, *Patterns in Nature* (Boston: Little, Brown, 1974), pp. 38–48.

CHAPTER 2   Premise

1. R. S. Crane, *The Language of Criticism and the Structure of Poetry* (Toronto: University of Toronto Press, 1953), p. 2.

CHAPTER 4   Character

1. Peter Brook, *The Empty Space* (New York: Atheneum, 1978); p. 76.
2. Ibid.

CHAPTER 6   Story World

1. Gaston Bachelard, *The Poetics of Space* (Boston: Beacon Press, 1969), p. 43.
2. Ibid., p. 201.
3. Ibid., p. 47.
4. Ibid., p. 4.
5. Ibid., p. 7.
6. Ibid., p. 51.
7. Ibid., p. 52.

8. George Sand, *Consuelo*, vol. 2, p. 116.

9. Bachelard, *Poetics of Space*, p. 150.

10. Ibid., p. 155.

CHAPTER 8 Plot

1. Brook, *Empty Space*, p. 91.

2. Peter Brooks, *Reading for the Plot* (Cambridge, Mass.: Harvard University Press, 1992), p. 168.

3. Edgar Allan Poe, in a review of Edward Bulwer Lytton's *Night and Morning*, *Graham's Magazine*, April 1841, pp. 197–202.

4. Northrop Frye, "The Road of Excess," in Bernice Slote (ed.), *Myth and Symbol* (Lincoln: University of Nebraska Press, 1963), p. 234.

5. Henrik Ibsen, "A Letter in Rhyme," in *Det nittende Aarhundrede*, April–September 1875.

acting stories, 8, 80, 260

action genre, 109; good-versus-bad moral argument in, 126; time endpoint in, 190; *see also titles of specific films*

actions, symbolic, 239–40, 253

Adam's Rib, 68, 87

adult-to-leader character change, 81–82

adventure stories, 109; outer space, 157 (*see also* science fiction genre)

adventure versus safety, visual opposition of, 163

Adventures of Huckleberry Finn, The (Twain), 11, 24, 50, 222, 419; characters in, 70, 79; designing principle of, 27; moral argument of, 110, 137; plot of, 261; story world of, 152, 162; symbols in, 222

Adventures of Tom Sawyer, The (Twain), 70, 79, 200

Aeschylus, 262

African Queen, The, 152, 158, 161–62

After Hours, 136

Age of Innocence, The, 126

Aguirre: The Wrath of God, 158

Alice in Wonderland (Carroll), 27, 152, 174, 175

Alien, 69, 151, 158, 224, 306–307

Alison, Joan, 142, 165, 415

allegory, 109

Allen, Woody, 187, 188

allies, 59–60, 281, 285–86; attack by, 121, 293–94; in buddy stories, 64; fake-opponent, 60, 91; moral argument in dialogue with, 138

Almost Famous, 169

Altman, Robert, 247

Amadeus, 126
Amarcord, 183, 186
Amélie, 181, 246
American Beauty, 167, 169, 319;
    characters in, 61–62, 66, 68, 70–71,
    96; moral argument in, 126, 132, 136
American Graffiti, 12, 13, 188
Amityville Horror, The, 167
animal symbolism, 230–31, 242;
    Christian, 243
antagonists, *see* opponents
antiplot, 263–65
Apocalypse Now, 158, 162
Apollo 13, 158
Apu Trilogy, The, 131
arbitrary endings, 419
archetypes, 67–71; artist, 70; clown, 70;
    father, 67–68; king, 67–68; lover, 70;
    magician, 69; mother, 68; queen, 68;
    rebel, 70–71; shaman, 69; trickster,
    69–70; warrior, 68–69; wise man or
    woman, 68
arena of story, 150–56
Argento, Dario, 238
Aristotle, 3, 4, 262
Arsenic and Old Lace, 167
Arthur, King, stories of, 68, 183, 235,
    245, 249–50, 255–57
artist archetype, 70
As You Like It (Shakespeare), 158,
    236–37
Atlantis, 157
attic versus cellar, visual opposition of,
    167–68
audience appeal, 36; of hero, 76–77
audience revelation, 297; reversal,
    305–306; thematic, 303–304
Austen, Jane, 92–93, 133, 134, 326,
    360, 387; *see also titles of specific novels*

Avventura, L', 264
Ayckbourn, Alan, 81
Aykroyd, Dan, 172

Bachelard, Gaston, 146, 156
backstory, 272
backward storytelling, 265
Balderston, John L., 231, 243
Ball, Alan, 61, 96
Ballad of Cable Hogue, The, 159
Barry, Philip, 63, 99, 229
bars, 164–66
Basic Instinct, 93, 307–308
Batman, 170, 222, 230
Batman Begins, 161, 171
battle, final, 39, 48, 90, 300; building
    conflict leading to, 94; crosscutting
    in, 330; gauntlet during, 299; moral
    argument in, 120, 121, 139; in story
    world, 192
Beau Geste, 152, 159, 235
Being John Malkovich, 133
Bellah, James Warner, 238
Beloved (Morrison), 24
Ben and Me, 174
Benchley, Peter, 24
Beneath the Rooftops of Paris,
    170, 171
Benson, Sally, 195, 396
Benton, Robert, 303
Bertolucci, Bernardo, 238
best character, determining, 29–30
Betrayal (Pinter), 265
Beverly Hills Cop, 69, 152
Bible, the, 27; *see also* Moses story
Big, 22–23, 49, 152, 175
Big Country, 161
big plots, 263, 264; genre, 265

black comedy, 135–36, 184

Black Rain, 152

Blade Runner, 158, 171, 231

Blair Witch Project, The, 158

Blake, Michael, 116, 155

blockbuster films: moral vision in, 137; *see also specific genres; titles of specific films*

Blood Simple, 151, 161

Blow-Up, 11, 81

Blue Velvet, 184

Blues Brothers, The, 126, 152, 190

Bob and Carol and Ted and Alice, 133

Body and Soul, 313, 317, 319

Boileau, Pierre, 94, 179

Boorman, John, 249

Borges, Jorge Luis, 79, 309

Borrowers, The, 174

Brackett, Charles, 153, 179, 200

branching story, 12, 264

Braveheart, 82

Brazil, 136

Brecher, Irving, 195

Brecht, Bertolt, 58

Brer Rabbit, 69

Bridge on the River Kwai, The, 126

Broadcast News, 63

Brokeback Mountain, 161

Brontë, Emily, 97, 128, 130, 239

Brook, Peter, 58, 76

Brown, Leigh, 187

Brueghel, Pieter, 164, 168

buddy stories, 62, 64–65

Burnett, Murray, 142, 165, 406

Butch Cassidy and the Sundance Kid, 65, 69; scene construction and dialogue in, 381–86, 405–406; story world of, 70, 99, 176–77, 183

"buzzing household" technique, 164

Cage aux Folles, La, 133

Call of the Wild, The (London), 159

Camille, 70

Canterbury Tales, The (Chaucer), 13, 32, 66

caper stories, 190, 265

Capra, Frank, 117, 153, 196, 273, 367, 391

Carrie, 167, 244

Carter Beats the Devil, 233

Casablanca, 17, 49, 380; characters in, 68, 70, 71, 82, 87; moral argument of, 115, 142–44; plot of, 269, 271, 274–77, 279–81, 283–84, 286–300, 302, 304, 306; scene construction and dialogue in, 406–10; story world of, 151, 165–66, 180

Cast Away, 159

Catcher in the Rye, The (Salinger), 70, 71, 224, 264, 389–90

Catch Me If You Can, 69

Catch-22, 136

cause-and-effect pathway, 30–32

cellar versus attic, visual opposition of, 167–68

central conflict, 30

challenges, identifying, 23

chaos theory, 172

Chaplin, Charlie, 203

character change, 8, 32–35, 77–87; in circular journey, 152; creating, 83–85; double reversal, 85–87; as expression of self, 78–83; in never-ending story, 420; plot and, 260–61; scene construction and, 374; story world as physical expression of, 178–79; symbols connected to, 233–34

characters, 9, 15, 56–107, 181, 221, 259,
    373; archetypes, 67–71; best,
    determining, 29–30; in buddy
    stories, 64–65; conflicting values of,
    117–19; extraneous, cutting, 66;
    genre, 265; individualizing, 71–75;
    in love stories, 62–64; main, *see*
    hero; in multihero stories, 13,
    65–66; in never-ending story, 435; in
    premise, 16; size change of, 174–75;
    story function of, 58–62 (*see also*
    allies; opponents); storyteller and
    depiction of, 310; in story world,
    153, 177; subplot, 60; symbolic,
    227–33, 252; variations on moral
    argument among, 115–17; *see also*
    character change
Chayevsky, Paddy, 238
Cheers, 164
Chekhov, Anton, 16, 78, 98, 117,
    167, 182, 401; *see also titles of specific*
    plays
Cherry Orchard, The (Chekhov), 182;
    characters in, 98; moral argument
    in, 117–18, 131, 133, 136; symbols
    in, 223
child-to-adult character change, 81
Chinatown, 22, 88; characters in,
    68, 69, 92; structure of, 39, 45,
    47–49
Chocolat, 181, 246
Christianity, 243, 245, 252, 253, 255,
    256
Christie, Agatha, 22
Christmas Carol, A (Dickens), 200;
    moral argument of, 113; premise
    and designing principle of, 29;
    story world of, 150; symbols in,
    226–27

Christmas Story, A, 164, 187
Chronicles of Narnia, 256; *The Lion, the*
    Witch and the Wardrobe, 175
Cider House Rules, The, 164
Cinema Paradiso, 131, 176, 183;
    storyteller of, 313, 316, 319; symbols
    in, 238–39
circular story: journey in, 152; seasons
    in, 185–86; single-day, 188–89
Citizen Kane, 68, 318, 319; moral
    argument of, 113, 126; premise
    and designing principle of, 29;
    story world of, 150, 173; symbols in,
    227
city, 169; natural settings combined
    with, 170–72
City Slickers, 126
Clark, Bob, 187
clichés, visual, 162, 171
cliffhangers, 66
climax, 3
Close Encounters of the Third Kind, 82
closed ending, 419
closings, 401–406
clown archetype, 70
Clueless, 132
comedies: black, 135–36, 184;
    circular time techniques in, 189;
    journey, 190, 261; plot of, 269;
    symbolic names in, 232; traveling
    angel in, 246; *see also titles of specific*
    films
comic books, 230
coming-of-age stories, 81
community start, 277
complex scenes, 376
conflict: with allies, 293; in buddy
    stories, 65; building, 94–101; central,
    30; dialogue and, 378; final, *see*

battle, final; in scene construction, 375; *see also* opponents

conflicting values, 90, 97–98, 391–400; in final battle, 300; moral argument and, 117–19, 391

Conformist, The, 81, 182, 319

Connecticut Yankee in King Arthur's Court, A (Twain), 69, 79, 200, 250

Conversation, The, 11, 51, 69, 81, 131, 182, 301

Cool Hand Luke, 230, 380

Copenhagen, 226, 317, 319; moral argument of, 113; premise and designing principle of, 28–29; story world of, 149

Coppel, Alex, 94, 179

Coppola, Francis Ford, 22, 54, 101, 229, 233, 320, 410, 412

cop stories, *see* crime genre

Count of Monte Cristo, The (Dumas), 263

counterattack, 289–90

Crash, 13, 66

creation myths, 82, 244

Creelman, James, 154

Crichton, Michael, 16, 333

Crime and Punishment (Dostoyevsky), 71, 93

crime genre: scene weave in, 341–54; story world of, 171, 179; *see also* specific films

Crocodile Dundee, 69, 126, 152, 181, 230, 246

crosscutting, 13, 329–32, 355–59; in multistrand plot, 266, 333–40; in story world, 151

Crucible, The (Miller), 184

cynic-to-participant character change, 82

Da Gradi, Don, 171, 181

Dances with Wolves, 49, 82, 231; moral argument in, 116–17, 126; story world of, 152, 155, 161, 183

David Copperfield (Dickens), 11, 228; characters in, 68, 70; plot of, 269; storyteller of, 388–90; story world of, 164, 182, 200

Days of Heaven, 161

Dead Poets Society, 212

Dean, Hamilton, 243

death: of hero, 182–83; storyteller and, 317–18; visit to, 192, 299

Death of a Salesman (Miller), 25, 68, 131; story world of, 151, 167, 177, 182

Deer Hunter, The, 161, 273, 277

defeat, apparent, 192, 294–95; visit to death during, 299

Dehn, Paul, 22

Deliverance, 152, 162

denouement, 3

deserts, 159

designing principles, 25–28, 181; plot and, 266; story world in, 147–50; symbols in, 224–27, 240; theme line in, 110–13; of Westerns, 245

desire, 7–8, 39, 43–45; of ally, 281; character change and, 84; in dialogue, 378; of hero, 87–88, 120; levels of, 280; in love stories, 62–63; in multihero stories, 65, 66; in never-ending story, 420; of opponent, 90; plan and, 47; plot and, 271–72, 279–80, 286–88, 295; in premature ending, 418; in scene construction, 374–76; story world and, 191 detective genre: desire in, 45; love interest in, 60; moral choice in, 36; opponents in, 47; plot in, 260, 263, 264, 283, 287, 305; scene weave in, 341–54; story world in, 171, 179; traveling angel in, 246; *see also specific films*

deus ex machina, 261, 419

Devotions upon Emergent Occasions (Donne), 111

dialogue, 9, 15, 259, 373, 376–81; in closing scenes, 401–406; key words, phrases, taglines, and sounds in, 380–81; masterpieces of, 406–15; moral, 138–39, 379–80, 391–400; of never-ending story, 420; in opening scenes, 382–86; self-revelation expressed in, 301; story, 377–79

Dickens, Charles, 11, 16, 74, 199, 200, 216, 232, 240, 263, 326, 388; *see also titles of specific novels*

Die Hard, 51, 69

digressions, plot, 264

Dirty Dozen, The, 190, 289

Dr. Strangelove, 136

documentaries, nature, 186

Dog Day Afternoon, 131, 133, 137

Donati, Sergio, 238

Donne, John, 111

Don Quixote (Cervantes), 11, 64, 131, 152

dopplegänger, 89

Dostoyevsky, Fyodor, 93

double, concept of, 89–90

Double Indemnity, 169

double reversal, 85–87, 301–302

Down and Out in Beverly Hills, 133

Dracula, 167, 231, 243–44

drama: moral vision in, 109; story world for, 179

dramatic code, 7

drive, 120, 269, 290–93; obsessive, 121, 295–96

Dubliners, The (Joyce), 204

Dumas, Alexandre, 263

Dune, 158, 159

dystopias, 178; settings for, 159, 165

Eames, Charles, 173

Eames, Ray, 173

Eliot, T. S., 146

Elizabeth, 68, 82

Ellroy, James, 116, 155, 341

Emerald Forest, The, 158

Emma (Austen), 132–35

emotions: correlations between weather and, 162; symbols and, 220, 221, 228

empathy versus sympathy, 76

Empire Strikes Back, The, 355–59

endings, false, 406

endpoint, 190, 374–75

English Patient, The, 70

Epstein, Julius J., 142, 165, 406

Epstein, Philip G., 142, 165, 406

ER, 333–40

Eszterhas, Joe, 93, 307

Euripides, 262

Everybody Comes to Rick's (Burnett and Alison), see *Casablanca*

evolution, theory of, 158, 159

Excalibur, 158, 183, 249–50

Exodus, Book of, *see* Moses story

Exorcist, The, 244

explosive story, 12–13

exposition, 273

extraneous characters, cutting, 66

fairy tales, 26; forest setting in, 158; metamorphosis in, 83; size change of characters in, 174

fake-ally opponent, 59–60, 285–86; revelation of true identity of, 298, 299

fake-opponent ally, 60, 91

fallacies of past and future, 184–85

Falling Down, 131

false endings, 418–19

Fantastic Voyage, 174

fantasy genre: city combined with natural settings in, 170–72; metamorphosis in, 83; moral vision in, 109; passageways between worlds in, 175–76; size change of characters in, 174; social, 12, 367–72; symbols in, 229; tools in, 176; *see also titles of specific films and novels*

Faragoh, Francis Edward, 231

farce, 265

Farewell to Arms, A (Hemingway), 36, 161, 224

Fargo, 159

fascinating characters, 75–76

father archetype, 67–68

Faulkner, William, 79–81

Ferris Bueller's Day Off, 188

Few Good Men, A, 82, 139

Field, Sally, 303–304

Fielding, Henry, 74–75, 261

Field of Dreams, 118, 126, 380; story world of, 152, 161, 180–81

Finding Nemo, 152, 157

Finklehoffe, Fred F., 195

Finnegans Wake (Joyce), 202

first sentence, 387–90

Fisher King, The, 250

fish-out-of-water stories, 152

Fitzcarraldo, 158

Fitzgerald, F. Scott, 24, 154, 232, 235–36, 404–405; *see also titles of specific novels*

Flashdance, 87

Flirting with Disaster, 11

Fly, The, 83

For Whom the Bell Tolls (Hemingway), 111, 222

Forbidden Planet, 158

forests, 158; cities as, 172; symbolic power of, 236

Forrest Gump, 23, 82, 126, 251, 319

Fort, Garrett, 231, 243

Fort Apache, 68

Four Weddings and a Funeral, 28, 148, 225

four-corner opposition, 94–101; moral argument in, 118

framing device, storyteller as, 312

Frankenstein, 70, 167, 231

Frayn, Michael, 81

freedom, move from slavery to, 178–84, 192

Frye, Northrop, 264

Fugitive, The, 126

Full Monty, 44, 88

future, fallacy of, 185

Gandhi, 109

gangster genre, 184; *see also titles of specific films*

garden, symbolic meaning of, 242

Gaslight, 168

gate, 299

gauntlet, 299

Gelbart, Larry, 21, 38, 63, 72, 116

genres, 5, 8; characters in, 62–65; multiple, 282; plan of action in, 47; plots of, 265, 267, 319; scene weave and, 327; symbols in, 229, 241; undercutting, 247; *see also specific genres*

ghost, 182, 272–75

Ghostbusters, 172

Gilgamesh, 64, 83, 318, 319

Gilligan's Island, 159

Glass Menagerie, The (Williams), 68, 167

Godard, Jean-Luc, 81

Godfather, The, 88, 137, 380; characters in, 68–70, 82–84, 101; plot of, 285, 320–25; premise of, 17, 22, 26, 31, 34–35, 84; scene construction in, 410–15; scene weave in, 327, 330–33; structure of, 39, 47, 48, 54–55; symbols in, 229, 233–34

God symbolism, 229–30

Gold Rush, The, 159

Goldman, William, 99, 382, 384, 385, 413, 414

Goldwyn, Samuel, 108

Gone with the Wind, 63

Good Morning, Vietnam, 181, 246

good-versus-bad moral argument, 126, 138; combined with other forms, 136; symbols in, 243, 245

Goodbye, Mr. Chips, 212

Goodfellas, 136, 184, 295, 316, 319

Goodrich, Frances, 117, 153, 196, 273, 367, 400

Graduate, The, 133

Grapes of Wrath, The, 82

Great American Fourth of July and Other Disasters, The, 187

Great Expectations (Dickens), 68, 74, 166

Great Gatsby, The (Fitzgerald), 24, 404–405; storyteller of, 316, 317, 319; story world of, 151, 154; symbols in, 232–33, 235–36

Great Santini, The, 69

Greek drama and mythology, 126, 161, 223, 241, 255, 262; archetypes in, 68–70

Green, Walon, 193

Greystoke, 158

Groom, Winston, 23, 251

Groundhog Day, 151, 189

ground versus sky, visual opposition of, 163–64

group events, 66

Guess Who's Coming to Dinner?, 109

Guiol, Fred, 240

Gulliver's Travels (Swift), 12, 159, 174, 175

Gunga Din, 240

Guns of Navarone, The, 190

Hackett, Albert, 117, 153, 193, 273, 367, 391

Hamlet (Shakespeare), 48, 126, 183, 252, 253, 310; characters in, 58–60, 68, 70, 71, 82, 96; plot of, 272–73, 282, 283

Hanks, Tom, 175

Hannah and Her Sisters, 13, 66, 187–88

Hanson, Curtis, 116, 155, 341

Harbou, Thea von, 329

Harris, Thomas, 61

Harry Potter books, 27, 69; moral argument of, 112; premise and designing principle of, 28; story world of, 145, 149, 158, 199, 215; symbols in, 225, 237, 256

Harry Potter and the Sorcerer's Stone, 212–19

Hashimoto, Shinobu, 100, 403

haunted houses, 166

Hawthorne, Nathaniel, 137, 184, 235

Heart of Darkness (Conrad), 27, 110, 111; storyteller of, 314, 315, 318, 319; story world of, 152, 158, 161, 162, 182; symbols in, 222

Hecht, Ben, 97, 239, 240

Hedda Gabler (Ibsen), 131

heist stories, *see* caper stories

Helgeland, Brian, 116, 155, 341

Helprin, Mark, 159

Hemingway, Ernest, 232, 402; *see also titles of specific novels*

Henry, O., 306

Hercule Poirot stories, 246

hero, 29, 58, 75–94; allies of, *see* allies; in buddy stories, 64–65; cause-and-effect pathway of, 30–31; character change of, 32–35, 77–87; desire of, 43–46, 87–88, 271–72, 279–81, 286–87, 295–96; in four-corner opposition, 94–101; meeting requirements of, 75–77; moral argument and, 72, 119–23, 291, 295; moral decision of, 35–36, 114–15, 302–303; more than one, 65–66; need of, 39–42, 120, 271–72, 276; new equilibrium reached by, 50–51; opponents of, *see* opponents; plan of, 47–48, 289; plot and, 259–63 (*see also* twenty-two-step story structure); premature ending and, 418–19; self-revelation of, 49–50, 271–72; storyteller as, 312; in

story world, 151–52, 177–84, 274; weakness of, 39–42, 45, 120, 276

high-concept premises, 17, 18, 57

Hill Street Blues, 265

historical characters, 233

historical fiction, 184, 185

Hoffman, Dustin, 56, 73

holidays, 66, 186–88

Home Alone, 69

Homer, 100, 125, 242

Honey, I Shrunk the Kids, 174

Hope and Glory, 250

horror genre: metamorphosis in, 83; story world for, 166; symbols in, 229, 231, 243–44, 247; *see also titles of specific films*

Hospital, The, 169

houses, 163–68; terrifying, 166–67; visual oppositions of, 163–64, 167–68; warm, 164–65

How Green Was My Valley, 27, 164, 183; storyteller of, 313, 319; symbols in, 223

Howards End, 68, 70, 71, 82

Hunt for Red October, The, 157, 190

Hustler, The, 138

Huxley, Aldous, 360

Ibsen, Henrik, 78, 272

iceberg opponent, 284–85

ice worlds, 159

identification with hero, 76

Ikuru, 131

Iliad, The (Homer), 68–71, 100, 115, 125–26

immoral actions, 120, 121, 269, 290–91; confrontation by ally over, 293; of storyteller, 317

Importance of Being Ernest, The (Wilde), 133

inciting event, 278–79

In Cold Blood, 161

Incredibles, The, 159, 169

Incredible Shrinking Man, The, 174

Indiana Jones movies, 69

individualization, 71–75

In God We Trust, All Others Pay Cash (Shepherd), 187

Innocents, The, 167

institution, city as, 169

irony, 109, 131–36

Island of Dr. Moreau, The, 159

islands, 159–60; symbolic power of, 236

It's a Wonderful Life, 12, 273; moral argument of, 113, 117, 138; premise and designing principle of, 29; scene construction and dialogue in, 391–96; scene weave of, 367–72; storyteller of, 314, 316, 317, 319; story world of, 150, 151, 153, 164, 182, 196–200; symbols in, 227

James, Henry, 122

Jane Eyre (Brontë), 167, 168

Jaws, 24, 157

Johnson, Diane, 173

journey, 168–69; circular, 152; comic, 11; as designing principle, 27; of learning, character change in, 84; moral argument expressed as, 110, 111; in outer space, 157; as plot form, 260–61, 263; river, 161–62; single-line, 151–52; storyteller of,

312; symbolic meaning of, 242; time endpoint for, 190

Joyce, James, 80, 136, 137, 202–204, 223, 229, 252–53; *see also titles of specific works*

Jung, Carl, 67

jungle, 158; city as, 171

Jungle, The (Sinclair), 171

Jurassic Park, 16, 158, 159, 184

Kafka, Franz, 79, 83

Kasdan, Lawrence, 355

Kelley, William, 21, 240

key words and phrases, 380

King, Stephen, 173

king archetype, 67

King Kong, 83, 110; story world of, 152, 154–55, 158, 159, 171, 174

King Lear (Shakespeare), 68, 70, 126, 130, 183, 283

Kinsella, W. P., 118, 180

Kipling, Rudyard, 240

Kloves, Steven, 212

Koch, Howard, 142, 165, 406

Kramer vs. Kramer, 87

Kubrick, Stanley, 173

Kurosawa, Akira, 100, 403

L.A. Confidential, 13, 66, 82; moral argument in, 116; scene weave of, 341–54; story world of, 151, 155–56, 184

labyrinth, symbolic meaning of, 242

ladder, symbolic meaning of, 242

Lang, Fritz, 329

Last of the Mohicans, The (Cooper), 126, 161

Last Year at Marienbad, 13, 81, 264
Lavender Hill Mob, The, 167
Lawrence of Arabia, 159
leader-to-tyrant character change, 82
leader-to-visionary character
    change, 82
learning stories, 8, 80–81, 260;
    character change in, 81
Legend of Sleepy Hollow, The, 158
Leone, Sergio, 238
life-changing premises, 19–20
Life with Father, 164
linear story, 10, 65; omniscient
    storyteller of, 310; seasons in, 185;
    story world surrounding, 147, 168
Lion King, The, 82, 182
Lion in Winter, The, 68
listener, 6–7
Little Big Man, 11
Little Mermaid, The, 157
Long Day's Journey into Night (O'Neill),
    68; moral argument of, 113; premise
    and designing principle of, 28; story
    world of, 149, 167, 189; symbols in,
    226
Lord of the Flies, 159
Lord of the Rings, The (Tolkien), 68, 69;
    story world of, 158, 182, 199;
    symbols in, 222, 237, 250,
    255–57
Lost, 159
Lost Horizon, 161
Lost in America, 133
Lost World, The, 158, 159
lover archetype, 70
love story genre: characters in, 62–63;
    double reversal in, 87; plot of, 269,
    291; scene weave in, 360–67; *see also*
    titles of specific films and novels

Lucas, George, 23, 71, 93, 137, 192,
    251, 355

M, 167, 171, 329–30
*M*A*S*H*, 133
MacArthur, Charles, 97, 239, 240
Macbeth (Shakespeare), 68, 69, 82,
    309
Machiavelli, Niccolò, 137
machine symbolism, 231
Madame Bovary (Flaubert), 68, 70, 71,
    131–33, 137, 319
Magic Mountain, The (Mann), 27, 161
magical powers, infusing places with,
    236–37
magician archetype, 69
Magnificent Ambersons, The, 131, 164,
    176, 184, 319
main characters: two, 62; *see also* hero
Malory, Thomas, 249
Maltese Falcon, The, 36, 115
Mamet, David, 123, 378, 400
man-made spaces, 162–76, 184; city,
    169–72; house, 163–68; miniatures,
    172–74; passageways between,
    175–76; road, 168; size change of
    characters in, 174–75; vehicle, 169
Mankiewicz, Herman J., 173
Marshman, D. M., Jr., 153, 179, 200
Mary Poppins, 68, 246; story world of,
    151, 164, 171, 175, 181–82
Master and Commander, 157
Matrix, The, 126; characters in, 68, 82;
    story world of, 151, 169; symbols in,
    230, 239
McCabe and Mrs. Miller, 131, 158,
    247–48
McDonell, Gordon, 405

McGuire, Don, 21, 38, 63, 72, 116
McKay, Brian, 247
McQuarrie, Christopher, 96, 250
meandering story, 11; journey as, 261
Meatballs, 181
Meet Me in St. Louis, 68; moral
   argument of, 113; plot of, 273, 277;
   premise and designing principle of,
   28; story world of, 149, 151, 164,
   183, 186, 195–96; symbols in, 226
melodrama: moral argument in, 126;
   story world for, 179
Memento, 11, 81
memory stories, 164
Men in Black, 69
mentor archetype, 68
metamorphosis, 83
Midsummer Night's Dream, A
   (Shakespeare), 158, 236
Miller, Arthur, 25, 184
Miller's Crossing, 158
miniatures, 172–73; symbolic, 236
Moby-Dick (Melville), 27, 157
modernization stories, 176
monologue, 400–401
Moonstruck, 17, 63, 237, 282
moral arguments, 9, 15, 108–44, 181,
   259, 373; basic strategy of, 120–22;
   in black comedy, 135–36; in
   character individuation, 71–75; in
   dialogue, 138–39; in double reversal,
   86, 302; drive and, 269; good-versus-
   bad, 126; in monologue, 400–401;
   of never-ending story, 420–21; of
   opponent, 90; in pathos, 130–31;
   plot and, 122–26, 291, 295;
   revelation of, 303–304; satiric-
   ironic, 131–35; split into
   oppositions, 114–19; symbols

encapsulating, 234–36; in tragedy,
   127–30; unique vision in, 137
moral decision, 35–36, 114–15,
   302–303; of storyteller, 317
moral dialogue, 379–80
moral need, 41, 77; creating, 42–43;
   plot and, 271–72, 277; self-
   revelation and, 50
moral weakness, *see* weakness,
   psychological and moral
Morrison, Toni, 24
Morte d'Arthur, Le (Malory), 126, 183,
   249
Moses story, 161, 216, 244; character
   change in, 82; moral argument of,
   112; premise and designing
   principle of, 27; story world of, 148;
   symbols in, 224–25
Mosquito Coast, 158
mother archetype, 68
motive, changed, 286–88, 295–96
Moulin Rouge, 70, 168
mountains, 160; cities as, 170;
   opposition of plains and, 160–61;
   symbolic power of, 236; terrifying
   houses on, 166
multihero stories, 12; cause-and-effect
   pathways in, 31–32; narrative drive
   in, 65–66
multistrand plot, 265–66, 333–40
Murder on the Orient Express, 22, 169
Murphin, Jane, 360
musicals, 246
Music Man, The, 87, 181, 246
Mutiny on the Bounty, 157
My Darling Clementine, 126, 159, 246
Mysterious Island, The, 159
mystery, 282–84
myths, 8, 11, 80, 109; circular time

techniques in, 189; creation, 82, 244; good-versus-bad moral argument in, 126, 136; opposition between house and road in, 168; plots of, 260; river settings for, 161; science fiction and, 157; size change of characters in, 174; symbols in, 229, 241–43, 247; visit to death in, 299; *see also* Greek drama and mythology; Norse mythology

Nabokov, Vladimir, 232
names, symbolic, 232–33
Narcejac, Thomas, 94, 176
narrative drive: multiple heroes and, 65–66; time techniques and, 188, 190
narrators: shifting, 264; *see also* storyteller
Nashville, 12, 13, 66, 151
natural settings, 156–62, 184, 185; city combined with, 170–72; desert, 159; forest, 158; ice, 159; island, 159–60; jungle, 158; mountain, 160–61; ocean, 156–57; outer space, 157–58; plain, 161; river, 161–62; symbolic power of, 236–37
natural time, 185
nature documentaries, 186
Naughton, Edmund, 247
need, 39–42, 120; character change and, 84, 85, 87; desire distinguished from, 43–45; in love stories, 63; in multihero stories, 65; of opponent, 90; plot and, 271–72, 276–77; self-revelation and, 50; story world and, 166, 191
Network, 136, 169, 223, 239

new equilibrium, 40, 50–51, 304–305; in closed ending, 419; in multihero stories, 65
Nightmare on Elm Street, A, 166
Nixon, 126
nonchronological time, 264
Norse mythology, 255; archetypes in, 69
Notes from the Underground (Dostoyevsky), 71, 167
Nugent, Frank, 238

O'Bannon, Dan, 306
objective correlation, 146
objects, symbolic, 240–51, 253
obsessive drive, 121, 295–96
ocean, 156–57; city as, 170–71; symbolic power of, 236
Ocean's Eleven, 190, 289
Odyssey (Homer), 11, 48, 69, 202–204, 252, 253; symbols in, 222, 236, 242–43
Oedipus the King (Sophocles), 51, 182, 301
Oguni, Hideo, 100, 411
Oliver Twist (Dickens), 70
Omen, The, 244
Once Upon a Time in the West, 159, 238
One Day in the Life of Ivan Denisovich (Solzhenitzyn), 189
One Flew over the Cuckoo's Nest, 223
O'Neill, Eugene, 78, 189
On the Waterfront, 278, 299
openings, 277–78, 381–86; first sentence of, 387–90
opponents, 58–60, 88–94, 260–63, 282–83; apparent defeat by, 294–95; battle with, 48, 300;

opponents *(continued)*
in buddy stories, 64–65; character change of, 86; fake-ally, *see* fake-ally opponent; final action against, 121; hierarchy of, 284–85; internal, 272; in love stories, 63; moral argument and, 72, 119–23, 138–39; in multihero stories, 65, 66; mysterious, 283–85; plan and main counterattack of, 289–90; plot and, 260–63, 282–86; in scene construction, 375; self-revelation of, 86–87, 301–302; story world of, 191; in structure of story, 39, 46

oppositions: four-corner, 94–101, 118; hidden, 60; moral argument split into, 114–19; symbolic, 228, 232, 243; visual, *see* visual oppositions

Orman, Jack, 334

Orwell, George, 185

Othello (Shakespeare), 68, 69, 92, 126, 283

Outbreak, 190

outer space, 157

Pallenberg, Rospo, 249

Paoli, Vanna, 238

participant, character change from cynic to, 82

past, fallacy of, 184

pathos, 130–31, 136

Patton, 69

Peckinpah, Sam, 193

Pepe Le Moko, 171

Percival, Robert Carson, 235

perfect-day technique, 189–90

Phantom of the Opera, 69

Philadelphia Story, The: characters in,

63, 68, 70, 99; symbols in, 221, 229–30

Phil Silvers Show, The, 69

Pinter, Harold, 265

Places in the Heart, 126, 303–304

plain, 161; opposition of mountain and, 160–61

plan, 39, 47–48, 288–89; in dialogue, 378; in multihero stories, 65; of opponents, 289–90; in scene construction, 375, 376

Platoon, 69

Player, The, 133

Pleasantville, 175

plot, 9, 15, 221, 258–325, 373; antiplot, 263–65; building blocks of, *see* twenty-two-step story structure; genre, 265, 267, 319; journey, 260–61; moral argument balanced with, 122–26; multistrand, 265–66, 333–40; of never-ending story, 419–20; organic, 259–60, 266–67; in premise, 16; reveals, 262–63; revelations sequence of, 305–10; storyteller and, 310–19; symbolic actions in, 239; three unities, 262

Plot Against America, The, 233

Poe, Edgar Allan, 167

Poetics (Aristotle), 4

Poetics of Space, The (Bachelard), 146

points of view, multiple, 264

Poisonwood Bible, The (Kingsolver), 158

Poltergeist, 166, 175

Portrait of the Artist as a Young Man, A (Joyce), 70, 223, 229

Portrait of a Lady, The (James), 122, 263

Positively True Adventures of the Alleged Texas Cheerleader-Murdering Mom, The, 136
possibilities, exploring, 20–23
power, balance of, 122
Powers of Ten, The, 173
premature ending, 418–19
premise, 14, 16–38, 181, 259, 373; audience appeal of, 36; best character in, 29–30; cause-and-effect pathway of, 30–32; central conflict in, 30; character change and, 32–35, 84; defining, 16–18; designing principle and, 25–29; exploring possibilities of, 20–23; life-changing, 19–20; moral choice in, 35–36; story challenges and problems of, 23–25; symbols and, 222–24
Presumed Innocent, 319
Pretty Woman, 51, 87
Pride and Prejudice (Austen), 87, 92, 132, 164, 387–88; film version of, 360–67
Prince, The (Machiavelli), 137
Prince and the Pauper, The (Twain), 79, 133
Private Benjamin, 133
Prizzi's Honor, 136
problem: identifying, 23–25; plot and, 276–77; in scene construction, 374; weakness manifested in, 42
progressive complication, 3
promises, inherent, 20–23
Psycho, 167
psychological need, 41–43, 77; plot and, 271–72, 277
psychological weakness, *see* weakness, psychological and moral
Pulp Fiction, 13, 66

purposeless hero, 278
Puzo, Mario, 22, 101, 229, 233, 320, 410, 412
Pygamlion (Shaw), 70

queen archetype, 68

Ragtime, 13, 233
Ramis, Harold, 172
Rebecca, 167
rebel archetype, 70–71
Rebel Without a Cause, 71, 278
Red River, 68, 82
Reds, 71
Reed, Barry C., 123, 378
religious stories, 109; horror stories as, 243; Westerns as, 245
Remembrance of Things Past (Proust), 224
Return of the Jedi, 158, 355
reveals plot, 262–63; journey plot and, 261, 263; *see also* revelations
revelations, 264, 269, 286–89, 295–98; audience, 297; impact on drive of, 291; mountain setting for, 160, 162; in never-ending story, 419–20; in scene construction, 375; sequence of, 9, 305–10; thematic, 122, 303–304; in three unities plot, 262; *see also* self-revelation
reversal, 305–306; double, 85–87, 301–302; in never-ending story, 434–35
Reville, Alma, 396
rising action, 3
rituals, 185–88
river, 161–62
River Runs Through It, A, 162

road, 168

Road Warrior, The, 83

Robinson, Phil Alden, 118, 180

Robinson Crusoe (Defoe), 159

Romeo and Juliet (Shakespeare), 70

Ronde, La, 66

Rose, Ruth, 154

Ross, Gary, 22

Roth, Eric, 23, 251

Rowling, J. K., 212, 213, 218

Royal Tenenbaums, The, 164

running start, 278

Run Silent, Run Deep, 157

safety versus adventure, visual
opposition of, 163

Salinger, J. D., 389

Sand, George, 168

satire, 131–36

Saving Private Ryan, 44, 45, 82, 88

Sayre, Joel, 240

Scarlet Letter, The (Hawthorne), 27, 111,
137, 184; symbols in, 223, 235

scenes, 15, 259, 373–417; closing,
401–406; complex or subtext, 376;
conflicting values in, 391–400;
masterful construction of, 406–15;
monologue in, 400–401; of never-
ending story, 420; opening, 381–90

scene weave, 9, 15, 326–73; crosscut,
355–59; detective or crime, 341–54;
juxtaposition in, 328–29; love story,
360–67; multistrand, 333–40; order
in, 328; social fantasy, 367–72

Scent of a Woman, 87

Schindler's List, 82

Schisgal, Murray, 21, 38, 63, 72, 116

Schulz, Charles, 203

science fiction genre, 157–58; fallacy of
the future in, 185; symbols in, 229,
231; technology in, 176; *see also titles
of specific films*

Sea Wolf, The, 157

seasons, cycle of, 185

Seinfeld, 203

self, concepts of, 78–79

self-exploration, 19

self-revelation, 40, 49–50; character
change and, 84–87; in false
endings, 419, 420; in journey plot,
260–61; moral, 121; in multihero
stories, 65; need and, 41; new
equilibrium following, 50–51; plot
and, 271–72, 301–302; of storyteller,
316; story world and, 182–83; in
tragedy, 127

setbacks, 294

settings, natural, 156–62

Seven Samurai, The, 69, 70, 100, 126,
183, 403–404

seven-steps technique, 14–15, 39–55;
battle in, 48; desire in, 43–45; new
equilibrium in, 50–52; opponent in,
46–47; plan in, 47–48; self-revelation
in, 49–50; subplots in, 282; visual,
191; weakness and need in, 40–43

sex, lies, and videotape, 87

Shadow of a Doubt, 139, 396–400

shadows, archetype, 67

Shakespeare, William, 92, 96, 130,
272–73, 309, 310; *see also titles of
specific plays*

shaman archetype, 69

Shampoo, 133

Shane, 69; story world of, 151, 161;
symbols in, 246–47

Shanley, John Patrick, 237

Shawshank Redemption, The, 182; plot of, 313–14, 316–19

She Wore a Yellow Ribbon, 159, 184, 238

Shelley, Mary, 231

Sheltering Sky, The, 159

Shepherd, Jean, 164, 187

Shining, The, 161, 166, 173–74

Ship of Fools, 169

Shoeless Joe (Kinsella), see *Field of Dreams*

Shrek, 158

Shusett, Ronald, 306

Sickner, Roy N., 193

Silence of the Lambs, 167, 231; characters in, 61, 68, 69, 91–92; structure of, 40, 51

simultaneous action, 12–13; in multistrand plots, 266; narrative drive and, 65–66; in plot digressions, 264; in story world, 147, 168; time techniques for, 188, 190

single-day technique, 188–89

single grand symbol, 111

single-line journey, 151–52

Sixth Sense, The, 167, 305–306, 403, 420

size of characters, changing, 174–75

sky versus ground, visual opposition of, 163–64

slavery, move to freedom from, 178–84

slow start, 278

Smiles of a Summer Night, 66, 188

Snows of Kilimanjaro, The (Hemingway), 161

social fantasies, 12; scene weave in, 367–72; *see also titles of specific films*

social forces, symbols for, 237–38

Song of Solomon, 158

Sophie's Choice, 35, 115

Sophocles, 262

Speed, 190

Spider-Man, 151, 171, 222, 230

Spielberg, Anne, 22

spiral story, 11

Stagecoach, 246

Stallings, Laurence, 238

Star Trek, 158

Star Wars, 47, 299, 355, 380; characters in, 68, 69, 71, 82, 93; moral argument of, 126, 137; premise of, 17, 23, 31, 34; story world of, 151, 158, 159, 182, 192–93; symbols in, 205, 251

Steel Magnolias, 164

stereotypes, preventing archetypes from becoming, 67

Stern, Philip Van Doren, 117, 153, 196, 273, 367, 391

Stewart, Donald Ogden, 63, 99, 229

Sting, The, 28, 225–26; moral argument of, 112; story world of, 149

Stoker, Bram, 243

Stoppard, Tom, 81

story, 7–9; arena of, 150–56; body of, 9; branching, 12; explosive, 12–13; functions of characters in, 58–62; linear, 10; meandering, 11; movement of, 9–10; never-ending, 418–21; spiral, 11; writing, 13–15

story dialogue, 377–79

storyteller, 6–7, 267, 310–19; as designing principle, 27; of never-ending story, 420–21

story world, 9, 15, 145–219, 259, 373; arena of, 150–56; comparison of settings in, 221–22; connected to hero's development, 177–84; in designing principle, 147–50; in explosive stories, 13; genre, 265; man-made spaces in, 162–76;

story world *(continued)*
natural settings in, 156–62; in never-ending story, 420; plot and, 273–75; through structure, 191–209; symbols and, 224–27, 236–39; technology in, 176–77; time in, 184–91; weather in, 162

Streetcar Named Desire, A, 17, 131; characters in, 68–70, 93–94, 103–107; story world of, 151, 167, 180, 182; symbols in, 230

Strindberg, August, 78, 167

structure, 14–15, 39–55, 181, 373; battle in, 48; desire in, 43–45; moral argument through, 119–26; new equilibrium in, 50–51; opponent in, 46–47; ordering scenes by, 328; plan of action in, 47–48; self-revelation in, 49–50; storyteller and, 314; story world and, 160, 171, 191–209; weakness and need in, 40–43; *see also* plot

Stuart Little, 174

subplots, 281–82, 327; characters in, 60; scenes of, 328

subtext scenes, 376

subworlds, passageways between, 175–76

suicide mission stories, 190

Sun Also Rises, The (Hemingway), 232, 402–403

Sunset Boulevard, 42, 278–79; storyteller of, 313, 319; story world of, 151, 153–54, 167, 179–80, 200–202

Superman, 222

surprise, maximization of, 263

Swept Away, 152, 159

symbols, 15, 220–57, 259, 373; actions as, 239–40, 253; and character, 83, 227–34, 252–53; as designing principles, 27; examples of, 248–53; grand moral argument as, 111–13; horror, 243–44; mythic, 241–43; in never-ending story, 420; objects as, 240–51, 253; plot and, 266; reversing, 247–48; of story, 222–27, 252; of story world, 236–39; themes as, 234–36; web of, 221–22; Western, 244–47

sympathy versus empathy, 76–77

Syriana, 13

taglines, 380; moral vision expressed in, 137

Tale of Two Cities, A (Dickens), 183, 230, 240

talisman, symbolic meaning of, 242

Tally, Ted, 61

Tarzan, 158, 230

Tati, Jacques, 152, 190

Taylor, Samuel, 94, 179

teacher archetype, 68

technology, 176–77, 184

teller, *see* storyteller

Tempest, The (Shakespeare), 27, 68, 159, 236

temporary freedom, 192

Terminator, The, 69, 126, 231

terrifying houses, 166–67

Thackeray, William Makepeace, 74

themes, 110–13; genre, 265; in never-ending story, 420; plot and, 266; symbols and, 224–27; *see also* moral arguments

"Theme of the Traitor and the Hero" (Borges), 309–10

Thin Man, The, 69

Thomas Crown Affair, The, 126

Thoreau, Henry David, 185
three-act structure, 4, 40, 258, 287
Three Musketeers, The (Dumas), 263
Three Sisters (Chekhov), 182
three unities plot, 262
thrillers, 11; plot of, 263, 283, 287,
    305–306; story world of, 179; time
    endpoint in, 190; *see also titles of
    specific films*
Through the Looking-Glass (Carroll), 175
Thumbelina, 174
ticking-clock technique, 190
time: as designing principle, 27;
    endpoint technique, 190; in
    multihero stories, 66;
    nonchronological, 264; story, 184–91
Titanic, 152, 157, 169
Tolkien, J.R.R., 255–57
Tom Brown's School Days, 212
Tom Jones (Fielding), 11, 74–75, 133;
    plot of, 261
Tom Thumb, 174
tools, 176–77, 184
Tootsie, 116; characters in, 56, 63–64,
    68–70, 72–74; plot of, 269, 271–72,
    275, 277, 279–81, 284, 286–90,
    292–300, 302–304, 306; premise of,
    21, 26, 38; structure of, 39, 40, 42, 50
Top Gun, 87
Tornatore, Giuseppe, 238
Touch of Evil, 126
Towne, Robert, 22, 92
Trading Places, 133
Traffic (1971), 152, 190
Traffic (2004), 12, 13
tragedy, 126–30, 136; connection
    between hero and story world in,
    182–83
training, 289

traveling angel stories, 246
traveling metaphor, *see* journey
Travers, P. L., 171, 181
Treasure Island (Stevenson), 159
Treasure of the Sierra Madre, The, 183
tree, symbolic meaning of, 242
trickster archetype, 69
Tristram Shandy (Stern), 13, 315, 319;
    plot of, 264–65
Tron, 175
Twain, Mark, 24, 73, 79, 199, 200, 261,
    434; *see also titles of specific novels*
twelve-hour single day, 188
Twentieth Century, 169
24 (TV series), 189
twenty-four-hour single day, 188; in
    three unities plot, 262
20,000 Leagues Under the Sea, 157
twenty-two-step story structure,
    267–71; ally or allies in, 280–82;
    apparent defeat in, 294–95; attack
    by ally in, 293–94; audience
    revelation in, 297; battle in, 300;
    desire in, 279–80; drive in, 290–93;
    fake-ally opponent in, 285–86; first
    revelation and decision in, 286–88;
    gate, gauntlet, and visit to death in,
    299; ghost and story world in,
    272–76; inciting event in, 278–79;
    new equilibrium in, 304–305;
    opponent and/or mystery in,
    282–85; opponent's plan and main
    counterattack in, 289–90; plan in,
    288–89; second revelation and
    decision in, 295–96; self-revelation
    in, 301–304; self-revelation, need,
    and desire in, 271–72; third
    revelation and decision in, 298;
    weakness and need in, 276–78

Twilight Zone, The (TV series), 158
2001: A Space Odyssey, 158, 231
tyrant, character change from leader to, 82

Ulysses (Joyce), 13, 70, 71, 264; moral argument of, 112, 136, 137; premise and designing principle of, 27–28; story world of, 145, 148, 152, 189, 202–209; symbols in, 225, 252–53
underground, symbolic meaning of, 242
Underwold, 233
unities of time, place, and action, 262
Usual Suspects, The, 403, 420; characters in, 70, 81, 96; plot of, 305–306, 313, 314, 318, 319; symbols in, 250
utopias, 178, 183; perfect day as time version of, 189–90; settings for, 157, 159, 165, 172

values, 120, 177; conflicting, *see* conflicting values; in historical fiction, 184; in miniature, 173; in Westerns, 245
Vanity Fair (Thackeray), 70, 74
vehicles, large, 169
Verdict, The, 88, 182; moral argument of, 123–25, 139; scene construction in, 378–79, 400–401; structure of, 41–42, 45, 48
Vertigo, 11, 51, 299; characters in, 69, 94; moral argument in, 115, 126; story world of, 179
Victor/Victoria, 133

victory, apparent, 295
Virginian, The, 245–46
visionary, character change from leader to, 82
visit to death, 192, 299
visual oppositions, 153–56, 177; ground versus sky, 163–64; mountain versus plain, 160–61; safety versus adventure, 163; symbolic, 243
voice, 311
Volpone, 69

Wachowski, Andy, 239
Wachowski, Larry, 239
Wag the Dog, 136
Waiting for Godot (Beckett), 264
Waiting for Guffman, 133
Walden (Thoreau), 185
Wallace, Earl W., 21, 240
Walsh, Bill, 171, 181
Waltons, The (TV series), 164
warm houses, 164–66
warrior archetype, 68–69
weakness, 39–42, 45, 120; of archetypes, 67–70; character change and, 32–35; fatal flaw, 127; in four-corner opposition, 95; in multihero stories, 65; of opponent, 90; plot and, 182, 276–77, 289; psychological and moral, 43; of storyteller, 313; story world and, 166, 179, 181–82, 191
weather, correlations between emotions and, 162
Webling, Peggy, 231
Wedding Crashers, 132
Welles, Orson, 173

Westerns: anti-, 176–77; symbols in, 244–47; *see also titles of specific films*

Who's Afraid of Virginia Woolf?, 167

Wild Bunch, The, 152, 159, 176, 183, 193–94

Wilder, Billy, 153, 179, 200

Wilder, Thornton, 139, 396, 398

Williams, Tennessee, 78, 93, 103, 180, 230

Willis, Bruce, 420

Wind and the Lion, The, 233

Wings of Desire, 170

Winter's Tale (Helprin), 158

wise old man or woman archetype, 68

wish list, 19

Witness, 21, 152, 190, 240

Wizard of Oz, The, 126, 152, 158, 175, 231

Wolf Man, The, 83, 158, 231

Wolfen, 83

Woolf, Thomas, 80

Wray, Fay, 83

Wren, Christopher, 235

writing process, 13–15

Wuthering Heights, 68, 70, 97, 166; moral argument of, 126–30; symbols in, 239–40

Yellow Submarine, 157, 164, 170

You Can't Take It with You, 164, 172